The Great Upheaval

NEW AFRICAN HISTORIES

SERIES EDITORS: JEAN ALLMAN, ALLEN ISAACMAN, AND DEREK R. PETERSON

David William Cohen and E. S. Atieno Odhiambo, *The Risks of Knowledge*

Belinda Bozzoli, *Theatres of Struggle and the End of Apartheid*

Gary Kynoch, *We Are Fighting the World*

Stephanie Newell, *The Forger's Tale*

Jacob A. Tropp, *Natures of Colonial Change*

Jan Bender Shetler, *Imagining Serengeti*

Cheikh Anta Babou, *Fighting the Greater Jihad*

Marc Epprecht, *Heterosexual Africa?*

Marissa J. Moorman, *Intonations*

Karen E. Flint, *Healing Traditions*

Derek R. Peterson and Giacomo Macola, editors, *Recasting the Past*

Moses E. Ochonu, *Colonial Meltdown*

Emily S. Burrill, Richard L. Roberts, and Elizabeth Thornberry, editors, *Domestic Violence and the Law in Colonial and Postcolonial Africa*

Daniel R. Magaziner, *The Law and the Prophets*

Emily Lynn Osborn, *Our New Husbands Are Here*

Robert Trent Vinson, *The Americans Are Coming!*

James R. Brennan, *Taifa*

Benjamin N. Lawrance and Richard L. Roberts, editors, *Trafficking in Slavery's Wake*

David M. Gordon, *Invisible Agents*

Allen F. Isaacman and Barbara S. Isaacman, *Dams, Displacement, and the Delusion of Development*

Stephanie Newell, *The Power to Name*

Gibril R. Cole, *The Krio of West Africa*

Matthew M. Heaton, *Black Skin, White Coats*

Meredith Terretta, *Nation of Outlaws, State of Violence*

Paolo Israel, *In Step with the Times*

Michelle R. Moyd, *Violent Intermediaries*

Abosede A. George, *Making Modern Girls*

Alicia C. Decker, *In Idi Amin's Shadow*

Rachel Jean-Baptiste, *Conjugal Rights*

Shobana Shankar, *Who Shall Enter Paradise?*

Emily S. Burrill, *States of Marriage*

Todd Cleveland, *Diamonds in the Rough*

Carina E. Ray, *Crossing the Color Line*

Sarah Van Beurden, *Authentically African*

Giacomo Macola, *The Gun in Central Africa*

Lynn Schler, *Nation on Board*

Julie MacArthur, *Cartography and the Political Imagination*

Abou B. Bamba, *African Miracle, African Mirage*

Daniel Magaziner, *The Art of Life in South Africa*

Paul Ocobock, *An Uncertain Age*

Keren Weitzberg, *We Do Not Have Borders*

Nuno Domingos, *Football and Colonialism*

Jeffrey S. Ahlman, *Living with Nkrumahism*

Bianca Murillo, *Market Encounters*

Laura Fair, *Reel Pleasures*

Thomas F. McDow, *Buying Time*

Jon Soske, *Internal Frontiers*

Elizabeth W. Giorgis, *Modernist Art in Ethiopia*

Mari K. Webel, *The Politics of Disease Control*

Kara Moskowitz, Seeing Like a Citizen

Jacob S. T. Dlamini, Safari Nation

Cheikh Anta Babou, *The Muridiyya on the Move*

Alice Wiemers, *Village Work*

Judith A. Byfield, *The Great Upheaval*

Laura Ann Twagira, *Embodied Engineering*

Matthew V. Bender, *Water Brings No Harm*

David Morton, *Age of Concrete*

Marissa J. Moorman, *Powerful Frequencies*

Ndubeze Mbah, *Emergent Masculinities*

Patricia Hayes and Gary Minkley, editors, *Ambivalent*

The Great Upheaval

Women and Nation in Postwar Nigeria

⤴

Judith A. Byfield

OHIO UNIVERSITY PRESS ⤳ ATHENS, OHIO

Ohio University Press, Athens, Ohio 45701
ohioswallow.com
© 2021 by Ohio University Press

Earlier versions of chapters in this book were published in the following articles:

"Taxation, Women, and the Colonial State: Egba Women's Tax Revolt" was originally published in *Meridians*, vol. 3, pp. 250–77. (c) 2003, Smith College. All rights reserved. Republished by permission of the copyright holder, and the present publisher, Duke University Press. www.dukeupress.edu.

"Feeding the Troops: Abeokuta (Nigeria) and World War II" was originally published in *African Economic History* 35 (2007): 77–87 © 2007 by the Board of Regents of the University of Wisconsin System. Reprinted by courtesy of the University of Wisconsin Press.

Judith Byfield, "Women, Rice, and War: Political and Economic Crisis Wartime Abeokuta (Nigeria)," *Africa and World War II* (Cambridge: Cambridge University Press, 2015), 147–65, © 2015 Cambridge University Press. Reproduced with permission of the Licensor through PLSclear.

Printed in the United States of America
Ohio University Press books are printed on acid-free paper ⊗ ™
29 28 27 26 25 24 23 22 21   5 4 3 2 1

Library of Congress Cataloging-in-Publication Data
Names: Byfield, Judith A. (Judith Ann-Marie), author.
Title: The great upheaval : women and nation in postwar Nigeria / Judith A. Byfield.
Other titles: New African histories series.
Description: Athens : Ohio University Press, 2019. | Series: New African histories | Includes bibliographical references and index.
Identifiers: LCCN 2019031415 | ISBN 9780821423974 (hardcover) | ISBN 9780821423981 (paperback) | ISBN 9780821446904 (pdf)
Subjects: LCSH: Women—Political activity—Nigeria—Abeokuta—History–20th century. | Women—Nigeria—Abeokuta—Economic conditions—20th century. | Women—Nigeria—Abeokuta—Social conditions—20th century. | Nationalism—Nigeria—History—20th century. | Nigeria—History—1900-1960. | Nigeria—Politics and government—To 1960.
Classification: LCC DT515.9.A17 B94 2019 | DDC 966.9230904—dc23
LC record available at https://lccn.loc.gov/2019031415

Contents

Illustrations

Acknowledgments

This book has been germinating a long time. It started as my original dissertation proposal. However, as I probed the questions that seemed relevant to understanding the relationship between the 1947 women's tax revolt and nationalism, those questions became other projects—*The Bluest Hands: A Social and Economic History of Women Dyers in Abeokuta (Nigeria), 1890–1940* (Heinemann, 2002) and *Africa and World War II* (Cambridge, 2015). The research and writing also had to be fit around teaching, advising, health issues, and the passing of many people near and dear to my heart. The long incubation period afforded many advantages. It allowed me to explore new literature, reread old classics with new questions and new eyes, and engage the stimulating work of a new generation of Africanist historians. Ultimately, this book is much better than what I originally envisioned.

While research and writing are largely singular endeavors, we are pushed to think more deeply or to question our assumptions as we share our ideas with students, friends, and colleagues. I have a special place in my heart for the students in my seminar on nationalism and decolonization in Africa. Their engagement with the readings helped me more than they can appreciate. I had the good fortune to be surrounded by generous, thoughtful colleagues who never hesitated to probe, ask difficult questions, or cheer me on as I wrestled with each chapter. I gained tremendously from the multiple conversations that began as a writing group and turned into fun-filled, raucous meals. For those moments, I especially thank Deborah Gray-White, Carolyn Brown, Natalie Byfield, Wanda Hendricks, and Donna Murch. I experienced similar boundary crossings and lively meals with participants of the Black Women's Intellectual History Project organized by Mia Bay, Farah J. Griffin, Martha S. Jones and Barbara D. Savage. Invigorating discussions also followed presentations to Columbia University's Women and Society Seminar and the Seminar in Contemporary African History. Those times were buttressed by the continued love and friendships forged at Dartmouth College with

Deborah K. King, Bryant Ford, Lourdes Guttierez-Najera, Celia Naylor, Annelise Orleck, and Craig Wilder. At Cornell University, I worked with wonderful colleagues in the History Department, the Feminist, Gender, and Sexuality Studies Program, and Africana Studies. I have valued the strong friendships of Ed Baptist, Sherman Cochran, Naminata Diabate, Grant Farred, Maria Cristina Garcia, Sandra Greene, Durba Ghosh, Salah Hassan, Saida Hodzic, Russell Rickford, Riché Richardson, Noliwe Rooks, Barry Strauss, Olúfémi Táíwò, Eric Tagliacozzo, Robert Travers, and Penny Von Eschen. Our administrators—Barb Donnell, Treva Levine, Renee Milligan, Claire Perez, and Judy Yonkin—helped me stay in compliance and in good humor.

Equally important, many people in Nigeria helped bring this book to fruition. I thank everyone who generously sat for interviews and shared their stories. My Nigerian "family"—especially Bisi and Kunle Adeniji, Joseph and Tope (Victoria) Ayodokun, Iyabo and Fasse Yusuf, and the late Olufunso Yoloye—made sure I was safe, comfortable, and nourished. Joseph and Tope Ayodokun were also my primary research assistants. Their insights, good humor, care, and dedication to this project helped keep me going as the years wore on. I also thank Bola Sowemimo, who had worked with me on *The Bluest Hands*, for contributing to this project as well. The staff at the National Archives in Ibadan and Abeokuta welcomed me warmly at each visit. In addition, I received great assistance from the staffs at the Kenneth Dike Library at the University of Ibadan, the Gandhi Library at the University of Lagos, and Special Collections at Obafemi Awolowo University. In the United Kingdom, the staffs at The National Archives in Kew and at the old Rhodes House Library and the New Bodleian Library in Oxford never failed to present a cheerful face as I requested an endless list of documents. Visiting the cousins in London and Manchester always added a special touch to these trips as we created new dimensions to our experience of the Jamaican diaspora.

This project could not have been completed without the financial assistance of several institutions. I deeply appreciate the support I received from Dartmouth College and Cornell University, especially from their history departments and Cornell's Society for the Humanities. I also thank the Fulbright Senior Scholar Fellowship program (2002–3) and the National Endowment of the Humanities (2003–4), whose generous support facilitated research in Nigeria. Residences at the National Humanities Center in the Research Triangle (2007–8) and the Institute for Advanced Study in Princeton (2013–14) proved pivotal to the reconceptualization of several chapters. I relished the warm, collegial atmosphere created at NHC and IAS and opportunities to think and learn from an amazing group of scholars.

I owe a significant debt of gratitude to Gillian Berchowitz and her successor, Stephanie Williams, and the editors of the New African Histories series at Ohio University Press—Jean Allman, Allan Isaacman, and Derek Peterson. Your unwavering support of this project still makes me emotional. In addition, I am deeply appreciative of the thorough attention to detail and the incredible patience of the editorial staff.

The period 2017–18 was an especially difficult one as health issues overwhelmed me, but I was sustained by small and big acts of kindness from my siblings, Natalie and Byron, niece and nephews; my sisters-from-other-mothers, Ellen, Margot, Carolyn, Deborah, and Funmi; students; colleagues; and friends. To all those who called to check in, listened to me sob, visited, brought food, took me to or accompanied me to doctor's appointments, drove me to the Cornell bus, or offered hugs—thank you from the bottom of my heart. I will do my best to pay forward all the love and support you showered on me. E ̣ ṣeé gan.

Abbreviations

Abe Prof	Abeokuta Provincial Office Papers
AG	Action Group
AHIS	Association of Headmasters of Ijebu Schools
ALC	Abeokuta Ladies Club
AUDC	Abeokuta Urban District Council
AWAM	Association of West African Merchants
AWU	Abeokuta Women's Union
CMS	Church Missionary Society
COLA	cost-of-living allowance
CSO	Chief Secretary's Office
DCI	Department of Commerce and Industry
ECR	Egba Council Records
ENA	Egba Native Administration
EUBM	Egba United Board of Management
EUG	Egba United Government
FNWS	Federation of Nigerian Women's Societies
KDML	Kenneth Dike Memorial Library, University of Ibadan
LUT	Lagos Union of Teachers
NAN Abeokuta	National Archives of Nigeria, Abeokuta
NAN Ibadan	National Archives of Nigeria, Ibadan
NCBWA	National Congress of British West Africa
NCNC	National Council of Nigeria and the Cameroons
NNDP	Nigerian National Democratic Party

NUS	Nigerian Union of Students
NUT	Nigerian Union of Teachers
NWU	Nigeria Women's Union
NYM	Nigerian Youth Movement
TNA	The National Archives, Kew, United Kingdom
TUC	Trade Union Congress
UAC	United Africa Company
UNIA	Universal Negro Improvement Association
WASU	West African Students Union

Introduction

To My Dear People,

After more than half a century of service to my country and people, twenty eight of which I have given in the capacity of Native Authority, conditions have arisen which completely obliterate from men's memory the efforts which I have made to advance in every way possible the interests of Egbaland.

That so fierce and unprecedented opposition should have been encountered at this hour in my career on the Stool of Egbaland is entirely beyond my capacity to understand; but as I have always placed the happiness of the people and the progress of my dear country above everything I cannot bear any longer the sight of turmoil, strife and discontent more particularly as there have been threats of damage to properties and attacks on persons which have become a reality.

I have therefore decided, after mature consideration and in order to avoid bloodshed, to leave the environs of my territory in the hope that after a time frayed tempers will subside and an atmosphere of calm prevail.

May God save Egbaland and bring it happiness prosperity and lasting peace.

Ademola II,
Alake, 29/7/48.[1]

With the release of this statement in July 1948, Ademola II, traditional king (*alake*) and sole native authority (paramount chief) of Abeokuta, abdicated. He spent the next three years in exile in Oshogbo.[2] Crafting the letter to elicit sympathy, Ademola specifically identified his disappointment in the men who had forgotten his achievements. Moreover, the letter pointedly failed to name those most responsible for this turn of events—the Abeokuta Women's Union (AWU), under the leadership of

Funmilayo Ransome-Kuti. We should not accept at face value Ademola's claim that he did not understand the grievances that led to this moment. However, Wole Soyinka helps us appreciate that there was an element of genuine surprise. No one had imagined that this organization, composed of market women and a few elite women, could force Ademola from office. For Soyinka, Ademola's abdication was "the Great Upheaval."[3]

Ademola's abdication followed a protracted tax revolt. Starting in 1947, the AWU began a lengthy series of protests, petitions, and confrontations with colonial officials as women complained about taxation, abuse at the hands of government officials, and Ademola's corruption, especially in the harsh economic climate after World War II. The AWU united thousands of women from all sectors—elite Christian women, Muslim women, teachers, and market women from the town of Abeokuta and its rural environs. The organization put forward three main demands: the abolishment of taxes on women, women's representation on the local governing council, and the removal of the colonial state's designated sole native authority, Alake Ademola II. The organization's demands indicated that the upheaval they inspired was both political and economic, for they called into question the political and economic underpinning of the colonial state and demanded redress for women's erasure from political office.

The AWU's demands resonated with an earlier generation of women's protests in Nigeria, when women in eastern Nigeria and Lagos challenged plans to impose taxes on them. Their economic concerns also mirrored the demands of labor unions during and after the war. However, the Abeokuta protests were distinctive because they became the foundation from which the first national women's organization in Nigeria, the Nigeria Women's Union (NWU), emerged. The AWU's success set off a firestorm of organizing, and Ransome-Kuti received letters from men and women around the country who wanted her to help them form women's unions. The letters demonstrated the desire of many women in Nigeria to participate in the political process and transform the socioeconomic and political landscape in which they lived. Building on this excitement, Ransome-Kuti convened the meeting in Abeokuta out of which the NWU was born.

On May 15, 1949, the members of the AWU accepted Ransome-Kuti's proposal to incorporate the organization into the NWU, thus making the former a branch of the new group.[4] Though often overlooked, the formation of the NWU was an important moment in Abeokuta's history as well as Nigerian political history. It reflected an expanding political vision and organizational networking as women activists moved from local arenas of political engagement to a national level coterminous with the Nigerian colonial state. This development was significant for several reasons. It emerged specifically to address the needs, demands, and aspirations of Nigerian women at the same time that the premier nationalist organization, the National Council of Nigeria and the Cameroons (NCNC), had become moribund. The NWU predated the political parties that would contest regional elections in the 1950s, and its leadership pointedly resisted pressure to bring the organization under any political party. The emergence of the NWU signaled a rejection of the idea that women would be silent and symbolic spectators to dramatic political changes on the horizon. In establishing an organizational space built on local organizations around the country, the NWU revealed women's desire and capacity to shape political agendas at multiple levels and to become active agents in creating a postcolonial nation.

The creation of the NWU just two years after the tax revolt attests to the changing material conditions, technological transformations, and political visions that made mobilizing on a national level entirely reasonable and possible for this generation of women activists. These activists played a critical role in knitting together the idea and reality of Nigeria as a nation. Despite the political work carried out by these women's organizations, their vision for the postcolonial nation was only partially fulfilled. The men who brokered independence shelved universal franchise and accepted the demand by Northern Nigerian leaders that women in this populous region be denied the right to vote. Northern women did not receive voting rights until 1979.

The Great Upheaval makes three main interventions in the scholarship on nationalism in Nigeria. It challenges the teleological orientation of much of the scholarship, which presumes that all nation-making centered on a Nigerian nation. Abeokuta's openness to European missionaries and African Christian converts created a distinctive history of nation-making that predated the imposition of colonial rule and continued into the interwar period. In fact, the early colonial period strengthened Abeokuta's sense of itself as a nation so that even as late as 1930, town leaders hoped to regain their independence as a sovereign state. *The Great Upheaval* demonstrates the longevity of Abeokuta's commitment to nationhood and explores the economic and political factors that gradually produced the shift in their political commitment. By the end of the decade, the town's leaders increasingly articulated support for a Nigerian nation-state and suppressed claims for the town's independence.

Narratives were central to Abeokuta's expression of nationhood. While scholars have explored many national narratives, few have called into question the ways in which those narratives were gendered. *The Great Upheaval* pays particular attention to the centrality of gender by exploring competing narratives of the nation as Abeokuta set aside its claim for independence and joined the movement for a Nigerian nation. This analysis is possible because I apply a multidisciplinary approach to my examination of the tax revolt. The tax revolt is much more than an expression of economic distress. It offers a rich symbolic and discursive landscape from which we can glean insights into women's political thoughts and their contribution to the cultural construction of nation. I show that the performative dimensions of the tax revolt—songs, protests, dress—as well as the thanksgiving celebrations after Ademola's departure created a counternarrative about colonialism in Abeokuta and an aspirational narrative for the newly emerging nation. The fruit of that aspirational narrative was the formation of the Nigerian Women's Union (NWU). It was to be the vehicle through which women across Nigeria would define their interests, desires, and needs while fulfilling the obligations and responsibilities of citizenship. The erasure of these events from studies of Nigerian nationalism only compounds the political marginalization women experienced at independence. *The Great Upheaval* ultimately challenges us to problematize rather than take for granted the limited franchise Nigerian women enjoyed at independence, despite the political energy and effort they invested in the nationalist era.

This study demonstrates that gender played a central, though consistently underappreciated, role in Nigeria's nationalist movement. The ignoble political deal that cemented Northern Nigerian women's disenfranchisement has not been subjected to a sustained analysis. Scholars have yet to examine the gender ideologies of political leaders and parties as well as the centers of resistance that challenged the gender inequalities codified in the constitution. Equally significant, there are no studies of the NWU during the critical period from its founding to independence. *The Great Upheaval* is a building block toward this endeavor as it brings a gendered analysis to Abeokuta's political history and affirms the town's critical role in the conceptualization of a national women's movement. It answers the question, why look at Abeokuta to understand gender and nationalism in Nigeria?

The Great Upheaval draws on many different literatures. It required revisiting texts I had read decades ago and venturing into new fields. The robust literature on gender and nationalism made it possible to reread the classics of Nigerian political history and the letters and speeches of the stalwarts of the nationalist era with new eyes. Literary theory and cultural studies prevented me from creating a reductionist account that would have robbed the story of its nuances, textures, and vitality. Nuance and textures exist on top of, between, and around structures. The centrality of taxes to this story ensured that political economy did not disappear from view. While this study benefited from the work of numerous fields and scholars, it contributes to the study of gender and nationalism broadly and in Nigeria specifically. It draws attention to women's activism across the decades of the interwar and postwar periods and demonstrates how political history is ultimately warped by the marginalization of women and gender. The erasure of women and gender reduces the complexity of Nigeria's sociological landscape and the range of contradictions embedded in its process of nation-building. Moreover, it restricts our ability to appreciate that as nationalist leaders called for unity among the country's major ethnic groups and minority populations, they simultaneously embedded gendered inequalities in the very structure and organization of the nation.

PURVEYORS OF ABEOKUTA'S IMAGINED COMMUNITY

In his important text *The Nation and Its Fragments*, Partha Chatterjee admonishes scholars for taking "the claims of nationalism to be a political movement . . . too literally."[5] He argues instead that we must distinguish the ideological and cultural process of imagining the nation from the political movements that challenged colonial regimes for control of the state. He encourages us to write what he calls "a cultural history of nationalism" in which the process of creating the nation does not begin or end with the political movements and the contest for political power against imperial states.[6] A cultural history of nationalism requires us to historically locate the "polyphony of voices, contradictory and ambiguous, opposing, affirming and negotiating their views of the nation" rather than succumbing to the "harmonized, monologic voice of the Nation."[7]

Identifying Prasenjit Duara's polyphone of voices has taken scholars into multiple spaces beyond newspapers and political manifestos. Critical studies by Marissa Moorman, Kelly Askew, and Thomas Turino demonstrate that cultural practices, institutions, and an expressive culture provide spaces where the nation is marked, defined, and contested by people of multiple social positions.[8] Culture is central to any analysis of the nation because, as Geoff Eley and Ronald Suny argue, it is the terrain where the nation is elaborated, "and in this sense nationality is best conceived as a complex process of cultural innovation, involving hard ideological labor, careful propaganda, and a creative imagination."[9] Nonetheless, for a nationalist consciousness to come into being, it requires political inter-vention. It is "creative political action [that] transforms a segmented and disunited population into a coherent nationality."[10]

Abeokuta's cultural history of nationalism and the spaces in which it unfolded are the product of a history that predates colonialism. The town's very existence is intimately connected to an earlier imperial history, that of the Oyo Empire. Oyo's collapse early in the nineteenth century trans-formed the political geography of western Nigeria and gave rise to new political communities such as Abeokuta, which was established in 1830. It was a city of refugees of the Yoruba Wars that housed approximately one hundred thousand people by the 1850s.[11] While the Egbas constituted the largest group, it had a sizable population from Owu, a major Yoruba town destroyed during the wars. Under the security of Olumo Rock, the refu-gees recreated their walled city-state. It comprised four quarters—Egba Alake, Egba Oke-Ona, Gbagura, and Owu—and each quarter recognized a king as the dominant political authority: the alake, *oshile, agura,* and *olowu,* respectively. Quarters had numerous townships and each township recognized a tripartite administration populated by male and female title-holders who controlled trade, security and civil government.[12] Townships had numerous compounds or residential units. They sometimes housed members of one patrilineage or multiple lineages as refugees settled to-gether, freeborn and enslaved. Each compound recognized a head of the unit, the *bale,* who was the most senior male of the founding lineage.[13]

Abeokuta was one of the first sites of missionary enterprise in Nigeria and home to a significant number of repatriated Christianized Yoruba speakers, the Saros. Liberated from slave ships and settled in Si-erra Leone, Saros lived among British, Jamaican, and African-American households where they adopted Christianity and western culture. From its inception, Abeokuta struggled to define itself culturally and politically. The town's cultural diversity and the continued military crisis during the nineteenth century created room for competing male and female power brokers to exercise considerable influence on its political organization and practice. They often challenged efforts to centralize power around the alake or tried to place their candidates in the position. Abeokuta's political and cultural struggles during the nineteenth century became more com-plicated as the British established their foothold in Lagos and gradually extended their influence inland. "Nation-ness" in Abeokuta evolved from a complex political and cultural landscape in which its architects sought to establish a nation that was first and foremost Egba as well as historically and contemporarily independent of both Oyo and British overlordship.

The idea of a Yoruba nation is also a product of the nineteenth century. The Yorubas occupy a region that encompasses sections of what today is Benin and southwestern Nigeria. Although the various subgroups shared a common language and culture, they lived in distinct political units. They recognized a common origin from Ile-Ife, considered the cradle of Yoruba civilization, but their cultural identity was more often contiguous with the subgroup to which they belonged—Ijebu, Ife, Ijesha, Egba, or Oyo.[14] The idea of all these subgroups composing a Yoruba nation emerged first among Yoruba exiles in Sierra Leone.[15] As J. Lorand Matory argues, the proximity of peoples—Oyos, Egbas, Egbados, Ijeshas, and so forth—that shared linguistic and cultural features helped reinforce their similarities as well as their shared differences from the local Sierra Leonean population. A pivotal development in the creation of a Yoruba nation was the publication in 1843 of Samuel Ajayi Crowther's *A Vocabulary of the Yoruba Language*. This dictionary standardized a "hybrid language predominantly Oyo in its morphology and syntax, and . . . Egba in its phonemes."[16] Furthermore, it took a term that used to be specific to those from Oyo and used it to now encompass all the communities from this cultural-linguistic region.[17]

Exile facilitated the crystallization of a Yoruba identity, but it did not operate alone. Christianity provided some of the ideological tools that hastened this process. J. D. Y. Peel argues that "at its height, 1890–1914, virtually all the key figures of cultural nationalism were clergymen or active Christian laymen."[18] However, insufficient attention has been given to the ways that Christianity shaped this development. Christianity did more than create a religious community. Political ideals and organization were embedded in the missionary project, and Christianity validated "the ideas of the ethnos, the pre-political foundation of the nation state."[19] Christian-dominated spaces were at the center of nationalist discussions. Peel notes, "It is . . . not at all surprising that two of the early venues of 'cultural nationalist' discussion were the Young Men's Christian Association of Breadfruit Church, whose pastor was then James Johnson, a Yoruba missionary, and the Abeokuta Patriotic Association, based at Ake Church and under the patronage of the English missionary J. B. Wood."[20] Even more specifically, "the missionary project envisaged an ethno-linguistic nation," thus the cultural nationalism that emerged in this period was a distinctly Yoruba nationalism.[21]

Christian-informed notions of the nation also embraced a distinctive set of ideas about gender roles and expectations. In public and in private, Christianity promoted male dominance and authority. The public work of politics and nation-building was male work. In the home, a husband was "naturally" the head of the household. Still, as Antoinette Burton argues, women were not merely subjugated—they performed equally important care-taking functions and transmitted culture. They were considered morally superior and ultimately responsible for the uplift and improvement of the national body politic.[22] Christian converts processed from the beginning a gendered understanding of the nation. These teachings were inculcated and reinforced through church teachings, newspapers, pamphlets, social clubs, school curricula, and marriage legislation.[23]

The concept of a Yoruba nation was gendered at its inception and had to be invested with meaning and history. Samuel Crowther launched the first effort to write a history of Yorubaland while still in Sierra Leone. This history was included in his Yoruba dictionary.[24] When Crowther and other Yoruba exiles began returning to Nigeria in the 1830s and 1840s, they imported the idea of Yoruba nationality. Interest in elaborating Yoruba history lay dormant for several decades, but by the 1880s a steady stream of histories began appearing in books and in the newspapers. Robin Law notes that the motives of the authors of these histories varied considerably. Some aspired to rescue and preserve traditions that would be forgotten; others hoped to use these histories to help foster unity.[25] The most notable is Samuel Johnson's classic *History of the Yoruba*, written in the 1890s but not published until 1921. Johnson claimed "a common origin for all Yoruba and an effective political unity which . . . endured until the wars of the nineteenth century."[26] Of the histories that stress unity, Michel Doortmont notes that Johnson's was the most holistic. He produced a "more homogeneous story," though it was strongly based on the history of Oyo and Ibadan. It was informed by the idea shared by many of the Christian and educated elites that "progress and civilization only had a chance if there was at least some sense of unison among all Yoruba. . . . *The History* . . . actually drew a blue-print of a future Yoruba nation."[27]

The period between the 1880s and World War I witnessed the production of a wide range of local histories that collectively challenged the notion that Africa lacked a history. These histories became the building blocks of ethnic nationalisms that together composed the first generation of nationalist thought in Nigeria. From their inception, these histories captured the multiplicity of voices competing to massage nations into being. Some authors, like Johnson, imagined nations that corresponded to the political templates created by nineteenth-century empires such as Oyo, while others, like the inhabitants of Abeokuta, seized the opportunity to assert the nation-ness of their communities and their autonomy from former empires.

Local histories operated in the service of what Law and Doortmont, respectively, call micronationalism or ethnic provincialism, in which they asserted their autonomy from Oyo's historical dominance.[28] The production of histories of individual towns and kingdoms increased in the twentieth century. The proliferation of these histories reflected the rapid social and political changes unfolding in the region. As schools spread across the region, local leaders wanted their own histories to be reflected in these texts, so local histories formed an important component of Yoruba-language textbooks used in the schools.[29] These texts also attempted to shape the political geography of the colonial state as chiefs challenged or advocated for the boundaries of administrative divisions.[30] Equally important, local histories revealed political tensions and fractures within the towns, for they often called for unity in the face of rising British power. Thus, local histories did not speak only of the past—they used the past to help construct the colonial present. In the case of Abeokuta, its political and cultural elites asserted their independence from Oyo, their demand to be independent of British control, and their distinctive nation-ness. The spirited political debates embedded in local histories were old political arguments that shifted from the battlefields to books and classrooms and had to be adjudicated by colonial officials.

Abeokuta produced several important historians who belonged to what Michel Doormont considers the second wave of Yoruba historians. They included Ajayi Kolawole Ajisafe, *History of Abeokuta* (1916); John B. Losi, *History of Abeokuta* (1920); Adebesin Folarin, *A Short Historical Review of the Life of the Egbas from 1829 to 1930* (1931); and Ladipo Solanke, *The Egba-Yoruba Constitutional Law and Its Historical Development* (1931). Ajisafe was an especially important figure because his history became the first local classic to be reprinted several times. Moreover, he was the first Egba historian to produce an anthropological study as well, *The Laws and Customs of the Yoruba People*.[31] Adrian Deese argues that Ajisafe is also an underappreciated intellectual of this period, whose approach in many ways anticipated contemporary concerns. Ajisafe argued, for example, that Abeokuta's modernity was not based on its leaders' acceptance of European ideals or ideas. Instead, its modernity evolved from its leaders' repudiation of elements of Oyo statecraft, specifically the centralized monarchy. Abeokuta developed a state system that was federal and had a weak monarchy.[32] While Ajisafe, like Samuel Johnson, subverted British ideas about African political and religious systems, he also subverted Johnson's uncritical rendering of Oyo by suggesting that Oyo's political structure had become an anachronism unable to grapple with the international and regional changes of the nineteenth century.[33] Thus, Ajisafe was not just following in Johnson's footsteps on a local level—he instead offered a different historical perspective through the lens of Abeokuta's history.

Literary works, broadly defined, augmented historical texts and played a critical role in the elaboration of national identities.[34] Nigeria's early cultural nationalists emerged from its ethnically, politically, and religiously diversified educated community. A disproportionate number were Saro, but it also included Blacks from the diaspora, particularly from Brazil and the Caribbean. They were spread unevenly across the southern region of what became Nigeria. As Philip Zachernuk notes, they were concentrated among the Yorubas and Niger Delta trading centers, especially Lagos and Calabar.[35] This educated community was mobile, circulating throughout West Africa, Brazil, and England.[36] The community was linked as well by a distinctive set of ideas. They shared a belief in the civilizing mission. They saw themselves as the natural leaders of Nigerian society and appreciated their membership in a broader intellectual community that included other parts of West Africa and the diaspora.[37]

The new imperialism of the late nineteenth century and the increasing acceptance of racist pseudoscientific literature that opined on Black inferiority altered the social and cultural landscape in which the intelligentsia lived. Like their counterparts in the United States and the Caribbean, the Nigerian intelligentsia had to assert their humanity, their ability to build a great civilization, and their modernity.[38] The onslaught of the new imperialism's racism sparked a cultural flowering among these "Victorian-mannered" elites. Zachernuk shows that "they began by asserting that Africa's culture was too substantial to be simply displaced by Europe's and that in any case their pride in being African would not allow it."[39] They demonstrated their pride in African culture by adopting African dress and African names and promoting African culture and histories.[40] They defended indigenous customs and institutions such as polygyny and the use of Yoruba language in education. The intelligentsia also played a central role in the creation of the separatist African churches, which began in the 1880s.[41]

Karin Barber argues that our understanding of the literary works that challenged the cultural pronouncements of imperialism should be an expansive category that includes much more than local histories, novels, and plays. Genres such as memoirs, diaries, and letters helped create new kinds of self and self-consciousness. While these texts recorded individual experiences and aspirations, the authors narrated moments of their lives in dialogue with and "under the shadow of colonial officialdom." Reading clubs and literary and debate societies became important spaces where young men practiced techniques of government, such as electing officers, taking minutes, and drafting reports, and demonstrated their eligibility for political participation. While only a small percentage of the population in Africa was literate, Barber argues that print helped make the constitution of an African civil society possible. Newspapers played an especially important role in shaping civil society.[42] By the 1920s, Lagos had nine English-language newspapers, five of which were dailies, and five Yoruba-language weeklies. The Yoruba-language newspapers were especially innovative as they included forms of Yoruba oral literature, individual travel narratives, open letters to prominent members of society, and serial novels. These papers often reproduced stories carried in the English-language papers; however, Barber notes that they utilized a range of textual forms to appeal to different audiences. The English-language papers primarily addressed the government and African elites, while the Yoruba-language papers specifically aligned themselves to the larger population they characterized as the poor or lower classes.[43] In the process of shaping civil society, the expanding category of literary works showcased the competing narratives of distinct political communities and evolving social classes.

Literary forms of nation-making did not replace other forms of elaborating the nation. Communities continued the symbolic work of representing and reinforcing existing political communities through ritual observances, even as new political ideas and associations emerged. Royal installations, for example, "validate the right of a king to rule and emphasize the unique identity and corporate unity of his kingdom." Andrew Apter argues that these ceremonies often reenacted the details that established the kingdom's founding and the authority of its political charter.[44] Such foundational exercises existed in dynamic tension with rituals that challenged these constituted authorities. For example, the Shango cult and Beere festival reflected Oyo's political centralization in the seventeenth and eighteenth centuries. However, rituals that commemorated kingdoms with ties to Ife in fact challenged Oyo's hegemony.[45]

Many different rituals participate in these contests of power and authority, and *The Great Upheaval* focuses on two critical events: the hundredth anniversary of Abeokuta's founding and the AWU celebrations after the alake went into exile. These events were staging grounds for competing narratives about Abeokuta's history. Wale Adebanwi argues that commemorations are rituals of ethnonational validation.[46] Abeokuta's centenary in 1930 is a powerful example of the political work performed by such activities, as it served multiple political agendas. It reinforced the dominance of Egba identity in Abeokuta as well as the dominance of the alake. The planning committee used the events to ultimately underscore Abeokuta's modernity and the reasons why its sovereignty should be restored. Colonial officials, though supportive of the centenary celebrations, imagined an entirely different set of meanings, for in it they saw confirmation of the colonial enterprise. Like other events crafted to reinforce collective identities, such as the centenary of the Great Trek in South Africa, Abeokuta's centenary was gendered.[47] The celebrations turned a spotlight on male leaders while ignoring female leaders, including the nineteenth-century merchant and kingmaker Madam Efunroye Tinubu.

The erasure of Tinubu during the centenary celebrations forms a stark contrast to her veneration during the tax revolt. *The Great Upheaval* juxtaposes these two events to demonstrate the ways in which questions of gender and agency shaped the tax revolt as well as Tinubu's iconic role in the process. Women often prayed at Tinubu's grave before protests, and they celebrated their victory by holding a picnic at her grave site, thus indicating that it held symbolic significance. Their use of Tinubu's grave site supports Adebanwi's contention that rituals around death and the ways in which the dead are memorialized can contribute "to the collective integrity and solidarity of the groups that use them."[48] By invoking Madam Tinubu in their struggle against the alake, the AWU attempted to reanimate the town's history of women power brokers and validate their demands. Moreover, history was on their side. Tinubu's funeral in 1887 attested to her significance. A biographer noted that the chiefs orchestrated "a fitting burial to the great woman who had been one of their own number." Her body lay in state for several hours, then a mile-long procession accompanied the corpse to the burial site, and celebrations continued for a weekend.[49] Her contemporaries understood that the scale of the celebrations following her death was an indicator of her importance to the Egba nation. The AWU edited the narrative of the nation that was created by the 1930 centenary celebrations, but its context was created by indirect rule as well as the material and economic conditions of the interwar depression and World War II.

The nineteenth-century architects of a Yoruba nation envisioned a landscape in which Yoruba-ness would come to dominate the other political identities that vied for significance. They could not have anticipated the ways in which the early decades of colonial rule animated sub-Yoruba identities as communities attempted to protect their hard-won independence from Oyo or its potential successor state, Ibadan, and claim access to resources from the colonial state. Thus, Yorubaland's complex political history in the nineteenth century was a critical component of the twentieth-century efforts to define Abeokuta as an Egba nation.

WOMEN, NARRATIVE, AND NATION

Building on the work of Benedict Anderson, an increasing number of scholars are exploring the centrality of narratives to the ideological and cultural construction of nations. Lloyd Kramer has characterized Homi Bhabha's edited volume, *Nation and Narration*, as one of the most forceful examples of scholars using a literary approach to nationalism. Its contributors argue that the nation "is constructed through narrative processes that resemble and include the narrative constructions of novels, film and history books." In fact, the nation is a text. Kramer suggests that the contributors expand on Anderson's work by stressing that the narrators of the text must contend with a range of contradictions, such as repressing issues, ideas, or people, while claiming unity and coherence.[50] Bhabha characterizes these contradictions as an ambivalence that haunts the idea of the nation. This ambivalence is created by a disjuncture inherent in "the language of those who write of it (the nation) and those who live it." As a result, the origins of national traditions are both "acts of affiliation and establishment as they are moments of disavowal, displacement, exclusion, and cultural contestation"[51]—in short, unity, which at the heart of all nations' narratives requires a nations' narrators to elide the people, races, classes, or ideas that do not fit easily or contradict the text they have created.

Nigerian scholar Wale Adebanwi uses Bhabha's insights productively as he combines literary theory and social science analysis of colonial and postcolonial political culture in Nigeria. Nigeria, he notes, "had the arduous task of forging a nation out of an amalgam of competing nations . . . [and] the Nigerian press has been at the center of the struggle for common nationhood." The press is also the site where hegemonic and counter-hegemonic battles of Nigeria's competing ethnic nationalities play out. Since the Nigerian press began before the colonies of Southern Nigeria and Northern Nigeria were amalgamated in 1914, newspapers expressed the African educated elites' strident criticism of this new direction in colonial policy. The press was also the battlefield on which the leaders of the country's three dominant political parties in the 1950s questioned each other's commitment to decolonization and unity. Through his analysis of the Nigerian press across the colonial and postcolonial divide, Adebanwi "interrogates meaning[s] in the press and how meanings[s] are mobilized in the service of the construction, deconstruction, or reconstruction of the idea of 'nationhood.'" His findings lead him to conclude that "narrative

[is] not just a process of bringing a nation into being through telling stories, but also as the nation itself. . . . The nation exists in and through its
narratives; thus the nation is a grand narrative."[52]

Whether the nation is text or a grand narrative, it still contains the
ambivalences Bhabha identifies. In Nigeria, this was apparent in a series of
editorials in which leaders of the Western and Eastern Regions simultaneously chastised and cajoled the leaders of the Northern Region to support
the call for independence in 1956:

> Now that the whole nation of "brothers" shared a "common
> destiny" and was separated from its foreign other, the "British
> imperialists," the *Pilot* argued: "Let us therefore make it plain
> to our brothers in the North that times have changed. The old
> form of propaganda which put a barrier between the Northern-
> ers and Southerners must now be exposed. Europeans may go
> and come, but Northerners and Southerners will continue to
> live together, work together and face the same destiny now or in
> the future.[53]

This quote is instructive as it reveals these politicians' efforts to create unity
as well as the ways in which Nigeria's grand narrative naturalized male
political dominance and elided women.

The idea of a "nation of brothers" dramatically supports Chatterjee's
argument that the hegemonic discourse of nationalism "was in its core a
male discourse."[54] Unfortunately, as Anne McClintock has charged, many
male theorists of nationalism "have been indifferent to the gendering of
nations," and "feminist analyses of nationalism have been . . . few and far
between."[55] Since the groundbreaking work of Chatterjee and McClintock
in the 1990s, studies on women, gender, and nationalism have grown exponentially as authors consider how women were represented in narratives of
the nation, the privileging of distinct forms of masculinity, femininity, and
sexuality, and the roles women played in nationalist movements.

Women were written into the nation in ways that were symbolic and
silencing. They were "typically constructed as the symbolic bearers of the
nation, but . . . denied any direct relation to national agency."[56] Scholars
have interrogated and looked beyond the symbolic representations that
offered a caricature of women's participation in nationalist movements in
Africa. The breadth of studies allows us to develop comparative analyses
of the multiple pathways that brought women into anticolonial and nationalist movements. Increasingly they are identifying the numerous ways
in which African women contributed to and shaped anticolonialist and

nationalist movements as well as the commonalities and divergences in what men and women hoped to be the outcome of these campaigns. This scholarship also calls our attention to specific ways in which local and national contexts shaped when, where, and how women contributed to these movements. Beth Baron, for example, vividly captures the paradox of women's marginalization while still a symbol of the nation, in her monograph *Egypt as a Woman*.[57] Preexisting women's organizations established the base from which women participated in the protests that undermined the legitimacy of the British. Despite the organizational infrastructure they brought to the protests, Egyptian women were denied any voice in the unfolding deliberations that led to self-government. In contrast to Egypt, Algerian women did not have a strong foundation of women's organizations at the beginning of the nationalist movement. In Algeria, the Algerian Communist Party helped create the first women's union in 1943, the Union of Algerian Women (UFA). It was the only party that championed equality of the sexes, though following the repression of popular demonstrations in May 1945, other political parties articulated greater interest in improving women's lives. By 1947, Muslim women had created the Association of Muslim Algerian Women (AFMA). Though their program focused on social issues—tending the sick, distributing clothes and food to the poor, and encouraging the education of both boys and girls—the leaders of both the UFA and AFMA joined the armed struggle.[58]

Even where women were part of male-dominated nationalist organizations, they held distinctive aspirations and goals. The late Susan Geiger's work on Tanzania demonstrated that women brought shared but not identical concerns to that country's nationalist discourse. Women were central to the expansion of the Tanganyika African National Union (TANU), Tanzania's main nationalist organization, but they saw TANU as a vehicle for transforming gender relations as well as one for moving the country toward independence. Women also shaped the ideological orientation of nationalist organizations. Elizabeth Schmidt's *Mobilizing the Masses* illuminates how women helped radicalize the nationalist movement in Guinea and forced Sékou Touré to turn down France's offer to remain in the French commonwealth.[59] In the former French Cameroon where the Union des Populations du Cameroun (UPC) led a guerrilla struggle against French rule, Meredith Terretta argues that women were the intermediaries that made decolonization imaginable. Women of the Democratic Union of Cameroonian Women "occupied strategic positions in reshaping social ideology until the UPC message became something 'thinkable' even in the humblest village home."[60]

Women were not an amorphous group, therefore their social status, religion, and competing notions of femininity also shaped women's political engagement. Abosede George and Saheed Aderinto, for example, consider the contributions of elite women in Lagos to the discourse on development, modernity, and nationalism in the 1940s and 1950s. Their studies document the ways in which Victorian class and gender ideals informed the issues these women engaged. Elite women played central roles in the debates around prostitution and street hawking by children and worked to shape colonial policies around these issues. However, their advocacy often put them in contention with poor women who relied on sex work, given the limited employment opportunities for women in Lagos, and on child labor for their trading enterprises.[61] Similar tensions also unfolded in Southern Rhodesia. There the dominant political organization from the 1930s to 1950s, the Reformed Industrial and Commercial Workers' Union, enjoyed a brief alliance between elite men and self-employed single women as they resisted the state's efforts to evict men and women who did not have proper papers. This cross-class alliance failed as the state met elites' demands for married housing that also separated them from migrant laborers and married women strongly opposed the presence self-employed single women in the townships. These studies underscore Timothy Scarnecchia's suggestion that it is "more productive to examine the historical evidence to show how groups of women attempted to apply their own specific struggles within a political framework." This will help us make sense of the wide range of outcomes—from women who pushed nationalist struggles to be more radical, to those movements that failed to attract women's active support.[62]

Excavating women's role in nation-building is only one dimension of a gender analysis of the nation. It is equally critical, as Joane Nagel argues, "to explore the fact of men's domination of the nation-state in order to see what insights . . . masculinity provides."[63] Lisa Lindsay's *Working with Gender: Wage Labor and Social Change in Southwestern Nigeria* does just that as it demonstrates how masculinity informed the labor movement that played such a central role in Nigerian nationalism. Lindsay's study of the 1945 general strike in Lagos contributes significantly to a more gendered analysis of the nationalist era in Nigeria, for it demonstrates the ways that gender ideals and notions such as the "male breadwinner" were woven into the constitutive elements of the nationalist agenda. Although the male breadwinner ideal was not adopted wholesale by Nigerian men and women, it heavily informed nationalist politics and sanctioned male monopolization of political space. Insa Nolte noted that "the division of labor between Obafemi and Hannah Awolowo reflected a gendered approach to politics, in which Awolowo himself acted officially in the public sphere while his wife provided access to and mobilized non-public political re-sources."[64] Their gendered approach to politics differed significantly with that of Rev. I. O. Ransome-Kuti and Funmilayo Ransome-Kuti, where both husband and wife played large public roles. The different approaches to political work between the Awolowos and the Ransome-Kutis remind us that gender ideals were dynamic and not rigid.

Increasingly scholars of gender are also calling our attention to competing masculinities at any particular historical moment. Thembisa Waetjens pushes our analysis further by arguing that "nationalisms are often forced to incorporate more than one vision of patriarchal social or-ganization into their narrative of the collective whole."[65] Focusing on the Zulu organization Inkatha, Waetjens shows how its leader, Chief Man-gosuthu Buthelezi, "employed a sophisticated and well-crafted masculin-ist discourse that referenced 'traditional' gender systems and identities to bolster its credibility as a nationalist politics based on deep-seated cultural traditions."[66] In their bid for regional power in postapartheid South Africa, Buthelezi hoped to use the appeal of Zulu masculinity and the history of the duty and valor of Zulu warriors to garner support among Zulu men who belonged to trade unions and the African National Congress. This strategy, while effective in the rural areas, was less successful in the urban areas, especially among workers whose identity as workers supported a competing framework of masculinity.

These theoretical insights are invaluable to an effort to understand women's agency in constructing the nation. Few historians, however, have drawn our attention to the ways in which women's political engagement tried to contribute to the narration of the nation or succeeded in doing so. Analyses of women's narration of the nation have been explored most thoroughly by literary scholars. Susan Z. Andrade, for example, challenges the assumptions that locked African literature in a public/private binary in which male novelists produced works that performed national narra-tives while women's novels focused on the family and the domestic realm in apolitical ways. Andrade convincingly argues that men and women both used the trope of the family, but whereas men used the family as an allegory of colonial resistance or national consolidation, women writ-ers, especially after the 1960s, used it to expose other fictions. For women novelists, "the family [became] the nation writ small." Andrade's insightful rereading of women's novels against each other and against the works of male novelists allowed her to illuminate women's counternarratives of the nation.[67] Elucidating women's narratives is a critical exercise because, as *Nation and Narration* reminds us, "the survival of nations depends on a narrative construction of reality, and the power for control of that narrative becomes a struggle over power, meaning and knowledge in every nation-state."[68] A struggle over power and meaning is at the heart of *The Great Upheaval* as it focuses our attention on the narrative the AWU attempted to craft in which its members' voices were not repressed but full-throated.

Although this power struggle extended to the national stage, much of the important political work conducted by the activists of the AWU and the NWU has been erased in the histories of postwar Nigeria and nationalism. James S. Coleman, for example, produced one of the earliest studies on nationalism in Nigeria that in many ways exemplifies the overarching narrative. The roots of nationalism, according to Coleman, are to be found in the different patterns of urbanization: increased mobility, physical detachment from traditional authority, and the concentration of economic power in the hands of the European trading companies, especially the United Africa Company (UAC).[69] Economic grievances contributed significantly to the rise of nationalist sentiment across Nigeria's social spectrum, especially during the interwar period and World War II. However, as he noted, "nationalism is not merely the sum of accumulated grievances; it is equally an awareness of greater possibilities and opportunities."[70] Those with a Western education were better positioned to articulate those possibilities and opportunities since they were endowed with "the knowledge and skills, the ambitions and aspirations, that enabled them to challenge the Nigerian colonial government."[71]

World War II brought forward new forces and a new militancy in the trade union and nationalist movements. Critical moments that identify this new militancy include the formation of the NCNC in 1944, the spirited demand for political participation and voting rights in 1945, the general strike in Lagos in 1945, and the coal miners' strike of 1949 that led to the shooting of miners at the government colliery in Enugu. These events inspired many of the individuals who were at the forefront of nationalist politics, in particular Obafemi Awolowo, a key figure in the Nigerian Youth Movement (NYM) and founder of the Action Group (AG), the Yoruba-dominated political party; Nnamdi Azikiwe, a newspaper publisher and one of the founders as well as the leader of the NCNC; and Michael Imoudu, who was considered to be "Nigeria's Labor Leader No. 1."[72] This narrative is heavily weighted toward the male actors who helped give voice to people's grievances and helped individuals and communities across the length and breadth of Nigeria imagine themselves as part of a unified, sovereign nation. The narrative normalizes male political dominance and glosses over the charged debate about gender and the appropriate roles for women both in the nationalist movement and the imagined nation-state.

Most scholars of this era did not consider the ways that masculinity shaped the evolving nationalist discourse or movement. Nor did they question the marginalization of women's voices among Nigerian nationalists. Nonetheless, women were not completely absent from the analysis. Coleman, in a brief discussion of Lagos market women, notes that "they were the mass base of Nigeria's oldest political organization, the Nigerian National Democratic Party," and that "market-women were constituents whom any urban politician or nationalist leader would ignore at his peril."[73] Richard Sklar's discussion focused on the formation of political parties and thus accurately reflects the way that the parties conceived of women members—as ancillary elements.[74] Thomas Hodgkin gave the most attention to women, especially highlighting women's associations in a number of different countries and the various ways they moved into nationalist politics.[75] He identified the Egba Women's Union and Funmilayo Ransome-Kuti as one of the most interesting cases.[76]

These scholars, Coleman, Sklar, and Hodgkin, acknowledged the important support women brought to nationalist organizations and the political momentum of the period. Although they did not consider how women, through their actions and organizations, contributed specifically to the intellectual ferment that typified the nationalist era, Hodgkin articulated a useful framework for such an analysis. He argued that associations were democratic "in the older sense, that they have been constructed by a *demos* which is slowly discovering, by trial and error, the institutions which it required in order to live humanly and sociably."[77] He challenged scholars to study associations because they were an outcome of the "discontent excited by the philosophy of life" of which, in this case, the nation was the symbol and expression.[78] Hodgkin moved women beyond the role of supporters and into the realm of contributors to a philosophy of life. Building on this insight, this study foregrounds the political work of Nigerian women activists instead of folding it into the history of the Nigerian nation-state and the nationalist movement.

THE POLITICAL AND ECONOMIC CONTEXTS OF REVOLT

This analysis of narration is grounded in material realities of the period and does not champion narrative or cultural productions at the expense of socioeconomic processes. Instead, it establishes the social and economic conditions upon which this struggle over nation and narration unfolded. *The Great Upheaval* excavates the circumstances that shaped the AWU demands. Thus, it traces the women's political position with each transformation of the Egba state. It demonstrates that male monopolization of the organs of power was not a natural process; rather, it was engineered with each failure to incorporate women into the council, which in theory shared power with the alake or to ensure that women's titles were filled as titleholders passed. This political engineering, however, did not erase the political transcript crafted by women such as Madam Tinubu in the nineteenth century.

Tinubu's historical role helped sustain the tax protests, but the AWU's deployment of this iconic figure should not be read as a harking back to a traditional past. She was being used to wage a contemporary struggle. Abeokuta's ideological landscape remained dynamic during the twentieth century. The colonial government could not dampen enthusiasm for new political ideals that challenged colonial thought and its attendant racism. *The Great Upheaval* makes note of the political ideas that took root in Abeokuta, especially in the interwar period, and also explores how women used the new political organizations that emerged. Many in Abeokuta followed events in Lagos, other parts of Nigeria, and Britain, and as a result they offered support or commentary to a variety of causes, including Ethiopian resistance to the Italian invasion of 1935 and the general strike in Lagos.

Equally important, *The Great Upheaval* explores the economic impact of the Great Depression and World War II on women in Abeokuta and Nigeria more broadly. The war is especially important because of the complicated ways in which it shaped the experiences of market women. Britain demanded resources from its colonies for the war effort. The list of resources included foodstuffs for civilians and the military as well as revenue either through voluntary donations, such as support for the Red Cross, or involuntary contributions, such as taxes. The war proved to be an especially challenging period for market women and farmers in Abeokuta, especially since the government forced traders and farmers to sell their goods at the low control prices. As their profit margins shrank, they confronted an increasingly coercive and efficient tax-collection regime. *The Great Upheaval* demonstrates how wartime conditions and policies in conjunction with a more strident nationalism set the stage for the tax revolt and the rising crescendo of women's voices in Abeokuta.

Since taxes lie at the center of this study, it is important to consider the larger historical and philosophical dimensions of taxes. Taxation in

Britain, as Jane Guyer notes, was ideologically naturalized by the late eighteenth century.[79] Benjamin Franklin's famous saying "In this world nothing can be said to be certain, except death and taxes" reflected the ubiquitous nature of taxes in Euro-American economic and political culture.[80] Taxes came in multiple forms, and while all systems of taxation raised revenue, taxes simultaneously satisfied economic as well as symbolic functions. The items taxed, who collected the taxes, and how taxes were used engaged political, social, economic, and philosophical questions since the collection and distribution of taxes helped construct relations of power within the state as well as between state and society, rich and poor, and men and women.

Control over tax collection facilitated centralization of the British state. By the late sixteenth century, the Treasury Board had extended oversight over state revenues and distribution. It brought uniformity to revenue collection and perfected fiscal measures that enabled it to establish "its authority over the monarch, the Privy Council and the spending departments" and defend itself against the expanding authority of the secretaries of state.[81] Taxes also bore direct links to political participation. For more than a thousand years, taxation and property profoundly shaped who had the right to exercise governmental authority in the political landscape. However, political reformers also used taxation to undercut propertied classes by linking it to ideas of a universal franchise. In British history, taxation and democracy became tightly interwoven.[82]

Colonial officials, however, did not export the linked discourse between taxation and democracy to Britain's African colonies. As Guyer argues, Britain's African subjects experienced taxation without representation for much of the colonial period. This historical experience had profound implications for democratic practice in postcolonial Africa because the "present African leadership has to seek consent first and enforce taxation afterwards."[83] The political role of taxes went beyond limiting democracy: they were central to controlling African political elites as well. While the state insisted that taxation would provide emirs and chiefs a regular source of income, thereby enabling them to maintain their estates and carry out their administrative duties, taxation also allowed them to control African political authorities more efficiently and directly. In Northern Nigeria, part of that control rested on the fact that chiefs no longer had the power to levy taxes; that power was given to the district officer.[84] While scholars explore the political implications of taxation, a significant literature already exists on the imposition of taxes, their importance to the fiscal self-sufficiency of the colonial state, and their role in the creation of a wage labor force.[85] In the settler colonies of East and Southern Africa, taxes proved critical to the development of migrant labor. Taxation also impacted African family structures and gender relations. In the Belgian Congo, officials used taxation to discourage polygynous marriage, while in South Africa women became legal minors because they were not legally liable for tax payment.[86]

Anthony Hopkins argued that research on taxation had become unfashionable.[87] However, new studies on taxation are appearing, and they are distinguished by their attention to culture as they explore the political, social, and economic consequences of tax policies at different historical junctures. Moses Ochonu uses an analysis of the methods colonial officials resorted to in collecting taxes in Northern Nigeria during the 1930s to explore the contradictions between the self-perceptions of these officials and the realities of their actions.[88] Taxation and fiscal policy more broadly also tell us much about the state and its governance. In a provocative article, Barbara Bush and Josephine Maltby draw our attention to the role of accounting and taxation in colonial/imperial contexts. Taxation was "a moralizing force, transforming the primitive and barbaric into good, industrious and governable colonial subjects." In short, it was a method for controlling and disciplining the colonized.[89] Lord Frederick Lugard, commissioner of Northern Nigeria and later the first governor general of amalgamated Nigeria, oversaw the extension of taxes across most of Nigeria. His insistence on direct taxation drew heavily on his belief that taxes were morally justified as "contributions towards the cost of Administration" as well as a moral benefit to the taxpayer because it "stimulated industry and production."[90] For Lugard, taxation was also a symbol of British suzerainty, and, as Janet Roitman argues, it "exemplified the materialization of colonial power in its fiscal form."[91] Drawing on her research in Cameroon and the Chad Basin, she shows that it turned the peoples in this region into consumers of French currency, "an incontrovertible sign of colonial power."[92] The methods of accounting and financial relations linked to taxation, according to Dean Neu and Monica Heincke, also made a domain of behavior visible and amenable to intervention based on the information gathered. They provided technologies of governance that allowed force to remain in the shadows, though readily accessible.[93] These new technologies of governance produced different consequences for different societies and social groups and therefore created different forms of resistance.

These recent studies on taxation bring new insights to our understanding of moments of tax resistance. Since colonial rule and governance varied considerably, it is necessary to examine the local context into which taxes were introduced as well as the local landscape of governance. The attempt to extend direct taxation during the interwar depression led to antitax protests in many parts of West Africa. However, in Nigeria and the Gold Coast, women were especially active because taxes threatened to undermine their already precarious marketing activities.[94] Moments of antitax protests also provide insights into African conceptualizations of taxation. Bush and Maltby note that during the interwar era, the African intelligentsia increasingly and more forcefully raised the question of taxation without representation. This demand highlighted one of the contradictions of colonial policy, but, more importantly, it illustrates that different segments of African society examined the political relationships established through taxation. Some accepted the idea that taxes were a civic virtue. They marked one's membership in a community as well as one's contribution to its upkeep and modernization. In Abeokuta, the administration that replaced the alake's government experimented with linking tax payment to political participation by requiring a tax receipt in order to vote. In other communities, people asked searing questions about the relationship between taxation and social reproduction. Roitman identifies tax resisters who took exception to French calculations that did not take food and other basic items of consumption into consideration. Her informants accepted that profits should be taxed, but they defined profits as what remained after the consumption of food and clothing for themselves and their families.[95] In many ways, tax policies mirrored the ambivalences of the nation. Although taxes were presented as an equally shared sacrifice, distinct social groups and individuals paid more than others and benefited much more substantially than others. Thus, arguments and disputes around taxes reveal the tensions and differences that challenge the nation's narrative of unity and coherence.

STRUCTURE OF THE BOOK

The book is organized into six chapters and a conclusion. Chapter 1, "The Birth and Demise of a Nation: The Egba United Government," examines the nineteenth-century promoters of nationhood in Abeokuta. It also reconsiders the creation of the Egba United Government (EUG) in 1898. In many ways, the EUG represented the sort of sovereign national government that European and African missionaries had envisioned. This chapter examines how women were represented in the national government and how they helped shape this important experiment. The end of the EUG came in 1914 when the Lagos government abrogated the Egba Treaty of Independence. The chapter considers the ideological and economic tensions as Abeokuta adjusted to life under the full mantle of British rule. Governor Lugard moved quickly to impose taxes, so the chapter examines the implications of the tax structure on Egba national identity and women's consciousness as well as the tensions that led to the Adubi War, a rural tax revolt in 1918.

Chapter 2, "Abeokuta's Centenary: Masculinity and Nationalist Politics in a Colonial Space," also analyzes the structure of the colonial state in Abeokuta, especially after the tax revolt and the ascension of Alake Gbadebo's successor, Ademola II. It demonstrates the tightrope colonial officials trod as they tried to undermine Abeokuta's sense of independence while relying on the political symbol of that independence, the alake, to reinforce their suzerainty. This challenge became most acute as Abeokuta looked to its centenary in 1930. The chapter highlights the plans and discussion around the celebration of the town's first hundred years, which focused attention on its sense of its history and national identity. This chapter draws attention to the local histories about Abeokuta, some of which were written for the centenary. It examines how the town's leaders selected the heroes to be memorialized and celebrated, in the process demonstrating how they attempted to construct and legitimize male political dominance. The centenary also encapsulated a political debate about colonial rule between colonial officials and Abeokuta's political elites. The very performance of the celebrations signified competing political goals. For colonial officials the centenary illustrated the efficacy of British colonial rule, while for the alake it demonstrated Abeokuta's progress and worthiness of independence.

While the centenary flamboyantly presented a case for Abeokuta's independence, other notions of independence and nationhood took root. Chapter 3, "Race, Nation, and Politics in the Interwar Period," examines the other political frames through which people constructed political and cultural identities and activism. It examines the evolving construction of Nigerian nationalism as new political parties emerged. Herbert Macauley's Nigerian National Democratic Party (NNDP) emerged in the 1920s, although Lagos was the center of its political activity. This chapter suggests that the emergence of the NYM in the 1930s represented an important political and organizational shift as it sought to mobilize people beyond Lagos. It also argues that the invasion of Ethiopia contributed to the expanding spatial dimension of nationalist thought during the interwar period. As NYM chapters established in other towns and communities organized to support the Ethiopians, these spaces facilitated discussions that deepened national and racial identity formation. This chapter argues that the 1930s was an important transitional period in Abeokuta as political identification and activism shifted from the search for independence within a British colonial framework to independence as part of Nigeria.

World War II deserves special consideration. Therefore, chapter 4, "Women, Rice, and War: Economic Crisis in Wartime Abeokuta," examines the broad impact of the war as well as the colonial government's efforts to regulate consumer prices and to obtain sufficient food to feed the enlarged population in Lagos. These actions had a direct bearing on the tax revolt because they exacerbated the economic crisis women traders faced. Chapter 5, "'Freedom from Want': Politics, Protest, and the Postwar Interlude," considers the impact of the postwar economic austerity on Nigeria more broadly and Abeokuta specifically. The discussion primarily focuses on a very narrow window of time, 1945–47, for it seeks to understand the multiple strands that came together to ignite the mass women's protests that unfolded in Abeokuta by the end of 1947.

The women often invoked the historical personality Madam Tinubu to give symbolic validation to their actions. Therefore, chapter 6, "Daughters of Tinubu: Crisis and Confrontation in Abeokuta," pays special attention to the deeper meaning and symbolic value that the women attributed to this complex icon and what she represented in women's cultural construction of the nation. It uses crisis as a lens to explore the competing ways in which the AWU, the alake, and his council, and colonial officials both saw and narrated the tax revolt. It relies on a wealth of documents crafted by the AWU and their supporters, the alake, and the top colonial official in the province, the British resident, especially John Blair. These sources provide a deep appreciation of the magnitude of the women's actions. The outcome could have mirrored that of the 1929 Women's War, in which sixty-nine women were killed, because on several occasions troops were brought to the outskirts of Abeokuta. Those in the moment understood the situation as a powder keg, and many faulted the AWU. The AWU's narration of the events is equally compelling, for it faulted the alake's authoritarian practice and articulated a challenge to the erasure of women in both colonial and nationalist renderings. In the process, the AWU's narrative revealed the kind of nation-state the women envisioned and their explicit or indirect ideas about the role of chieftaincy.

Finally, the conclusion considers events after the alake's departure and subsequent return in 1951. That year is equally impactful on the national stage because a new constitution, the Macpherson Constitution, moved the country along the path of self-government and opened the door for the formation of political parties. The creation of political parties catapulted women into a new political landscape that lacked the gender and ethnic idealism of the immediate postwar years. Ransome-Kuti became increasingly marginalized as she resisted ethnic mobilization and women's subservience to a political agenda established without recognition of women's needs. In many ways, developments in Abeokuta after the new constitution exemplified the reconfiguration of political space in broader Nigeria. The panethnic coalition under the broad umbrella of the NCNC in the years before 1951 quickly lost ground to the regional and ethnic parties that competed for elections. The conclusion also brings us back full circle to the pivotal emergence of the NWU and highlights the increasing tension between the organization and the political parties. It illustrates how women's political independence was increasingly undermined by nationalist success as the country moved toward self-government. As a result, the women's political organizations that survived the rise of the political parties were largely transformed into women's wings of the parties, a far cry from the aspirations of the NWU.

1 ⮜ The Birth and Demise of a Nation

The Egba United Government

THE POLITICAL landscape in Abeokuta had changed dramatically since the Egba and Owu refugees established this new town in the shadow of the geological formation known as Olumo Rock. From its location, which offered good security and ample farmlands, Abeokuta became one of the leading political and economic centers in Yorubaland as well as a center of missionary activity. This chapter considers competing political ideas as military chiefs, traders, European missionaries, and Christian converts wrestled to control and shape the town's political, economic, and social landscapes. Critically, it identifies the main proponents of the nation in Abeokuta and the corresponding nation-state they envisioned in the decades before British control of Yorubaland. It underscores the fact that Abeokuta had an ongoing internal conversation about nationalism that would be significantly augmented by the expanding British presence by the end of the century.

Abeokuta's chiefs created a new political structure in 1898 under great pressure from British colonial officials, the Egba United Government. The EUG in many ways seemed to be the fruition of the nation that many Egbas and non-Egbas had imagined over the course of the nineteenth century. On the surface, this new government appeared to achieve the centralization of Abeokuta's political structure that many had failed to secure before. The four quarters that composed the town were united under the leadership of the alake, the king of Ake quarter. Educated men played a central role in the EUG and helped transform Abeokuta's political structure into a modern monarchy that combined elements of the indigenous political structure with practices that would deliver the benefits modernity promised.[1]

Britain's recognition of Abeokuta as a self-governing kingdom facilitated the efforts of political elites in Abeokuta and in Lagos to craft a nation out of this polity. As the rest of Yorubaland fell to colonial imposition, Abeokuta became the space from which an African modernity and independence could be created and modeled. Colonial officials expected the alake to serve as the political center of this nation in the way that the *kabaka* (king) functioned as the political head of a self-consciously culturally and politically defined Buganda.[2] However, their efforts to construct the alake as the final arbiter of local politics were met with constant challenges in the remnants of the town's heterogeneous political structure. Moreover, Britain's recognition of the EUG did not allow the autonomy African elites had imagined. Thus, the alake's government was actively constrained by British needs and demands as well as local Egbas' demands for redress against destructive policies.

This chapter examines the emergence and subsequent demise of the EUG. It is especially concerned with the social and economic consequences of the EUG on men and women, the wealthy and poor as they navigated the new political landscape. It considers the articulation of nationalist thought in Abeokuta as this nineteenth-century city-state struggled to define and defend itself against the cultural and political onslaught of British colonialism. Finally, the chapter highlights the numerous ways in which Abeokuta's sovereignty and modernity assumed greater significance beyond the town's inhabitants because it became a symbol of African and racial pride. Thus, many experienced its loss of independence in 1914 as a seismic shift. That sense of loss further deepened when the colonial government imposed taxation, leading to a peasant tax revolt in 1918. These events collectively helped to solidify a national identity at the same time it deepened inequality and stratification across multiple layers of society. The chapter highlights the distinctive ways in which colonialism and British gender ideals shaped the inequalities embedded in this evolving nation.

REFORM AND EXPERIMENTATION

In a 1904 article for the *Journal of the Royal African Society*, the governor of Lagos, William MacGregor, noted that Abeokuta was engaged in "a most interesting experiment in native government." Furthermore, the "Alake is well aware of the difficulties and of the great importance of this task. If he and his colleagues are given a fair chance, it may safely be predicted that the experiment will succeed to such an extent that it will be extended before long far beyond the limits of the Lagos Protectorate."[3] The subject of this experiment, the EUG, enjoyed the greatest degree of independence of all the Yoruba provinces.[4]

In the article, MacGregor also painted Abeokuta and its political leadership in glowing terms. Abeokuta had "taken the lead in industrial development and progress. . . . The Alake presides over his own Council [which] . . . exercises legislative, executive and judicial functions. . . . The members are allowed complete freedom of speech. The meetings of the Council are conducted with the greatest decorum and regularity."[5] It would be remiss to believe, as MacGregor suggests, that this experiment in a centralized form of government with modern elements began only at the end of the nineteenth century. It is important to understand the length and depth of the antecedents to this government.

Within the first decade of the town's existence, Saros—Yorubas rescued from slave ships and settled in Sierra Leone—began returning to Egba towns. In Sierra Leone a few liberated Yoruba adopted Islam, but the majority accepted Christianity and elements of British culture. The first Saros arrived in 1839 and soon requested Christian missionaries to support them in the practice of their new faith and to help expand its membership.[6] The first missionary to visit Abeokuta was Thomas Birch Freeman, a Wesleyan missionary of African and English ancestry. Sodeke, the *balogun* of the Egbas (paramount military chief), welcomed Freeman and invited him to settle in the town.[7] Freeman did not accept the offer, but in 1846 the Church Missionary Society (CMS) established the first permanent station. Sodeke and his successors received the Saros and the missionaries warmly because they brought critical resources in the form of access to European traders, and therefore guns and ammunition from the coast, as well as new skills. One of the most important missionaries in Abeokuta was Henry Townsend, who visited the town in 1842 and then returned in 1846 to head the CMS station. Townsend acted as secretary to the alake for over ten years and directed "Anglo-Egba policy from the Egba side."[8] As Agneta Pallinder-Law argues, his position was very similar to that of a war chief or lineage head. In the eyes of the town authorities, Townsend was responsible for the Saros, the converts, the missionaries, and visiting Europeans—traders, missionaries, or representatives of the British government. Townsend is also important in the annals of Abeokuta's history because he established the first mission schools, introduced the printing press, produced a bilingual newspaper, encouraged the development of cotton exports, and established an industrial institute that produced the first bricks.[9] Townsend imagined that his influence would bring his political vision to fruition. He hoped to centralize political power in Abeokuta around the alake and set in motion the evolution of a Christian Egba theocracy. This theocracy would become the nucleus of a united Yoruba state.[10] European missionaries' influence evaporated, however, after 1867, when civil unrest forced them to leave Abeokuta.[11]

Townsend was not the only person to imagine a Christian state in Abeokuta. G. W. Johnson shared similar ideas, but he did not support the missionary presence there. Johnson, a tailor by profession, was born in Sierra Leone of Egba parents. He studied music in England for three years and tried a business venture in Liverpool.[12] After it failed, he returned to West Africa, eventually visiting Lagos in 1863 and Abeokuta in 1865. He "saw as his goal the creation in Abeokuta of a 'Christian, civilized state,' independent of foreign leadership."[13] Like Townsend, he believed Abeokuta needed a central government. In 1865, he devised the Egba United Board of Management (EUBM), through which he hoped to bring chiefs and Saros into one governing body. His ally, Bashorun Shomoye, became the president-general of the board, while Saros were given executive posts.[14] Johnson also composed a hymn to national unity,[15] and he created a flag that "contained the names of the four Egba kingdoms, but had in the middle the insignia of the crown of Queen Victoria."[16] The insignia clearly suggests that he hoped the new state would continue to share political relations with the British. The EUBM attempted some innovative developments. Johnson organized a postal service to Lagos, opened a secular school, and tried to persuade the mission schools to teach in English instead of Yoruba. The EUBM also tried to generate a central revenue stream for the board by collecting customs duties.[17] Although the late Egba historian S. O. Biobaku characterized the EUBM as "little more than an empty bureaucracy, parading sovereign pretensions, and issuing largely idle threats,"[18] he noted that it fostered some constructive developments. He identified two significant outcomes of Johnson's initiative: (1) the stress on the federal aspects of the Egba constitution and (2) the establishment of "the right of the immigrant elements, the Egba Saro, to participate in, and to direct, the affairs of the Egba."[19] Despite its weaknesses, it has to be recognized as one of the earliest political experiments to combine the legitimacy of traditional rulers with the knowledge of a Western-educated, Christianized elite.[20]

Johnson was the main spokesperson between the Egba chiefs and the Lagos government from 1865 to the 1880s.[21] However, the EUBM did not gain the widespread support within the Christian community or among the chiefs, nor did it have the support of the Lagos government. In Abeokuta,

Johnson competed against CMS-affiliated Saros for influence with the Egba chiefs. Although many converts fled from Abeokuta with the European missionaries during riots in 1867, many returned within a year. The presence of Christians remained strong in Abeokuta in part because they had the support of Ogundipe, the head of the *olorogun* (military chiefs) and "the uncrowned King of the Egbas from 1867 to 1887." He brought the outbreak against the Christians to an end by sending around his staff, the symbol of his authority.[22] In addition to protecting the lives and property of the converts in his township, Ikija, he saved the Abeokuta church.[23]

Johnson's influence weakened soon after his main supporter, Bashorun Shomoye, died in 1868. He tried to sustain the prospects for the EUBM by adding his support to the candidate for alake in 1869 backed by the military chiefs and leading traders, Oyekan.[24] However, Oyekan lost to Ademola I, who was supported by Henry Robbins, a layman within the CMS and the richest trader in Abeokuta.[25] Oyekan, who ultimately assumed the throne in 1879, supported Johnson's initiative because he was very poor when he assumed the office. Reports in the *Lagos Times* noted that previous kings brought their own personal wealth to the office since they were barred from trade and farming. Lacking substantial wealth, Oyekan stood to benefit from Johnson's plan to create a new port and levy export duties on cotton that would belong exclusively to the alake. The plan received swift condemnation from chiefs in the Owu quarter, who controlled the port and, traditionally, any fees collected, as well as by Saros and Lagos immigrants who argued that the duty would predominantly fall on them since they dominated cotton production. Ironically, after Oyekan's death, Chief Ogundipe resurrected the idea in 1881. He hosted a meeting of chiefs and people where it was decided to open a new port-of-entry and tollgate specifically for the alake. Ogundipe's second proposal, that G. W. Johnson collect the tax, was quickly dismissed by the CMS-affiliated Saros, but more people beyond the Christian elite were invested in the idea of a financially secure kingship.[26]

CMS-affiliated returnees remained an important factor in Abeokuta politics despite the absence of Townsend and other European missionaries from 1867 to 1875.[27] Saros maintained their political role because they continued to support the military rulers of the town. Robbins and Rev. William Moore, for example, provided ammunition from their own funds for the Egba military.[28] Military chiefs in turn accepted converts into their ranks. John Okenla, was a warrior, a devotee of the Yoruba deities Obatala (god of creativity) and Sango (god of thunder and lightning), and a high priest of Ifa (god of divination) before converting to Christianity. His conversion did not weaken the respect and support he enjoyed on the battlefield. Okenla became the first to hold a Christian warrior title, when Reverend Townsend installed him as balogun of the Christians in 1857.[29] Other military chiefs, including Chief Ogundipe, had tremendous confidence in him. Okenla was credited with defeating the Dahomean army in 1876; he spent his own money on his soldiers, rarely losing any in battle; and shortly before his death he "called some of his important friends together and advised them to subscribe towards procuring more ammunition for the defence of Abeo-kuta."[30] Though he was a Christian, Okenla was fully integrated into the so-ciopolitical structure of Abeokuta's military elite. When he died, the *Lagos Times* reported that "many heathen men of influence came from different parts of the town to witness the last honour that the Christians bestowed on their Balogun. Many heathen war-boys willingly joined the Christian war-boys. . . . Never had such a large concourse of people of every class and rank come together at a funeral at Abeokuta."[31]

In part to augment the important role that the Saros played, the CMS assigned Saro rather than European missionaries to Abeokuta. In 1868, John F. King resumed mission activities in Ake after he was interviewed and granted approval by Ogundipe and Madam Tinubu.[32] Tinubu—the highest-titled woman in Abeokuta, the *iyalode*, earned her title after helping to defeat Dahomey's army in 1864, having contributed soldiers, guns, and ammunition and helping to organize the women. She was one of the largest merchants in Abeokuta, having made a lateral transition from the slave trade to legitimate trade. Like her male counterparts, Tinubu had her own army and used her economic wealth to support or undermine those vying for the alakeship. Fr. Pierre Coquard, a Catholic priest based in Abeokuta, argued that Ogundipe and Tinubu were the two main political leaders in Abeokuta at this time.[33] Tinubu's participation in the interview with Reverend King indicated the significant political roles open to women of great wealth.

During this period, the Egba chiefs transferred their trust from Euro-pean missionaries to the Saros. Reverend Townsend observed the strong political relationship between the chiefs and the wealthy Saro leader when he returned to Abeokuta during 1875–76. Partly in recognition of this new reality, the CMS appointed Rev. James Johnson—a Saro of Ijesha and Ijebu parentage—superintendent of all the CMS stations in the interior of Yorubaland in 1876. Johnson settled in Abeokuta in February 1877,[34] and he was instructed to "extend the missionary frontier, to improve educational institutions with the aim of developing a native agency, and to encourage the churches to become self-supporting and self-governing."[35] Committed to the idea of a self-sustaining church, Reverend Johnson argued for an independent African church and tried to put in place practices that would support it. During the short period he served in Abeokuta, he doubled the revenue from Egba converts in preparation for a time when they would not have to take funds from the main mission body.[36] As a result of Johnson's vocal support for an African-led church, white missionaries actively worked against him.[37] Johnson also attracted the ire of slave-owning Saros and Egba chiefs when he tried to enforce the CMS circular calling for members to dismiss their slaves. Although this directive was intended for the CMS community, the Egba chiefs interpreted it as another attempt by Europeans to bring an end to domestic slavery. Johnson was ultimately removed from Abeokuta in 1880.

Despite Johnson's missteps in Abeokuta, the CMS faction enjoyed a political boost when a second generation of European missionaries, led by Rev. J. B. Wood, assumed the influence Henry Townsend had enjoyed in the 1840s. Wood became a confidante of Ogundipe. He "consulted regularly with the three chiefs who dominated Egba politics especially on Anglo-Egba relations, and he drafted all Egba dispatches to the Lagos Government in 1886."[38] Wood's relationship with Ogundipe was the most significant because, in many ways, Ogundipe was the de facto alake who was effectively shaping and affirming the town's sociopolitical landscape. He corresponded with the Lagos government on the town's behalf, warriors did not pursue military campaigns he did not support, and he symbolically supported the Christian community by abstaining "from certain works on Sunday" because it was their Sabbath.[39] The close relationship between the European missionary and the military elites encouraged Christian leaders to assume that Abeokuta's destiny depended on them. One observer noted that "if the Christians united, 'they would revolutionize Abeokuta; they have an indefinite power.'"[40]

While their power was not infinite, European and Saro Christians hoped to revolutionize Abeokuta in different ways. Whether their vision called for Abeokuta to be the nucleus of a larger Yoruba state or an independent state, they all imagined a state that would be based on Christian ideals and in which Christian men would play paramount roles. Townsend and Wood assumed Europeans would have a commanding position in this state, while both G. W. Johnson and James Johnson challenged the role Europeans ascribed to themselves and argued for an African-run polity.

GENDER, RELIGION, AND REVOLUTION

For the missionaries, a political revolution was not sufficient. This theocracy would have to conform to Christian social values, especially those concerning women and marriage. Christian missions required monogamy of their converts and that women in thought and practice be subordinate to their husbands. Nonetheless, individual missionaries promoted these ideals with different levels of zeal. James Johnson stands out in particular because he was less tolerant of polygamists participating in the church than his European and African counterparts, and he tried to purge them from the church.[41] Johnson's letters reveal his frustration with the ways converts flouted Christian ideals and simultaneously provide a lens into the competing social visions. He noted that husbands were losing control of their wives.[42] He expressed concerns about the practices of Christian wives most clearly in a letter stating his disapproval of the wife of one of the town's Egba pastors, a Reverend William Allen. The pastor's wife, Mrs. Allen (given name unknown), did little to identify with her husband and the work of the church. She "scarcely resides in her station . . . sometimes sleeping there only at nights or other times spending only a few hours on Sundays out of a whole week. She resides chiefly at Iporo township, where they have a house of their own, where she does her own business . . . keeps her own slaves, different from her husband's."[43] Egba/Yoruba society expected wives to care for themselves; therefore, when the church hired male agents, they hired the man alone and not his wife. For Johnson, this meant that "church work is treated as a commercial concern" comparable to women's economic enterprise.[44] While Johnson appeared to be offended by the characterization of church work, he supported the idea of women's economic independence. In a debate on European marriage in 1888, he condemned the "idea that woman is to be a burden on her husband" as an evil introduced by European marriage. He charged, "Let him who has the money make his wife a queen; and let the woman who has the money spend it on her lord. But let not those who have not the means do the same. It is an evil."[45] Johnson championed Yoruba women's economic independence but wanted to dictate how they expended their funds.

Mrs. Allen's lifestyle did not have Johnson's complete support, but it contrasted significantly with that of European missionary wives. Anna Hinderer, who accompanied her husband, Rev. David Hinderer, to Yorubaland, provides one of the few accounts of a European missionary wife. Reverend Hinderer had been serving in Abeokuta since 1848 when he decided to marry in 1852. Although the Hinderers would spend much of their time in Ibadan, Anna's account gives us important insight into her activities.

Anna Hinderer claimed that from a young age she had a "desire to become a missionary, to give myself up to some holy work."[46] Marrying David Hinderer brought her wish to fruition. Letters and diary entries reveal that

Anna shared her husband's commitment to spreading the gospel. She was his able companion on the home front. She described her day as "never long enough for her."[47] It was filled with housekeeping and tending to the children who lived on the mission station and to visitors who stopped by often.[48] She nursed her husband and others associated with the mission when they became sick, and when she was ill she fretted that they "might think that she was a lazy white woman."[49] She supervised the first Christian wedding in Ibadan,[50] and after they built a British-style house she gave the bale, the head chief of the town, and several of his wives a tour of it. She showed off their sitting room and bedroom and then took the women off by themselves for a lesson on washstands.[51] The domestic sphere of the mission station defined Anna Hinderer's role. She did not preach, though she shared information about her faith. She organized a meeting with the iyalode of Ibadan in which she explained why she had come to Yorubaland and "entreated them [the iyalode and her attendants] to come and hear the Word of God for themselves, and send their children to us to be taught."[52] Anna Hinderer felt that she had established a strong friendship with the iyalode since the iyalode had designated her the iyalode *fun* (white iyalode), accepted a velvet head tie and a silk bag from her, and reciprocated a few days later with a goat and a calabash of yams. However, it does not appear that the iyalode attended the Hinderers' services or sent any of the children in her household to their school. In assisting her husband in these ways, Anna Hinderer modeled the supportive wife as well as European mores and cultural practices. Her account does not suggest that she chafed in this role; nonetheless, she expressed an appreciation for the political power enjoyed by the iyalode.[53] It appears that she was equally committed to furthering the goals of the mission and to being a strong but dependent partner to her husband.

Anna Hinderer modeled one example of Christian womanhood. Phillis Fry, who accompanied her husband, Ernest Fry, to Abeokuta in 1893, offered another. Ernest and Phillis ran a dispensary in Abeokuta that treated on average 126 patients per day.[54] Their letters to parishioners in the United Kingdom do not reveal their training, but they do provide rich details of their activities. Phillis managed the household staffed by young boys the couple trained, cared for patients in the CMS leper facility, and accompanied her husband on visits to villages up to forty miles from Abeokuta. Even after her husband died in 1906, she continued to travel to distant villages to preach. She sometimes traveled with women converts who were part of a band of preachers who traveled to visit and preach in different places each week.[55] Phillis Fry was fully engaged in spreading the gospel beyond those who encountered her in the parsonage.

Some African women fully embraced the domestic values of their new religion. The testimony that Rev. James White gave of his late wife, Anne, stands in stark contrast to Johnson's description of Mrs. Allen. White described her as "'a faithful and affectionate wife, a competent associate, an able assistant, a tender Mother, and above all a devoted and conscientious Christian' . . . [with an] 'amiable disposition' . . . 'straightforwardness and faithfulness in reproving vice' . . . a mother to her household—a mother to the Otta church-nay, the heathen themselves style her the mother of all Otta."[56] In this testimony, as J. D. Y. Peel argues, we see the "Victorian ideal of the Christian wife, the helpmate of her husband within the framework of a singular marriage . . . combined with a Yoruba emphasis on her status as mother, the paradigm of realized female potential."[57] In sum, Anne White reflected a Yoruba version of Anna Hinderer.

Mrs. Allen's lifestyle was a radical contrast to that of Anna Hinderer and Anne White. She had her own business. This fell fully within the expectations of Yoruba society. Yoruba gender ideology, like British, presumed that all men and women would marry. All women were expected to be obedient to elders and husbands, to procreate, and to be economically independent. Upon marriage, a husband was expected to provide his wife with trading capital.[58] In Yoruba marriage, historian Kristin Mann noted that husbands and wives exercised considerable autonomy. Once they had fulfilled their obligations, "each could pursue economic activities. Neither had a right to use the other's property, nor interfere in its management."[59] Through trade, some women like Mrs. Allen became extremely wealthy and like men invested their wealth in slaves. Slaves brought in income, and they expanded the productive and trading capacity of their owners. Husbands of female slave owners were not entitled to their wealth or property. Therefore, Mrs. Allen had an investment in Yoruba gender ideology as well as Yoruba systems of inequality. In some ways, Mrs. Allen's actions anticipated those of Christian elite women in the twentieth century who rebelled against the Christian expectation of women's economic dependence in marriage and pursued trade as well as education in order to broaden their economic opportunities.[60]

Mrs. Allen was not alone within the community of converts. Johnson described other Christian women who also held slaves. He wrote of Betsy Desola, for example, the iyalode of the *parakoyi* (trade chiefs) and an "old communicant of the Ake congregation who has been over 20 years in the church."[61] He noted that she was "not encumbered with a family of children of her own . . . [and] was a trader and an owner of a number of slaves."[62] In addition, she demanded and received fifteen strings of cowries (approximately 3½ p.) daily from her slaves who worked on their own account. Annually, she received about £2 10s. from each slave. Lydia Yemowi, Mary Coker, Fanny Fisher, and Susannah Lawolu—old communicants of the Ake congregation—made their fortunes from trade and also invested in slaves.[63] These women attracted Johnson's attention because they opposed his efforts to increase church dues. He was taken aback by their disobedience to their pastor, the male authority of their religious "family." The daily transactions of their lives aligned more closely with that of Madam Tinubu than Anna Hinderer or Anne White. As a result, they also failed to conform to Johnson's idea of the economically independent but dutiful female congregant.

The social revolution that missionaries hoped to inspire needed many more women to replicate the lives of Anna Hinderer and Anne White. But missionary success with women was limited in the period before 1870. Peel noted that men, especially young men, predominated among the converts. He identified two factors that contributed to women's slower acceptance of Christianity. The first had to do with their reproductive and domestic roles. Yoruba culture prescribed bearing children and child-rearing as critical markers of womanhood. Women's concern to bear and successfully rear children made them "anxious seekers for any spiritual agency" that could assist them. These important tasks did lead some women to seek out the Christian god, but it locked the majority of women more deeply into Yoruba religion.[64] Families also persecuted women who attempted to follow the Christian god. Anna Hinderer wrote of several young women whose husbands divorced them and who endured beatings or were threatened with sale to slave dealers because they refused to stop attending church.[65] Peel suggests that young women were especially vulnerable to persecution because they played a key role in propitiating a lineage's *orisa* (deity), ensuring that the lineage was extended.[66] Thus, a significant number of the women who joined the missions in the first four decades tended to be older and therefore able to exercise greater autonomy within their households.[67]

The social revolution that European and Saro missionaries hoped to create was still conditioned by their political goals and the political climate in the town. This was especially apparent in their relationship with Chief Ogundipe. Stories abound about his mistreatment of enslaved men, women, and children in his household. In several instances, slave wives were forced to drown their children because he doubted the children's paternity. A scathing editorial in the *Lagos Times* offered numerous examples of his cruelty and noted that these actions were contrary to Egba law. The editorial pointedly charged the missionary community with failing to admonish the chief or speak out on behalf of the oppressed, especially after its members wrote a letter to the Lagos government on behalf of Ogundipe, requesting the return of an escaped slave. It charged that the Christians had "prostituted their religion before heathens." Yet the editorial also reported that Ogundipe had threatened to close schools and churches if the Christian community did not assist him.[68] There were very real limits to the sorts of transformations that the Christians could implement if they wanted to remain in the good graces of the powerful chiefs. Nonetheless, the missionaries' presence created opportunities for some to transform their position in Abeokuta's fluid social structure.

By the end of the century, tremendous social changes had occurred in Abeokuta. However, they did not unfold at the rate or in the ways that missionaries had anticipated. Women such as Madam Tinubu, Betsy Desola, and Mary Coker involved themselves in politics, welcomed the missionaries, and took advantage of new economic opportunities. They continued to live by Yoruba gender ideals and to support institutions such as slavery that enabled them to accumulate resources during this period of immense change. As a result, European missionaries, in particular, welcomed the extension of British power into the interior in the last decade of the nineteenth century because British political control would facilitate the political and social changes they desired.

MARKERS OF PROGRESS:
THE EGBA UNITED GOVERNMENT

When G. W. Johnson, the architect of the EUBM, left Abeokuta, his departure did not signal an end to his efforts to create an Egba nation consolidated around a centralized state led by the alake. In 1896, J. B. Kenny, who identified himself as a representative of the alake, published a letter in the *Lagos Standard* inviting all the "children of the Egbas residing in Lagos, at Home and abroad: who are in blood relation with the Alake, Olowu, Osile and Agura of the United Kingdom of Abeokuta" to join the Egba Deputation Club. The club wanted to build support for the EUBM, but its work was not confined to Abeokuta—it embraced the "general good, for the Race and Fatherland." Membership was open to men and women who were "willing to unite, in carrying out this noble object, for repairing our broken up Nationality caused by the Foreign slave trade, which has deprived us of our children, who are now weeping over the Atlantic, that from and hence forth, the sphere of this club will be enlarged; in consequence of which the name is to be called, *Egba Deputation and National Club.*"[69] A diasporic racial identity was interwoven into the club's expression of Egba nationalism. This sentiment was not unique to the members of the club. During his coronation as alake in 1898, Gbadebo "urged on the maintenance and support of the Independence of the Kingdom which if properly upheld would confound the opinion of the detractors of the Negro race."[70] Thus, for many people, a robust Abeokuta kingdom held significance well beyond the borders of Abeokuta and the Lagos colony.

When the British colonial government began to extend its control beyond Lagos, literate Egbas helped the chiefs in Abeokuta to negotiate a relatively favorable treaty. They guaranteed open trade routes through Egba territory in exchange for the Lagos government's recognition of the town's independence and its borders.[71] They also promised "complete protection and every assistance and encouragement to all ministers of the Christian religion."[72] This agreement, in theory, retained Egba control over its government and economy. It also gave the Christian community a free hand to expand. Nonetheless, the town's political independence was soon compromised when the Lagos government used a political crisis in 1897 as a lever to intervene. The then governor of Lagos, Sir Henry McCallum, threatened to actively interfere in the town's affairs if it did not reorganize its political structure.[73] The structure in place at the time of the treaty still recognized the preeminent role of the town's military chiefs; however, the basis of power shifted substantially under the newly reorganized government, the EUG.

Under the EUG, the multiple councils and kings who ruled each township in Abeokuta were streamlined into one dominant council headed by the alake, the senior *oba* (king) of the Ake quarter.[74] The *Lagos Standard* lauded Gbadebo as "the first king constitutionally elected, installed and crowned under the new regime."[75] The new council also included representatives from the town's Christian and Muslim communities as well as holders of senior *ogboni* (civil authority) and *olorogun* (military) titles. The architects of this new council excluded all women titleholders. It is unclear who the key female titleholders were in this period. We know, for example, that Madam Jojolola, who made her fortune from agriculture and the *adire* (tie and dye) industry, succeeded Madam Tinubu as iyalode, but none of the local histories indicate when this was. A report prepared for the British commissioner in 1906 acknowledged women as political actors but discounted the significance of their political positions: "Women . . . hold political position, as 'Olori Erelu' (chief of the women in the township). 'Olori Erelu' is not present when serious matters are discussed at Township councils. The Head trading woman in a township is called 'Iyalode' (mother of the public). 'Iyalode' may attend minor meetings, and her opinion is consulted on matters affecting trade; it is a high position amongst women. Women hold considerable influence politically, and behind scenes bring great influence to bear on the Chiefs in almost every big palaver."[76] Women were reduced to anonymous behind-the-scenes political players not at all like Madam Tinubu, the kingmaker of the nineteenth century. This rendering reflected a new political reality in which male authority increased.

The EUG, often at the encouragement of the Lagos government, developed Abeokuta's political and economic infrastructure to mirror the developments taking place across Nigeria as Britain consolidated its rule. The town was discouraged from rebuilding its town walls, and its demography changed as Abeokuta's inhabitants took advantage the diminishing insecurity. Farmers established cocoa farms farther and farther away and contributed to a pattern in which an increasing number of the town's population began to live in rural areas semipermanently.[77] The EUG invested heavily in the construction of roads and markets, especially in the villages and hamlets that extended beyond the town's metropolitan center.[78] Abeokuta area farmers produced several major export items for the international economy (palm oil, palm kernels, and cocoa), and the regional economy (kola nuts and indigo-dyed cloth). The town's inhabitants imported large quantities of manufactured items, especially cloth and spirits. Commercial activities received a tremendous boost when the railway, which reached Abeokuta in 1899, attracted droves of European merchants.

Abeokuta's new economic and political landscape contributed to rising incomes for both men and women. Cocoa production provided incomes for an expanding base of producers, wage laborers, and buyers. Women made up an important segment of the buyers who purchased small quantities of cocoa from farmers and transported it to bulking centers.[79] The expanding kola nut market brought revenue to farmers as well as to the women who dominated its retail trade. Women processed the palm oil from the palm fruit and also dominated its retail sale. By custom, women owned the palm kernel, so they profited from the expanding market for palm kernel oil as well. Women also dominated the retail trade in cloth and foodstuffs in the town's markets.

Many people perceived the changes unfolding in Abeokuta as exceedingly positive. The alake's visit to London in 1904 provided proof of the town's advancement. At the invitation of Governor MacGregor, Alake

Gbadebo, EUG secretary Mr. Edun, heir presumptive Prince Ladapo Ademola, and Lagos merchant Richard B. Blaize sailed to London on May 4, 1904.[80] The group met King Edward VII, the Duke of Marlborough, and representatives of the Colonial Office and the Church Missionary Society. They traveled to Scotland to visit Aberdeen College, Governor MacGregor's alma mater. Photographs of Gbadebo, Edun, and Ademola showed them in sumptuous gowns.[81] Edun in many ways appeared to personify the modernization Abeokuta desired. He had changed his name from Jacob Henryson Samuel to Edun shortly before the trip to London; he wore Yoruba robes during the entire time and worked assiduously to be "an Egba chief in looks . . . and a cultured English gentleman in speech and demeanor."[82] Press stories confirmed his success. The *Westminster Gazette* reported "Mr. Edun is as dark as a dark man can be, and in his gorgeous robes of gold embroidery might well have walked out of some Arabian Nights story; while his courtly manner, perfect English and diplomatic attitude are suggestive of St. James of today."[83]

Many saw an independent "Egbaland as a certain special symbol,"[84] and discussions in the Lagos press reflected the general sense of pride: "A wishful smile plays across our face at the mention of the fact that the Egba kingdom stands alone today, the only independent native state in this part of West Africa"; "Abeokuta is sailing as a self-dependent barque on the ocean of politics. . . . We in Lagos take a special pride in the autonomy and progress of the Government of Abeokuta as demonstrating to the world at large the resources for self-government . . . possessed and practiced by the Native and sincerely pray that nothing may ever happen to weaken that autonomy or hinder that progress."[85]

The changes unfolding in Abeokuta became signifiers that marked the sense of progress Egba and non-Egba alike associated with the town. Ernest Fry, an Abeokuta-based missionary, recounted many of the changes that had taken place by the beginning of the twentieth century. In February 1900, a new church in Ake was dedicated to Reverends Townsend and J. B. Wood. Following the dedication, the alake and some of the chiefs began attending church regularly.[86] Fry and his wife also visited the houses of several chiefs, including the alake, to preach. He noted as well that daily living changed "with the railway and telegraphic communication, and three posts in and out a week, and one to the interior too. It can no longer be styled 'bush life.'"[87]

Progress could be marked also by the expanding numbers of literate men and women as well as the critical role of educated elites in the semiautonomous government. Both Ransome-Kutis were Saro-descended members of this educated elite. By the time Funmilayo Thomas was born in 1900, her family had been Christian for two generations, and both of her parent had trained at mission schools. Israel Ransome-Kuti was born into one of Abeokuta's most prominent Christian families. His father, J. J. Ransome-Kuti, was a priest in the Anglican Church and also held secular administrative posts for the EUG.[88] A wealthy Egba trader with links in Lagos and Abeokuta, C. B. Moore was appointed treasurer, and a Brazilian repatriate, P. P. Martins, also well established in Lagos and Abeokuta, became secretary of the government.[89] In 1904, David Sokunbi became the first *oshile* (king of Oke-Ona) in Abeokuta. More importantly, he was the first educated and baptized king in Abeokuta.[90]

By far the most important educated official within the government was Adegboyega Edun, the executive secretary of the government. Edun had come to Abeokuta in 1902 after a well-established career in Lagos as a clergyman and headmaster of the Boy's High School (Lagos). Pallinder-Law credits him with quickening the pace of administrative modernization in Abeokuta.[91] In 1898, the EUG employed only 20 people, but by 1908 it employed about 350, 85 of them in clerical positions. Its components included a secretariat, a treasury, an audit office, a customs department, a judicial department, a public works department, medical and sanitary departments, a police department, a prison, a printing office, a post office, a forest and agricultural office, and an education department.[92] Certain groups in Abeokuta celebrated Edun's administrative skills. Upon his return from his second trip to London in 1913 as part of the Yoruba delegation to the West African Lands Committee, a Committee of Abeokuta Young Men honored him at a special function. The participants included "nearly everybody who was anybody in Abeokuta": the British commissioner, the alake, all members of the Egba national council, other chiefs, European missionaries, and African missionaries including Rev. J. J. Ransome-Kuti (father of the future Rev. I. O. Ransome-Kuti). Though the event was characterized as a plebiscite—"a true index of the peoples' opinion of Mr. Edun's service"[93]—it was most reflective of the social ambitions of this group of young men.

Many perceived the availability of schools as clear signs of progress. As one of the earliest centers of missionary education in Nigeria, Abeokuta had excelled in providing educational opportunities from the nineteenth century. In 1877, Abeokuta had six elementary schools and a high school, with a combined student body of 283 students.[94] Demand for education only increased during the era of the EUG, and new facilities opened. Richard B. Blaize—founder of the *Lagos Times*,[95] a wealthy trader, a member of St. Paul's Church Breadfruit in Lagos, and a strong supporter of Rev. James Johnson[96]—bequeathed £3,000 "for the training of lads in technical work."[97] His gift launched the Abeokuta Industrial Institute, which opened on February 14, 1908.[98] Reverend Fry noted that Muslims were learning to read for the sake of trade.[99] In the alake's estimation, education had surpassed military tools as the town's most pressing need. In a letter to the governor of Lagos, the alake stated, "We do not need now to protect our walls, we do not need to spend our revenue in the purchase of guns and powder, but we need now to protect the country against ignorance—intellectual, social and political—against stagnation in trade; we need to look after the proper sanitation of the town; the construction of good roads, the development of trade and agriculture, the education of the people."[100] The EUG supported education by giving grants to the mission schools. These schools were not restricted to Christians; they accepted students who practiced the Yoruba religion as well as Islam.[101] By 1904, approximately two thousand children attended schools in Abeokuta.

In 1908, Christians and non-Christians alike pooled their resources to found the Abeokuta Grammar School (AGS), "the first secondary school in Nigeria that was not directly founded by an alien Christian mission."[102] The founders of the AGS wanted to create an institution to train young men for the world beyond the clergy, a world in which its students would help move Nigeria toward independence. Thus, from its inception, a sense of nationalism infused the mission of the AGS. Education supporters recognized the need to create a good secondary school for girls as well. However, girls' education was intended to prepare them "to occupy the position of teachers in our local school in the future and wives of our agents, and . . . play an important part in the development of the Church."[103] Ernest Fry viewed their work as contributing to the enlightenment, uplift, and spiritual welfare of the Egba nation; however, it was also their task to prepare men and women to play different roles in the nation.[104]

This combination of factors led many to believe that Abeokuta had in fact surpassed Lagos in several measurable ways. In a 1913 article, the *Lagos Weekly Record* commented, "Abeokuta vies with Lagos in her road making; her waterworks is not only cheaper but is calculated to be in working condition before that of Lagos. Railroads in a part of the country has been undertaken and completed by Abeokuta alone and with local resources to the wonder and astonishment of the Lagos Authorities."[105] The Egba government also recognized that, in order to ensure its continued rate of development, it had to secure its revenue base. Moreover, it had a substantial citizenry on which to base its revenue collection. Officials estimated Abeokuta's population as 265,000 in 1912.[106]

In June 1914, the alake met with representatives from Christian organizations and the Egba Citizen's Association to discuss the town's financial footing. The sale and distribution of gin provided a significant portion of the town's revenue; however, the Lagos government had raised the duty to 10s. 6p. per gallon, which increased the cost of a case of gin by at least £1. Since only the wealthy would be able to afford gin at this cost, he argued that the government would become insolvent and be forced to put the country under British control. In order to prevent this scenario, he argued for a system to collect revenue from each compound. He reasoned that in the past during time of war, the leaders used to collect money from every compound, and they used those funds to purchase gunpowder and shot.[107] In essence, the EUG began laying the groundwork for a more systematic system of revenue collection in part to safeguard the town's independence. The alake recognized that protecting the revenue base was critical to extending and consolidating control over this modernized monarchy, and he reached out to these organizations because they were invested in the institutional success of the EUG and its plans to modernize the town.

THE CONTRADICTIONS OF PROGRESS

The political and economic changes that unfolded under the EUG had contradictory consequences for men and women and different social classes. The expanding trade in cocoa, palm kernels, and kola nuts increased opportunities for both men and women. Cocoa production in particular encouraged more people to move beyond the town as they expanded the range of cocoa farms. Yet both men and women were subject to forced labor as the state oversaw the construction of roads to carry these goods to market. As early as 1901, the EUG had begun using forced labor for road construction.[108] The order of council that established the Department for Construction of Roads in 1905 gave further legitimacy to its use. It stated that, based on ancient native custom, the alake or officers appointed by him could call on chiefs or headmen to supply the labor necessary to construct and maintain roads. Refusal to work or provide substitute labor or money without sufficient excuse was punishable by a fine of £5 or three months of imprisonment with hard labor. "Free" labor was only demanded from inhabitants of the rural areas because the people of Abeokuta town were excluded.

Demand for Abeokuta's exports also created a labor crisis for farmers. The early cocoa planters had established plantations on which they used migrant laborers, but the majority of cocoa was produced on small farms.[109] For smaller producers, marriage became an important strategy for acquiring labor. Rev. J. J. Ransome-Kuti, who was superintendent of the Abeokuta Church Mission in Soren-Ifo, a rural district, found that as the price of produce increased, "people rushed to accumulate wives so as to get helpers in the field."[110] This rush to get wives did not abate even though the bride price increased substantially. The demand for labor made it difficult for Ransome-Kuti to persuade church members to send children to school or to give up "extra wives." This demand for labor limited the ability of some women to participate in the new social and economic opportunities, but it was not universal.

The increasing reliance on wives for agricultural work likely reflected the unavailability of slave labor. Numerous sources called attention to the disappearance of slaves. A correspondent to the *Lagos Standard* noted that when the Lagos government demanded that the Egba government prepare roads for the installation of telegraph poles and wires between Ibadan and Abeokuta, the Egbas reported that "all their slaves had run away and the few men in town are busy preparing Palm Oil and Kernels for the markets."[111] Six years later, in 1903, Reverend Fry also identified the labor shortage as he contemplated the declining number of clients who visited his dispensary. "Very many slaves have run away to Lagos, and obtained their freedom, and now the people have to work their farms themselves, and if I am not mistaken this labour question is going to be a big problem when the country opens up."[112]

The large-scale departure of slave labor appeared to be one more snag in the fraying social fabric. There was a general perception that the expanding economy and the presence of Europeans also contributed to a breakdown in social control over dependent women and men. The 1906 Report on Egba Native Law argued that

> the family system is breaking down, owing to the influx of civilisation, which has produced the following effects: *a)* The parent's hold over grown-up children, formerly absolute, in now practically extinct, except from a moral point of view; *b)* Husbands not having absolute power over their wives as heretofore, seduction and adultery are more prevalent; *c)* Children will not allow themselves to be pledged for debt, as has been customary; *d)* The chiefs and elders of the country do not now receive the same respect from the younger generation, and their personal influence is greatly reduced.[113]

Many commentators called specific attention to the increasing number of divorces, suggesting that it had become a social revolution in the interior countries.[114] Divorce invited attention because it became an option for many more women at a moment when the demand for labor was at a premium. Yoruba sociologist N. A. Fadipe specifically attributed the great state of flux in native marriage to the diffusion of foreign ideas, the process of rapid economic growth, and the advance of the railway.[115] Many women and girls visited the railway camps in pursuit of trade and established relationships with men employed in the camps. Economic considerations no doubt played a role in cementing these relationships since railway workers earned nine to ten pence per day and were paid in silver coins at the end of each week.[116] The camps provided a sanctuary from lineage authority, new relationships, and economic opportunities as well as an alternative judicial space since they fell under the railway commissioners' jurisdiction.[117]

Members of the Christian community also expressed this sense of social unease. Reverend Fry warned against the "alarming increase of worldliness and immorality among the rising generation."[118] An editorial in the *Lagos Standard* illustrated that this unease with the young generation was not limited to Abeokuta. The author argued that the average Christian girl in Lagos attended school up to the third or fourth standard, which was insufficient. Once she completed school, "the bent of her energies are now directed to the all-important object of securing a desirable partner in life. Marriage becomes the *ultima thule* of her ambition. . . . Having no useful occupation and with no mental resources, is it to be wondered at that her life degenerated into one of idleness and frivolity—a round of balls, parties, gossip, and it is to be feared less innocent amusements taking up the most of her time? The passion for dress and display amounts almost to a mania with her." He contrasted the life of the Christian girl in Lagos with her sister in the interior, "who is brought up to some useful occupation, is bethrothed in childhood, and has her life mapped out for her."[119] However, the women in Abeokuta who fled to the railway lines did not live by the social maps assigned to them. These snapshots illustrate the unease and social tensions as dependent men and women experimented with or took advantage of the new opportunities of the era. Progress created change, though not always the change that was desired.

ABEOKUTA'S LAST DAYS OF INDEPENDENCE

Abeokuta's political class was greatly affected by the political changes under the EUG. The new structure weakened the predominant position the military chiefs had exercised for much of the nineteenth century,[120] and it invested greater power in the alake. Nonetheless, British power grew in large measure as Alake Gbadebo relied heavily on the colonial state's recognition, loans for development projects, and military support. In exchange for financial support, the British commissioner in Abeokuta sat on the town's Financial Advisory Board, thereby enhancing the tremendous power he already exercised.[121] During Gbadebo's reign, the Lagos government staunchly supported Edun; as a result, he essentially ran the government. He alienated important chiefs in the town and the rural districts as he enthusiastically imposed policies that weakened their authority and access to revenue but were encouraged by the Lagos government. Tensions came to a head in July 1914 following the arrest of Ponlade, a minor chief from Ijemo. Edun, in the company of Commissioner Pelham Young, the representative of the Lagos government, had ordered Ponlade to repair the road to his village. Ponlade rebuffed their order, claiming that he was a subject of the alake and did not take orders from Edun or the British,[122] a response that was somewhat ironic since Ijemo had long been a center of unrest and agitation against the alake. Ijemo residents' grievances focused on the EUG's control of functions that had formerly been carried out by township ogboni councils, the excessive force used by EUG police in making arrests, and inadequate representation in the EUG.[123] Agitators, however, singled out Edun for most of the policies they disliked; thus, Ponlade's response reflected this thread of anti-Edun sentiment.

Ponlade's arrest was politically motivated and intended to dramatize Edun's power and that of the British. However, events spiraled out of control after the elderly chief died from abuse suffered during his detention. The chief, "who was not in good health when the police arrested him on June 17, was made to lie prostrate before Young and outside Young's house for a considerable time." Edun and the commissioner's carriers beat him with "stout sticks" and then tied him to a tree overnight. Following this abuse, the court charged Ponlade with assaulting the police and demanded a fine of £2 or two weeks of imprisonment as well as a separate fine for an offense under the Road Construction Ordinance. Either unable or unwilling to pay these fines, Ponlade went to prison and died shortly after, on July 1.[124]

Following Ponlade's death, protests "in accordance with the customs of country" ensued. Adebesin Folarin noted that "whenever the people felt aggrieved by the act of the Government or any important personage and sought for redress," they demonstrated and chanted in front of the *afin* (the alake's palace), a practice known as *kirikiri*.[125] They called for Edun's dismissal and an inquiry into the old man's death. People from Ijemo along with some educated Egbas demanded that Edun be punished for past activities as well for the Ponlade case. Both the British and the alake viewed these demands as tantamount to restricting the alake's power and British influence and in essence refused to respond to their demands. The climax of the protests came on August 7 when about one hundred Ijemo women gathered near the afin. Led by a woman who claimed to be Ponlade's daughter, the women rushed the palace, yelled insults at Gbadebo, and accused him of murdering Ponlade. The group also threw stones at the secretariat building and Edun's office. Somewhere during this series of events, a European trader was knocked from his bicycle.[126] Finally, the ogboni chiefs intervened and brought an end to the protests.[127]

While putting pressure on the alake to act, the people of Ijemo had also sent a petition appealing to the colonial government in Lagos. Colonial officials decided that the events in the township warranted a strong show of force. Troops were brought up from Lagos on July 14, but since things still seemed relatively calm, they were sent back on July 27. Despite its willingness to send troops, the Lagos government did not choose to intervene in the dispute between the alake, Edun, and the people of Ijemo. Maj. Harry Moorhouse, secretary of the Southern Province, who visited Abeokuta on July 28, met with the alake and Young, the British commissioner, but did not attempt to meet or confer with the people of Ijemo. Instead, he used the opportunity to press the alake to accept the Provincial Courts ordinance that was intended to further restrict the town's independence.[128]

The Lagos government's decision to ignore the Ijemo petition and the alake's refusal to dismiss Edun contributed to the escalation in tension touched off by the women's protest. The ogboni stepped in again, telling the alake that he had three days to dismiss Edun. Otherwise, they threatened to kill Edun and depose the alake. To increase the pressure on the alake to act, the ogboni chiefs sanctioned the performance of *oro* rites, and traders were directed not to sell food to the alake's wives or servants.[129] Oro, a spirit who represented the collective male dead among the Egbas, was the ogboni's enforcer. Therefore, Oro could be asked to proclaim curfews, punish those accused of witchcraft or sorcery, or execute criminals. When the rite of oro was performed, women and uninitiated men were expected to go into hiding.[130] The spirit's appearance signaled to the alake that Edun's life and his tenure were at stake. On August 8, troops from Kaduna arrived in Abeokuta. Commanded by a Lieutenant Wilson, who was new to Africa, the soldiers set off to the compound of the head of the obgoni chiefs in Ijemo, the *oluwo*.[131]

Strikingly different versions of what ensued exist. The official records state that the soldiers found that approximately fifteen hundred people had gathered at the compound of Aluo, the oluwo of Ijemo. Wilson claimed that three-quarters of the people present were armed with guns, sticks, and machetes. He ordered them to disperse. Instead, a man standing next to him drew his machete, and another discharged a gun. Wilson had no choice but to give the order to fire.[132] Using a Maxim gun and rifles, the soldiers fired on a largely unarmed group, killing from thirty-four to fifty-five people, including the oluwo.[133] Other witnesses disputed this account. A corporal in the Nigerian police force, Belo Bida, stated that none of the people in the compound had guns and that the crowd was nonthreatening.[134] Writing two years after the massacre, Folarin argued that the crowd had assembled at the request of Commissioner Young in order to amicably settle the issue of Ponlade. The soldiers, on the other hand, had been briefed that they were going to the oluwo's compound to arrest twenty-two men identified as leaders of the protests.

Violence did not end with the massacre at the oluwo's compound. The soldiers looted the compound, set the houses on fire, and "battered [the walls] to the ground." They also dynamited the homes of several Ijemo chiefs as well as the "Ijemo house of parliament."[135] After learning that many people had fled to their farms, the troops went to the farms and "proceeded in a show of power to destroy a number of houses."[136] The soldiers' actions following the massacre displayed colonial violence for public spectacle and consumption. To further reinforce Britain's hegemony, the commissioner guided three provincial kings, the alake, the oshile, and the agura, to the Oluwo's compound where the "bodies of the slain were . . . collected and piled in a heap in the front of the debris of the . . . compound for public view."[137]

For the Lagos government, long unhappy with Egba independence, the Ijemo massacre supplied the excuse they needed to formally cast aside Egba independence.[138] Although the Alake clearly expressed no desire to invite armed assistance if it would destroy the town's independence, the British government misled him.[139] He was ultimately forced to renounce Egba independence. On September 16, 1914, Frederick Lugard and Alake Gbadebo signed a new treaty that placed Abeokuta under the jurisdiction of the Protectorate of Nigeria.[140]

The demise of Abeokuta's independence was a blow to supporters well beyond the town's borders. The Lagos press debated as it analyzed the actions of all parties involved and the legitimacy of the colonial state's decision to abrogate the treaty.[141] Nonetheless, the sense of loss was palpable.

An editorial in the *Lagos Weekly Record* best summed up the general feeling: "That the hopes and aspirations of the Egba people, their heroic struggles for the maintenance of their independence should have ended thus ingloriously presents a lurid picture that is disheartening to their best friends and well-wishers."[142]

For Egbas at home and abroad, the Ijemo conflict laid bare the fragility of Abeokuta's independence. Townspeople assumed they had the right to recall and remove officials who did not serve their best interests. However, that power had long been compromised as the colonial government accumulated authority over the town's political leaders. For colonial officials, the abrogation of the treaty finally clarified their relationship with Abeokuta. Governor MacGregor, who had lauded Abeokuta as a great experiment in native government, did not champion it consistently. In 1902, in an interview with representatives from the Aborigines Protection Society, MacGregor denied the independence of the Egba government. He charged that "it would be a most dangerous idea to put into the heads of a protectorate State that they are an independent Sovereign Power. They are not independent as a State, although they are held responsible for the maintenance of peace and order in their provinces."[143] For Governor Lugard, on the other hand, there had never been any ambiguity: Abeokuta was always an outlier in his plans to consolidate British control over southern Nigeria.

UNDER THE PROTECTORATE

In the wake of the Ijemo massacre and the abrogation of the treaty, Abeokuta town became a division, the Egba Division, in an administrative province, Abeokuta Province, that also included Ijebu, Ilaro, and Meko. The EUG was restructured to conform with Lugard's theories of colonial governance. The system of indirect rule that Lugard first systematized in Northern Nigeria relied on the incorporation of indigenous political institutions and officeholders into native administrations that received advice from British political officials—the resident and the district officer. In Abeokuta, the resident replaced the British commissioner and moved from the outskirts into the town. These political officers exercised much more power than the commissioners who preceded them, even though their role was defined as advisory. The alake remained the head of the newly constituted Egba Native Authority, which later also used the name Egba Native Administration (ENA), and Edun, his primary adviser, became its secretary.[144] The three other obas remained in the government, but British officials worked to lower their authority and prestige in relation to the alake.[145] The inhabitants of the Owu quarter felt especially aggrieved under this new structure because their king, the olowu, became the lowest-ranking king.[146] Equally important, the British curtailed the power of other ranks of chiefs, especially the ogboni.

The colonial government slowly began to develop the foundations for more substantial changes, specifically the imposition of a system of direct taxation. Contrary to Britain where taxation sat at the nexus of property, democracy, and expanding political rights, taxation in Abeokuta Province and the rest of the southern provinces was exclusively associated with British hegemony.[147] Taxes were the fiscal expression of colonial power and reached deep into African households.[148] Yet even in the colonies, taxation was never only about revenue. Taxes helped create a wage labor force, induced involvement in cash crop production, and helped shape the social landscape. Tax structures that required men with more than one wife to pay supplementary taxes for each additional wife was a method to discourage polygyny while "extracting a greater contribution . . . from those who were assumed to have greater wealth, and wealth gained and expressed immorally in the colonial sign, polygamy/wealth (slavery/prostitution)."[149] Even where women were not taxed directly, the tax structure could still have significant impact on their status. In South Africa, Sean Redding shows that the tax structure accorded all men adult status while relegating women to the status of legal minors. Although women were not legally liable for tax payment, the migrant labor system forced women to increasingly assume the responsibility of paying taxes in order to hold on to land and other property.[150] Thus, the state extracted resources from women while rendering them politically and juridically invisible.

Colonial officials primarily discussed the tax structure in Abeokuta merely in terms of revenue generation, but the conflict around taxes revealed competing ideas about state-society relations as well as gender relations. In advance of creating the tax structure in Abeokuta, the colonial government sent Edun on a tour of Northern Nigeria so that he could become acquainted with the native administration system as well as the tax structures there. In the north, the tax system borrowed heavily from the precolonial tax structure of the Sokoto Caliphate, which included a "land and rough native income tax." Officials claim that they "merely took the [tax] system over from the Fulani, pruned it of the abuses which had grown up, & made various improvements."[151] Nonetheless, Andrew Barnes argues that they introduced several European notions that transformed the theoretical underpinnings of tax collection and fiscal administration. First, they introduced the idea of taxes as an annual payment of cash to the government and, second, the notion that the amount of taxes paid should be based on income; third, they equated taxpayer with the householder.[152] Neither Yorubaland nor eastern Nigeria had developed a land tax or equivalent income tax systems from the precolonial period, so Lugard ordered the supervisor of native revenue, H. R. Palmer, to tour the southern provinces in order to discern if there were cultural practices or institutions on which they could build a system of direct taxation.[153] Yoruba towns had a long history of tolls on trade goods, and Palmer concluded that the introduction of a direct tax would not be novel because the communities were practiced in paying tribute and fines to local chiefs. He did note, however, that "if there was any real objection to taxation it is evident that nowhere would that objection be likely to be more apparent than at Abeokuta."[154] One week after the outbreak of World War I, Governor Lugard asked for permission to "introduce a system of direct taxation into Southern Provinces such as exists in the Northern Provinces." He had hoped to introduce it gradually, but the war made it necessary "in order to reinforce the Revenue."[155] The Colonial Office was stunned by this request. One Colonial Office staff member commented, "Only Sir F. Lugard would raise a question like this at the outset of a European war and demand an answer immediately."[156] Citing fear of revolt, the Colonial Office refused his request in 1914 and again in 1915.

As the war wore on, the government had to contend with a significant decline in revenue. Most government revenue in the southern provinces came from import duties and railway freights. Before the war, the greatest share of import duties was from "trade spirits," especially German liquor. Until 1899, duty stood at 3s. per gallon, but from 1901 until the outbreak of World War I, it was 5s. 6d. per gallon.[157] Even though duties on other imports increased during this period, none of them increased at the same rate as the duty on spirits; furthermore, the duty on spirits contributed the greatest share to the total custom revenues collected each year. From 1904 to 1913, import duties on trade spirits averaged 65 percent of the total customs revenue.[158] However, the war had a considerable effect on revenue in Nigeria. The absence of German spirits, the difficulty and cost of shipping other available spirits, and further increases in duties led to a dramatic fall in the amount of liquor imported into Lagos. In order to offset the corresponding shortfall in revenue, the government imposed export duties on palm oil, palm kernels, and cocoa toward the end of 1916.[159] But, export duties alone were not sufficient, and the colonial government was forced to consider other initiatives.

In Abeokuta the financial picture mirrored the national one. The vast majority of revenues came from licenses, native courts created after annexation, and tolls, especially on spirits, tobacco, and salt. Table 1.1 indicates the precipitous decline in revenue derived from tolls.[160]

TABLE 1.1. REVENUE FROM TOLLS

Year	Total revenue	Amount from tolls
1911	£40,280	£31,695
1912	£40,113	£29,200
1916	£21,533	£7,383
1917	£22,987	£3,646

Given this context, Lord Lugard yet again urged the Colonial Office in 1916 to allow him to impose direct taxation in Yorubaland. The Colonial Office still feared revolt but acquiesced to the proposal because of the dire economic situation. Moreover, with the end of the Cameroon Campaign, during which British and French forces seized Cameroon from Germany, companies from the Nigeria Regiment could be made available in the event of unrest.[161]

Letters between Governor-General Lugard and Alake Gbadebo show that Lugard had been preparing the ground for the tax system before he received permission from the Colonial Office. In a letter written in 1915, Gbadebo noted that in the previous year he spent considerable time meeting with the public and with chiefs and other important persons to "educate them in their civic duties and prepare them for direct taxation in the near future." In the letter the alake reaffirmed his support for direct taxation and proposed to leverage taxation against the capital improvements the EUG had made in the town—water, electricity, and a corn mill. Lugard had threatened to sell the electric works and corn mill because of the poor state of the town's revenue, and in order to forestall the sale of these facilities, the alake and his council

> guaranteed an annual revenue of £20,000 half of which was to be available to the Native Administration. . . . We propose that an extra £5,000 should be raised, making all £25,000, and that this £5,000 should be placed to a capital account and be used annually for (1) the upkeep of the corn mill, (2) the extension of the water supply and electric lighting in the town and (3) general improvements in Egbaland.[162]

These facilities had affirmed the town's sense of progress both within and beyond its borders; furthermore, they made a substantial difference in people's lives. The alake explained that the corn mill in particular served the needs of both urban and rural women, especially makers of *agidi* (a corn porridge). A large delegation of women had appealed to him to save the mill, which was the only facility that serviced the urban and rural communities; light and water did not extend beyond the town. When Lugard finally received permission to impose taxation in 1916, the alake and his council were already invested in the process.

The resident and the alake conducted more meetings in 1917 to prepare the general population for the implementation of the tax scheme. They were told that the tax would be approximately five shillings, but the well-to-do would pay more than the less well-to-do. They were also promised that other forms of taxation and demands would be withdrawn, specifically "custom tolls, various license charges, charges for water at the public fountains, obligation to work on roads and all irregular levies by the chiefs."[163] The government also introduced administrative changes that in theory should have facilitated tax collection. For the purpose of tax collection, colonial officials divided Abeokuta and its rural environs into seven districts that more or less conformed to the native court districts and assigned a high-ranking chief to each tax district as district head. The alake was made district head of Abeokuta town, which was considered Central District, while the three other obas—the oshile, the agura, and the olowu—were assigned to rural districts and had to relocate to them. These officials had some relationship to their districts, for they included villages that belonged to the sectional quarters they controlled. This was not true for all the other districts. One district head in particular, Seriki Onatolu, had no cultural or political relationship at all to his district, the Western District; he was, however, a close friend of Edun.[164]

Abeokuta's citizens began paying taxes on January 1, 1918. The tax plan was essentially a collective tax on the adult population assessed at an average of five shillings per head. Based on the estimated number of adult men and women in a compound or in a village, compound heads and chiefs were given a figure that the entire group was responsible for paying.[165] From the inception of the tax scheme, Egba women were assessed independently of men. The decision to tax women independently was contrary to the model used in Northern Nigeria. It also contrasted with earlier draft proposals as officials debated the tax in Yorubaland. Earlier proposals called for taxes to be imposed on "every able-bodied adult, male native to pay a tax of £1 per annum to the Government. This tax will include his first wife and he will pay a further tax of 10/- [ten shillings] per annum for each additional wife."[166] This proposal used women as a proxy of men's wealth and strengthened household patriarchal relations, but the tax scheme in Abeokuta did not subordinate women to men. In fact, it reinforced Egba/Yoruba women's historical economic autonomy by establishing an avenue for women's direct engagement with the state through the Treasury.

It is important to ask why Egba women were taxed contrary to established models. Abeokuta's assessment plan was created by the secretary of the Egba Native Authority, Adegboyega Edun, and fully supported by colonial officials. Edun's plan may well have borrowed heavily from the tax structure in Northern Nigeria,[167] but it was informed also by Yoruba cultural practice that expected women to work and have independent incomes. Since most women were involved in the trade of manufactured goods or foodstuffs and predominated in the markets across Yorubaland, there was a shared perception by Yoruba and European men that women often had money. A resident made the latter point explicit in 1927 when the acting secretary of the southern provinces inquired why women in Abeokuta were taxed independently.[168] The resident responded that "the taxation was first instituted on the basis of a village assessment. Both men and women contributed to the village quota. Therefore when an individual receipt taxation was substituted women were made to pay as a matter of course."[169]

The resident opposed any effort to change the system because it spread taxation over a larger population. Furthermore, he noted that Egba women were considerable traders and independent of any husband. Therefore, he saw no reason why women who had definite incomes should not contribute to the state. He also theorized that it gave men "a little extra hold on their wives," although he did not elaborate on the advantages men derived from this.[170] He suggested that if women were exempted and the tax on men raised to ten shillings, there would be a great deal of opposition from young men, while women and those men with multiple wives would probably be in favor. Taxing only men might have made tax collection easier; nonetheless, the resident still felt such a change was not justified and that it would be "a retrograde step" to remove women from the tax rolls. He noted that even in England the growing tendency was to tax women separately. Egba women's economic independence clearly informed the decision to impose independent taxpayer status on them. Women were not party to these discussions, so the decision to tax them directly resulted from male political monopoly.

In spite of assurances to the Colonial Office that taxation would go smoothly, Abeokuta was by June 1918 in the throes of a major revolt that would become known as the Adubi War. Serious discontent manifested first in the Western District, the district headed by Edun's friend Seriki

Onatolu. Adubi, a farmer from Owu quarter, was recognized as a leader of the revolt for he had organized a number of meetings with rural bales. He ordered them to collect information from meetings arranged by the district head and instructed them to send their grievances in a letter to him.[171] On June 13, 1918, thirty thousand rebels, all men, many armed with dane guns, first destroyed the railway line in Wasimi, then moved on to destroy much of the railway and telegraph lines south of Abeokuta. They killed a European trading agent and an oba, the oshile, who refused to support them. The rebels hoped to take the battle from the rural areas directly into Abeokuta, but the governor-general had access to Nigerian troops of the West African Service Brigade who had not been demobilized from their service in East Africa. Twenty-eight hundred Nigerian soldiers, seventy British officers, and a full complement of machine guns arrived to suppress the revolt. In the end, about one thousand Egba peasants were killed. Casualties among the British-led forces, on the other hand, were very low, with eight rank-and-file and two civilian carriers killed and four Europeans and sixty-seven Nigerian soldiers wounded.[172]

CIVIC EXPECTATIONS IN AUTHORITARIAN SPACES

The tax revolt was a vote of no confidence in colonial officials and Abeokuta's political leaders. The items the rebels destroyed could be seen as symbols of modernity and progress. Railway lines transported the goods that assured Abeokuta's position as a thriving commercial center in the colonial economy. However, these networks of modern transportation and communication were also the physical manifestations of the expanding colonial state that sought to extract increasing amounts of goods, capital, and labor from Abeokuta town and its rural villages. Taxes were at the heart of an existential debate on how the extraction of capital and labor would proceed, for taxation had been presented as a civic duty as well as a means of lowering the demands on Abeokuta's citizens. They had been told that once taxation began, they no longer had to pay customs duties and shop and butchers' licenses. Furthermore, they were promised that forced labor would effectively end because "the introduction of tribute . . . would cancel compulsory road construction."[173] In spite of the assurances, forced labor continued after taxes were imposed.

Forced labor had increased significantly after the abrogation of the treaty in 1914. A commission of enquiry into the tax revolt estimated that in the areas where most of the road construction occurred in 1917, only a small number of the assessable adult male and female population of 120,000 supplied a total of 435,716 working days.[174] Several witnesses before the commission of enquiry stated that people worked as much as three weeks continuously and the same villagers could be called on several times a year.[175] Government correspondence confirms that villagers were pulled away for long stretches of time. In a meeting with the alake, council members, and three thousand men from 136 different villages, the *asipa*, an ogboni chief and council member, spoke about the importance of road construction and advised people "not to grudge against it simply because they will be deprived of few months to attend to their cocoa plantations, palm trees and crops which otherwise might bring them a loss of few shillings."[176] In fact, some villagers were told that the amount of work that was performed weighed most in deciding when they returned to their villages rather than the amount of time they spent away.[177]

Correspondence between residents and the alake showed that at any given time, several hundred people were involved in road work. In a letter complaining about a decline in the supply of labor, one resident wrote, "With reference to the construction of the road head on the Abeokuta-Ijebu-Ode Road, I am sorry to see that the labour has dropped from 717 down to 318. . . . Kindly use your influence to restore the labour on this road to 700."[178] This stands in stark contrast to a report in which the Abeokuta resident, W. C. Syer, stated, "The number of men working is very small, and their hours very light: 10–11 a.m. to 2–3 p.m. only, and they stay only 3 or 4 days a week on the work."[179] In addition to road construction, villagers were called upon to supply labor for road maintenance, the construction and maintenance of government rest houses, and an odd assortment of tasks. In a letter to the alake, a resident passed on complaints he had received from villagers in Oba District who turned out for road construction but were made to collect firewood, shoot game, fetch palm wine, and collect herbs.[180] Failure to report for work was punishable by prosecution in the native courts as was refusal to live in the construction camps.[181] Workers were also fined for tardiness. One informant recounted, "A servant of mine named Lawani went one day to work on the Oba road. He was accused of being late and fined £3. He failed to pay the fine and he was sentenced to a term of imprisonment which he served in the Ake Prison."[182] In some instances, villagers also contributed money to these construction projects. One witness, E. A. Vaughan, a former president of the Ifo Native Court, testified that during the construction of "Court houses, Rest House and . . . Quarters for Presidents of Native Courts . . . the elderly men in the country have to subscribe so that qualified mud-builders may be engaged. In some cases from £25 to £50 had to be subscribed. Those who were too old to be called upon for free labor have to subscribe for the upkeep of those working on the roads."[183] Forced labor clearly disrupted farming and other economic activities and competed with income generation precisely when the state demanded a portion of producers' income for taxes.

Testimony gathered during the commission of enquiry made it clear that forced labor continued after January 1. The head of one village testified that during a meeting with the district head, Seriki Onatolu, two hundred bales were given the tax assessments for their respective villages *and* informed that they had to supply eight hundred laborers for road construction. Moreover, they had to pay within nineteen days or they would suffer the same fate as the people in Ijemo. The bales took this threat seriously, and it directly contributed to armed meetings across the district.[184] Another respondent told the committee that after his village received an assessment of £80, villagers were then ordered to erect court buildings.[185] These actions were condoned by the administration. In one instance, thirty-eight town chiefs, "many of them very old men, were ordered out of Abeokuta at a moment's notice, under threat of arrest if they did not make their people in the villages turn up for road construction and also make them pay their tax."[186]

The system of assessment also contributed to the revolt. The resident claimed that the adult population was assessed at an average of five shillings per head.[187] There were two critical discrepancies. At a public meeting to discuss the tax scheme, resident Syer informed the assembly that the tax would be about two shillings, sixpence. When collection was implemented, the flat rate was higher, leading the members of the commission of enquiry to charge that Syer had deliberately misled the populace.[188] In a number of instances, the assessments imposed on a village were frightfully high. In cocoa-growing and oil palm districts, or where there was a good deal of trading such as near a railway station, a substantial tax was imposed on the entire village. In theory, traders and wealthy farmers were to pay more, but the tax was divided evenly across the population without attention to income.

Native courts provided a third major contributing factor. In Abeokuta, sanitation fines imposed and collected through the courts became the backbone of local revenue collection. In addition, their collection led to greater police involvement in people's daily life.[189] Sir Hugh Clifford, confirmed widespread and excessive use of court fines. In his confidential memo to Viscount Alfred Milner, the secretary of state for the colonies, Clifford stated that Resident Syer had "conveyed to the Presidents of the Native Courts the idea that the infliction of substantial fines was desirable in the interests of the local revenue."[190] Such action was encouraged in light of the decline in toll revenue. Until the end of April 1917, sanitation cases were few, the fines did not exceed two shillings, sixpence, and no costs were charged. From May 1917 onward, however, the number of sanitation cases increased dramatically and fines were raised to five shillings. Defendants were forced to pay the cost for being summoned to court, an additional eight shillings, thus bringing the total fine to thirteen shillings.[191] In some courts, defendants were fined as much as thirty shillings.[192] In a total of 1,406 criminal cases tried in eleven native courts in the districts in 1917, 556 cases were for sanitary offenses, and out of a total fines and costs of £1,624, £752 were from these sanitary cases. In the two town courts, there were 106 sanitary cases out of a total of 172, and the fines and costs amounted to £103 out of £149.[193] These summonses were given only to women by court messengers who traveled around collecting names and summoning those "who in their opinion, did not keep their compounds sufficiently clean."[194] Specific charges included not sweeping the ground in front of their houses or keeping pots of water in which mosquito larvae could breed. Even in cases where several women from one compound were named on a single summons, each had to pay the fine.

These prosecutions were primarily on women living in small farm villages, but market women were also subject to these excessive fines. The harassment was such that, according to historian Ajayi Kolawole Ajisafe, Itori one of the principal rural markets, closed as a result.[195] Sanitation fines continued after tax collection began. However, it appears that the fines became a strategy to punish villages when they refused to provide free labor. One informant told the committee, "We said we are against doing free labour and when they cannot get us to do free labour police bring summons and our women were fined 13/."[196] Although it was later determined that levying these sanitation fees was illegal, its successful practice in Abeokuta helped establish for the architects of the tax scheme that women were an important source of revenue.[197]

The native courts were an additional point of contention because they redirected revenue that in the past went to ogboni chiefs. In the past, ogboni chiefs gained much of their income from fees and fines as they adjudicated disputes and from dues associated with the rites and ceremonies at death. However, the establishment of native courts usurped the ogboni's judicial functions. Very few ogboni chiefs served as assessors in these courts, and court fines went directly into the administration treasury. In addition, the administration abolished the fees ogboni chiefs collected when someone died.[198] Governor Clifford later charged that a decision by the resident to remove the roofs from all the ogboni meeting houses across

Abeokuta, where township ogboni chiefs met to discuss business or hear cases, created the impression that the administration was waging war on this important society.[199]

Rural-urban tensions provided a fourth contributing factor. Writing in 1959, Akin Mabogunje noted that the human geography of Egba Division, which included Abeokuta and two other settlements, Otta and Ifo, differed substantially from that other Yoruba communities. Specifically, Egba Division had the greatest number of small rural settlements and fewer settlements that could be considered urban.[200] As the insecurity of the nineteenth century lessened, people in search of additional farmland moved out of the town. As the distances increased, they built more permanent structures and spent most of their time in the rural settlements, thus giving rise to a new type of landscape—"a single large town surrounded by a whole litter of small, insignificant villages and hamlets."[201] Abeokuta, nonetheless, remained the permanent home of all Egbas. People returned to town for important cultural events, ceremonies, and rites, and they maintained their political affiliation to their township and sectional oba within Abeokuta. This settlement pattern contributed to some of the problems with the tax system. Many people faced double assessment since both their rural and urban homes were assessed.[202] Furthermore, while rural residents suffered exclusively from demands for free labor and paid a great percentage of illegal court fines, the revenue generated from these activities were disproportionately invested in the town. The realities of this uneven development created resentment among rural residents who were called on to pay a water tax even though the water system did not extend beyond the town. Rumors also circulated that houses in Abeokuta itself were assessed but that nobody ever paid.[203] To those in the countryside, it appeared that the state was much more efficient in collecting taxes from them than from the urban population.

The nature of the grievances and the clearly disproportionate demands on the rural community explains why this revolt was concentrated in the rural areas. As a result of the revolt, the tax scheme was modified. A poll tax was imposed on those who earned less than £40 per year, with men paying five shillings and women two and a half shillings. Those whose income averaged £40 or more paid 1 percent of their income in taxes, and those who derived income from rents were assessed 5 percent on rental income.

In large measure, women's voices were absent from the records that resulted from the Adubi War, even though women were integral to the discussion on taxation and to the grievances that led to the revolt. The only woman's voice recorded was that of Madam Jojolola, the iyalode of the Egbas. Following the revolt, the commission of enquiry investigating its causes asked Madam Jojolola if the women had any grievances. She replied, "The women all complained that they derived no benefit from the government. We make no profit on the goods we sell, and yet we have been called upon to pay taxes."[204] Her statement reveals that women had certain expectations of the state that were in part based on their status as taxpayers. In exchange for paying taxes, women expected the government to extend benefits in the form of protecting their interests as producers and traders so that they earned profits. However, by mid-1918, it was clear to them that the state was not living up to these expectations, though it continued to extract revenues from them. In short, practicing civic duties yielded no returns.

The silences in the commission of enquiry's testimonies and reports are equally compelling. Taxing women as a principle was not challenged or called into question.[205] It appears from the testimony taken during the enquiry that Abeokuta's citizens did not object to taxation in principle or to men and women being taxed independently. Their grievances were against the exploitation they suffered from the excessive taxes and court fines coupled with forced labor. Thus, the revolt made clear that they would not accept forced labor or other forms of extraction dressed up as civic duty.[206]

෨

Adebesin Folarin, who provided one of the few contemporaneous accounts of the Adubi War, had studied law in Britain and qualified as a barrister-at-law in Lincoln's Inn Middle Temple on April 16, 1913.[207] He published a short book on his observations of London and of British manners, habits, pastimes, and government institutions that included a list of ten wishes for Abeokuta and Nigeria. Although the publication date is not listed, the wish list suggests that the booklet was published while or soon after he completed his studies. His first wish, for example, stated, "I wish to see the amalgamation of Northern and Southern Nigeria, with Lagos as Capital." Governor-General Lugard and the Colonial Office made this a reality in 1914. Several wishes called for greater investment in education, specifi- cally "a system of Compulsory Education in the Egba United Kingdom," as well as the introduction of colleges and universities. He also wished "to see the Egbas initiated into the system of paying taxes for the welfare of the country," the establishment of "a Parliament after European models," and "the confederation of all Yoruba countries under the suzerainty of Great

Britain, with Abeokuta as Capital." Finally, he wished to see "full rights of a Sovereign State, similar to those granted to certain minor States in Europe, to be accorded to the Egba United Kingdom."[208] Unfortunately, the dream of an independent Egba nation could not withstand the pressure of British imperialism or the internal contradictions it generated.

By the end of 1914, all semblance of Egba independence had evaporated. The alake and Adegboyega Edun retained their positions, but the alake was forced to renounce the earlier treaties that recognized the town's independence. For many people in Abeokuta and Lagos, the town's independence was real and its loss traumatic. In response to Governor MacGregor's claim in 1902 that Abeokuta was a part of the protectorate, an editorial writer noted, "The Egba government has for many years now, after the fashion of European Governments, had its own national flag, marking and proclaiming thereby its independence." Moreover, "it is as an independent native State that the Egba Government has for long asserted, with a keen sense of its own rights, its claim to land on the mainland Lagos, reaching to the edge of the Lagos lagoons, as a part of the Egba territory."[209] Abeokuta therefore conformed to contemporary definitions of nation—imagined and limited by finite boundaries[210]—and, critical to the writer, the bearer of a flag.

Unlike Buganda, whose nation-ness was vested in the strength and historicity of its consolidation under the kabaka, notions of progress, civilization, and Christianity deeply informed the architects of Abeokuta's nation-ness. Egbas championed Abeokuta's standing as an independent state in part because they had created an infrastructure that combined elements of the town's indigenous political structures with institutions of the modern state as modeled by Britain. Over the course of seven decades, with input from Saros, military chiefs, missionaries, women, and British officials, Abeokuta's inhabitants had created a modern monarchy with ancient roots that they anticipated would sustain them through the colonial present. The racial ideology that Europeans used to justify their political control over African polities further deepened the symbolic significance of Abeokuta's independence.

The EUG best expressed Abeokuta's sense of national identity. As this chapter demonstrates, the consolidation of the EUG also transformed the town's political culture, especially for women. Whereas women could hold significant political authority in the nineteenth century, under the EUG women were gradually marginalized from the institutions of governance, a practice that comported well with British gender ideals. Some women still held titles; however, as a group, women were increasingly dismissed in official reports as ancillary, behind-the-scenes actors in political discussions. The resident C. W. Alexander captured this well when he concluded that women exercised considerable influence but they, like the educated Christians and Muslims, could "be ignored or placated by granting them in part what they wanted."[211]

2 ∽ Abeokuta's Centenary
Masculinity and Nationalist Politics
in a Colonial Space

IN THE wake of the Ijemo massacre and the abrogation of the treaty with the Lagos government, Abeokuta became a part of the Southern Nigeria Protectorate. It was already integrated into the colonial economy, especially through the establishment of the railways and the networks of roads and telecommunications. The most pressing issue for the colonial government lay in the political realm, for it had to, in theory and practice, impose political and administrative control over the town. This required that colonial officials break up nodules of opposition but still keep elements of the precolonial structure intact. Abeokuta had to produce revenue for the colonial state as well, therefore Gov. Frederick Lugard moved to introduce taxes into the town as part of his larger strategy to introduce an income tax system in the Southern Protectorate. As we saw in chapter 1, taxes were introduced in 1918, and within months a tax revolt erupted in the rural environs.

Eighteen months after control was reestablished, Alake Gbadebo died. Colonial officials faced a new alake, Ademola II, who brought a different set of qualities to the office as well as a different set of expectations. He was literate, had been recognized as the heir apparent shortly after the turn of the twentieth century, and was expected to restore Abeokuta's independence. Thus, the 1920s was distinguished by political intrigue and tension as colonial officials tried to stamp out the remaining fires of opposition and Ademola attempted to keep the embers of independence lit. As a result, 1930, the year of the town's centenary, became a defining moment in its history.

FIGURE 2.1. Centenary Hall, Ake, Abeokuta. (Photo by Joseph Ayodokun, 2014.)

Centenaries and anniversaries of this nature are never only about the past. They, as Anne McClintock argues, are spectacles where collective identities are created and reinforced.[1] They are opportunities to deploy the past in the service of contemporary political and cultural concerns, and they are gendered. These moments of commemoration are cultural productions that are simultaneously nation-building and state-making. Scholars who examine events such as independence-day celebrations note that they become "sites and arenas for the performance of nationhood . . . where individuals can perform national identity and belonging."[2] Carola Lentz argues they also present an opportunity for the state to stage itself and make it palpable to its citizens and potentially to a wider international audience. Though the focus may be on unity, national commemorations often inspire debate about the norms and values making up national identity and offer opportunities for the articulation of new demands for public recognition. Ultimately these events are not only for the political or intellectual elites—they invite the broader public to engage in debates about the country's past, present, and future.[3] Abeokuta's centenary was an unusual event because in spirit and practice it was more reminiscent of national days celebrated in postcolonial Africa. It was not an imported colonial reinvention like the durbar in Northern Nigeria or an older cultural ritual such as the Odwira festival in Asante.[4] Instead, it was a display of state-making intended to illustrate Abeokuta's readiness for a return to independence as well as an exercise in nation-making cementing Egba national identity.

Alake Ademola II also appreciated the significance of texts in which to ground the claims for Abeokuta's sovereignty. He specifically commissioned several historical texts to address key political questions such as the dominance of the alake over the other kings and Egba constitutionalism. The texts, written by Egba lawyers Adebesin Folarin and Ladipo Solanke, were in dialogue with the earlier histories produced by A. K. Ajisafe. Collectively, they established the historical context that provided the supporting arguments for the town's bid for independence.

This chapter is most concerned with the symbolic role the occasion served in Abeokuta as well the gendered nature of this nationalist spectacle. It shows that a gendered discourse was already embedded in the very planning phases of the centenary and revealed most conspicuously in the final program of events, which read like a parade of masculinity. While the chapter illuminates Partha Chatterjee's argument that the hegemonic discourse of nationalism is fundamentally a male discourse,[5] it also exposes the tightly woven power differentials inflected in this male discourse. The centenary was an opportunity to reinforce British paternalism, the alake's dominance of the Egba political structure, and male monopolization of politics.

CAUSE FOR CELEBRATION

Prices for the three major exports from West Africa—palm oil, cocoa, and ground nuts—began a precipitous decline in 1920. By 1926, the prices African producers received for their exports was half of what they received in 1920.[6] Across Nigeria, producers increased production in order to maintain their incomes, and the colonial state increased taxes or tried to make tax collection more efficient. In Abeokuta, the colonial government created a chain of responsibility to oversee tax collection in the 1924–25 season. In the rural areas, bales were made responsible for collecting taxes, while in the towns the heads of compounds were responsible for tax collection. Bales and compound heads answered to specially appointed district heads, who ultimately answered to the sectional obas and the alake. The state followed this reform with a tax reassessment in 1926.[7] Taxation posed an even greater problem for producers in Northern Nigeria because the colonial state took a much greater share of its revenues from income taxes in the north than in the south, where import and export tariffs generated the bulk of government revenues. In 1928–29, the state took 5 percent of farmers' income as taxes in the north but only 1.5 percent from producers in the south. By 1933–34, the government collected 30 percent of net incomes from farmers in Northern Nigeria and only 2.5 percent from farmers in the south.[8]

African societies were already experiencing an economic crisis before credit markets collapsed in the United States and Europe in 1929. Furthermore, the impact was uneven. The worldwide scope of the Depression encouraged Britain and other countries to adopt protectionist economic policies; however, Britain's protectionism incorporated its empire. As a result, African consumers would be hurt further by the protectionist policies implemented across the British Empire because "tariff agreements . . . all but closed the empire to non-empire goods, while promoting exports and imports, even at uncompetitive price, between empire countries."[9] This manifested in different forms across economic sectors in Nigeria: indigo dyers and cloth merchants lost access to less expensive cloth from Japan while tin miners became unemployed following the closure of tin mines in the middle of the country.[10]

One year following the collapse of the credit markets, the annual report stated that "the finances of the Egba Native Administration have been tried rather hard during the year." To make matters worse, locusts attacked the crops of the Egba Division. The minutes of the Egba Council spoke of impending famine, and the bellman was sent around the town to notify its inhabitants that export of food from Egba Division should cease.[11] Nonetheless, colonial officials sanctioned a special expenditure of £3,000 toward the completion of Centenary Hall and £750 toward the centenary activities pending a reserve fund of £1,100.[12] In support of these massive outlays during this period of sustained economic distress, Folarin noted that despite "the world wide commercial depression, the people were determined to pursue the preparation without a flinch."[13] Therefore, it is important to consider why in the midst of this period of profound economic crisis the ENA would want to and be allowed to set aside a substantial amount of revenue to mark the town's hundredth anniversary.

Sources do not indicate earlier celebrations of Abeokuta's founding. The most comparable political celebrations were Ademola II's Coronation Day, September 27, and Empire Day, May 24. The late Egba historian Saburi Biobaku offered a recollection of Coronation Day:

> We would have a children's rally at the grounds of the Ake Palace in the morning and as Oba Ademola II . . . came forth in his resplendent regalia, we would all break into

Kábíyèsí, Ọba Aláké Ademọ́lá Kejî
Ọmọ Erín Jogún olá
Ọmọ Otenikan
Kábíyèsí Ọba wa, Kábíyèsí o

the Egba Royal Anthem set to the same tune as British National Anthem God save the King. The Alake would address us; we would march past and then disperse only to assemble again at the Ijeja playground to have our sports, with the Alake gracing the occasion with his august presence.[14]

Whereas Coronation Day underlined the supremacy of the alakeship and reinforced Ademola's political authority, the centenary provided an opportunity to recast and rewrite Abeokuta's patriotic history. Patriotic histories, as John Lonsdale argues, are historical, comparative, and argument inducing. They edit the plural traditions of the past in order to tell a single narrative. Authors use the golden era of seniors and ancestors as a reference point to "evaluate the public governance of, and personal honor within, their moral community." Patriotic histories are a tool for individuals and communities to meditate on a range of social issues, including the correct relations between the powerful and the weak, the obligations owed to patrons, and the sanctions each has at their disposal. Equally important, these histories are contingent on the context that makes "such patriotic thought relevant to political program and public action."[15]

Organizers of the centenary would not allow the Depression to stand in the way of the political and ideological work the event was intended to fulfill. The 1930 resident's annual report revealed much of the inner dialogue underlying the event and the political programs it addressed. C. W. Alexander noted, "Any-one acquainted with Abeokuta is well aware that there is among a large class a hankering after the measure of independence enjoyed before 1914. The abrogation of the treaty is without doubt looked upon as a somewhat disgraceful episode for all concerned."[16] Though he noted that "local patriotism" had been fully inflamed and there had been an increase in the open expression of a desire for independence, he did not think that the government had to worry about the manifestations of this during the centenary celebration. He was far more concerned about the discussions regarding local government that emerged during the year. The colonial state justified its control on the idea that the British had developed the best system of governance and the native administrations were a vehicle to teach Africans "the art of Local Self-Government."[17] Political elites in Abeokuta worked with this logic because it held the promise of a return to their independent status. The planning of the centenary provided an opportunity to revisit the question of independence as they took stock of the town's development, especially in relation to other parts of Nigeria. Some, particularly among the educated elites, argued that Abeokuta had made significant progress and was ready for self-government; however, it was being unfairly held back by the lack of political development in other parts of Nigeria. In many ways the centenary festivities were to be an affirmation of Abeokuta's sense of itself as a center of progress and therefore a space that should enjoy independence.

The centenary also provided an opportunity to affirm the leadership of Ademola and the native administration system. The resident reported,

> The Egba Council is certainly improving. A few years ago the Council was looked on as a secret assembly and seemed to consider itself as such. . . . This is gradually changing and the people are beginning to look on the members of Council as the natural mouth-piece through which they can make their desires known. . . . Moreover the Native Administration has nothing to hide; the more people understand its workings the better for everyone.[18]

This report captured the assumptions about the efficacy of indirect rule and revealed competing investments in Abeokuta's progress. In short, the resident reassured his superiors that indirect rule in Abeokuta was secure and could withstand the exuberant patriotism of the centenary because officeholders within the ENA and those subject to its policies had learned to understand the structure and what was required of them. In short, they had learned to think and operate bureaucratically in the ways that allowed the British to project the appearance that they were not directly ruling the colonies — they were merely advising.[19] The resident's use of "understand" also reflects the colonial state's confidence in its efforts to reshape Egba political culture to fit the ideal image of aristocratic rule — a strong political center, the alakeship, and limited channels for political expression. Colonial officials wished to make the ENA the pipeline through which all politics flowed. The British used two strategies to accomplish this goal: first, the restructuring of the Egba Council and the process for selecting members, and, second, the suppression of any group or individual that tried to challenge or circumvent the alake and council.

In 1926, the governor approved a proposal to increase the Egba Council from thirteen members to twenty-eight — seven life members and twenty-one elected members with three-year terms. The life members included the alake, the other three sectional obas, and three senior ogboni and military titleholders.[20] By 1929, the council had expanded to thirty members—"the four Obas, eleven War Chiefs and thirteen Civil Chiefs, with two new members to represent the more enlightened party in the town."[21] Christians, Muslims, and the parakoyi also had representation on the council. Election was a bit of a misnomer, for the process was entirely based on a highly structured and narrowly controlled procedure. Chiefs controlled the entire selection because colonial officials argued that given the high rates of illiteracy, the general population was not ready for elections.[22] Each quarter received a number of "elected" council seats based on the number of townships under their control. Ake had many more townships than all the other quarters combined, with forty-seven, while Oke Ona had seven, Gbagura seventeen, and Owu seven.[23] The chiefs within each quarter met separately to discuss which townships would be asked to put forward a candidate for the council seat. The leading chiefs of the townships then selected three or four names for each vacant position. If the list of candidates met the approval of the chiefs of the quarter, the names were forwarded to the alake, who, with the permanent members of the council, selected the most suitable candidate for each vacancy. Those selected had to "hold recognized titles, . . . be men of accepted good character who have not been to prison and are not in debt as far as can be ascertained."[24]

This selection process reinforced the political significance of civil and military titles and contributed to their resilience. However, relatively few men could meet the wealth requirements to be viable candidates. Furthermore, the selection process completely excluded women from consideration and contributed to the weakened state of women's titles. As early as 1920, the iyalode, Madam Jojolola, had expressed her desire to be on the council and complained that women's titles were allowed to lapse. She also appealed to J. K. Coker, the head of the Christian trade guild, the *olori parakoyi*, to create new titles for women. The council did not act on her request to be a member, and Coker refused to help create new women's titles because the alake had not sanctioned their creation.[25] It was only during the planning for the centenary that the council addressed women's titles by deciding that all of them would be filled to synchronize with the celebration.[26] They created a Women's Centenary Celebration Committee that represented the three main religious sections—"Christians, Muslims, Pagans"[27]—and tasked its members to submit names of candidates for general titles from the pool of daughters "of title bearers and other influential women."[28] The records do not indicate any discussion to include women titleholders on the council. The lack of discussion suggests that

women's titles were honorific instead of a means toward political participation. In addition, their status as daughters paved the path toward titles,
unlike the older political practice from which women derived titles by
virtue of their work and accumulation of capital. By both omission and
commission, the Egba Council was an exclusively male domain. Colonial
officials were complicit in creating a political structure that was simultaneously autocratic, patriarchal, and paternal.

Political officers and council members vigilantly monitored any activity that directly or indirectly posed a challenge to the alake or the council.
For example, in 1924, several chiefs from Ishere Township were fined £10
10s. by the Judicial Council for installing new chiefs.[29] The following year,
the *osile* (king of Oke-Ona), Suberu Adedamola, was called to task during
a council meeting for forwarding a petition to the resident about the condition of his palace without first consulting the council. The annual report
notes that "the Osile in defending his conduct used most insubordinate
language to the Alake, and also cast reflection on the Resident and Political Officers."[30] For his insubordination, the council, with the support of
the government, suspended him for three years. During his suspension he
was accused of rape and then deposed. Subsequent investigation appeared
to prove his innocence; nonetheless, the alake and the council refused to
reinstate him.[31]

By 1930, attempts to bypass the council had declined considerably.
In the annual report, the resident compared the improvement in the political system to a "few years ago . . . [when] frequently important chiefs
were not summoned to meetings even in their own township because they
were members of the Council."[32] Colonial officials also trumpeted the
expanded machinery of government. In the 1929 annual report, Senior
Resident F. B. Adams noted that the ENA was "fully organized" and well
advanced. He further elaborated:

> The Egba Native Administration has all the machinery and the
> personnel to manage its own affairs and the Alake and chiefs
> have been told over and over again that that is what is expected
> of them. . . . I think it is important that Government Depart-
> ments should regard the Egba Native Administration, not as a
> mere collection of quasi-government officials under the orders
> of Government, but as a Yoruba State with an individuality of its
> own, and with the power to give expression to that individuality.[33]

Throughout the report, the resident identified the many features of the
ENA that made it a real government. The ENA ran an Infant Welfare

Center staffed by a British nurse, Jane McCotter; issued its own liquor licenses; managed a voluntary registration of births, deaths, and marriages; appointed produce examiners; and had a police force. In addition, the alake inspected all the native institutions at intervals, visited the districts, and personally heard many complaints.[34]

The optimistic notes struck in the 1929 and 1930 reports indicate that the colonial state also had an investment in the centenary celebration. The ENA appeared to be a model native administration that demonstrated the progress promised of indirect rule. The discussion also revealed that colonial officials and Abeokuta's political elite attributed entirely different meanings to "progress." For Abeokuta's elites, progress cleared the path toward a return of independence, but for the colonial state, Abeokuta's progress substantiated the claims of indirect rule while self-government remained in the distant future.

Abeokuta's place as a model native administration was championed within and beyond Nigeria. Since colonial officials perceived Abeokuta as "an example of the highest development of the principles of indirect rule to be found in the Southern Provinces,"[35] it became the training ground for future traditional leaders. The 1925 annual report noted that Godfrey Eweka, the heir of the oba of Benin City, was sent to Abeokuta to be trained under the ENA. It appointed him to the alake's office so that he could accompany him on inspections of the native administration institutions,[36] and he remained in Abeokuta from December 1925 to July 1927.[37] Sir Donald Cameron, governor of Nigeria from 1931 to 1935, shared Abeokuta's success story beyond Nigeria in an article published in 1937. Discussing native administration in Tanganyika and Nigeria, Cameron spoke glowingly of ruling through indigenous institutions and liberally used Abeokuta as an example of this system. He argued that it would have amounted to vandalism to smash the institution through which the alake of Abeokuta ruled over the Egbas. He characterized Abeokuta as a well-run native administration,[38] and he called the alake his "good and respected friend."[39] Ademola achieved this status and high praise because he internalized and practiced indirect rule as colonial officials imagined, and correspondingly he knew how to use it to his best advantage.

BECOMING A "GOOD AND RESPECTED FRIEND"

On May 28, 1920, Alake Gbadebo died after twenty-two years in office. Informants told British officials that he was poisoned.[40] This was not an auspicious beginning to the reign of his successor, Ladapo Ademola. Ademola's candidacy received unanimous support; as a result, the colonial

FIGURE 2.2. Ademola II, alake of Abeokuta, 1923. (CO 1069/65/11 C. T. Lawrence, 1910–39, TNA.)

government decided not to challenge his nomination. Nonetheless, officials worried because Ademola had the support of key members of the Lagos-based educated elite, especially J. K. Coker. They had long experience with Coker for he continually tried to influence developments in Abeokuta during Alake Gbadebo's tenure. However, by 1920, British officials felt that Gbadebo's government had become increasingly independent of Coker and the Lagos Egbas.[41] The political officers' interaction with Coker no doubt influenced how they described his activities on behalf of Ademola. For example, they characterized Coker's campaign on Ademola's behalf as violent and suggested that he "no doubt used every means in the nature of intimidation and bribery . . . to influence the Egba Alake Ogboni."[42] Their concerns were heightened during the preparations for the coronation. The same confidential memorandum claimed that "Bolshevik" elements dominated the committee in charge of the coronation ceremony for they erected "a higher platform . . . for [the] Alake, and a lower one at the side for His Excellency."[43] Claims of communist influence was one of many ways in which the British discounted any rhetoric or action read as critical of the colonial state.[44] In addition to seeking out signs of resistance in the coronation plans, they anticipated a range of troubling developments in the near future, including attempts to exalt the alake as an independent sovereign and Abeokuta as at least a semi-independent state, attempts by educated persons to pose as chiefs, arousal of chiefs' hopes to regain some of their lost privileges, and proposals to create administrative positions for educated elites.[45]

These fears were not unwarranted. Colonial officials procured a letter crafted by the Lagos Egba Society in which Ademola promised to address certain demands once in office:

> Prince Ladapo Ademola hereby declares that he on his accession will in co-operation with the Lagos Egba Society see that:—
>
> (a) First and foremost the abrogation of the Treaty of 1914 is effected and Abeokuta independence restored.
>
> (b) The native system of Government as in the days of yore be re-established. The country will be governed entirely by the Kings of the four provinces with the aid and assistance of the Ogbonies, the Ologoruns and the Parakoyis.
>
> (c) The Residency will be removed to Aro. . . .
>
> (d) With the exception of tolls and fines (which will be duly shared with the chiefs . . .) no tax will be imposed on any house, land, farm, sheep or goats in Egbaland.[46]

Furthermore, Ademola did not waste any time asserting himself as alake. He demanded £90 from the treasurer to cover entertaining expenses, he called general meetings in Abeokuta and villages beyond the town without consulting political officers, and he requested £17 worth of fuel from a European firm and charged it to the account of the ENA. He held meetings with educated Egbas and J. K. Coker to decide the proposals to present to the council,[47] and he asked the resident to receive a deputation of ogboni chiefs that included two Christian ogbonis. Upon meeting the group, the resident refused to allow the two Christian ogbonis to attend the meeting because their titles were not township titles and therefore not accredited by the state.[48] These incidents appeared to confirm colonial officials' suspicions of Ademola, the educated elites, and the Lagos Egbas.

Challenges to colonial control became more ominous as the year progressed. Following Ademola's coronation, longtime European residents in Abeokuta reported aggressive anti-European feelings in the town, especially the singing of abusive songs to Europeans, a practice that had been abandoned for a long while. In addition, on Christmas Day 1920, chiefs held a "hostile" demonstration to protest Ademola's failure to close the courts. Agitation continued to foment in the new year. Informants reported that during a meeting held on January 29 with ogboni chiefs, the three sectional obas, and the alake, they decided to demand the immediate abolition or halving of the tax and resolved to resort to arms if the government did not accept their demands. The participants also decided to send messages to the inhabitants of Ijebu and Ilaro Divisions, with whom Egba Division shared Abeokuta Province, to join them. The resident crafted several responses to the political tension. First, he requested a half company of troops in order to double the number of soldiers at the barracks.[49] Second, he called a general meeting with the obas and the ogboni chiefs in which he declared that political officers would entertain no further discussion on the three main concerns behind the agitation—the abolition or halving of the tax, the abolition of native courts created by the British and a return to private courts, and the removal of troops from Abeokuta.[50] The increased military presence proved effective because subsequent intelligence reported that the alake told the ogbonis he could not assist them further. In addition, the majority of people in Abeokuta did not support a military effort.

In addition to charges of conspiring with the ogboni chiefs, Resident Alexander alleged numerous instances of misconduct in which Ademola was directly implicated: "receiving of money from market women in circumstances which amounted to extortion, the improper detention of women, extortion by messengers, the dispatch of an orderly and chauffeur to collect and receive tax in return for unofficial receipts, the retention of small amount of forest fees and tax until the retention came to light, and connivance in the holding of an illegal Court within a few miles of Abeokuta."[51] While the investigation into these charges unfolded, the alake made a speech "in which the tone was unfortunate throughout, and in the course of which he stated that what the Government want is to see that the Alake and Council carry on their affairs in such a way that the interference of Political Officers will be practically unnecessary." Added to this, Ademola had been in contact with the Lagos-based activists Herbert Macaulay and J. E. Shyngle.[52] The colonial government regarded these actions as so threatening that Resident Alexander was ordered to personally convey to the alake "a severe warning of the disastrous results which must follow the pursuance of evil courses." To underscore the depth of their displeasure, officials delayed a planned increase in his stipend for twelve months.[53] This action substantiated an earlier warning issued to Ademola in late 1920 when Alexander informed the alake that his "personal interests were bound up with the satisfactory progress of real native administration" and that he would have the "fullest support and sympathy from all Political Officers" only if he "directed his energy to good ends."[54]

The warnings and vigilant monitoring of any action that could be subversive transformed Ademola's relationship with the colonial officials over the next two years. The 1924 annual report noted his willingness to work with the political officers. District Officer J. H. Kirk acknowledged that

> during the year important changes have taken place in respect to the relationship between the Political Department and the Native Administration. The policy introduced, and successfully adopted, now brings the machinery of Government more into line with the system of Indirect Rule, and leaves the Political Staff free to act as an advisory body unencumbered with the minor details of direct control. . . . The Alake and Council and the Administration Staff, fully realize their new responsibilities, and they show a command which gives every encouragement. The Alake has given the political staff willing assistance.[55]

In order to bring Egba Division more in line with indirect rule, Ademola received greater autonomy and control of the affairs of the administration. The report noted that he personally ensured that all minor details were observed. While the machinery of government appeared to run more smoothly, the report also called attention to two problems—the passive role of the members of the council and absence of independent political organizations in the districts. As a result, political power was concentrated in Abeokuta and in the alake.

The concentration of power was in part a by-product of the increasing centralization of political authority that proceeded swiftly after the creation of the Egba United Government in 1898. As we saw in chapter 1, nineteenth-century alakes were not powerful. They lacked a revenue source, and their ability to exercise political power paled in comparison to that of wealthy and powerful ogboni and military chiefs. Although Ademola's immediate predecessor, Alake Gbadebo, was in a stronger position in the EUG, he nonetheless was plagued by challenges from individual chiefs and townships as he put in place policies that undermined the authority and revenue bases of chiefs—such as the right to hear court cases privately, maintain private prisons, and control the revenue from customs houses within their area of control.[56] In 1901, the people of Itori Township installed a "kingling" and seized a customs house; in 1903, Odowu, an ogboni chief from Kemta, was arrested for holding a private court in his own house. In both cases, Gbadebo sought military assistance from the Lagos government, and the townships were fined £200 to defray the cost of the troops.[57] The effort to simultaneously restrict the power and independence of chiefs while implementing policies advocated by Lagos provoked the crisis in Ijemo Township in 1914 that led to the abrogation of the 1893 treaty.

Gbadebo's death and Ademola's ascension to the throne in 1920 was a transitional moment that reopened political possibilities in an ongoing process of state formation. As alake, Ademola was enmeshed in the inner conflicts of a heterogeneous Egba elite and the competing agenda of the colonial state.[58] Political officials tried to control this process of consolidation around a new alake and still have the ENA conform to the ideals of indirect rule. However, chiefs marginalized during Gbadebo's reign and the Lagos Egbas, who were marginalized in Abeokuta and in Lagos, envisioned Ademola as their ticket to the center of Egba politics. The unfolding struggle to define the ENA under Ademola is reminiscent of efforts in other parts of the continent where educated elites formed coalitions with indigenous elites to claim the political space of the native administrations.[59]

During his first two years in office, Ademola tried to meet his political commitments to the chiefs and the Lagos Egba Society while creating some autonomy from the colonial government. He revealed that he struggled to satisfy these competing constituencies, in a meeting with the acting resident, Maj. W. Birrell Gray, where he "rather despairingly stated that he was being pulled one way by the Resident" and the opposite way by supporters such as the wealthy Muslim trader Madam Subuola Egberongbe, who was charged and heavily fined for illegally adjudicating court cases.[60] Ademola's relationship with colonial officials improved significantly as he distanced himself from chiefs still opposed to the political restructuring of the Egba state and from supporters such as J. K. Coker and Subuola Egberongbe. A further expression of his deepening relationship with colonial officials can be seen in the decision to extend an ogboni title and the full complement of regalia to the resident in 1925, Capt. E. A. Brackenbury.[61]

While Ademola's relationship with colonial officials improved, some of these chiefs and their Lagos-based supporters continued to challenge his authority. The 1926 annual report noted that the ex-osile Adedamola had filed a libel suit against a Lagos newspaper that supported the alake's decision to remove him from office. This was seen as a deliberate effort to embarrass the native administration, and although Adedamola won the suit, he was deported from Abeokuta and sent into exile in Offa.[62] The agitation around the ex-osile did not end with his deportation in 1926. In numerous stories in the Lagos press, members of the Lagos Egba group attacked Ademola. With the support of Captain Brackenbury, the alake filed libel suits against his former collaborator J. K. Coker and Egba historian A. K. Ajisafe. The court fined Coker £100 and £75 for costs, while Ajisafe was found not guilty and fined costs of £25.[63] Later that year, colonial officials learned of a plot to depose Ademola and install a former candidate for the alakeship, D. O. Mann, as the new alake. Six men were tried in the Ake Grade "A" Native Court, the senior court in the district, and sentenced to one to two years in prison.[64] In light of the multiple attacks on Ademola, the Egba Council passed a unanimous vote of confidence in the alake and the ENA on November 10, 1927.[65]

Those challenging Ademola could not be easily compiled into monolithic groups; instead, they represented Abeokuta's increasingly complex social and economic landscape. The discussion during the Egba Council meeting on November 27, 1927, is especially enlightening, for it revealed the weakness of the social categories in common use—chiefs, Muslims, Christians, and "pagans." James Ajayi, a council member from Kemta Township, with broad support within the council, proposed a motion to temporarily close the ogboni house in Itoku. Many confirmed his report that a section of ogboni chiefs, Christians, Muslims, and pagans met with messengers of Coker and lawyers in the Itoku ogboni house. In the past, only ogbonis from Itoku met there unless there was need for a general meeting of all the ogbonis across the city. However, the current meeting was not exclusive to Itoku ogboni chiefs or open to all ogbonis, since some chiefs who tried to attend were prevented from entering. Council members assumed the meeting, which was not discussed with the alake, was to plan further intrigues against the alake.

During the ensuing discussion, numerous claims and counterclaims flew: the ogbonis had caused the Adubi War, the Muslims and Christians were responsible for the war,[66] Muslims and Christians had initiated the current crisis and provoked a faction of the ogbonis. The balogun of the Christians declared that any Christian who attended the meeting should be ashamed, while another prominent warrior title holder, the seriki of the Egbas, stated that all the war chiefs supported the closure of the Itoku ogboni house.[67] Collectively, they demonstrate that even though council members in theory represented specific constituencies, individuals involved in these political disputes were not defined exclusively by title, status, township, or religion. The alake's challengers often combined multiple factors and cut across numerous social lines. They included wealthy Muslim merchants such as Subuola and her father; chiefs who had lost their revenue base when tolls, courts, and prisons were removed from their purview; chiefs who had weathered the economic changes and became large landowners; Saro landowners, especially cocoa farmers in Agege like Coker; educated elites; and Owu chiefs and townships that fought to maintain their distinct identity. The interests of these constituencies were not identical. Large landowners expected greater power because of their vast holdings. Oluwatoyin B. Oduntan argues that the scale of land accumulation in the early decades of the twentieth century actually enabled Abeokuta to retain its old imperial boundaries and to expand beyond them. He suggests that "the idea of an Egba kingdom with an affixed territory became more real during colonial rule than in the period before."[68] While landowners wanted political power by virtue of their landholdings, the Owus chaffed at the fact that their king was made subordinate to the alake and that they did not have a free hand in selecting him.[69]

Literacy further complicated the social and political landscape. Colonial officials relied heavily on Ademola's literacy. They pointed out that he read newspapers and periodicals to keep in touch with outside events and that his effectiveness was in large measure due to his literacy.[70] He could read estimates and budgets and understand all the problems the ENA confronted. Moreover, only two members of the council could read, write, and speak English.[71] Literacy thus amplified the concentration of responsibilities on Ademola. Adding other literate members to the council might have helped, but colonial officials had a strong antipathy toward the town's educated elites. In a rather disparaging tone, the resident wrote in the 1924 annual report that "a number of persons in Abeokuta have a very small smattering of education and a slight acquaintance with the Christian religion. They consider that because of these facts they are highly civilized and capable of managing the elaborate machinery of modern Government. They want to run before they can walk."[72] Though another officer grudging acknowledged that there existed "a body of educated and loyal citizens . . . [who] put forward suggestions most of which are quite reasonable."[73] The antipathy toward the educated elite was nurtured by Lugardian ideas about indirect rule. Even though Governor Lugard had resigned from the colonial office by 1918, Anthony I. Nwabughuogu argues that even those who had been critics of Lugard had become doctrinaire about applying indirect rule and its essential component, direct taxation.[74]

The colonial government tried to finesse restricting the political participation of the educated elite while lessening the appearance of autocratic rule. Thus, they introduced a reform in 1927 by which the alake heard complaints and held some discussions with administrative officers in the presence of four council members—an oba, an Egba chief, and two ordinary members.[75] On the surface this created the impression that council members were more engaged in the day-to-day management of the administration. Resident Adams also agreed to some concessions demanded by the Abeokuta Society of Union and Progress in 1927 by which more educated men would be given admission to the council as long as they had titles.[76] None of these changes, however, radically altered the balance of power between the alake and the council.

Given the challenges to his authority and the state's efforts to erase any semblance of autocracy, Ademola had a personal investment in the centenary celebration. They provided an opportunity for him to address his critics and recast for posterity the history of the alakeship as well as the first decade of his rule. Toward this end, he commissioned a text on the history of Abeokuta by Adebesin Folarin, the president of the Abeokuta Grade "A" Native Court, and one on Egba constitutional law by Ladipo Solanke, a London-based Egba lawyer and founder of the West African Students Union (WASU). These books were very much in dialogue with other historical texts about Abeokuta as well as the political issues that dominated this period.[77]

A CELEBRATION IN SEARCH OF HISTORY

Folarin's text, *A Short Historical Review of the Life of the Egbas from 1829 to 1930*, appeared in 1931. The text offers an important example of patriotic historiography, for it is replete with national heroes and narrative reductions. His narrative begins with the homestead, where "the Alake was universally acknowledged head of the Egba tribes."[78] He lays out their history of intimidation under the Oyo empire and their hard-won independence led by a farmer, Lisabi, who is credited with organizing the revolt that freed the Egbas from Oyo's control.[79] Interestingly, he stated that Lisabi and his achievements are historical and not in "the realm of romance."[80] The Yoruba Wars forced their migration to Abeokuta, but he argues that it did not transform Egba political geography because Ake remained the dominant quarter and the alake the dominant leader. Following the move to Abeokuta, "government . . . was carried on in a most regulated orderly and methodical manner. . . . Ake was the capital of the country where the head of the whole nation in the person of the Alake had his residence."[81] He also addressed the town's diversity and noted that the Owus were not Egbas; however, circumstances of the nineteenth-century wars caused them to fuse with the Egbas.[82] As Oduntan suggests, authors such as Folarin appropriated a sectional historical experience and used it as the basis to create a national Egba history. In this national narrative, the Owus and other refugee communities from the nineteenth-century wars, and Egba dominance of groups such as the Egbados to the south of Abeokuta, were subsumed and folded into the Egba nation.[83] This historical erasure of ethnic complexity allowed for Egba history and Abeokuta's history to be coterminous and seamless.

Folarin's discussion of Ademola is revealing for it was crafted to address Ademola's critics and favorably frame the alake's personal and political history. Folarin identified three periods of Egba history: the first period was in the homestead; the second period, 1830–1914, incorporated the Egbas' relocation to Abeokuta and the end of their independence; and the third extended from 1914 under direct colonial rule. He characterized the second period as "a very glorious epoch in the history of Abeokuta,"[84] in which he emphasized Ademola's activities and contributions.

As recounted by Folarin, Ladapo Ademola was born in 1872, the son of Ademola I. He was educated at the Ake School in Abeokuta and the Breadfruit School in Lagos, after which he apprenticed in the printing office of J. B. Benjamin. He later joined the printing office of J. P. Jackson, the editor and owner of the *Lagos Weekly Record*, a newspaper. He augmented his salary by conducting petty trade from his home, and as his trade grew he opened a shop and got into moneylending. In contrast to his predecessor Gbadebo, Ademola was wealthy before he assumed the title of alake. Ademola also served in an advisory capacity to several alakes. For example, he accompanied Alake Osokalu to Lagos to see Gov. Henry MacCullum, who later helped to reorganize Abeokuta's political structure, creating the EUG. Consequently, Ademola served "as the natural representation of Egba interest in Lagos."[85] During the reign of Alake Gbadebo, he helped to resolve the rebellion by some chiefs in Itori in 1901; in 1903, he accompanied Governor MacGregor and the troops from Lagos to put down the rebellion in Kemta; and he accompanied Gbadebo, EUG secretary Edun, and Egba merchant Richard B. Blaize on the state visit to London in 1904 organized by Governor MacGregor. Ademola also helped to mediate the tension between the Lagos government and the Abeokuta authorities over the railway agreement. Folarin noted that Ademola, Blaize, and MacGregor formed a unique "triumvirate," suggesting that they were ultimately the power behind the throne.[86] After being so politically active, Prince Ademola "for some occult reason thought it best to quit the colony and retire to private life for . . . nearly eleven years."[87]

Folarin's discussion of Ademola revealed that he was engaged in two of the most lucrative economic sectors in the early colonial period—trade and moneylending. Council minutes tell us that he also owned farmland and buildings that he rented to European firms.[88] He sat at the nexus of the local and international economies as he facilitated and primed the exchange of imported consumer goods and local products. His relationship with Blaize was equally significant because Blaize was one of the most important merchants of the nineteenth and early twentieth centuries. Blaize founded the *Lagos Times*, as mentioned in chapter 1, and bequeathed £3,000 to found the Abeokuta Industrial Institution. His store was located on one of the best sites in Lagos's commercial center, Marina. By the twentieth century, this store dealt in hardware, automobiles, provisions, and cotton and fancy goods as well as produce. His son, C. O. Blaize, attended school in England—Christ's College, Queen's College, and Birmingham University.[89] In highlighting Ademola's wealth and his association with wealthy individuals such as Blaize, Folarin attempted to discount the rumors of financial misdeeds that circulated at the time Ademola went into seclusion and during his early administration. Given his fortune and his economic and political connections, Folarin theorized that only an occult reason or imperceptible factors could explain why Ademola retired from public life.

Folarin also dedicated one chapter to the tension between Ademola and J. K. Coker. The chapter is very short—just two pages—nonetheless, its placement in a text ostensibly about the history of the Egbas underscores the role of this text in recasting Ademola's place in Egba history. Folarin acknowledged that Coker was one of the leading advocates for the succession of Ademola II; however, he suggests that Coker's attachment to the ogboni chiefs demonstrated a fanatical type of patriotism.[90] Moreover, he characterized Coker as dictatorial in tone and deportment. As a result, even when Coker offered reasonable advice, it was conveyed in a tone that suggested mockery and insult. He pointed out that Coker had never lived in Abeokuta and had allowed his home in Agege to become a resort for complainers and gossipers from the town. Due to these actions as well as Coker's publication of libelous material in a Lagos newspaper, *Eko Igbein*, Folarin argued that the decision to strip Coker of his ogboni title was justified. Coker had demonstrated disloyalty and a tendency to foment rebellion against "constituted Authorities."[91]

Solanke's text, *The Egba-Yoruba Constitutional Law and Its Historical Development*, which also appeared in 1931, grew out of two lectures he gave on Egba constitutional law during the centenary celebration.[92] It formed an ideal companion to Folarin's history because in it Solanke attempted to define and validate the constituted authorities who oversaw

Abeokuta's centenary. He located Egba constitutional law in a longer historical trajectory by arguing that its antecedent lay in Muslim-influenced northern Yorubaland, specifically Oyo.[93] Solanke identified seven components to the constitution developed in Oyo:

(i)   The necessary dread that every citizen should entertain for the sovereign Head of the State;

(ii)   The idea and utility of a strong central Government

(iii)   The Oba Household development

(iv)   Attempt to distribute the Sovereign powers among Separate bodies

(v)   An attempt for a separation of the Judiciary from the Executive

(vi)   The Basorun (Alias Premier's Office).

(vii)   Introduction of Islam into the constitution.[94]

Since 1830, advances in constitutional law moved south to cities strongly influenced by Christianity, especially Abeokuta and Lagos. Solanke claimed that the constitutional advances in the south were much more rapid that those in the north because religion informed the development of government and Christianity was a higher form of faith than Islam. Moreover, constitutional law developed most rapidly among the Egbas because they also adopted Western learning and education and were the last group to be "reduced to the British Power."[95]

While Solanke did not cast the period between 1830 and 1914 as a glorious epoch, it is clear that he also saw it as a vital period in the development of Egba structures of government. He described seven major improvements to Yoruba constitutionalism introduced by the Egbas:

(a)   The clean Separation of the Judiciary from both the Executive and the Legislature.

(b)   The Strengthening of the Central Government at Ake.

(c)   The imposition of customs duties on all foreign Merchandise imported and the institution of modern forms of customs Departments.

(d)   The re-organisation of the National Council with a larger number of representative Chiefs from various townships.

(e)   The introduction of the Egba National Flag.

(f)   The re-organisation of the Courts of Justice, on modern lines.

(g)   Re-organisation of the Police on modern lines.[96]

Multiple political values are embedded in this text. As Philip Zachernuk demonstrates, Solanke was articulating a new direction in Nigerian political thought that discounted unique racial qualities in need of protection and preservation and instead stressed processes of development that could be considered universal. Solanke sought to continue the efforts of the Egba government that led toward modern forms of democracy.[97] Nonetheless, Solanke's explication of democracy conformed to the political needs of the alake. For example, he noted that "in a standard civilized democratic form of Government there must be one and only one determinate Head of the State in whom is vested the bundle of all rights and powers of the citizens of that State to exercise on behalf of the people."[98] He then argued that only the alake could be the head of state based on the antiquity of the title, the acknowledged paramountcy of the alake by "kinglets" in the original homestead, and the approval of the Ifa oracle.

Solanke completely rejected the idea that the alake was just one among other kings (*primus inter pares*), and used Samuel Johnson's *History of the Yoruba* to support his claim that the alake was the head (*primus*) of the Egba chiefs. Moreover, he noted that the kings of the other three quarters in Abeokuta had to be granted permission by the alake before they were crowned.[99] Progress and democracy also required replacing sectional loyalties with national unity.[100] Here, too, Solanke subordinated democracy and national unity to the paramountcy of the alake:

> Since 1830 it would seem that the Alake's paramountcy through-
> out Egbaland has become more and more effective and pro-
> nounced in its development, whilst the status of each of the
> other subordinate "Obas" continues to disappear gradually from
> the constitution as the Egbas continue to develop that necessary
> civilized spirit of National Unity and cohesion which is a *sine
> qua non* in the progress of any people towards the attainment of
> modern nationhood.[101]

Both ideals—national unity and the paramountcy of the alakeship—were visually represented on the flag of the EUG. At its center stood the "Alake's Sceptre . . . representing the Head of the Nation, while the other Sectional Obas were holding the Sceptre, thereby depicting their subordinate position to the Alake as the Paramount Chief or the Natural Sovereign Head of the Nation."[102] Conceptualizing the alake as a natural sovereign effectively erased the history of power struggles in Abeokuta.

Solanke also erased Britain's critical support of the alakeship. In his discussion of the 1914 treaty that abrogated Abeokuta's independence,

Solanke argued that article 5, which reads "the Alake and his successors shall be *the recognized Head of the Egba People* and shall continue with *the approved chiefs of Egbaland* to carry on the Native Administration of Egbaland subject to the control of the Governor of the Colony and Protectorate of Nigeria," removed any doubt of the alake's elevated position over the other obas. Therefore, the treaty did not change any aspect of Egba customary law—it only transformed that law into a written constitution.[103] In essence, colonialism affirmed and provided positive proof of longstanding practices. Solanke also elaborated on this idea when he suggested that since 1920, the beginning of Ademola's tenure, colonialism had served as an incubator of sorts for the improvement of the customary system of democracy. This customary democracy included:

4 (b)   Development of representative system in Egbaland i.e.:

(iv)   The introduction of what may be termed (advisedly) "Egba Electoral Law" whereby 21 out of the present 28 Members of Council, after three years in office are to vacate their Seats for new election.[104]

Other improvements included the institution of "a sort of Egba Cabinet system," improvements in the judiciary, and the constitutional development of the ogboni house. He argued that the constitutional developments among the Egbas were a far cry from the oligarchic form of government that was the trajectory of Oyo's customary law. If the other Yoruba states modeled their constitutional development on the Egba state, Solanke anticipated that "a modern Federal Constitution may be possible throughout the whole of Nigeria in no distant future."[105]

Solanke's analysis of Egba constitutional law buttressed the major political goals of key constituencies of the centenary. He affirmed the alake's paramount position to the other sectional kings and the claim of its long historical tradition and practice. Furthermore, he validated the claims of Egba progressiveness and affirmed that it did not begin with colonialism. Since its foundation, Abeokuta had been on a path of modernization evidenced by Egba political leaders' early alliance with Christianity and Western education. The loss of independence, though distressing, did not divert the Egbas from their trajectory because colonial officials recognized their progressive goals and helped to advance them. The way in which he framed Egba history also satisfied the political goals of British officials for it cast indirect rule in a favorable light. The British were positioned as contributors to a project of African advancement instead of conquest and exploitation.

Ademola was at the apex of this Egba government that brought together the best of the old and the new. He was clothed in tradition and custom and simultaneously the embodiment of advancement. Solanke listed twenty improvements implemented in Abeokuta by the native administration and several specifically attributed to Ademola. General improvements included maintenance of the Church Missionary Society leper settlement; resuscitation of general or national titles; introduction of the registration of births, marriages, and deaths; a child welfare program; water and electric light programs; and support to the agricultural sector through the organization of the Egba Farmers Association. In addition to overseeing these developments, Ademola introduced a number of educational initiatives. Specifically, he inaugurated the Alake's Scholarship to provide secondary education to children from impoverished families; personally supported another fund, the Ademola Scholarship, which augmented the Alake's Scholarship; and initiated the Egba Science Scholarship and the Girl's Education Movement.[106]

Finally, Solanke's text was a call to action for the educated elite in Nigeria and Britain's other West African colonies. He tasked all educated Nigerians to give loyal support to all

> Constituted Native Authorities throughout Nigeria; . . . to devise practical ways and means whereby all the Native Farmers and Traders shall organize themselves first into small combines later into federated combines and lastly into a single great combine with a view to protecting their interests as well as to advancing the trade and the general prosperity of the country and the people. . . . The time has come for every educated Yoruba to put into actual practice the principle of Self-Help, Unity and Co-operation as daily preached by . . . WASU throughout West Africa; for this is the first and indispensable step to take towards realizing that most ambitious, legitimate and desirable goal of a "United States of West Africa."[107]

He challenged educated Yorubas, Nigerians, and other anglophone West Africans to form political and economic coalitions with "traditional" rulers, traders, and farmers. Solanke simultaneously engaged multiple levels of identity, demonstrating the fluidity of political nationalism during the interwar period. Although the centenary was a celebration of Abeokuta and Egba nationalism, Solanke used this moment to remind everyone that Egba nationalism coexisted within a diverse universe of political thought and possibilities that was also male-centric. Women were completely absent in their debate about the kingship and the relationship between the obas and titled chiefs. Their absence worked to naturalize the Egba Council as a male space and suggests that women's titles were perceived as ancillary to the real business of politics, political history, and nation-making. Women's absence from the council also meant that they were marginal to the planning of the centenary program and the face of Egba nation-ness that would be revealed through its activities.

CENTENARY ACTIVITIES

In his *Short Historical Review of the Life of the Egbas from 1829 to 1930*, Adebesin Folarin provided substantial detail about the centenary's activities. Tremendous energy and time—three years—went into planning the celebration. Invitations were sent far and wide—to the *shehu* (hereditary ruler) of Bornu, King Fuad of Egypt, and Emperor Ras Tafari (Haile Selassie) of Abyssinia.[108] In addition to meetings in Abeokuta, Egbas living in Lagos, Zaria, Jos, Ibadan, Oshogbo, Kaduna, and Ife also held meetings to help plan the celebration.[109] In Abeokuta, hundreds of women participated in meetings discussing general titles. Three hundred and eighty-four women attended the meeting on July 30, 1930, and 645 women attended the meeting on September 24, where they were informed that the

FIGURE 2.3. Olumo Rock, Ikija, Abeokuta. (Photo by Joseph Ayodokun, 2014.)

candidates for titles would "be installed 26 days hence."[110] The centenary's events stretched over nine days, from October 26 to November 2, 1930, and thousands of Abeokuta's citizens joined the festivities as well as kings and chiefs from other parts of the colony. The Yoruba-language weekly paper, the *Akede Eko*, printed the complete program listing the daily events.[111] The colonial government granted vacation time to Egba workers on the Nigerian Railway so that they could return home for the events, and British officials, including the resident, district officers, and their assistants, attended the celebration. Similarly, British merchants, missionaries, and representatives from *West Africa* magazine joined the festivities.

On Saturday, October 25, the train departing from the Lagos station at Iddo for Lafenwa, the station in Abeokuta was "full to the brim with people, young and old, male and female."[112] On Sunday, a preface to the celebrations began with worship in churches and mosques throughout the town and "invocations to the Immortal gods for its success."[113] The ogbonis performed their own comparable ceremony, *porun*, also calling for success. Monday began with the war chiefs firing dane guns on Olumo Rock to signal the start of the celebration. The general thanksgiving service brought out hundreds of people. St. Peter's Church in Ake was packed beyond capacity, the alake wore a specially made crown of pure silver, and the featured speaker, Bishop Isaac Oluwole, preached with such zeal that he fainted and had to be helped down from the pulpit.[114] The resident, B. W. Macpherson, unveiled the cenotaph created at Bada Square in Itoku in the memory of national heroes such as Lisabi and Sodeke and personally financed by the alake.[115] The alake delivered his centenary message at Ake Palace Square, and acting governor, Capt. W. Buchanan Smith, pardoned some prisoners from the 1918 Adubi War.[116]

On the following day, Tuesday, the acting governor officially opened Centenary Hall and unveiled photographs of prominent Abeokuta citizens—Dr. O. Sapara, Hon. S. H. Pearse, Dr. A. Savage, and Barrister A. Alakija. Additional activities included Solanke's lectures on Egba customary laws and two "Dramatic Entertainments entitled, Freedom of the Egbas from Oyos and The Foundation of Abeokuta." Events were held at the palace where the alake welcomed "native and European Ladies and Gentlemen of note from Lagos, Abeokuta and other parts of Nigeria."[117] Wednesday, October 29, was set aside as Ogboni Day. Activities included "a general display of various kinds of Native Dances by the Ogbonis at Ake Palace Square, where Igba and Gbedu (State Drums)" were brought out.[118] The chiefs continued the festivities with drumming in ogboni houses throughout the town.[119] The celebration concluded with a service at St. Peter's Church, Ake, followed "in the small hours of Monday by Oro play."[120]

Folarin noted that all the events were captured on film and in photographs taken by British and African photographers. People purchased numerous souvenirs, including a specially designed national standard and flags, centenary medals, and badges with the image of the alake.[121] Given the significance of the event, people spent heavily on velvet, silk, and cotton cloths with special emblems marking the centenary. Council minutes recorded the prices of the textiles ordered for the celebration: velvets, £2 10s. for ten yards; silk head ties, £1 5s. for eight yards; and cotton prints, 6s. for six yards.[122] To mark the occasion, all schoolchildren received a specially made mug that featured the emblem of the EUG—two clasped hands symbolizing unity in strength. The late Egba historian Saburi Biobaku recalled that the children paraded, sang, danced, and attended the lectures by Solanke. His autobiography aptly captured the excitement of the week:

> For us . . . the climax of the Centenary Celebration . . . was the Woro, the procession of singers and dancers in successive nights of the four sections of the Egbas, each starting from its own area and culminating at the Ake Palace. As each competing group, gaily dressed, carrying gas lamps and other illuminating devices, singing songs praising their section and deriding others, with each group trying to surpass all others, the atmosphere was simple electric.[123]

To further enhance the symbolism and pageantry, the event was commemorated in songs, including what has become known as "the Egba anthem"—"Lori Oke Ati Petele" (On the hills and in the valleys).[124]

Canon J. J. Ransome-Kuti is credited with composing the anthem.[125] It was written before the centenary, but several verses specifically reference the festivities celebrating their century in Abeokuta. However, it was not recognized as the defining national anthem in 1930 because the centenary committee commissioned a Mr. T. K. E. Phillips from Lagos to compose a national anthem for the occasion.[126] Nonetheless, "Lori Oke Ati Petele" was in circulation at the time of the centenary and like all anthems, it is suffused with patriotic imagery. Its historical trajectory charts a progression from bondage to freedom as its founding fathers, Lisabi and Sodeke, gave their lives to buy the Egbas' freedom from Oyo and establish a new home under Olumo Rock. Ransome-Kuti identified Abeokuta as "a town of freedom" where everyone is Egba and a child of Lisabi. Implicitly it suggests that strands of an Egba nation existed in their original homestead, but it became concrete when blood was shed in the overthrow of Oyo's imperial control and the migration to Abeokuta. The physical terrain of Abeokuta is intertwined with Egba nationalism, for every verse references Olumo Rock. Although the original homestead is acknowledged, it is not the space in which Egba identity consolidated.

In a similar way, the founders of the homestead are not the founding fathers of Egba nationalism. Each verse in the anthem ends with the phrase "child [or children] of Lisabi." This phrase performs several important tasks. Lisabi's resistance purchased their collective freedom; therefore, as children of Lisabi, the Egbas inherited a commitment to resistance and to anti-imperialism. Ransome-Kuti created a subtly subversive text that celebrated both Egba nationalism and their history of anti-imperialism, which the Egba attendees sang enthusiastically while in the company of British colonial officials. "Children of Lisabi" also erased all the political and social divisions that divided Abeokuta and imagined a unity that was unchallenged.

Ademola's centenary message presented a fascinating contrast to Ransome-Kuti's anthem. In it, he elided the history of Oyo's imperial control of the Egbas and began with the wars that forced the Egbas to abandon their original homestead. He argued that those conflicts, the Fulani invasion, and the internecine wars among the Yorubas resulted from the transatlantic slave trade. Ademola praised those leaders who brought the Egbas to Abeokuta and their struggles to assert their existence, identity, and independence. They established such a firm foundation that by 1844 "the Egbas had not only proclaimed to all the Yoruba Nations their self-sufficient entity but also created a nucleus of territorial expansion to which several conquered kingdoms have been annexed."[127] Whereas Ransome-Kuti's anthem did not acknowledge Egba imperial actions, Ademola celebrated the Egbas' expansionism and their reputation as a "Military Power, and a force to be reckoned with in every capacity among the Yoruba Nations."[128] Ademola avoided any critical judgment of imperialism, whether Egba or British. He praised the British government for its "humanely persistent efforts and kind assistance" that suppressed the slave trade and restored "peace, order and good government . . . gradually throughout the whole of Yoruba Country."[129]

Ademola also credited the first generation of leaders with creating a national government. He argued that one of their very first measures was to reestablish the Egba National Council. Initially military leaders dominated, "but no sooner they became better settled down than the Civil and proper Constitutional Power was reinstated, when in 1854 Chief Okukenu was installed the first Alake of this new Settlement and the old customary constitution was gradually restored." He also celebrated their foresight in embracing Christianity. As a result of their "noble action . . . Christianity formed part of the foundation stone upon which the Egba Political Society was re-erected in this Settlement."[130]

Ademola's framing of Egba history achieved several important goals. First, it imposed a centralized political structure on Egba history with Ake and the alake at the center. Furthermore, he minimized the role of the missionaries as well as the British government in creating the centralized structure that existed. He credited Egba chiefs with being the primary engine behind this form of government, arguing that they had only recreated something that had already existed in their original homestead. Colonial rule had not brought political innovations to the Egbas; it only created the security necessary for the Egbas to resume their already modern political structure. The wisdom of the ancestors also allowed Abeokuta to maintain its independence until 1914 and to receive a measure of autonomous native administration since 1924.[131] Embedded in the celebration of the Egbas' hundredth year in Abeokuta was a celebration of their foresight, political acumen, and wisdom, qualities they possessed before colonial rule.

Ademola further suggested that the Egbas were fulfilling Ifa's prophecy. He stated that it "is either not yet known to many of us or not yet sufficiently stressed by writers of our history . . . that in 1830 our Ancestors having consulted our ancient Ifa Oracle had been foretold of the advent of the British people (the Missionaries and the Government)." Ifa had revealed three predictions to Chief Tejuoso of Ikija, the chief Ifa priest: "(i) that prosperity would be the lot of the Egba people on the proposed Settlement, (ii) that most of their lost children would be found, and (iii) that a Nation from over the sea would come to raise the Egba Nation on the proposed site."[132] Nonetheless, Ademola acknowledged that their success in fulfilling Ifa's prophecy was predicated on having the support of "educated sons" and the "broad sympathy" of good British political officers. Finally, he defined civic duties for the citizens of Abeokuta:

> First and foremost it is the duty of every citizen of our beloved country to acquire the soundest possible learning and education grounded upon strong moral character, for, this constitutes the arms, ammunition and other weapons of warfare in these modern days with which every citizen should be properly and duly

armed to fight manfully to success, the present modern warfare in order to preserve intact the identity and solidarity of our Administration. Hence the Institution at these present Centenary Celebrations of "The Egba Science Scholarship and the Education of our Girls." . . .

It is the duty of every Egba educated man to impart in his or her illiterate brother or sister what we may describe as the "right type of mass education." So that our country may advance rapidly along the road of progress."[133]

Unity and cooperation constituted a second civic duty, and he provided specific examples:

Again, whenever any one of you learns about any rumour in connection with this Administration, it is his or her duty to acquaint the Alake through the proper and constitutional channel with such rumour in order to obtain the truth of the situation before any credence should be attached to such rumour.[134]

Strikingly, both duties revolved around support of his administration. He conflated the preservation of Abeokuta and its advancement in the future with the preservation of his administration. While the celebration marked the town's hundredth year, they also provided an opportunity for Ademola to inscribe his administration into the town's providential history.

By most measures the centenary was a success. Folarin estimated that about four hundred thousand people visited Abeokuta, and each event witnessed large crowds. He claimed that all the clergy from Lagos, Ibadan, Abeokuta, and other parts of Nigeria attended the state service at Ake Church. At the cenotaph, the "the crowd was so thick that it was almost impossible to see the very ground that was being trod." He noted that the events were so picturesque that only a trained artist could truly convey them, such as the procession to Olumo Rock "when the war chiefs and the 'Kila' Society mounted on beautiful charges [sic] arranged themselves on the two sides of the Cars conveying the Alake and his other chiefs."[135] The grandness of the event was relayed across Nigeria and to Britain. West Africa, a London-based magazine, discussed the centenary in four separate issues. The October 25 issue carried a brief paragraph announcing the upcoming events. One month later, the November 29 issue included a full-page discussion of the activities and a summary of the alake's centenary message. In the December 6 issue, it printed a letter to the alake from A. A. Cowan, a codirector of United Africa Company, and several pictures from the events. The magazine published a final picture from the centenary in the December 13 issue.

It is important to consider the ways in which *West Africa* packaged the Abeokuta centenary for consumption in the metropole. The article that provided detailed discussion of the celebration began with the alake's message to the king of England: "Egba people celebrating the 100th anniversary of their settlement in present capital city of Abeokuta present their dutiful obedience to your most gracious Majesty and tender their deep appreciation of your Majesty's unfailing interest in their national well being. The Egbas most humbly beg to assure your Majesty of their loyalty and attachment to your throne and person."[136] The text of the message clearly reaffirmed Abeokuta's loyalty to Britain and the colonial project. Using thick description, the author tried to convey to the readership the pomp of the event. The alake, for example, wore "a crown of solid gold, massive in design, and beautiful in workmanship, a gold chain from which hung two elephants, carved in African gold; heavy gold bracelets, encircling his wrists; and robes of exquisite silk, embroidered with golden threads. A Rolls-Royce, landed in time for the Centenary, conveyed him to the various ceremonies."[137] This description invoked a visual image of the alake virtually wrapped in gold. His adornment and the Rolls-Royce signaled splendor of a magnitude that was exponential given the economic conditions of the period. The article also provided other details absent in Folarin's text such as Ogboni Day, when dancing began in the morning in Ake Palace square and ogboni drums were played in the Ake ogboni house. It underscored the significance of the presence of the state drums because these drums were only used on special occasions, the last being fifty years before.[138]

The special correspondent also noted that the alake visited the European Club and signed the visitors' book and hosted a garden party in honor of the resident and European guests. Following the party they attended a ball at Centenary Hall sponsored by the Lagos Egba Society. The article offered a brief summary of the alake's centenary speech, noting the special thanks he gave to the missionaries and the European firms that set up shop in Abeokuta, especially John Holt, the first to arrive in 1903. The firms also offered their thanks to the alake. The senior general manager of UAC, a Mr. Henderson, added to the alake's collection of gold by presenting him with a gold watch with the alake's coat-of-arms engraved on the back. The article focused on features that seemed to illustrate colonial success: the role of missionaries and commercial agents, preservation of indigenous institutions, acculturation of British practices, and the generation of wealth for loyal Africans who gave themselves over to the process. The photographs in *West Africa* captured these elements in an even more compelling manner. They showed, for example, the alake and the resident, Captain Macpherson, at the unveiling of the cenotaph; the alake, chiefs, and princes in the throne room; Mr. Henderson presenting the watch to the alake; the alake inspecting a police honor guard; and an overhead view of the crowd walking up to Olumo Rock. By far the most striking picture was one of the alake and Captain Macpherson walking toward St. Peter's Church for the thanksgiving service. The caption underneath read, "As it should be: African and British leaders side by side."[139]

The centenary celebration integrated large segments of Abeokuta society—Christians, Muslims, schoolchildren, ogbonis, war chiefs, inhabitants of all four quarters, Europeans, and the Egba diaspora. In this lengthy display of national pride that featured several events honoring important past and current Egba citizens, women were conspicuously absent. Neither the program nor the press coverage leading up to or after the centenary mentioned Abeokuta's first iyalode, Madam Tinubu, or its iyalode at the time of the celebration, Madam Jojolola.

Despite the fact that the centenary celebration brought many people together, there were critical voices. In a letter to the editor of *Akede Eko*, the author praised the alake for his accomplishments in bringing education and development to Abeokuta but criticized him for the continued injustice to the ex-oshile Suberu Adedamola.[140] A. K. Ajisafe also published a critical letter in *Akede Eko* in the months leading up to the celebration,[141] but in 1931 he expanded his critique into a small pamphlet, *Abeokuta Centenary and Its Celebrations*. The author of several books on Abeokuta's history, Ajisafe used the centenary as an opportunity to reflect on the past and compare it to the present. He argued rather forcefully that Abeokuta's past was, in fact, a better and more prosperous period than its present. He dated the town's decline to 1902, when Abegboyega Edun was hired as the secretary of the EUG. It was under Edun's tenure that Abeokuta lost its freedom, its people turned into slaves, and its king into a chief.[142] Given these developments, Ajisafe questioned the cause for joy and celebration of the centenary.

Ajisafe directed most of his criticisms to Alake Ademola. He challenged Ademola's self-presentation, and indirectly Solanke's characterization of the alake, as the only rightful and constitutional oba of Egbaland. Furthermore, he argued that it was unfair that the alake received £3,000 annually in salary while the other obas received less than £500 each. Ademola also received a number of allowances, including funds for the renovation of his court and the upkeep of his car. The other obas did not receive any allowances and were forced to use their small salaries to maintain the prestige of their positions and palaces. In addition, Ajisafe charged that Ademola engaged in a number of practices intended to undermine the prestige of the other kings. These included demanding that in the council room the three obas sit on mats instead of on chairs and remove their crowns.

Ajisafe also questioned the high praise given to Christianity and Western education. He stated that there is no substantive progress associated to Christianity; instead it fostered immorality and many diseases unknown to their ancestors. Similarly, education had brought no progress, and the "educated few are the productions of the artificial decadent civilisation and consequently are absolutely subservient."[143] The people of Abeokuta lived in more deplorable conditions under an educated king than before under illiterate kings. He took the administration and the alake to task on economic issues as well. He observed there were fewer prominent Egba traders than in the past, in part the result of the access European trading companies now enjoyed to Egba farmers. Few employment opportunities existed; nonetheless, each year the administration generated new schemes to extract money from people. While Solanke listed the birth, death, and marriage registration and the electricity and water programs as improvements, Ajisafe charged that they were just moneymaking ventures by the administration. Other such ventures included a plan to tax women oil venders five shillings. He also accused the alake of using his position to compete with traders of all levels:

> The present Alake Ademola II has at Abeokuta so many houses, and the houses are tenanted by European Firms. This shows that the Alake rivals his subject in the petty trade of the land. . . . How will the petty traders of any land fare whose king and ruler, through his Agents or personally, competes with them in their petty trade like Adire cloth making, cattle trading and meat selling, Gari and Vegetable selling and trading in palm oil and farm products?[144]

As further evidence of the alake's disregard for the economic well-being of the people of Abeokuta, Ajisafe cited the creation and distribution of the centenary cloth. The cloth had the alake's name, *oriki* (praise poem), a portrait of him, and a stamp. It did not include the other obas at all. Moreover, despite the "financial famine," the alake visited the rural districts with samples of the cloth and induced poor farmers to purchase it: "Some had to sell their valuable properties to meet up the costs of the cloths and those who were supplied on credit are now smelling and experiencing the worry and sting of the debt. Many did not buy the cloths by free-will; they were intimidated that the Alake will punish them severely if they failed to buy."[145] Ademola was taking advantage of the Yoruba practice of *aso ebi* (family cloth) in which participants at social functions, most often weddings and funerals, dress in outfits made from a cloth selected by the host. Wearing aso ebi expresses solidarity, but it can also reflect intimidation, as Ajisafe suggests.[146] Thus, for Ajisafe, the centenary was yet another money-making scheme from which Ademola benefited.

Ajisafe also criticized some of the cultural aspects of the program. He charged that the anthem should not have included specific names of any individual king or ruler. Furthermore, it should have been in Yoruba rather than English, and it should not have been set to English or any foreign music. He called attention to the many great heroes who were not recognized in the pantheon created in Centenary Hall. Among the list of contenders, he included several women: Madam Tinubu, Mrs. J. B. Wood (wife of CMS missionary J. B. Wood), Madam Jojolola, and Madam Subuola Egberongbe. Ajisafe concluded that the centenary celebration was not really for Abeokuta or the Egbas—instead it was "formulated to fan fame and for self aggrandizement."[147]

Ajisafe's critique did not go unanswered. Folarin devoted thirty pages in his history to respond to Ajisafe's pamphlet.[148] He cited evidence from a variety of sources, including Ajisafe's own *History of Abeokuta*, to refute the characterization of Ademola and the state of progress in Abeokuta. Collectively, Folarin, Solanke, and Ajisafe were engaged in a battle to frame and contextualize Abeokuta's past, present, and future. Equally important, they represented competing factions in the town's heterogeneous elite. While each also claimed to speak on behalf of "the people" and to champion leaders and policies that would bring improvement to their lives, the voices of the people were absent from the historical records of this discourse.

⌐

The centenary celebration was a signal achievement in part because it brought together multiple modes of history-telling and history-making. The documentary evidence taught us much more about the production of the celebration than its reception by the participants. Nonetheless, as Wendy Griswold and Muhammed Bhadmus argue, we cannot assume that the reception was bipolar or unidirectional.[149] While organizers sought to convey specific meanings and messages through the structure of the program, they likely conveyed multiple messages to different segments of the audience. The organizers of the centenary celebration wanted to evoke unity; nonetheless, parts of the program demonstrated Mikael Karlström's suggestion that in these events local groups often do not stage themselves as solidary and undifferentiated.[150] Differentiation and competition lay at the heart of the Woro dances Biobaku witnessed. Even though many wore the centenary cloth, Ajisafe's suggestion that some people did so under duress means that the very picture of solidarity their dress invoked was fragile.

This spectacle of nation-ness was deeply gendered. The photographs unveiled in Centenary Hall tell us a great deal about the values that undergirded this display. The photographs featured men who also shared certain characteristics. They were Christian, highly educated professionals, self-made men whose fortunes and status existed outside of spaces controlled by the colonial bureaucracy or British capital. Collectively, they reflected the new social hierarchy that marginalized men who were not Christian and literate. These men were also family men with wives who were Christian, literate, and socially engaged. Like the alake, they valued education for their daughters and girls in general. However, they did not envision a political role for women, whether educated or not. On multiple levels the centenary celebration affirmed the singularity of nation and masculinity. The first planning meeting of the Centenary Celebration Committee occurred on March 14, 1927, but women were invited for the first time on June 9, 1930, to inform them of the arrangements and to suggest that they form a committee.[151] Egba women were completely absent from the program; they were not present among the heroes honored in the cenotaph or among the photographs in Centenary Hall. The program did not mention the installation of women's titles. Women, however, appeared only in the scenery of the centenary's festivities. They populated the crowds that traveled from Lagos, witnessed the unveiling of the cenotaph, moved in a procession to Olumo Rock, danced at nighttime competitions, and enjoyed the garden party and balls. They remained anonymous, undifferentiated, and virtually invisible in the cultural representations of the nation.

The centenary celebration also affirmed a process of state-making that was highly gendered. With each expansion of the Egba Council, officials claimed they were widening the scope for democracy and narrowing the space for the alake to exercise autocratic rule. However, only men were brought onto the council to represent geographically or culturally defined constituencies. Women were not perceived as a constituency that needed representation or as possible representatives of an accepted constituency. Thus, colonial practice entrenched the idea that the institutions of government were exclusively male preserves.

3 ∽ Race, Nation, and Politics in the Interwar Period

Abeokuta's centenary celebrations highlighted the major power blocks in Abeokuta—colonial officials, the alake and his council, and the ogboni. Each used tradition to legitimate its authority. The display of chiefly power and the cultural performances satisfied the colonial state's claim of preserving indigenous practices and institutions. The alake's sartorial display drew on Yoruba aesthetics of power, while the ogboni performances and use of the state drums underscored their continued centrality to the exercise of power. Through these symbols of tradition, the alake, ogboni, their respective supporters, and colonial officials exercised competing political discourses. They modeled the long-term continuities in political language that Steve Feierman argues transformed over time as people struggled with radical social change and conflicts.[1] The critical concern at the center of the centenary celebration revolved around sovereignty. For colonial officials and the larger British audience, the centenary championed their long-term commitment to colonial rule. However, for the alake, the chiefs, and the majority of citizens who attended the celebrations, the centenary events showcased Abeokuta as a blend of old and new political customs and practices and ready to regain its sovereignty. It had a modern, progressive leader who valued education, and, as Ladipo Solanke argued, the town was well on the way to developing a modern democratic state that incorporated indigenous institutions. This moment projected what Oluwatoyin Oduntan suggests was the highpoint of Egba nationalism, but it also contained elements of the developments that would shift Egba nationalism from a quest for sovereign independence to independence as part of a larger nation.[2]

This chapter demonstrates that shifts in political thought and political identification did not follow a linear trajectory where one succeeded the other. Rather, they were overlapping processes jostling each other in the same temporal moment. Prasenjit Duara captures it well when he explains, "Identities are forged in a fluid complex of cultural signifiers: symbols, practices, and narratives. The process of community closure is the process of fixing certain signifiers within this fluid complex and authorizing them to mobilize the affective strength of the others."[3] The crisis of capital in the interwar period shaped the material conditions that made more people attentive to the increasing political and ideological challenge to racism and imperialism.

Much of this intellectual ferment was based in Lagos where people experienced an upsurge in newspapers and increased political agitation after World War I. The newspapers, some now published in Yoruba, helped create and nurture a public that extended beyond the educated elites and became vested in new political practices—political parties and elections.[4] Abeokuta was influenced by the new political discourse and practice in Lagos. Increasingly some of the individuals who in 1930 argued that Abeokuta should regain its political independence gradually shifted their geographical scope. By the end of the 1930s, new organizations emerged that demanded independence for Nigeria, and even Solanke ceased calls for an independent Abeokuta. This chapter examines those voices within Abeokuta who championed a broader political landscape than Egbaland. It is especially concerned with men and women who encouraged the citizens of Abeokuta to engage in political thought and imaginings on a national and international stage. While much of the literature on nationalist thought in Nigeria during this period focuses almost exclusively on Lagos, this chapter demonstrates that Abeokuta was not just a satellite of intellectual developments in Lagos; rather, it was also an important crucible of intellectual thought and debate. The new inflections in political thought were shaped by the deepening global economic depression that for African commodity producers and consumers defined the interwar period. Thus, the chapter also pays attention to ways in which the economic crisis informed the search for new political leaders, new political goals, and new forms of political mobilization.

TOWARD A NEW NARRATIVE OF NATION

Lagos, as Philip Zachernuk argues, was the "cosmopolitan center of education and the educated community in the interwar years." The majority of newspapers were concentrated there, and it "served as center stage for the explicitly political organizations that multiplied after World War I."[5] As early as 1920, a branch of Marcus Garvey's Universal Negro Improvement Association (UNIA) emerged in Lagos. Zachernuk estimates that the group had about four hundred members at its height. However, Rina Okonkwo notes that West Indians dominated the membership, for few Nigerians joined. The majority of West Indians in Lagos in the early decades of the twentieth century attempted to maintain their cultural distinctiveness. Many belonged to the West Indian Association, and they did not adopt African dress or languages. Nonetheless, some, like Amos Shackleford, one of the founders of the Lagos chapter of the UNIA, were part of Lagos's educated elite and contributed to Nigerian politics. Shackleford was also a cofounder and vice president of the Nigerian National Democratic Party, formed by Herbert Macaulay, proprietor of the *Lagos Daily News*.[6] While it does not appear that the UNIA extended into Abeokuta, some inhabitants of Abeokuta were aware of the organization.

The records do not reveal the alake's views on the UNIA. Nonetheless, he interacted with members of the organization. In 1920, Ademola invited the pan-African activist, member of the UNIA, journalist, and publisher of the London-based paper *African Times and Orient Review*, Dusé Mohamed Ali, to visit Abeokuta during a trip to West Africa. Ali shared Garvey's vision of Africa's economic emancipation and visited West Africa in an effort to build commercial relationships between Nigerian cocoa farmers and British banks. When that effort failed, he tried to establish links between West African cocoa farmers and American banks and chocolate manufacturers. Although these efforts were also unsuccessful, Ali moved in 1931 to Nigeria, where he worked for several newspapers—the *Nigerian Daily Telegraph* and the *Nigerian Daily Times*—before launching his own Lagos-based weekly magazine, the *Comet*, in 1933.[7] It is not clear if Ali and the alake maintained communication after his visit to the town in 1920, but he went on to play an important role in Nigerian politics during the 1930s and 1940s. Through the *Comet*, he supplied much international news to Nigerian newspaper consumers and was at the forefront of the country's support of Ethiopia following the Italian invasion. Moreover, he became a patron of the Young Muslim Society, lectured widely on Islam, and chaired the inaugural meeting of the National Council of Nigeria and the Cameroons, Nigeria's first nationalist organization. Though Mustafa Abdelwahid's suggestion that Ali transformed "the political interests of Nigerian intellectuals from a narrow focus on local Nigerian politics to embracing the politics of the entire continent" is hyperbolic, Ali contributed significantly to the increased political agitation of the interwar period.[8]

Educated elites in Abeokuta were aware of the pan–West African mobilization closer to home because a local branch of the National Congress
of British West Africa (NCBWA) emerged in 1921. The Gold Coast lawyer J. E. Casely Hayford and Dr. Akiwande Savage (from Nigeria though
working in the Gold Coast) first circulated calls for a West African conference in 1914.[9] Territorial committees formed initially in Sierra Leone
and the Gold Coast, and the Gold Coast section took the lead in organizing the Conference of Africans of British West Africa from March 11 to
29, 1920, in Accra.[10] The organization argued for the creation of a united
British West Africa that would be self-governing within the British Empire. The organization's political objective emerged largely in response
to indirect-rule policies that marginalized educated African men in the
legislative councils and colonial administrations and centered authority
on traditional rulers.[11] The actions of European powers in the wake of
World War I also informed the deliberations at the meeting in Accra as did
the occurrence of pan-African meetings in Europe and America — the 1919
Pan-African Congress in Paris and the New York establishment of Marcus
Garvey's UNIA.

Writing in the *Africa and Orient Review*, Ali affirmed the importance
of this conference: "We have all along said . . . that unity among West Africans is an essential to commercial and political prosperity. . . . This being
an age of combinations of one kind or another, it behoves the coloured
people of the world to show a solid front."[12] Conference participants passed
resolutions that created the foundation for self-government.[13] The constitutional proposals envisioned a much larger role for the educated elites
and expressed a clear critique of colonial rule. They demanded a Legislative Council with half of its membership nominated by the Crown and
the remaining half elected by the people, a House of Assembly composed
of the members of the Legislative Council, and financial representatives
elected by the people. The assembly would have the right to discuss and
approve the annual budget proposed by the governor as well as the power
to impose all taxes. Each British West African community would have
the power to elect members to the Legislative Council and the House
of Assembly. They also suggested the creation of municipal corporations
that would have local self-government in each principal town. Taxpayers
would elect four-fifths of the members of the corporation, and the colonial government would nominate one-fifth. Both nominated and elected
members of the corporation would select a mayor from among the elected
members. In addition to proposals that clearly created spaces for educated
African men in government, conference participants demanded an end to

the color bar in hiring in the West African Civil Service and the creation of a British West African University.[14]

The dominant Nigerian chapter of the NCBWA was in Lagos. However, by 1921, the Abeokuta annual report noted that a group, mostly Christians, had formed a branch of the NCBWA in Abeokuta. Both the Egba Council and the resident expressed reservations about the group. The council claimed that some members participated in undesirable activities, while the resident argued that they could introduce "unnatural institutions at the expense of those founded upon custom." A deputation representing NCBWA-Abeokuta appeared before the council during a session attended by the resident. Although they received "a somewhat unfriendly" response from council members, the branch continued to meet. The resident, C. W. Alexander, sanctioned the group's operation for "any attempt at initial repression might attach to them an importance they do not deserve."[15] The decision to allow the group to meet without interference reflected colonial officials' insecurity about their ability to maintain the peace in Abeokuta, for it was only three years since the peasant tax revolt, the Adubi War. In his disquiet, Resident Alexander stressed the necessity of sending only experienced district officers to Abeokuta in response to a confidential memo from the secretary of the Southern Provinces in 1922.[16]

Abeokuta also became more integrated into national politics when the town was allotted a seat in the Legislative Council in Lagos in 1922.[17] The Legislative Council was first established in 1862, a year after Lagos was ceded to Britain. Ironically, Tekena Tamuno argues the council was not intended to be a training ground for self-government. It had an official majority and unofficial members who represented the African and European communities in Lagos. The governor nominated the unofficial members who represented the African community, thus further marginalizing any African input. Moreover, despite the small size of the European population for most of its history from 1862 to 1913, the African and European communities had the same number of representatives on the committee.[18] Adult African men in Lagos gained the right to elect African representatives in 1922, a policy shift that led to the creation of Nigeria's first political party, the Nigerian National Democratic Party.[19] The NNDP grew out of the Ilu Committee, "a body traditionally organized out of the Oba's council . . . and responsible for duties associated with welfare and self-government." The committee was composed of representatives from a vast network of associations that dominated religious, social, and economic life among the city's popular classes—artisans, traders, wage earners, and the poor. There were representatives from Muslim and Yoruba religious groups as well as market women's associations from different wards of the city. The NNDP was a new form of political organization that from its inception reflected a coalition that was multinational, multiclass, multireligious, and critical of the colonial government.[20] While the NNDP and the Legislative Council were based in Lagos, citizens from across the country reached out to Macaulay and the NNDP to bring issues to the council's attention, thus giving a national character to the party.[21]

The proliferation of schools contributed as well to the development of a national consciousness. In the 1920s, several teachers' organizations emerged. In 1925, Rev. J. O. Lucas and T. K. Cameron formed the Lagos Union of Teachers (LUT). The following year, Rev. I. O. Ransome-Kuti formed the Association of Headmasters of Ijebu Schools (AHIS). Unlike most teachers' unions of this time, the AHIS included headmasters of primary schools. By the end of the decade, Lucas and Cameron had helped initiate the beginnings of a truly national organization. At the initiation of the LUT, the AHIS, and the teachers' unions of Abeokuta, Agege, Ibadan, and Ijebu joined together to create a federated Nigerian Union of Teachers (NUT). Local organizations would become branches of the central organization, which would speak with one voice for the teaching profession. The organization was formed on November 8, 1930, and during its inaugural meeting on July 8–9, 1931, Reverend Ransome-Kuti and Reverend Lucas were elected president and vice president, respectively.[22]

The union underwent substantial philosophical and political changes over the course of the decade. At the beginning some of its supporters felt that the union needed to be cautious, especially in its dealings with the colonial government and the missionary bodies, and "convey to the authorities the professional character of the teachers' union."[23] Raymond Smyke and Denis Storer suggest that the unsettled political period in which NUT emerged, the year following the Women's War in eastern Nigeria, contributed to this caution.[24] Caution also included maintaining a safe distance from the developing nationalist movement. This fear of upsetting the authorities resulted from two intersecting concerns. First, several missionary societies forbade their members from joining the union. Second, teachers were part of a small but growing class of African professionals who felt compelled to organize in order to protect their interests but who nonetheless expressed some ambivalence about the roles of the organizations they had created. However, as the Depression worsened and the colonial government cut educational subsidies and teachers' salaries, the caution advocated by people such as Henry Carr, the first African educational officer in Lagos, dissipated. Teachers felt compelled to make increasing demands on colonial authorities. In 1933, for example, a resolution offered by the Calabar branch demanded that teachers be paid as civil servants, and the central organization petitioned the lieutenant governor of the Southern Provinces to place a representative of NUT on the education committee of each province.[25] NUT affiliated with the National Union of Teachers of England and Wales and cultivated support from several members of the Legislative Council in Lagos, especially Dr. C. C. Adeniyi-Jones. While professionalizing and organizing teachers, NUT forged new political linkages nationally and internationally and demanded a role in shaping education policy.

By the end of 1934, NUT had twelve branches and four hundred teachers as its very effective general secretary, E. E. Esua, encouraged other teachers' associations around the country to join the union.[26] NUT's attempt to reverse the salary cuts over the decade and its sympathy toward strikers, such as the teachers in Calabar and Creek Town who called a strike on April 1, 1936, brought new members to the organization. New branches of NUT opened primarily in the southern provinces; however, by 1938, several branches existed in the north, specifically Zaria and Kaduna. Even though many of the branches in the north represented southerners who lived there, it provided a national character to the organization.[27]

The Abeokuta branch of NUT also established a strong relationship with the West African Students' Union. Reverend Ransome-Kuti was a childhood friend of Ladipo Solanke and a strong supporter of WASU from its inception. Both Reverend and Funmilayo Ransome-Kuti were individual members of WASU, and the teachers' union actively supported WASU. West Africa reported, for example, that Abeokuta celebrated "WASU Week" from November 16 to 21, 1931. It noted that the success of the week was "chiefly due to the local branch of the teachers' union, especially Mrs. F. Kuti, Mrs. B. K. Gibson Roberts, and Aderemi Ademola."[28] The relationship between WASU and NUT deepened over the course of the decade, for education sat at the center of nationalist thought.

During the 1941 WASU annual conference, for example, members passed a number of resolutions on education because education was central to the nationalist project. They wanted to ensure that "the average Nigerian attending school became more aware of the social and economic conditions" in which he or she lived and more politically responsive to the country's future needs. However, in order to create a politically engaged citizenry that could "appreciate current social changes and . . . pass informed judgment on all government policies," mass education had to be implemented. WASU also wanted assurance that those young Africans

pursuing education had job opportunities, so they called for the employment of Africans in the civil service.[29] These resolutions lent tremendous
support to the work carried out by NUT. Through its alliances with the
British teachers' union and WASU, NUT helped to create international
support for the development of a robust educational system in Nigeria as
well as the evolving nationalist project.

The emergence of the Nigerian Youth Movement in 1934 offered a
significant transformation in political thought. The NYM began life as
the Lagos Youth Movement in 1934 in response to the limited social vision
projected in the creation of Yaba Higher College, a vocational institution. Opponents wanted institutions of higher learning modeled on British
universities. The NYM became a force in Lagos politics, for it ended the
electoral monopoly of the NNDP, which had controlled the three African
seats since the creation of the Legislative Council.[30]

Most of the leaders of the NYM were educated, professional men, and
many were Yoruba, but it also included Lagos-based Igbo professionals
such as Nnamdi Azikiwe, the Nigerian journalist who returned to Lagos
in 1937 and launched the *West African Pilot* in 1938. Nonetheless, scholars
argue that the organization was not sectarian, because it had branches in
urban centers throughout Nigeria and it stressed the notion of national
unity among all regions and ethnic groups. Equally important, the NYM
crafted a new political template. It issued a Youth Charter on May 2, 1938,
in which it articulated a set of goals and demands that would be incorporated by later nationalist organizations. For example, it called for complete
autonomy within the British Empire, equal partnership with members of
the British Commonwealth of Nations, universal adult suffrage, abolition
of the indirect-rule system, equal economic opportunities for Nigerians and
foreigners, improvements in wages and working conditions, emancipation
of women, and progressively free and compulsory elementary education.
The NYM established a women's wing and very early became involved in
strikes such as the Motor Union strike in 1937 and the campaign against
the cocoa price-fixing schemes of the British trading companies in 1938.[31]
The NYM's activism illuminated its larger criticism of the leaders in the
1920s and early 1930s who, in its estimation, did not pay sufficient attention
to the economic grievances that animated most Nigerians. By establishing
a platform that was both national and populist, the NYM refashioned the
political landscape to reflect the issues that were central to the majority of
the population.[32] The NYM offered more radical leadership for the times;
moreover, its leadership emerged from different social locations. Zachernuk notes that a significant number came from provincial families rather

than the elite Christian, often Saro families. Many were professionals—lawyers, doctors, journalists—and businessmen; however, their careers were threatened by the economic crisis and job retrenchment in the 1930s, thus creating a sense of urgency for change.[33]

By 1941, there were Abeokuta branches of the NYM and the NNDP. Press coverage of the NNDP called particular attention to women's participation. The first meeting of the group that became the Abeokuta branch of the NNDP took place on Saturday, January 26, 1941, in Centenary Hall, as recounted in the newspaper *Egbaland Echo:* "The third meeting was held on Saturday the 23rd August, 1941, was largely attended by representatives of the different sections of Abeokuta and there were no less than 14 to 16 representatives of women societies in Abeokuta in attendance. . . . Several speakers—women not excluded—spoke and expressed their desire and determination to establish the Abeokuta Branch of the Demos."[34] The article did not provide any details of the women in attendance or the societies they represented. Nonetheless, their active recruitment indicates that women were a part of the new political discourse emerging in Abeokuta. During the formal inauguration of the group as the Abeokuta branch of the NNDP on May 15, 1943, they were addressed by Herbert Macaulay as well as by Madam Animotu Pelewura, leader of the Lagos Market and Trading Women Association. The president of the Abeokuta branch, Chief I. A. Sodipo, noted that although the current number of women in the NNDP was small, he knew many women who were anxious to join. Pelewura offered to return to Abeokuta to speak to the women "so that they may know what important part they can take in the political affairs of the Country."[35]

Pelewura's visit to Abeokuta under the umbrella of the NNDP was critical, in part because it offered an important political model. Macaulay's and Pelewura's political association since the interwar period demonstrated that market women aligned with nationalists could restrict the reach of the colonial government. Lagos in the 1920s, as Karin Barber notes, was a time of "intensifying political agitation." The administrative and financial capital of colonial Nigeria, the city experienced continuing mass protests against the water rate, the "crisis in the majority Muslim community, and above all the deposition of the traditional ruler, the Eleko."[36] Although colonial officials saw the *eleko*'s power as largely symbolic following the British takeover in 1861, the colonial government and the holder of the title in 1920s, Esugbayi, had a tempestuous relationship. Esugbayi first earned the ire of colonial officials, but widespread popular support among Lagos residents, in 1915 when he challenged the imposition of water rates. He was suspended in 1916 but reinstated following mobilization by the royal house of Lagos, Saro-descended Christian elites such as Herbert Macaulay, the Muslim community, and market women's associations. Nigerian lawyers worked with prominent politicians to intercede with the governor, Sir Hugh Clifford.[37]

Esugbayi fell afoul of officials again in 1925 when he was asked to denounce Macaulay for publicly criticizing the colonial government in London while carrying one of the eleko's official staffs. Colonial officials interpreted Macaulay's criticism as a quasi-official act on behalf of the eleko. Esugbayi sent a denial of Macaulay's statements to the newspapers in Lagos, but he refused the government's demand that he "send his bellman and town crier round the town to read a denial statement prepared by government officials."[38] He was detained by force, deposed, and exiled to Oyo in 1925. His removal reenergized his political coalition, and in a long, sustained legal battle, Nigerian lawyers took his case to the Privy Council twice. Although the Privy Council referred the case back to the Nigerian courts, Bonny Ibhawoh argues that their ruling was an indictment of both the Nigerian government and judiciary. In 1931, the new governor, Sir Donald Cameron, announced that the government would no longer pursue the eleko case in court, and Esugbayi was reinstated as eleko. Lagosians marked Esugbayi's return to Lagos with an unofficial public holiday by closing shops, markets, and offices and composing songs, dances, and plays. His return represented a clear victory over the colonial government.[39]

The eleko affair was significant for several reasons. Barber argues that the mobilization around the eleko fostered a formative moment in the development of the Nigerian press, for as newspapers lined up behind the eleko or the colonial government, they experimented with new genres, expanded their reach even beyond literate audiences, and created a more diverse and multiscalar public.[40] Over the course of the decade, the eleko's battles with the colonial government brought together cultural associations, workers' guilds, market women's associations, lawyers, and other educated elites who attended public meetings and raised funds on his behalf. Many of these organizations supplied representatives to the Ilu Committee. Furthermore, they taxed themselves so that the committee could pay the eleko's stipend from 1920 to 1931 to allow him greater autonomy in his dealings with the colonial government and finance his case before the Privy Council.[41]

These associations became the building blocks of the NNDP voting lists that enabled the party to win the seats in the Legislative Council from its inception in 1922 and then hold on to those seats until the late 1930s. Market women were central to the campaign supporting the eleko and turned out in the hundreds for NNDP mass meetings. Market women's support of the political party meant that they could rely on assistance from Macaulay, the NNDP's coalition partners, and newspapers when they challenged colonial policies that threatened their livelihoods. Thus, when rumors circulated in 1932 that women in Lagos would be taxed, colonial officials assured the market women's delegation that the rumors were incorrect. A second delegation revisited colonial officials in 1941 because the issue of taxing women rose again. In a letter addressed to Madam Alimotu Pelewura and Madam Jiromi Barikisu sent care of Macaulay, the acting financial secretary wrote,

> His Excellency has no intention, at any rate for the present, of interfering with the custom by which the lower incomes of women in Lagos are exempt from separate taxation, although in Abeokuta and elsewhere the incomes of all women are liable to separate taxation. At the same time His Excellency cannot agree that wealthier women, such as doctors and barristers and owners of large properties, should be forever immune from taxation. Indeed His Excellency feels sure that such women will themselves agree that it is their duty to contribute to the public services of the country.
>
> Nevertheless His Excellency has decided to propose to the Legislative Council at the session due to be held in March next that the minimum annual income on which women should be liable to separate taxation shall be raised from £50 to £200.[42]

In spite of the dire need for revenue during the war, the vast majority of Lagosian women did not pay taxes. Thus, Pelewura's visit to Abeokuta as a representative of the NNDP communicated the efficacy of membership in a nationalist party and more specifically the NNDP.

Market women's support of the NNDP also reflected the challenges illiterate inhabitants of this colonial capital faced as they tried to push back policies that affected them negatively. Approximately twenty-six markets existed in Lagos by the 1920s. Each market had a leader, the *alaga*, who was responsible for the maintenance and upkeep of the market. Within each market, traders organized by commodity associations. As the colonial government imposed an increasing regime of taxes and fines on the markets and households, market women used numerous strategies to convey their concerns to the government. In 1908, for example, they supported the traditional chiefs in a campaign against the water tax by closing markets and shops and joining a protest march to government house. By the 1940s, many commodity associations employed secretaries, who tended to be men, given the disparity in education, or hired lawyers.[43] However, their most successful strategy by far was their affiliation with Herbert Macaulay and the NNDP.

ELITE WOMEN, MARKET WOMEN, AND THE INTERWAR CRISIS

A number of elite women had the literacy skills necessary to assist market women, but ideals of colonial femininity restricted the nature of their political and social activism. Elite women focused their activism on service projects with broad goals of social and racial uplift. Abosede George argues that the emergence of organizations such as the Lagos Ladies League in 1901 "marked the beginnings of a new vision of what elite women's clubs could represent and accomplish and what elite women's roles could be in the larger society." Their organizations became spaces where they could imagine transforming elite gender expectations well as the broader society in Lagos. For example, the Lagos Ladies League's support of the government's infant mortality reduction campaign charted a different course for elite women. It enabled them to gain status in a public role while they still satisfied the expectations of colonial femininity. Moreover, it made the organization quasi-governmental since its members implemented government policy by visiting different parts of the city to distribute medicine and advice on child-care, among other things.[44] The league's public works on behalf of the government generated hostility among the households they visited because occupants saw them as "spies who came to inspect the houses in order to report the unhygienic conditions to the government."[45] This hostility contributed to the league's demise by 1908.

In 1924, the Lagos Ladies League reemerged as the Lagos Women's League. As George notes, the name change did not reflect a change in the demographic composition of the organization. The members were elite, Christian women of wealthy Saro and other diaspora families. However, they no longer administered colonial government policies. They concentrated on advocating for Lagos's poor and working populations. Their concerns revolved around infrastructure, especially drainage, health care, universal education for girls, and greater government support for non-denominational schools. They also demanded government attention to quality-of-life issues such as rudeness, lewdness, and prostitution. They were especially exercised over young girls engaged in trade—child street hawking—which they perceived as a cover for child prostitution. For elite women, underage prostitution and hawking "threatened to undermine the moral uplift of women in Nigeria . . . and seemed to flout the value system that would lead toward what women reformers considered respectable modern womanhood."[46]

Respectable womanhood overtly shaped debates about adult prostitution and venereal disease in Lagos. Saheed Aderinto shows that class, gender, race, and ethnicity informed the discussion about adult prostitution. While some elite men supported the regulation of adult prostitution, elite women reformers advocated strongly for its prohibition. They also envisioned women playing an important role in ending prostitution. Elite women had long advocated that the colonial government hire educated Nigerian women, and they put the idea forward again when they proposed that the Nigerian police force hire women, especially to rescue young girls engaged in sex work.[47] While these women perceived their actions as beneficial to all Lagosians, their positions on child hawking and adult prostitution put them in tension with market women and poor women struggling to survive the Depression and the war era.

Child hawking socialized young girls and helped them develop the skills to be successful traders, but, as George demonstrates, it was also economically vital to many households.[48] No doubt some girls were involved in sex work, but given their youth, elite reformers believed that these girls could be redeemed. They held no such expectations for adult women involved in prostitution. Lagosians insisted that many of the adult women involved in sex work were not indigenes of the city. The distinction between indigene and foreigner mattered because the Lagos Town Council had the power to "repatriate 'foreigners' to their native homes for offenses ranging from prostitution to public disorder."[49] For impoverished women migrating to the city, such as those from Cross River Basin, sex work provided sufficient funds to assert economic and social autonomy, build homes, and finance male and female relatives back home in petty trading or other ventures.[50]

Elite women focused on girl street hawking and prostitution as existential threats to the moral fabric of the city, thus these topics dominated the agenda in their meetings with colonial officials. The discussions between elite women and colonial officials stand in contrast to the topics that dominated interactions between market women and colonial officials. Market women were overwhelming concerned with issues that threatened their livelihood—market fees, taxation, arrests for profiteering, and infringement by traders from outside Lagos.[51] Since elite women reformers and market women were not galvanized by the same issues, they maintained separate and distinct organizational spaces during the interwar period. Nina Mba noted that World War II initiated the greatest period of cooperation between elite women and market women when the Lagos Women League and the recently established Women's Party (1944) supported market women's protest against the government's efforts to control food prices through the Pullen market system.[52]

The social and political distance between market women and elite educated women existed in other parts of southern Nigeria. In eastern Nigeria, the first major women's protest to colonial rule emerged in 1916 in Onitsha when market women protested the state's decision to move them to a new market location in which they had erected updated stalls. Women would have to pay an annual rent of £1 to government-appointed men given control over the market. The plan removed women's long-standing control of markets and was at a cost that few could afford.[53] Market women played pivotal roles in the 1929 Women's War, the most significant expression of women's activism during the interwar period. They had major grievances against the capricious power of the warrant chiefs, who represented the colonial state at the village level. Economically, they had already been burdened with the expansion of produce inspection in 1926 and European trading companies' purchase-price agreements in 1928 when the rumors of taxation began.[54] Utilizing leadership structures and networks of market associations, secret societies, and other women's organizations, Igbo and Ibibio women across eastern Nigerian protested the economic and existential threat colonial rule imposed on their societies.

These women fully grasped the threat taxes posed to their economic well-being; however, they were more than economic actors. The women who participated in the protests subscribed to a worldview that did not separate "public" and "private" and in which their physical and symbolic roles as producers and reproducers were intertwined. Caroline Ifeka-Moller argues strongly that reproduction shaped the impulse to organize as well as the nature of the protests and the techniques the women used.[55] Moreover, Misty L. Bastian notes that women reinforced the connection between production and reproduction during their testimony before the commission of inquiry where their spokeswomen often linked the evils of falling produce prices and rising bride-wealth prices. Taken together, the lack of consumers of their products and the financial inability to contract marriages put human fertility at risk.[56]

Market women were also at the forefront of protests in Abeokuta during the interwar period. Although women were absent from the Egba

Council, they nonetheless claimed political space through their activism. During the interwar period, women indigo dyers, producers of adire, dominated the political stage. Since 1929, they had been challenging the alake's decision to ban the new technologies they introduced into the industry—caustic soda and synthetic dye.[57] Their confrontation reached a critical point in 1936 when police began arresting women who continued to use the banned substances, and dyers kept the alake under siege in the palace. The unrest that resulted from the dyers' protests forced the colonial government to convene a commission of inquiry into the industry that ultimately removed the bans. In this instance, this group of women reacted to government policies that undermined their economic position. The dyers' protests were not anticolonial, but they challenged key aspects of the colonial economy and indirect rule.

Indigo dyers also challenged policies of the European trading companies, such as shortening the length of credit extended to cloth buyers and efforts to take over the trade in indigo-dyed cloth between Abeokuta and Ghana. These policies effectively protected the companies but at great expense to dyers. The dyers also challenged the efforts by the alake to control the industry. Although he argued that his decision to ban caustic soda and synthetic dyes were in the best interest of the industry, he failed to take into consideration the economic realities the dyers experienced. Dyers retained lawyers to help them challenge the alake's rulings. Ultimately, the lawyers successfully took the issue out of the hands of the alake and deposited it in the lap of the chief secretary of government, despite the government's insistence that this was a local issue. Dyers did not question the existence of the colonial state, but they interfered with the preferred functioning of indirect rule by directing their complaints above the alake. The creation of the commission inquiry into the industry and its overturn of the bans on caustic soda and synthetic dye exposed the ambiguous and limited authority of the sole native authority system that made local rulers the first rung of the colonial administration. The dyers' actions also demonstrated that British power and its political apparatus could be circumvented.[58]

The interwar period generated a diverse set of responses to the economic and political conditions on the ground. Even though organizations that suggested a national character had emerged, most were focused on local issues. Italy's conquest of Ethiopia in 1936 helped transform the political landscape because it contributed to a deepening sense of national consciousness at the same time that it put Nigeria into a global discussion about race and imperialism.

STRETCHING THEIR HANDS FORTH
TOWARD ETHIOPIA

One of the most important examples of political mobilization in Nigeria, and in Abeokuta, emerged in the wake of Italy's invasion of Ethiopia in 1935. While Britain, France, the United States, and the League of Nations stood on the sidelines and effectively sanctioned Italy's occupation of Ethiopia, Abeokuta became part of a global resistance movement.[59] This movement mapped a political consciousness and practice that was shaped by imperial boundaries but not defined by it, for it brought together Black peoples from multiple empires. Across Africa and the African diaspora, men and women organized petitions in defense of Ethiopia's sovereignty and raised funds for the Ethiopian Red Cross as well as guns and munitions, and some joined the resistance in Ethiopia.[60] However, much of the scholarship that examines the African and African American responses to the Italo-Abyssinian War has focused on leading male political figures. Few have paid attention to how women in Africa and the diaspora were specifically mobilized in the struggle against Italy, fascism, and imperialism.

In 1936, Princess Tsaha, the youngest daughter of Ethiopia's emperor, Haile Selassie, sent an appeal to women around the world. In response to Tsaha's appeal, women in western Nigeria collected money on behalf of Ethiopia and wrote petitions to the governor of Nigeria. They may have been motivated by the brutality and flagrant racism of the Italian forces as well as the peripatetic life imposed on Haile Selassie and his family. Anthony Mockler reports that Tsaha, her youngest brother, Prince Sahle Selassie, and their mother, Empress Menen, joined her father in England on September 20, 1936. However, due to illness, Empress Menen moved to Jerusalem, and the children divided their time between England and Palestine.[61] Or Nigerian women may have been moved by Tsaha's age, for she was only seventeen at the time. Regardless of the inspiration, Nigerian women's response to Tsaha's appeal provides a small glimpse into their internationalism during this period of heightened pan-African activism.

In the introduction to the appeal, the princess credits her mother and the first attack on Ethiopia as her inspiration:

> I was inspired to write this soon after the first attack on the Abysssinians with poisonous gas by their Civilized Foe—The Italian. So shocked, horrified, and grieved was I, that as I sat at the Radio listening to the Broadcast of the Empress of Abyssinia to the Mothers of the World—I became lost in thought, and I

imagined that I saw Her—sad, but calm poised. Then with out-stretched hands, she said:

The Emperor Sleeps Not Day or Night![62]

The introduction suggests that the princess felt inspired by her mother's broadcast to contribute to the war effort in some way. The statement appears to be in large measure a reproduction of the empress's broadcast, "Appeal to the Mothers of the World."[63] However, its title offers a slightly different but significant variation. Whereas the empress appealed to the mothers of the world, the princess appealed to all women of the world. It was circulated prior to her father's speech before the League of Nations, for it reached Nigeria in early June. Nonetheless, it reflects similar rhetorical inflections as well as the broader diplomatic efforts of the government in exile.

Comparing Italian and Ethiopian war tactics, the appeal questioned the humanity of the Italian aggressors. It noted, "We Abyssinians are warriors, not cowards. We do not slaughter innocent and defenceless women and children and use others as cannon fodder! Unprepared for war . . . defenceless . . . but unafraid we face the Aggressor . . . the green eyed-monster, whose arms are long, and whose tail possesses a sting." Their monstrous behavior was further exemplified by the use of bombs and poisonous gas to ravage Ethiopian women and children. Through these acts, the Italians "violated one of our sacred codes. . . . In war women must be protected." The author assumed a universal commitment to this code and ironically noted, "Savages we are called." The appeal made clear that Italy's actions had brought all of Western culture into question: "If this wanton attack upon us be civilization . . . then let us die resisting it." Therefore, Ethiopia's resistance was not only against Italian aggression—it was also against the hypocrisy and immorality hidden behind the veneer of Western civilization.

The appeal also argued that Ethiopia's resistance to Italian aggression was being fought for the entire Black world. The document is rife with references to racial kinship, in particular male kinship. It suggests that this war was a test for all Black people—"All eyes are upon us as a race"—and even God was watching them to see what they will do. It exhorts Black people to believe in themselves, for "WE MUST NOT LET OURSELVES DOWN." More specifically, the document is a call to Black men, for it declares, "BROTHERS! Men of my race, you have bled and died for others. For your King and Country you say? What greater love than this that a man should give his life for his brother?" It challenges Black men to privilege racial identity over that of national identity as it reminds them of what they gave up for king and country in the Great War:

> Why did you fight in the World War . . . What did you give . . . how much did you give . . . and how often? You gave of your all . . . your time . . . your money, and your lives. You gave your Fathers, your Sons, Brothers, Sweethearts . . . yea, even your Mothers, your Daughters, and Sisters. YOU bled physically, mentally, and financially. Some will say, I was compelled . . . I was conscripted. But most you have said and will say, we were patriotic. We had to fight for our King and Country . . . to face a common foe. Aye! But was she defenceless. Did the foe ravage her land. You loved her and were loyal. Brothers we suffer and die. . . . Does this not pull at your heart strings. We your brothers need less than they. Heed our cry!

The appeal does not condemn Black men for fighting for their countries voluntarily or under conscription. Instead, it suggests that the desire to fight for their "brothers" should be greater than that of their nations: after all, "we do not die for ourselves alone . . . but for you." Furthermore, the cost of fighting for Ethiopia is much less than the cost of fighting for their nations: "Does thou not remember, that you were sadly disillusioned, for many of our people were worst off, after the war, than ever before. WAR TO END WAR. Oh, God, what a price? We ask not for so much. . . . We ask not for your lives, may we ask you to live . . . to live . . . to earn . . . to give. Give to us of your utmost . . . even as you did when others called. SAVE YOUR LIVES AND OURS. . . . Give for he that giveth . . . receiveth . . . a thousand fold. The open hand must receive even as it is outstretched to give." Therefore, fighting for Ethiopia did not require their physical death.

Multiple moments throughout, the appeal reinforced the idea of racial kinship and solidarity, but there were contradictory moments when the document suggested solidarity did not have to be exclusively race-based. The latter was used to challenge claims that Ethiopians did not consider themselves Black: "Our enemies are spreading the propaganda, that we are not brothers . . . not of the same race. Let us assume, it is so. In previous wars were those whom you served the men of your race? Are we not worthy of your love, your interest, your sacrifice, even as they? Ethiopia has stretched forth her hands!!! The Prophecy is fulfilled!!" The author did not try to define the enemies spreading propaganda, though it was well known that Italians and some British journalists, including editorial writers for *West Africa*, argued that Ethiopians were white. This allowed them to suggest that race was not a factor in Mussolini's designs on Ethiopia and therefore Africans on the continent and in the diaspora had no cause to become involved in the conflict. Questions about Ethiopian racial identity inspired different responses. S. K. B. Asante argued that it inspired several West African newspapers to publish articles on Ethiopia's history and achievements. The issue could not be dismissed outright because Selassie affirmed in an interview with Chief H. O. Davies of the *Nigerian Daily Times* that Ethiopians did not think of themselves as Africans.[64] The issue of racial identity also informed the scathing critique Marcus Garvey wrote of the emperor for refusing to meet separately with the Black activists who waited for him at Waterloo Station on the day he arrived in London.[65] Rather than engage the question of Ethiopian racial identity, the appeal reminded them that the king and country for which they fought in World War I belonged to a different race.

While the document both valorized and problematized racial solidarity, it reflected a more consistent gender construction. It reinforced a masculinity based on the idealized male protector of the homestead, women, and children. Simultaneously, it idealized women as mothers who sacrificed by giving up their husbands and sons to the "Lords of War." Even though the husbands and sons of Italian women were ravaging Ethiopia, the appeal did not vilify Italian women. It suggested that Italian women had set an example of sacrifice that could be emulated. The idealization of a passive motherhood where women sacrificed husbands and sons was completely at odds with the reality of the scores of women who served in the resistance in both Ethiopia and Italy.[66]

Finally, the appeal drew heavily on biblical references. The many references to "heed our cry" recalled a lamentation, while verses from the Bible peppered the document. It invoked the shared practice of Christianity across Africa with many Blacks in the diaspora as it called on individuals to pray and to fast unceasingly "for ETHIOPIA HATH INDEED STRETCHED FORTH HER HANDS." This phrase held great significance among Blacks active in the abolition movements since the eighteenth century and the rise of Black independent churches around the world. It is from Psalm 68:31—"Ethiopia shall soon stretch forth her hands unto God"—and was widely viewed as "a holy vow of black redemption and was repeatedly invoked in calls on blacks to reclaim their usurped human rights."[67]

THE BLACK WORLD AND NIGERIAN WOMEN RESPOND

Even before war broke out in Ethiopia, observers around the globe noted that fascist threats had produced very strong reactions among Black populations globally. Riots between American Blacks and Italians had erupted, and simultaneous prayer services in Ethiopia and African American churches were planned, while in London the International African Friends of Abyssinia met. There was a tremendous amount of pro-Ethiopia activism as well in Paris, where figures such as Paulette Nardal, a key literary figure in the *négritude* movement, participated in support work.[68] In Jamaica, with its long history of Ethiopianism, including the Rastafari religion, over fourteen hundred men in the UNIA volunteered to fight in Ethiopia. The British Colonial Office stopped volunteers' plans across the empire.[69] Following the collapse of the Ethiopian army and his flight into exile, Haile Selassie appointed his cousin and personal physician, Malaku Bayen, to be his representative in the United States and his special envoy to Black Americans. Bayen eventually formed the Ethiopia World Federation (EWF), which became one of the most important Ethiopia support groups in the United States, especially with its weekly tabloid, the *Voice of Ethiopia*.[70] Both efforts attracted a number of women. Fikru Negash Gebrekidan suggests that the strong involvement in the EWF of Bayen's wife, Dorothy Bayen, encouraged heavy participation by women, especially contributors to her column, "Friends of Ethiopia."[71]

In London several organizations spoke out strongly against Italian aggression against Ethiopia. C. L. R. James and Amy Ashwood Garvey, from Trinidad and Jamaica, respectively, formed the International African Friends of Ethiopia, in her International Afro Restaurant. Marc Matero suggests that Ashwood Garvey was the center of gravity of mobilization around Ethiopia. Moreover, he credits her with motivating the WASU to join the campaign after speaking at a meeting in October 1935.[72] In time, WASU became "the focal point of West African protest" in Britain.[73] Matera credits the women members with first responding to Ashwood Garvey's call to action by creating the Ethiopia Defence Committee to raise funds among members. All the members of this fund-raising committee were women: A. M. Cole (chair), Irene Howe (vice chair), Omoba Remi Ademola (treasurer), and Gladys Franklyne (honorary secretary).[74] WASU's journal acknowledged that they were the "motive force of this and many of the group's other activities."[75]

European-led organizations also arose in support of Ethiopia. One of the most important was the Circle for the Liberation of Ethiopia, founded and led by the Sylvia Pankhurst. This organization also published a weekly newspaper, the *New Times and Ethiopia News* (*NT & EN*). Pankhurst's paper stood out because of its distinct attention to women. For example, it regularly featured references to the role of women in the pro-Ethiopian campaigns and highlighted the role of Ethiopian female patriots in the underground resistance.[76] While highlighting the agency of Ethiopian women, the paper also focused on Italian atrocities to Ethiopians in general and women in particular. Readers contributed numerous articles to the NT & EN; they included Ethiopian and Italian refugees, British citizens who had served in the Red Cross in Ethiopia, and the Ethiopian minister in London, Dr. Warqenah Eshete (alias Dr. Charles Martin), as well as American academics and anti-Nazi refugees from Central Europe. Metasehia Woldemariam argues that the NT & EN was widely quoted in newspapers elsewhere for news about Ethiopia and was distributed in the United States, the United Kingdom, English-speaking Africa, and the Caribbean. It was also translated into Amharic and circulated clandestinely in Ethiopia.[77]

Swift responses to the Italian invasion also came from across Africa. In Nigeria, the first Ethiopia relief fund formed in Lagos. Inaugurated as the Lagos Ethiopia Defence Committee (LEDC) on December 10, 1935, it established ten branches in major towns around Nigeria, including Ibadan, Ife, Abeokuta, Jos, and Kano. The LEDC's women's section, which adopted the name Save Abyssinia Society, was led by G. S. Wynter Shackleford, a Jamaican-born resident of Lagos and wife of Amos Shackleford. Mrs. Shackleford, accompanied by traditional dancers and drummers, solicited donations in workplaces, markets, trading houses, and government departments. Her group also organized social activities—concerts, dances, fetes, and carnivals—to raise funds. Asante estimates that by the end of 1936, the Save Abyssinia Society had collected over one hundred guineas.[78] Other relief funds independent of the LEDC also emerged. The Enugu Ethiopia Relief Fund Committee received support from ex-servicemen and several ethnic unions: the Ogidi Tribal Union, the Bende District union, and the Owerri Union Society. Dusé Mohamed Ali, the Egyptian born pan-Africanist as well as founder and publisher of the Comet magazine, led one of the most successful committees.[79]

Britain's recognition of Italy's conquest of Ethiopia drew its first response from the Prominent Women of Lagos Society led by G. S. Wynter Shackleford. From her base in Lagos, Shackleford reached out to Abeokuta.[80] On June 10, 1936, she sent a letter to several Christian ministers in Abeokuta, requesting that they read the letter to the class meetings of women and girls. The letter read:

> The Princess Tsaha of Abyssinia, a girl of only 17 years of age, has written an appeal to all women in the world to help in getting

the League of Nations to condemn and forbid the use of poison gas, laterite etc: by Aeroplanes or otherwise in war-fare.

We women of these parts should support her by sending through our Governor to the League of Nations our own agreement with her protest. We should also urge the League not to allow Italy to annex Abyssinia as the Italian war was an aggressive one and carried out by the violation of all rule of warfare.[81]

Shortly after sending this letter, Shackleford visited Abeokuta to speak with the alake, the town's religious leaders, and the heads of women's associations. Alake Ademola II hosted Shackleford while women leaders and religious authorities collaborated to organize a women's meeting on the Abyssinian question. The iyalode of the Christians, Mrs. Modupe Moore, chaired the meeting.[82] Speakers such as the Reverend Ransome-Kuti and Rev. S. A. Delumo spoke on topics such as "the part already played by men as a challenge to the women to play their own part" and "the women's position and duty in relation generally to the peace of the world, and particularly to the future of Abyssinia," respectively. Following the presentations the participants passed a resolution:

> That this meeting of representative women of Egbaland both in hearty response to the appeal of Princess Tsaha, and in the interest of the world peace, do most solemnly and emphatically appeal to the nations of the world and particularly to the League of Nations (1) to condemn and prohibit the manufacture and use of poison gas . . . in warfare, (2) to regard as a public enemy any nation which oppresses or suppresses the weak because it is strong, and prefers war to arbitration, and (3) on no account to permit the annexation of Ethiopia by Italy.[83]

In response to this program, 174 women donated amounts ranging from one penny to two and a half shillings, which totaled £3.2.1. They represented many religious denominations—CMS, Methodist, Baptist, African, Roman Catholic, Aladura, Seraphim, and Salvation Army.[84] Over time the women collected 503 signatures for the petition that would be forwarded to the League of Nations through the governor of Nigeria, Sir Bernard Bourdillon, and a total of £10. Princess Tsaha's appeal initiated the meetings called by Mrs. Shackleford; nonetheless, their resolution demonstrated that their concerns were broader. It demonstrated that they were looking beyond the immediacy of poison gas to the question of Ethiopian sovereignty after the war and world peace more broadly. In addition, it suggests that the women shared consensus on the idea that they could and should play a role in international issues and that they had a political investment in questions of sovereignty.

Anthony Eden, the British foreign secretary, rejected the petition relayed to him on Mrs. Shackleford's behalf by Governor Bourdillon. He argued that the government could not forward communications to the League of Nations on behalf of private individuals or organizations.[85] So, the women's actions did not impact the colonial government or the League of Nations. Nonetheless, this is an enlightening moment for what it reveals about gender and women's political activism. Shackleford belonged to a highly politicized segment of Lagos society; however, it was the specific appeal to motherhood that galvanized this mobilization of Nigerian women. She also worked through male authority figures—the king and clerics—to reach out to women. Shackleford enjoyed a degree of prominence and respect that gave her access to a wide cross section of male elites in colonial Nigeria. In a letter to the alake of Abeokuta, she mentioned that the colonial chief secretary promised her a donation. She also expressed a degree of playfulness with the alake: "We the 'Three Musketeers' (feminine gender—the new era) wish to pay our obeisance to His Highness the Alake Abeokuta and wish him a long life and prosperity. Pardon my fun—we were so bold, so what else are we?"[86] The letter did not identify the other women who constituted the Three Musketeers, but her reference to the new era suggests that these women belonged to the new generation of Christianized, elite women who were increasingly moving into more public roles and occupations.[87] The gentle teasing embedded in this letter highlights her awareness that she was simultaneously transgressive and respectful of the power structure. If the alake or colonial administers held any fear of colonized women mobilizing, it was neutralized by the terms of the appeal—motherhood. Motherhood did prove an effective way to mobilize women because women across Nigeria's diverse ethnic, religious, and socioeconomic landscape contributed funds to assist Ethiopia despite the economic distress they faced during the Depression.

Mobilization around Ethiopia had a deep impact on nationalist thought. In 1938, the subject of Ethiopia gained more attention when it appeared that the British government "was ready to sign an agreement including the grant of full recognition to Italian sovereignty in Ethiopia."[88] This development redoubled efforts to support Ethiopia. The *West African Pilot* carried a report of a meeting of the Friends of Abyssinia League at the Abeokuta Grammar School. Chaired by Reverend Ransome-Kuti, the members had a lively discussion "about recent happenings in Abyssinia." They proposed "to organize a 'wake up' campaign in Nigeria through the medium of the press, to draw the attention of Africans in Nigeria, who might happen to be still indifferent to their duty in the matter."[89]

In addition to following events in Abyssinia, the people of Abeokuta followed diplomatic discussions in Europe. The *West African Pilot* reported that on November 21, 1938, "an immense crowd of people, the kind of which is unusual in this town besieged the Centenary Hall, Ake . . . to register their protest . . . against the possible transfer of the whole or any part of Nigeria to the rule of Nazi Germany."[90] In response to the rumors, the alake constituted the Nigeria Anti-Transfer Committee, composed of a lawyer, O. Moore, Rev. I. O. Ransome-Kuti, and council member J. B. Majekodunmi, among others.[91] Clearly before fighting began in Europe, Nigerians and, more specifically, residents of Abeokuta were paying attention to the buildup of the global conflict. By and large it appears that the leadership of this effort came from the town's Christian and educated elites, but it garnered support from a wide cross-section of men and especially women.

The atrocities against Ethiopia invited a substantial questioning of colonialism. The mobilization around the continent engendered significant discussions about fascism and an increasing distrust of the intentions of Europeans as well as fuel to nationalist sentiments. In the Gold Coast, the British Ex-Service Men's Union and its affiliates passed a resolution stating that if Britain recognized Italy's sovereignty over Ethiopia, "they would never again take up arms to defend European nations in the event of any future war which may arise out of their diplomatic bargains contrary to the spirit and letter of the Covenant of the League of Nations."[92] Just as this conflict was also an important turning point for African veterans of the British army in the Gold Coast, S. K. B. Asante suggests that it intensified the nationalism of aspiring nationalist leaders such as Kwame Nkrumah and Obafemi Awolowo.

⌒

The interwar period is critical to our understanding of the shifting political templates that undergird the postwar nationalist movement. In Abeokuta, men and women followed local, regional, and international events. Inspired by Princess Tsaha's appeal, women mobilized and shared scant resources in an attempt to impede Italy's imperial efforts in Ethiopia. Their response did not prevent Ethiopia's defeat or Europe's recognition of Italy's African empire, but their critical stance put them in the midst of a worldwide conversation about imperialism, race, and sovereignty. They remained so engaged with developments in Ethiopia that when Haile

Selassie was restored to the throne, Ademola sent him a congratulatory message on behalf of the people of Egbaland.[93] Tsaha's brief appearance on the international stage generated an important political moment whose relevance continued beyond the war. Unfortunately, her life was cut short. After Ethiopia was liberated, Tsaha returned to England to train as a nurse. She later married Abiye Abebe and, sadly, died in childbirth in 1942, only twenty-three years old. After her death, her friend Sylvia Pankhurst raised funds in London to establish a hospital in Addis Ababa in her memory.[94]

The multilevel political activism in Abeokuta did not erase the interwar depression. The challenges of the economic crisis engendered a variety of responses to the colonial political economy. The analysis in this chapter demonstrates that factors such as social position, gender and cultural prescriptions, regional location, and local leadership structures shaped how groups rose to offset the economic, social, or political crises they faced. In eastern Nigeria and Abeokuta, long-established market women's associations confronted the local representatives of the colonial state. The Women's War in eastern Nigeria necessitated a radical restructuring of the colonial apparatus and brought an end to the warrant chief system. In Abeokuta, dyers did not challenge the alake's right to rule, but they questioned the autocratic way he exercised power and forced the overturn of some of his policies. In some ways they foreshadowed the women's tax revolt a decade later.

The interwar period was also an era of experimentation, and new types of organizations arose. In Lagos, the multiclass, multireligious alliance of men and women that supported the eleko became the core from which the NNDP emerged. The NNDP was produced in part by the change in colonial policy that extended a limited political franchise to African men of means in Lagos. By the close of the 1930s, Yoruba political discourse incorporated a lexicon of national identity that was increasingly coterminous with Nigeria. Though the idea of a Nigerian nation remained ephemeral, bodies such as NUT began to ground the concept as it developed branches across western, eastern, and northern Nigeria.

Abeokuta experienced all of these tendencies. The dyers' protest, for example, was not a comprehensive movement by all market women; it remained exclusive to their trade. While NUT sought to professionalize and protect the interest of teachers, it contributed to a developing national and international discourse about trade unionism, development, and the role of education. The town's connection to WASU further ensured that it participated in the global movement against Italy's imperial aggression against Ethiopia. The new political discourse emerging by the end of the

1930s challenged the core values emphasized during Abeokuta's centenary celebrations. The centenary emphasized a political identity forged around the precolonial polity, the centrality of the alake to the exercise of power and male monopolization of political space. As the British Empire plunged into war in 1939, those values became increasingly unstable.

4 ⤳ Women, Rice, and War

Economic Crisis in Wartime Abeokuta

BRITISH OFFICIALS anticipated that Africa would be tangentially affected by the war, and many general histories of World War II continue to perpetuate this idea. Timothy Parsons argues that Africa's marginalization is conditioned by the focus on the European and Asian theaters as well as "the imperial powers' explicit efforts to downplay and obscure the extent to which they relied on their African subjects to fight and the win the war."[1] Britain's African colonies supplied funds, soldiers, and food as well as resources necessary to create armaments, clothes, and vehicles, including cotton, diamonds, rubber, and uranium.[2] Africanist historians have long noted the resources utilized for the war effort and the war's impact on local communities, but they often treat the war as a monolithic event that was primarily a precursor to decolonization. This chapter, in conversation with scholarship reexamining World War II, calls attention to key developments during the war and their impact on Abeokuta.

World War II had distinctive phases that generated specific outcomes for different parts of the continent. The fall of France in 1940 suspended fighting for French West African soldiers in Europe and created an enemy across the many borders shared by British and French colonies. Japan's conquest of Britain's Far Eastern colonies after 1942 led to the expanded recruitment of African soldiers in the British colonies and increased production of rubber and copra across the continent. In many colonies, forced labor and forced production increased significantly. Officials created a command economy in which they set production quotas, rationed imports, imposed wage freezes and price controls, and increased tax revenue.

In Lagos, market women provided stiff resistance to price controls. Lagos was also the epicenter of strikes as workers demanded wages that kept up with inflation. The *West African Pilot* became the leading champion for their grievances and demands. Agitation by workers, market women, and the press in the colony's economic and political nerve center invariable focused attention on Lagos. This chapter shifts our attention inland and illuminates the distinctive ways in which World War II shaped economic and political developments in Abeokuta. It highlights how the state reached deeper into the social and economic fabric of Abeokuta to meet demands for food, manpower, and revenue. It also illuminates the impact of these policies on taxpayers, farmers, and traders. As inhabitants of an agricultural area, Abeokuta's farmers endured forced cultivation requirements. The alake and the Native Authority police enforced these heavily resented policies, thus the war exacerbated the political tensions between the alake and different segments of Abeokuta's rural and urban populations. This chapter argues that as the colonial state extracted foodstuffs and taxes and tried to control prices, the combined actions created particular tensions and economic distress for women in Abeokuta. Ultimately, it illuminates the ways in which the war shaped and contributed to the political and economic conditions that propelled the women's tax revolt in the immediate postwar era.

IMPERIAL STRATEGIES, LOCAL ACTIONS

Planning for the war began before hostilities actually broke out. By July 1939, Britain already had in place secret plans to restrict imports and exports. The goal was to conserve foreign exchange, secure access to certain commodities required by Britain and the other Allies, and to restrict enemy access to those goods.[3] To coordinate these plans, the government established a central purchasing organization in London, the Ministry of Food and Supply,[4] while the Nigerian colonial government established the Nigerian Supply Board to control trade and coordinate production.[5] In addition, the Nigerian Defense Regulations of 1939 conferred tremendous power to the supply board and officials such as the food controller to regulate the distribution of imports as well as local foodstuffs.[6]

When Germany invaded Poland on September 1, 1939, officials remained confident that the war would not have a great impact on Africa. On September 15, the secretary of state communicated to colonial governors that he wanted social services and development activities to continue with little disruption and to avoid personnel retrenchment. Nine months later, his successor sent a circular in a much more grim tone, noting that the German blitzkrieg had transformed their thinking. They now concluded that the war would require a supreme effort from all people in the empire in the "next few months." That effort included maintaining production of materials needed for the war effort, substantially reducing demand for nonessential imports from sterling and nonsterling sources, maximum development of foodstuffs to meet local demand, curtailment of existing social and other services, postponement of plans in the Colonial Development Bill, and the imposition or increase of direct taxation.[7]

The blitzkrieg that led to the surrender of Norway, Belgium, and France transformed Nigeria's engagement in this growing conflict, for Britain was essentially fighting alone.[8] The administrative machinery put in place now had to deliver manpower and resources to meet the needs of this empire-wide effort. The Nigerian Supply Board directed food production in Nigeria and played an instrumental role in ensuring that food also reached other parts of West Africa. Representatives of the supply board participated in meetings with representatives from the other West African colonies during which they debated the quantities of foodstuffs that would be exported from one colony to another to meet civilian and military requirements.

Rice was high on the agenda because it was in great demand: troops in the Gold Coast and the Gambia alone required three thousand tons. The Gold Coast representative noted that they needed rice to feed workers in the mines and on ships. While they had taken steps to increase local production, they could not become self-sufficient in rice. Similarly, the Gambia could not meet the demand for rice for civilians and the military. Sierra Leone produced a significant amount of rice, but since rice was the main staple of its population's diet and the colony also had to satisfy military requirements, it restricted rice exports. Therefore, it fell largely to Nigeria to supply rice to the Gold Coast and the Gambia.[9] In addition to rice, Nigeria supplied salt, groundnut oil, egusi oil, ghee, gari, potatoes, and onions.[10]

Colonial officials also undertook military recruitment. They enlisted technicians into the Royal West African Frontier Force, though potential recruits were disappointed that the colonial government did not want them for the combat forces. The 1941 annual report noted that recruitment was steady, and they had successfully enlisted 883 men from across Abeokuta Province for the signal corps, transport duties, and mechanic and other noncombat roles. The report also noted that it was impossible to fill the quota allotted to the province by the military authorities. Recruitment posed a challenge because the province was in the midst of a labor shortage, as many men had migrated to work on the extensive military construction projects in Lagos. Furthermore, it was particularly difficult to recruit educated men.[11]

Colonial officials tried to encourage recruitment by creating a recruitment campaign, a group of seventeen specially selected soldiers/tradesmen who toured the provinces for six weeks, demonstrating their trades and giving physical training as well as exhibits of drills and unarmed combat. The recruitment campaign did have a slight effect on the enlistments in Abeokuta itself and some of the rural villages; however, its impact was not sustained, as borne out in the recruitment figures.[12] The total number of recruits declined in 1943 to 305, but the pressure to recruit eased after 1943 because the army discontinued recruitment in certain categories.[13] The total number of recruits fell from 176 in 1944 to 61 in 1945.[14] So, Abeokuta did not contribute much in the way of manpower to the prosecution of the war. Its greatest contribution was in the production of agricultural products needed for the war effort and foodstuffs needed for the civilian and military populations in Lagos and Abeokuta.

Economically, World War II was a period of both continuity and change. Nigerians had experienced a prolonged economic crisis due to the worldwide depression in commodity prices and the collapse of credit markets. The crisis deepened during the war; Robert Pearce argues that the terms of trade were worse during the war than in the worst years of the depression.[15] This was most obvious when you examine the fate of cocoa prices. The government purchased the entire cocoa crop in 1939 and set the price below 1938 levels. Before the outbreak of the war, cocoa sold for £22.50 per ton, but the Ministry of Food set the price at £16.50 per ton, and by September 1940 it fell further to £11.00 per ton.[16] The government justified the low prices because the German market was closed and the US market had contracted. The low price of cocoa contradicted official claims that the first few months of the war, characterized as the "phony war," did not have a significant impact on the colonies.[17] The impact of the war was uneven; therefore, generalizations about its effects were misleading. David Anderson and David Throup argue that in Kenya the phony war situation was only transformed in 1941 following the Japanese advances and US entry into the war. In those first two years of the war, settler agriculture remained at the same level as in the late 1930s.[18] While the time lag of the phony war may apply in Kenya, Nigerian producers of cocoa felt the consequences of the war immediately.

France's collapse was a major turning point, for it "imposed new burdens and some drastic changes in the economic life" of Abeokuta.[19] The

Gambia, the Gold Coast, and Nigeria shared borders with French colonies, and once France surrendered, Britain closed the borders between French and British colonies.[20] Residents of the western section of Abeokuta Province felt the changes most acutely for they bordered Dahomey. In addition to closing the border between Nigeria and Dahomey, troops from the Gold Coast, Britain, and Belgium were stationed in Ilaro Division (western Abeokuta Province).[21] The most significant turning point came after the fall of the Far Eastern colonies in 1942. Characterized as "a profound shock," this event radically altered colonial policy in West Africa.[22] It was then that the "Resident Minister took over the supreme direction of West Africa's war effort," creating, "for the first time in its history, a regional machinery, for the administration, control and direction of economic affairs directly associated with His Majesty's Government in Great Britain."[23] Britain's experience over the progression of the war required corresponding shifts and different phases in the restructuring of West African economies.

EXPERIENCING THE WAR

Ronke Doherty (née Williams), a descendant of merchant traders on her maternal and patrilineal lines, attended the Church Missionary Society grammar school and Queens College in Lagos before going to England for further training. She attended University of London and Southland College from 1935 to 1939, returning to Nigeria the first week of the war. Doherty recalled that many Nigerians were leaving London to escape the war. She was fortunate that she left when she did for she knew of others whose ships were torpedoed as they made the return journey.[24]

While others were returning to Nigeria, some Nigerians were departing for United Kingdom. Dolu Ransome-Kuti traveled to England in 1943 to attend school. Her ship was part of a convoy accompanied by a warship. She recalled sending her parents a message in code, such as "the books arrived safely," to let them know that she had arrived safely.[25] The year 1943 proved to be a significant year for Egba historian Saburi Biobaku as well, for he received one of two scholarships set aside for Nigerian students to study in England that year. Due to the war and the limited space for passenger travel, it was February 1944 before he was given space on a Dutch troop carrier, the SS Stuyvesant. Biobaku noted, "The S.S. Stuyvesant, was the Commodore ship in a splendid convoy of some seventy-six barges which were destined to take part in the proposed allied landing in North Africa. . . . We heard detonation of bombs far away behind us and we joyfully received the subsequent news that an enemy ship or submarine had been accordingly eliminated."[26]

Prince Adegbola Ademola was only two years old when war started in Europe. He recalled being in Lagos and covering the light bulbs with paper to lessen the illumination. He also remembered alarms sounding around Marina. He learned later that salt was rationed, but he recalled, "I was too young to feel any real economic impact. And I guess also as a result of belonging to the privileged family."[27] Ronke Doherty remembered the rationing in Lagos very well: "There was an awful lot of blackmarketing going on. . . . You could get everything—meat, beef, duck, fish . . . but . . . at a price."[28]

For many people in Abeokuta, scarcity of food items dominated their recollection of the main years of fighting (1939–45). For the late justice Adewale Thompson, the shortage of butter stood out most, but for many other people the scarcity of salt was especially difficult.[29] Chief Emanuel Sorunke recalled that "during that war, there was scarcity of salt and I had to travel because salt was being supplied through John Holt and UAC which are located at Ibara and my parents are in the district."[30] Christopher Agboola Ajao, a boarding student at the Abeokuta Baptist Boy's School, also remembered the scarcity of salt and collecting palm kernels in order to extract the oil.[31] One needed a ration card to obtain items such as tinned milk, flour, and butter, and rationing remained in force as late as 1948.[32] In addition to food, the government rationed gasoline, which imposed a severe burden on transportation.[33]

The war seeped into social life and practices. Wole Soyinka noted that "the greeting Win-The-War replaced some of the boisterous exchanges which took place between Essay [Soyinka's father] and his friends." Barbers invented new styles that referenced the war, and women created a "Win-de-woh" for their repertoire of braided styles. Food sellers used the war as a standard response to complaints about the quantity of food they served. People reused envelopes as often as possible. Windows had to be blacked over, with household heads risking court fines if they exposed a naked light at night.[34] Soyinka suggests that in order to reinforce the charged atmosphere under which the town lived, an airplane flew over Abeokuta for the first time. Soldiers from other parts of Africa, including the Belgian Congo, were stationed at Lafenwa Barracks and drew attention when they visited the shops in Abeokuta. While some storeowners were afraid to do business with Congolese soldiers, Soyinka's mother did not fear them at all and did a brisk business with them.[35] The war also brought soldiers from America to Nigeria. Justice Thompson recalled seeing Black Americans for the first time, many who seemed to be very big—over six and a half feet tall. It appeared that the Americans did not enforce segregation, for he noted that Black and white American soldiers and Nigerians all attended the same cinema.[36]

Several people knew men who joined the army. Pa Michael Adeyinka lived in town, in Totoro Township, where he heard updates on the war from the radio. Three of his brothers went to war. He recalled that while some men volunteered at the beginning, others were forced to join the army. As a result, some men ran away. His mother prevented him from going because he was her only son still in Abeokuta.[37] Recruiters also applied force in the rural areas. Isaiah Adebayo was very young but recalled that it was a scary time for young men. He reported that they could not move freely for they were sometimes pressed into serving in the army.[38] There were those, however, who enlisted, such as Soyinka's maternal uncle.[39]

Those in the army served in the Eighty-First (West Africa) Division, created March 1, 1943. Along with soldiers from the Gold Coast, the Gambia, and Sierra Leone, they were trained at sites in southwestern Nigeria in preparation for battle in Burma. British officers established the division headquarters in Ibadan and training camps in Ibadan, Abeokuta, Ilaro, and Ede, in theory to develop their capacity for jungle warfare. No manual for jungle warfare existed, but the commander of the Eighty-First, General Woolner, thought it essential that troops learn to live as well as fight under jungle conditions. Unfortunately, the areas selected for camps were not suitable. According to Woolner, "in the South it was mostly dense forest and cocoa farms but around Abeokuta it was much too open, being largely cassava farms and thin scrub and grassland. In the north around Ede, it was even more open with only isolated patches of forest. . . . Bns of 5 Ede transferred themselves entirely to tented camps hidden in the jungle round Ilaro."[40] The weather further complicated the men's training. A. F. Giles reported that their training coincided with the start of heavy rains in April, thus they "lived and trained in intervals of torrential rains and steamy sunshine." Nonetheless, these conditions ultimately proved to be perfect preparation for what followed in Burma.[41]

While these plans unfolded, rumors circulated about Britain's impending defeat. The alake and colonial officials worked diligently to limit the spread of rumors and took advantage of new technologies in this effort. The 1940 annual report noted "the Alake set a splendid example not only by the outspokenness of his public declarations but by his prompt action in preventing the spreading of false defeatist rumours."[42] The Egba Native Administration issued weekly news bulletins that it distributed to all districts and especially to schools. When touring, the administrative officers informed people of the latest developments in the war, and the information officers provided illustrated pamphlets that were very popular. Without elaborating, a reporter noted that the propaganda films were disappointing. Nonetheless, radio was a success. On June 1, 1943, a local radio diffusion service opened in Abeokuta and was highly popular, but its reach was limited by the fact that the town had only 150 sets.[43] Over the course of the war, the number of sets increased dramatically. By 1946, there were 589 sets and a waiting list of 100 subscribers.[44] Radio, which offered programs in both Yoruba and English, became an important tool for disseminating information about the war and assisting recruitment. The station played BBC programs for ten hours daily, produced local programs for broadcast between 6:00 p.m. and 7:00 p.m. weekdays, and provided a Yoruba version of the news each day.[45]

Newspapers also carried information about the war and tried to boost support for the Allied forces. The *Yoruba News* included a box with the statement "V—Allies Victory over Axis Forces is Inevitable" in many issues. An editorial on August 11, 1942, argued that Germany, Japan, and Italy were fighting to enslave the people in the rest of the world. It implored people in rousing language to give the government money to make guns and airplanes and to produce the commodities needed by the Allied armies—palm oil, palm kernels, and rubber:

> Go into the bush with your wives and your children, and remember that every bunch of palm nuts that you cut down is like cutting down a German soldier; every tin of oil and kernels that you make will help to spoil a German or a German aeroplane. . . . Every cup of rubber that you fail to collect is a help to Hilter; every sheet of rubber that you make will help to destroy him and his soldiers.[46]

The *Yoruba News* also suggested indirect ways Nigerians could help ensure that soldiers had sufficient clothing:

> Take care of your clothes so that they will last longer
>
> Sleeves should be as short as possible
>
> Do not wear a coat if you can, do without it
>
> Wear shorts rather than trousers
>
> Keep some old clothes to wear when doing work that will soil your clothing
>
> If your work is of a technical nature, wear overalls or an apron.[47]

To be ready in case fighting did come to Nigeria, different groups organized defense measures. In June 1940, colonial officials organized a Local Defense Volunteer Force, while the Abeokuta Union of Teachers, led by Reverend Ransome-Kuti, developed plans for an air-raid precaution program. Individuals demonstrated their support of the war effort in multiple ways. Oladipo Somoye launched the Roosevelt-Churchill Club, which hoped to foster equality, fraternity, and mutual understanding.[48] Several fund-raising schemes emerged as well. A Captain Mason of the United Africa Company took the lead in organizing the Win-the-War Fund, and within six months it had collected £2,756. The alake alone contributed £500, and much of the remainder came from the rural districts, including Ilaro Division, which donated £456. The residents of Abeokuta Province also contributed £392 to the Nigeria War Relief Fund and £74 to the Comforts for Nigerian Troops Fund.[49] These monetary contributions continued throughout the war. For example, the alake tried to raise funds from residents in town as well as Egbas abroad to purchase a Spitfire plane to be named *Abeokuta*.[50] In 1942, he remitted a portion of the Spitfire fund, £500, to Clementine Churchill, the prime minister's wife, for her Red Cross Aid to Russia Fund. In his letter to Mrs. Churchill, Ademola characterized the contribution as "a token of our admiration of this splendid sustained effort of the people of the U.S.S.R."[51] It does not appear that they were ultimately able to secure the funds to finance the Spitfire *Abeokuta*, so they contributed to the purchase of the Spitfire *Nigeria*, which cost £105,000.[52] In addition to these individual and local fund-raising efforts, the Nigerian government also gave money to Britain. The *Yoruba News* reported that the governor, on behalf of the Nigerian government, offered the British Government a free gift of £100,000 to assist in the prosecution of the war.[53]

The 1943 annual report noted that since the beginning of the war in 1939, the Egba Division alone contributed £8,307.[54] The following year, citizens of Egba Division demonstrated even greater support. Organizers sent out a special appeal for contributions to the Nigeria War Relief Fund and hoped to raise £700. By the conclusion of the appeal, they had almost doubled their total, raising £1,381—£1,000 of which came in during the first month. In addition, they collected £71 on June 6 from the sale of flags for the Red Cross and £38 on "Poppy Day."[55] The archival records do not disaggregate the information by gender, but it is safe to assume that women contributed to these fund-raising campaigns just as they contributed to the fund-raising campaigns for Ethiopia. These monetary contributions to the war effort occurred in spite of the economic conditions that followed from the Depression into the war era.

The war also led to the reallocation of funds and manpower in some instances. These decisions had noticeable consequences on the town. In 1941, Ademola and the newly constituted Egba Central Council entertained a discussion to cut the police force by 50 percent. Commentators in the *Egbaland Echo* roundly dismissed the suggestion, charging that burglaries had spiked during the war. Burglars took advantage of the blackout, though they did not limit their activities to nighttime raids only: robbers boldly burgled the mission house of the Gbagura Anglican Church while the catechist conducted the morning service in the church. Commentators called on the alake and resident to take necessary steps to protect "the peaceful taxpayers both in person and in properties."[56] The war enveloped people's daily experiences, shaping what they could purchase, the cost of their consumption, and even their daily security. The war also shaped their experience as taxpayers, for it required the state to employ a variety of measures to ensure the collection of revenue to support the war effort as well as general administration.

WAR AND TAXES

At the start of the war, Britain was forced to purchase equipment from the American government. Since the Lend-Lease program that allowed Britain and other Allied nations to avoid becoming indebted to each other did not take effect until 1941, the first two years of the war proved to be a tremendous financial drain on the Treasury, for it owed the American government approximately $6 billion for armaments.[57] The British government claimed that the war would be tangential to its African colonies; however, these claims did not take into consideration the degree to which Africans would be forced to share the fiscal burden. When the governor of Nigeria called on all Nigerians to support the war effort, he identified paying taxes on time as one of the three main ways in which Nigerians could show their support.[58] Although the Colonial Office did not create an administrative structure comparable to that controlling and monitoring food prices and distribution, colonial officials at all levels understood the centrality of revenue collection to the war effort.

Minutes of Egba Council meetings as well as annual reports hold numerous discussions about tax collection. Critically, they reveal that Africans' fiscal obligations increased during the war because the alake and council members agreed, reportedly with great enthusiasm, to loan funds to the central government. The plan called for transferring a portion of the surplus of the ENA—up to £3,000—in three installments to the central government, with the understanding that the funds would be replenished after the war.[59] This was not unique to Nigeria, similar plans were put in place in other colonies.[60] These discussions also revealed that there was a great continuity of practices around tax collection in the period before the war and during the war. For example, after the collapse of the American and European markets in 1929, the administration experimented with numerous measures to keep tax collection consistent despite the downturn in trade.[61] In 1932, for example, the ENA for the first time used olopa (native police) to track down tax defaulters. They went house to house to detect tax evaders, but, as collection improved, the alake halted the house-to-house searches and only had them search the markets and streets. The alake justified these levels of intrusion by arguing that they avoided enforcement through the courts and payment of court fines.[62] Just as the Depression did not lead to any mitigation of taxes, World War II did not lead to any tax relief.

A report on tax collection in Egba Division for 1938–39 by I. W. E. Dods captured a snapshot of the economic climate as Britain moved toward war. Dods arrived in Abeokuta on August 25, 1938, and the resident, Capt. E. A. Miller informed him that he and an assistant, Cadet W. M. Milliken, would be responsible for tax collection in the entire Egba Division. They were expected to collect a gross total of £36,571, which reflected an increase of £1,297 over the previous year's total. Of the 1938–39 total, 70 percent (£25,600) would be kept by the ENA and the remainder sent to the central government.[63] Dods noted that collection was exceptionally slow and blamed compound heads for not aggressively collecting taxes from the members of their compounds even though they received 5 percent of the tax they collected. He lamented that "during the first week of September tax came in at a rate of only £5 a day and all payments that were received were made by individuals."[64] To motivate the compound heads, he received permission to make a small change in the structure—specifically, compound heads would not receive credit for taxes paid directly by individuals from their compounds. Yet tax collection did not improve, and receipts fell to £3 per day.

Dods acknowledged that "prices for produce have been low for two years and money is seriously scarce." Nonetheless, he opined that the failure to prosecute tax delinquents played a central role in the poor state of tax collection. On December 1, 1938, he began prosecuting tax defaulters. The prosecutions led to a significant increase in collection; by December 25 they collected £254, averaging £42 a day.[65] Dods's enthusiasm dissipated after Christmas because collection slowed once again; however, court revenue benefited "£56 from fees and fines."[66] By the end of the tax season he was virtually despondent, for collection ended with a shortfall of £3,672: "So discouraging has been the result of my labours that I am almost inclined to recommend that we should admit frankly that the Egbas are not sufficiently advanced to be treated in the present civilized manner and must therefore have their tax dragged out of them in the manner which the Alake suggests."[67] The old system the alake encouraged was the one in practice during 1932 when native police accosted people in their houses or in the markets and demanded to see their tax receipts. Officials had declared the system unlawful, and Dods did not want to resurrect it. He considered the former practice a "retrograde step" and instead advised that they continue the new "civilized" system and the prosecutions. While Dods characterized the current system of tax collection as civilized, he failed to note that it was equally coercive. The only difference lay in who carried out the coercion—the courts or the police.

Tax collection in 1939–40 remained equally dismal. In the annual report, the resident noted that tax collection had almost come to a standstill during the period June–September because the districts had not started paying the 1939–40 taxes and payment in the town had ceased.[68] To help the collection process, the alake announced in a council meeting on August 31 that bench warrants rather than regular summonses would be issued for heads of compounds who did not collect all the taxes from taxpayers in their compounds.[69] However, the resident noted that "the real jump forward was made when severe prosecution of defaulters was introduced towards the end of September."[70] Severe prosecutions proved successful, for in a council meeting on October 26, the alake informed the members that tax collection "was getting on very well in town and in the districts."[71]

Despite these assurances, the 1941 tax season began with arrears of £200 in the town and £2,400 in the districts. To collect both the current and back taxes, the local government introduced a new tax-collection plan that affected the composition of the central council. The government created village group councils, which were given representation on the central council. All township members of the council were appointed tax collectors, village heads had to compile tax rolls, and both township and village councillors had to personally collect taxes. People paid their taxes based on the township in which they lived and received a ticket as proof of payment.[72] Collectors received a percentage of the gross amount of taxes collected—7.5 percent in the districts and up to 12.5 percent for those in town. The resident noted that tax collection was more efficient in 1941–42, in large measure due to the updated nominal rolls.

The 1943 collection proceeded smoothly and brought extra revenue into the Treasury through special assessments on residents who paid the income tax rather than the poll tax. At the end of the fiscal year, the Native

Authority had a surplus on hand and used the funds to pay off the loans the council had taken to finance the electrical system and waterworks.[73] The following year, tax collection went smoothly again. The government kept the flat tax rate constant but increased the income tax rate.[74] Although it did not raise the flat tax rate, the improvements in the nominal rolls helped tax collectors keep better track of taxpayers as they moved between their farms and township homes.

The discussions on tax collection in the annual reports provide little indication of how it actually impacted people's lives. From the state's vantage point, the primary concern was whether or not tax collection occurred smoothly and on time. However, an examination of a few tax cases provides insight on why collection may have gone relatively smoothly. Records of the criminal courts provide brief summaries of the majority of tax cases, specifically noting the charge, plea, and sentence. This cursory information nonetheless reveals important data. For example, it showed that the fines imposed by the court had little bearing on the economic capacity of those accused; furthermore, the sentences varied substantially. The flat rate applied to individuals at the lower end of the economic spectrum because they did not meet the minimum taxable annual income of £40. Nonetheless, four individuals—Adebayo, Safuratu, Madam Jola, and Ibitomi—who pleaded guilty to nonpayment of taxes for 1939–40, received a sentence of a fine of 11/- or one week of hard labor.[75] D. M. Dalley was fined £2 or one month of hard labor for also pleading guilty to "persistently neglecting to pay flat rate tax for 1939–40."[76] Alfa Lawal received a criminal summons to court for "failure or neglect to pay tax for 42–43." After pleading guilty, he was sentenced to pay ten shillings or two weeks of hard labor.[77] Officials seemed to target those who benefited from the cost of living increase in 1942–43. In a case heard February 26, 1943, Adesanyo was charged with "neglecting to pay 4/9 added . . . on C.O.L.A. for 42–43." He was fined ten shillings or two weeks in prison.[78] The cost-of-living increase granted by the colonial government was quickly absorbed by the local government.

These cases demonstrate that for people already financially strapped, the cost of nonpayment could be devastating. The detailed tax rolls and the prosecutions enabled the state to become an increasingly efficient tax collector because it was in a better position to both identify and locate taxpayers, whether they lived in town or in the districts. Officials were most efficient at collecting taxes from the poor because those with the least paid the vast majority of the total tax bill as well as the court fines and fees. Dods's report documented the amount of money extracted from each of the four categories of taxpayers in 1937–38 and 1938–39 (see table 4.1).

TABLE 4.1. MONEY EXTRACTED FROM TAXPAYERS, 1937–38 AND 1938–39

Category of taxpayer	Amount collected, 1937–38	Percentage of total tax, collected 1937–38	Amount collected, 1938–39	Percentage of total tax, collected 1938–39
Flat tax in town	£3, 967	11.25%	£2,965	9.38%
Special assessment tax in town	£484	1.37%	£602	1.90%
Miscellaneous tax in town	£513	1.45%	£514	1.62%
Flat tax in districts	£29, 397	83.34%	£26,107	82.61%
Special assessment tax in districts	£913[a]	2.58%	£1,414[b]	4.47%
Total	£35,274	99.99%	£31,602	99.98%

[a] I. W. E. Dods, Report on Tax Collection in the Egba Division for the Year 1938–39, 3, 15, 17, 19, 26, ECR 1/1/12, vol. 1, NAN Abeokuta. Those who paid the miscellaneous tax did not live in any of the four sections of the town and likely were not from Abeokuta. They included laborers on the railway and in the public works department and domestic servants.

[b] I. W. E. Dods, Supplementary Report on Tax Collection in the Egba Division, 9, ECR 1/1/12, vol. 1, NAN Abeokuta.

In both years the vast majority of taxes were collected from individuals who paid the flat tax, the overwhelming majority in the districts. Ninety-six percent (£33,877) of the 1937–38 tax came from the flat tax, and in 1938–39 the flat tax accounted for 93.6 percent of the total (£29,586).

While political power was concentrated in Abeokuta's urban core in spite of the overwhelming amount of taxes paid by rural residents, taxes laid another cornerstone in the distribution of political power among the town's quarters. Colonial officials used taxes as a part of the formula to determine representation in the expanding Egba Council. The alake noted that

> the number of appointments in town to the Central Council is governed by the amount of tax collected in each Section as follows:
>
> | | | |
> |---|---|---|
> | Egba Alake: | £2, 296.19.0 | 29 members |
> | Egba Oke-Ona: | £752.13.6 | 9 members |
> | Egba Agura: | £698.18.0 | 9 members |
> | Egba Owu: | £279.13.0 | 3 members |
>
> The Olowu on special request was allowed 4 members as an act of grace. This new method of election is representative according to tax paid in each section and has undoubtedly given more satisfaction to all concerned.[79]

While it is difficult to discern the precise formula that determined the relationship between the amount of taxes paid and the number of members, it is clear that representation meant many different things. Representation remained tightly framed by the town's political geography. Regardless of claims of expanded representation, this formula ensured the continued dominance of the urban center over the rural areas and of the Egba alake section over the central council.

Income and poll taxes were not the only taxes inhabitants of Abeokuta paid. Those who lived in town also paid taxes on water. Dods reported a significant migration from the town to the districts because many people could not afford to pay the additional water rates—two shillings, six pence for men and one shilling for women—on top of their taxes.[80] Nonetheless, in April 1940, the resident announced that water rates would have to be raised to make the system financially solvent. He argued that the system had always operated at a loss. It cost £5,000 to maintain the system annually, but revenue collected totaled £1,500. Therefore, in order to make the system solvent, they would have to raise the rates to five shillings for men and two shillings for women—thus, the total tax bill would be ten shillings for men and four shillings, six pence for women.[81] Newspapers and council minutes reveal strident debates on the ways in which the water rates were determined. In some instances, the ongoing debates led to popular agitation such as a mass meeting at Centenary Hall on June 18, 1940.[82] An article in the *Daily Times* called for abolition of the water rate in favor of rates on a tenant, or individual, basis. This plan would ultimately charge those who used the taps instead of the general population.[83] The water rate was such an incendiary topic that it brought people out into the street.[84] And it was not only the poor who complained about the water rate. Those who enjoyed direct access to water in their home paid an additional fee on top of the water rate. A petition from educated elements asked the council to abolish the additional £3 the signatories paid for private taps.[85] It is not a surprise, then, that water-rate collection was often poor.[86]

Abeokuta residents also paid a tax for electricity, but it did not generate the sort of protest that accompanied the discussion about the water rate. Reports also circulated that market women paid additional taxes to men who were called market masters. An article in the *Egbaland Echo* raised concerns about these men who demanded money or kind from market women and their relationship to the administration. The author asked a series of pointed questions:

> (2) Who clothes these market masters with authority to demand and collect money and kind from the market women who are already tax payers? (3) Under what Government Ordinance or Administration Rules are these market masters empowered

to impose extra taxation on the market women? (4) How are the money and things they collect disposed of? . . . (6) Are the money and sales proceeds realized from 1931 to date paid into the Treasury as part of our Revenue? . . . (12) If they are not servants of the Administration directly or indirectly, what right have they to demand and collect money and kind from Egba market women who are already taxpayers and are loyally making direct contribution toward the Administration revenue? . . . (16) Are Egba Women British Protected Persons? (17) Are Egba market women entitled to British Protection? (18) If so, will His Honor the Chief Commissioner give the due protection and relief to these women, suffering . . . and impoverished Egba Market Women?[87]

Whether or not these men's actions were legitimate, their demands were interpreted as an additional tax burden that specifically targeted market women. Collectively these taxes consumed an increasing percentage of people's incomes during a period when opportunities to increase one's income were severely restricted. More importantly, the author wanted to illustrate his appreciation of the multiple layers of political rights and duties embedded in taxation. Taxation did not confer civilization; it created a reciprocity between colonized peoples and imperial powers. In exchange for loyalty, as evidenced by paying taxes, the market women had earned the right to be protected from exploitation.

WOMEN AND THE WARTIME ECONOMY

Women's critical role within the economies of Abeokuta and the other Yoruba provinces meant that very few economic decisions failed to impact their livelihood. Yoruba women not only processed cassava into gari, palm fruit into palm oil and palm kernels into palm kernel oil, but they dominated the retail sale of all these products. Although they did not process cocoa, women played a critical role in bulking each year's cocoa crop as they moved through the rural areas purchasing cocoa.[88] Women dominated the retail trade of imports such as salt, matches, and textiles. As mentioned earlier, they controlled the manufacturing of indigo-dyed cloths, one of the Abeokuta's major economic activities and an industry heavily dependent on imports of cheap textiles, caustic soda, and synthetic dye.[89] As a result of their varied economic activities, many women traders were connected to the international markets through the import or export of commodities. This meant that women traders were hit hard by the loss of international markets as well as the limited availability of shipping space.

The outbreak of war immediately led to the loss of the German market for cocoa and palm products. All exports to Germany were banned since the British wanted to deprive Germany of war materials and "strangle German trade as a war measure." Although the government purchased the entire crop, officials used the decline in demand, the acute shortage of cocoa storage in Lagos, and the shortage in shipping space to London to justify their prices. Low prices meant that farmers were producing at a loss, and agricultural officers noted that many farmers abandoned their cocoa farms. The storage crisis was so acute that the government destroyed part of the 1940–41 crop after it was purchased. Low prices also meant that profit margins for women traders who collected cocoa from the farms were equally small. Cocoa was £11 in September 1940. It increased to £13.10 in October 1940 and fell precipitously to £10 in May 1941. It rose to £14.10 in 1941–42, declined to £12.10 in October 1942, and hit another low of £10 in 1943.[90]

Difficulties with storage and shipping also contributed to the state's decisions on palm products. In August 1940, the government announced that it would not purchase palm kernels on its previous large scale because all the "continental sources . . . had passed into enemy hands."[91] Nonetheless, palm kernels were a high-valued item and had priority for available storage space. To discourage a glut of palm kernels on the market, the government banned the export trade in palm kernels from the cocoa-producing areas in western Nigeria. Although some people "did not fully appreciate the reason behind the prohibition," officials argued that this regional ban was fair since producers in Yorubaland already benefited from government's purchase of the cocoa crop.[92] To help offset the impact of the ban, the government encouraged the expansion of the domestic palm oil market by increasing rail shipments to Northern Nigeria.[93] The export ban on palm kernels did not last very long. In fact, the government reversed itself after the Japanese occupation of British colonies in Southeast Asia in 1942 and launched a production drive instead.[94]

The policies on cocoa and palm kernels hurt some women, but others benefited substantially from the state's decision to create an export market in cassava starch.[95] Since the war made it difficult to obtain starch from Java and Brazil, the two major sources for the British market, Britain looked to the colonies as alternatives. In Yorubaland, where starch was used for laundry purposes, women dominated its production. Starch production increased substantially in Abeokuta, Oyo, and Ibadan Provinces as producers responded to the government's promotional efforts as well as the higher price offered for starch. The 1940 annual report noted that "a new industry commenced during the year, shipments being sent to England." The UAC completely dominated the trade since it was the only shipper of starch, and it purchased freely because no limits were placed on how much could be shipped to England.[96] Increasing starch production seemed to correlate with declining attention to palm products. In response, the Nigerian government reduced the price of starch in February 1943 and prohibited its export the following month. After May 1943, the purchase of starch for export ceased.[97] Consequently, women traders involved in the export sector experienced tremendous ups and downs as the colonial government directed the economy.

The state was equally, if not more concerned, with food. The government had to ensure that there was sufficient food for the civilian and military populations, especially in and around Lagos, and that the food was available at affordable prices for consumers. To meet these requirements, the government attempted to control the movement of foodstuffs between provinces in addition to controlling prices. Regulations restricted the movement of gari and rice from Abeokuta to the colony of Lagos and created a license system that by definition greatly restricted those who could take advantage of the more profitable bulk sales between these two cities. The ban did not end the efforts by unlicensed traders to move gari and rice to Ibadan or points beyond, but it made those efforts illegal. Traders caught smuggling were tried in the criminal courts and sentenced to either a substantial fine or imprisonment with hard labor. For example, a survey of criminal court records from 1939 to 1946 shows fourteen cases of smuggling rice and forty-two cases of gari smuggling. Most of the rice cases were tried in 1943, while the majority of gari cases clustered around 1946.

Officials also tried to enforce price controls by prosecuting some traders for profiteering by selling items above the control prices. A trader from one of the rural villages of Abeokuta Province, Feyisitan, was charged with selling two tins of palm oil for fourteen shillings instead of eleven shillings, the control price. For making a profit of three shillings, the judge sentenced him to a fine of £2 or one month in prison with hard labor.[98] The enforcement of profiteering appeared to be more rigorous than that of smuggling, for from 1939 to 1946, the Ake courts heard 478 profiteering cases. Yet some cases of profiteering escaped government sanction. This was seen most clearly in the case of salt. The European firms sold salt at the control price, leaving no room for retailers to gain any profit while staying within the law. Multiple charges were made against a group of women salt traders who were arrested and charged with trying to bribe the chief of the Native Authority police to ignore their illegal actions. In addition, they were accused of reducing the amount of salt they sold at the control price.[99] The alake was also implicated in practices that undermined the position of most market women. The Abeokuta Women's Union charged that he purchased large quantities of items that moved quickly but under different names. The volume of his purchases meant that limited quantities of those items were then available for market women. They highlighted his actions around salt. In 1947, he purchased ten tons of English salt from the UAC, and G. B. Ollivant and sold it through his agent, a Mrs. Olaosebiken, the wife of a Baptist Church traveling teacher. They estimated that Ademola paid about 12s. / 5 ½ d. per bag but sold it for approximately £1 per bag, gaining a profit of £100. While Mrs. Olaosebiken conducted business on behalf of the alake, other market women had difficulty obtaining salt. Funmilayo Ransome-Kuti visited the alake and the European stores trying to secure salt for these market women. After putting pressure on them, she was able to obtain two tons of salt for the women.[100]

Ensuring abundant and affordable food cannot be minimized, and without doubt some people did try to take advantage of the circumstances. Nonetheless, profiteering has to be considered against the economic pressures that faced many Nigerians. With limited transport available, the cost of imports increased substantially and contributed to inflationary pressures across the entire economy; however, neither wage nor price freezes took inflation into consideration. As a result, food became a site of tremendous political contention, and in Abeokuta the most contentious food item was rice.

THE STRUGGLE FOR RICE

This discussion focuses on rice because rice sellers appeared to be at the forefront of the protests that began in 1947. The documentation from this period shows that there was tremendous demand and competition for foodstuffs. Different actors with competing loyalties jostled each other for food to feed the expanded population in Lagos and in Abeokuta Province. Correspondence from the chief secretary's office shows that demand for foodstuffs became increasingly critical since the entire requirements of the armed forces had to be met in full in West Africa.[101] The deputy chairman of the West African Governors Conference informed the chief secretary that Nigeria would supply three thousand tons of rice to feed the troops in the Gold Coast and the Gambia for the next twelve months beginning in 1941. In addition, Nigeria would supply one thousand tons of rice indefinitely for the civilian population in the Gambia. In the event that Nigeria could not meet the expected amount, "the requirements of the Military should first be met unless overriding circumstances, such as an acute shortage of all other forms of foodstuffs, arose."[102] An overriding circumstance unfolded in 1945 when Nigerian unions demanded a cost-of-living increase to offset the high cost of living. The Nigerian government concluded that it could not send rice and maize to the Gold Coast in the autumn of 1945 and the spring of 1946 because it hoped to reduce the prices of staple foodstuffs.[103]

The concern with food production also revealed tensions within the larger colonial administration. Officials in the Department of Commerce and Industry (DCI) believed that provincial administrators had underestimated the food crisis.

In a series of communications about the shortage of maize and the possible smuggling of maize from Abeokuta Province to Dahomey, an official from DCI noted:

> The point I would like to stress is that an immense amount of pressure has had to be brought to bear from Lagos in order to get things done at all. The general inference—though if may be a wrong one—is that the administration regards grain bulk purchases as taking an inferior place when compared with other administrative preoccupations. The particular inference drawn from p. 14 is that the administration would like to be free of the whole business as soon as possible, in order to get on with more important matters. In plain terms, such information as I have, tends to point to the fact that provincial administrations—this does not refer to Abeokuta alone—tend to regard the various economic duties that now have to be performed, as a most irritating distraction from their duties, and that the more pressure there is from this department, the greater becomes the cleavage between it and the provincial administration. Would it not be possible to clear up any possible misunderstanding by issuing a clear directive to the effect that the most immediate need of this country is attention to economic matters, and that native courts, complaints, politics, and all the normal preoccupations of the administrative staff are secondary, though inevitably to some extent, complementary to the economic effort?[104]

Pressure was being applied and felt through all levels of the colonial regime as it tried to mobilize enough food for the military and then the civilian populations. Moreover, Nigerian officials looked to Abeokuta to play a central role in food production. The resident noted in the 1942 annual report that "the main war effort in the province is . . . food production for the military." In addition to increased military personnel in Lagos, there was a substantial military presence in Abeokuta Province, since a section of the province shared a border with the French colony Dahomey. Troops from Britain, the Gold Coast, and Belgium were stationed in Abeokuta, Ilaro, Ajilete, and Meko.[105] A large number of military units were all around Egba Division specifically.[106]

In a secret report, officials noted that "rice is going to play an important part as a Nigerian food reserve to meet War requirements." "Rice," the report declared, "is our emergency reserve," and it tasked the agriculture department to increase production at "the earliest possible moment."[107] Within a short time, the principal agricultural officer who happened to be an expert on growing rice, R. R. Glanville, visited the rice-producing areas in Abeokuta Province and recommended plans to experiment with the three varieties of upland rice he identified. As a result of this interest, the 1940 Abeokuta annual report noted that rice cultivation was proving increasingly popular.[108] Historically, Abeokuta was not one of the main rice-producing regions in Nigeria. Officials claimed that the province produced approximately three hundred tons of rice of annually before the war.[109] By 1943, however, agricultural officers estimated that the province could easily harvest three thousand tons.[110]

The 1941 season appeared to have been a bumper year: a food-production report stated that Abeokuta's production "exceeded local requirement by some 2,000 tons of which 1,200 tons were supplied to the Army."[111] Despite increased production, the availability of rice, especially at the control prices, was a major concern, and officials took increasingly extreme measures to address the situation. Orders prohibited the export of rice from the province except by special permit.[112] By October 1943, the resident of Abeokuta Province, Capt. A. R. A. Dickins, signed an order under the General Defense Regulations requisitioning rice from farmers. The order created a system of forced cultivation because it gave officials the authority to assign production quotas to villages and prosecute bales if the quotas were not met.[113]

Officials also contemplated sending the army to physically requisition the rice.[114] A Captain Pullen, in particular, supported these measures because Abeokuta's rice was central to the bulk-marketing program he oversaw in Lagos. This system was part of a larger strategy to control the price of food during the war. Pullen and a team of price-control officials established prices for foodstuffs in the Lagos markets, but Lagos prices were predicated on obtaining sufficient quantities of foodstuffs at the control purchase price.[115] Abeokuta Province clearly loomed large in Pullen's plans for feeding Lagos because he argued that "the whole scheme of bulk marketing will break down at the outset unless he can secure adequate supplies" from Abeokuta.[116] Native Authority police and certain chiefs applied additional pressure on farmers and women traders by confiscating their rice. In a letter to the district officer, A. M. Salami charged that two Nigerian police officers confiscated his rice, sold it to the G. B. Ollivant store, and then pocketed the funds.[117]

Despite these efforts, officials still had difficulty obtaining sufficient rice at control prices. Some officials recognized as early as 1941 that the military presence contributed to the difficulty. That year's annual report stated that the "military have caused the prices of agricultural products to soar to a ridiculous level by placing contracts in Lagos instead of in the producing areas, no regard being paid to Food Price Control Order."[118] The military bureaucracy as well as individual soldiers flouted price control measures. In 1943, the resident reported that military personnel with "healthy stomachs and long purses provided a constant temptation to break the rule."[119] Primarily, colonial officials blamed the "black market" and farmers' resistance to producing rice as the main factors behind the difficulty they faced getting sufficient rice in a timely manner.

Indeed, a substantial unofficial market existed in Lagos. In 1943, three thousand tons of rice "disappeared" from Abeokuta.[120] The low official price played a significant role in these developments. Farmers complained that the price did not cover their cost of production, but the state used requisition orders to compel them to continue to produce rice rather than switch to other crops.[121] Officials insisted that low prices were necessary to counter inflation. They would not acknowledge that inflation grew nonetheless or that the increasing price of imports contributed to it.

Jostling between rice buyers compounded market tensions as well. The Association of West African Merchants (AWAM), which represented the European trading companies, competed with licensed local merchants for the purchase of rice for the military and the Lagos market. The records identify the main local purchaser as a Mr. Shodipo. Axel Harneit-Sievers argues that Shodipo and his counterpart in Ijebu, Timothy Adeola Odutola, flourished in the food-procurement business because they had much lower overhead costs than the AWAM firms. However, residents of Abeokuta offered other reasons for Shodipo's success.[122] Farmers, women traders, and AWAM agents alleged that Shodipo had extremely close ties to the alake, who put the Native Authority police at his disposal. The produce secretary of AWAM, J. C. Graham, suggested that Shodipo's relationship with the alake gave him an unfair advantage. Graham reported that when he tried to buy rice at ten shillings above the control price from the Ifo Farmers' Association, it refused to sell the rice to him. He was told that the rice was being "forwarded to Shodipo and Co., on the instruction of the Alake."[123] AWAM agents also insisted that Shodipo had "one foot in the black market and one foot in the government scheme."[124] The AWAM agents did not present any concrete evidence of these charges, but farmers reported that Native Authority police warned them that they had to sell their rice to Shodipo and not to the AWAM agents.[125]

These allegations about Shodipo implicated the alake, and they found sympathetic ears among some colonial officials. Captain Pullen, for example, insisted on several occasions that the alake was not doing all that he could to assist the rice effort.[126] Accusations about the alake using his political power for personal profit also cropped up in relation to other commodities. Traders charged that his store was profiteering on salt.[127] In many people's minds, war profiteering and the alake became linked. Although the governor did not believe that the alake was obstructing the purchase of rice, he felt "there is little evidence of support from the Alake in the past in this matter of rice."[128] As a result, communication from the top level of the colonial government and supported by the secretary of the western provinces conveyed to the alake that it was "his personal responsibility" to see that rice reached the appropriate organizations at the control price and was "not diverted to other clandestine and undesirable channels."[129] The pressure placed on the alake bore fruit, for at the end of the 1943 harvest, Abeokuta supplied a total of 2,095 tons of rice. It was below the target of 3,000 tons, but "in consideration of the fact that last year we obtained only 188 tons against the same target figure, the position is not unsatisfactory."[130]

The citizens of Abeokuta did not experience the violence of war that those of Britain sustained. Nonetheless, World War II had a profound impact on them. For men, the war presented opportunities to join an expanding work force in Lagos or join the army. Soldiers from Abeokuta who were part of the Eighty-First (West Africa) Division put into practice an experimental theory of warfare that would win accolades for its developer, Maj. Gen. Orde Wingate.[131] Invariably some of the men did not survive the war, but some did and were proud of their experience. The 1945 annual report noted that by October it was not uncommon "to see ex-soldiers from Burma walking about Abeokuta Town in their dull green battle dresses [sic]."[132]

World War II reshaped the economic and agricultural landscapes of Abeokuta, especially as rice became a significant crop. More importantly, the war sharpened political tensions in the town as men and women struggled to dominate or defend themselves in the grim economic climate. The struggle over foodstuffs during the war made the market an extremely contested space. In the process, it exposed struggles between the state and local producers as officials tried to obtain commodities below the cost of production and producers tried to resist this exploitation. The struggle over foodstuffs also exposed tensions between distributors. European trading companies with the support of the colonial state maintained their hegemonic position in trade, but they had to strategize against local African authorities who supported African traders. In Abeokuta, it is clear that small traders were caught between these two power blocs. Market women were vulnerable to the demands of the military and the food controller in Lagos and equally vulnerable to the alake and his agents, especially the Native Authority police.

Ademola was a central figure in this unfolding drama. Despite his best efforts to manage his public role as the father of Abeokuta, the alake became increasingly associated, in the minds of women traders, with duplicitous economic activities. No doubt these activities contributed significantly to their demand for his removal from office in the postwar period. Yet these events make clear that his power was not supreme. As he was a functionary within the colonial bureaucracy, pressure could be brought to bear on him to ensure that he privileged the state's priorities. The dramatic increase of rice for the government coffers in 1943 raise questions about how it was achieved. Did the alake and his agents redirect rice from the illegal market to government agents, or did the alake and his agents bring more coercive pressure to bear on farmers and traders? We may never know the full answer, but it is clear that the colonial government gave the alake and the police license to use whatever methods they had at their disposal to collect rice. The colonial state also rewarded him for his loyalty and duty. On November 27, 1945, the governor, Sir Arthur Richards, presented him with the "insignia of an Honorary Companion of the Most Distinguished Order of St. Michael and St. George" on behalf of the King George VI.[133]

World War II extended and in some ways deepened the economic crisis that had begun with the Depression. Nonetheless, significant differences existed, and the economic crisis during the war reflected much greater state intervention. The state, more so than market forces, determined commodity prices and often set them below the cost of production.

The war precipitated a severe shortage of shipping space that put inflationary pressures on imports and the economy as a whole. However, workers, traders, and farmers could not redress the inflation because the state imposed wage and price freezes. The state also raised taxes, which meant that it collected a larger percentage of the income from those most affected by the wage and price freezes—workers, farmers, and traders. In Abeokuta, since every stream of tax collection recognized women as independent economic actors, their historic economic roles in trade and production became even more significant. Women also belonged to households, and as the tax burden increased for both men and women, it invariably affected household economies and decision-making.

Colonial officials championed tax collection as a mark of civilization. Furthermore, they expected Africans to dutifully pay their taxes, demonstrating their conformity to colonial policy.[134] They desired colonial subjects whose acceptance of colonial policy and British social thought occurred without critical engagement. They failed to appreciate that many residents of Abeokuta had accepted their status as taxpayers as well as the extent to which "taxpayer" had become a central part of the lexicon of political discourse. Since taxes subsidized state expenditures and investment in infrastructure, they were the vehicle through which citizens claimed their right to press demands on the state. As taxpayers they wanted protection from criminals and con artists, and they looked to the state to provide certain resources out of the taxes they paid. However, officials did the exact opposite: they cut expenditures and services, executed tax collection more aggressively, and planned rate increases.

5 ~ "Freedom from Want"

Politics, Protest, and the Postwar Interlude

ALLIED FORCES celebrated victory over Germany on May 8, 1945. World-wide, the global conflict left millions dead or destitute, cities destroyed, and national economies as well as the international economy in crisis. Tim Rooth notes that the United Kingdom "emerged from the war as the world's greatest debtor."[1] Britain's weakened economic position forced the metropole to rely even more heavily on the empire and to continue the economic austerity measures put in place during the war. It requires different spatial units of analysis to fully reveal the intersecting and dynamic relationship between events in the metropole and in the colony. Nonetheless in many ways, World War II generated the conditions that both deepened and ruptured colonialism.

This chapter begins with a consideration of the challenges Britain faced following the war's conclusion. It illuminates the importance of the colonies, including Nigeria, to Britain's reconstruction plans and draws attention to the ways in which reconstruction shaped the austerity policies that continued in Nigeria after the war. The discussion primarily focuses on a very small window of time, 1945–47, for it seeks to understand the multiple strands that came together to ignite the mass women's protests that unfolded in Abeokuta in 1947. Even within this small temporal slice, the chapter illustrates the ways in which the continued austerity contributed to both national and local political developments in Nigeria and to the volatility of the crucial half decade after the end of World War II. Massive labor strikes emerged around the continent, including a general strike in Lagos in 1945 and a mine workers' strike in Enugu in 1949. These actions against low wages, inflation, and promises of increased taxes enhanced the political appeal of the newly founded nationalist organization the National Council of Nigeria and the Cameroons. Its political activities in the immediate postwar period helped to create a political moment that was more national than anything before. While the NCNC expressed an inclusive politics, it also carried within it the seeds of future conflicts. Most of its support in Northern Nigeria, for example, came from southerners based there. In this time period, those conflicts remained submerged as labor unions challenged colonial economic policies.

Colonial economic policies and the resistance to them assumed a distinct face in Abeokuta. The chapter explores the intersections of national and local issues in Abeokuta in order to explain why women were so galvanized in postwar Abeokuta and why their activism crossed religious, social, and economic lines. The political crisis between the alake and the women in Abeokuta allows us to bring a gender analysis to the examination of this critical moment in Nigerian colonial history. Most studies of the immediate postwar period have focused on the labor movement and the significance of the strikes to the evolving nationalist movement. The crisis in Abeokuta affords us the opportunity to understand how women experienced the postwar conditions and by extension their relationship to the nationalist movement. It also enables us to understand the dynamic ways in which imperialism, nationalism, and local politics intersected in this postwar moment.

BRITAIN'S POSTWAR ECONOMIC CRISIS

During the war, Britain introduced reforms to counter the anticolonial voices within the United Kingdom and across the Atlantic in the United States. Like France, Britain did not intend to give up its colonies after the war but nonetheless felt compelled to begin to polish the image of empire. New literary tropes populated colonial documents as "partnership" replaced "paternalism" and "trusteeship."[2] Michael Crowder argues that the passage of the Colonial Development and Welfare Act in 1945 and the £120 million set aside for postwar development and welfare over a ten-year period reflected acceptance of John Maynard Keynes's ideas as well as an effort to demonstrate to America that it had indeed reimagined empire.[3] However, factors such as Britain's sterling debt, lack of confidence in the pound sterling, and the country's weak productive capacity led to greater integration of its African colonies into the sterling area in the immediate postwar period—the very opposite of what the United States desired.[4]

In order to understand why the colonies became more integrated into the imperial economy and how this development affected local African communities, it is important to appreciate the financial crisis that enveloped Britain. By the end of the war, Britain owed £3,688 million, of which £2,605 million belonged to countries in the sterling area. Britain owed its largest creditor, British India, £1,177 million. It accumulated much of this debt by deferring payment for supplies needed to build military installations in India, Egypt, Palestine, and other countries along the southern fronts of the war.[5] Britain also needed tremendous capital infusion to rebuild its own productive capacity as well as the homes and neighborhoods destroyed during the war. In December 1945, Britain signed loan agreements with the United States in which it promised to abolish discriminatory trade practices, to make the pound sterling freely convertible with the dollar from July 15, 1947, and to reduce its sterling balance of payment. To balance these demands against its own self-preservation, Britain divided the sterling debts into three categories: "those to be released at once; those to be released by installments over a period of years beginning in 1951; [and] balances to be adjusted as a contribution to the settlement of the war and post-war indebtedness."[6] In addition, officials used informal methods, as during the war, to impress on members of the sterling area the necessity to restrict dollar expenditures.

Despite Britain's attempt to limit expenditure in dollars, a series of bilateral agreements with dollar-area countries led to the drain of dollars from the country's reserves before the loan agreement took effect. Already in 1946, the Treasury was losing $75 million per month. As convertibility extended in 1947, the monthly drain reached $315 million. Allister E. Hinds argues that "the implementation of free convertibility of sterling was tantamount to a referendum on the stability of the pound sterling as a major currency in world trade," and participants unanimously voted no. Doubts about the pound was reflected most dramatically in the net drain on Britain's gold and dollar reserves, which increased from £226 million for the year in 1946 to £381 million from July to September 1947.[7] In order to stem the flow of its gold and dollar reserves, Britain suspended free convertibility of the pound after five weeks. The run on its reserves brought forward more sustained discussion about the role that the colonies could play in Britain's reconstruction. As Hinds illustrates, this policy was confirmed by Ernest Bevin, the secretary of state for foreign affairs. Bevin instructed the secretary of state for the colonies to establish an interdepartmental committee to handle balance-of-payment questions. In a minute to Prime Minister Clement Attlee, Bevin noted, "The same committee should have its terms of reference widened to take into consideration the development of the Empire, as well as development at home; so as to earn by production of raw materials, a large contribution to the balance of payments."[8] In multiple communications, officials linked the development of African resources to the rehabilitation and strengthening of not only Britain but all of Western Europe. Even more important, African raw materials would enable Britain to either save or earn dollars and to maintain its independence from the United States. Of course, Africans would benefit too.

The enthusiasm for the new imperial policy led to changes in the structure of the Colonial Office and the passage in February 1948 of the Overseas Resources Development Bill, which created two corporations— the Colonial Development Corporation and the Overseas Food Corporation. Both corporations had the power to raise capital—£100 million and £50 million, respectively—to promote development of colonial resources.[9] As Africans stayed abreast of the creation of these new corporations, an editorial in the *West African Pilot* condemned the fact that they were developed without the consultation or participation of people on the continent.[10]

This new imperial policy relied heavily on the marketing boards established in British colonies during World War II. The boards averted complete economic disaster by purchasing in bulk commodities, such as cocoa, whose markets were disrupted by the war. These boards paid producers low prices and by the end of the war were accumulating surpluses as prices improved. Colonial officials offered many excuses for not increasing commodity prices. For example, they suggested that high prices would discourage production, boost the money supply, and accelerate inflation. However, scholars show that imperial fiscal policies actually contributed to inflation. African consumers had difficulty obtaining imports because of the restrictions placed on purchasing goods from dollar areas. They were restricted to the sterling zone, but British producers were often hampered by shortages of materials. These factors hurt African consumers, but officials were not inclined to address them because, as Rooth demonstrates, Britain benefited in multiple ways from the low produce prices paid to African producers. For example, Britain's importance as a source of imports increased, African producers effectively subsidized British consumers, and the marketing board surpluses contributed to the accumulation of sterling balances in London and helped back the money in circulation in the United Kingdom. Ultimately, Britain's fiscal and imperial policies created conditions in which the net flow of resources went from the colonies to the metropole.[11]

NIGERIAN POSTWAR POLITICS

The end of the war presented an important moment for the colonial government to reward those who had diligently supported the war effort. On November 27, 1947, the governor of Nigeria, Sir Arthur Richards, and his wife joined a number of well-wishers in Abeokuta to present a new title to the alake. Guests at the event included the entire cadre of colonial officers, missionaries from multiple denominations, heads of mercantile houses, and representatives from the army as well as Dr. C. P. Murray of the African Hospital and Jane McCotter, the sister in charge of the Infant Welfare Center. They were there to watch the alake receive the insignia of "an Honorary Companion of the Most Distinguished Order of St. Michael and St. George," conferred by King George VI.[12] It also smoothed over the strained moments during the war when officials had agonized over acquiring enough rice. This investiture reaffirmed the state's support of paramount chiefs like the alake, whom colonial officials expected to help them navigate the postwar period, for the war had fostered dire economic conditions as well as a new political era and new political discourse.

The new discourse reflected the language of the Atlantic Charter and its defense of the right to self-determination. Nigerians at home and in Britain adopted it as they offered more concrete plans for an end to colonial rule. The West African Students Union in the United Kingdom, led by Ladipo Solanke, first articulated a demand for constitutional reform on a territorial basis and interterritorial unity. In 1943, Nnamdi Azikiwe led a press delegation to Britain that put forward a plan to the secretary of state for the colonies for independence in fifteen years. The plan created by a small study association, the Nigerian Reconstruction Group, called for ten years of representative government followed by five years of limited tutelage with fully "responsible" government.[13]

This new political era was best reflected in the formation of the NCNC. Conceived as a national front that would coordinate the political activities of existing organizations across the country, it organically emerged from a meeting organized by the Nigerian Union of Students (NUS).[14] In response to NUS's summons, over forty associations met on August 24, 1944, to discuss Nigeria's political future. Participants included political parties, ethnic unions, trade unions, literary associations, professional associations, religious groups, social clubs, and women's organizations. Together they adopted a resolution "to work in unity for the realization of our ultimate goal of self-government within the British Empire."[15] From its inception, the NCNC planned to exert populist pressure to accelerate the political development of the country, but unlike earlier organizations it specifically articulated a call for self-government within a specific time period.[16] The NCNC married populism, independence, and internationalism, for it brought together a political agenda shared by Nigerians at home and abroad as well as organizations with a mass base. The inaugural meeting reflected its composite character—Dusé Mohamed Ali, the Egyptian founder and editor of the Lagos newspaper the *Comet*, chaired the event, Azikiwe was elected general secretary, and Herbert Macaulay president. Equally important, the organization had access to two media outlets that served as its mouthpiece—the *Comet*, owned by Ali, and the *West African Pilot*, owned by Azikiwe.[17] The emergence of the NCNC also reflected some of the political tensions of the period. In 1944, internal disputes led to Azikiwe's departure from the NYM. As a result, the NYM did not join the new umbrella organization.

The NCNC continued the practice of forging strategic alliances with workers as the NYM did. It included trade unions such as the Nigerian Union of Teachers, led by Reverend Ransome-Kuti.[18] NUT had undergone significant changes by the postwar period as well. In 1941, the union underwent an internal reorganization, wrote a new constitution, and registered as a trade union. Equally important, more teachers began to realize that "they were not organizationally attached to the missionary movement" and that they constituted a separate and distinct profession.[19] This militant period strengthened teachers' self-perception as a salaried work force especially as the economy remained in crisis after the war. NUT's militancy reflected the increasing political engagement of its leadership. Ransome-Kuti was in communication with the Fabian Colonial Bureau, which shared its memos and white papers with NUT while its general secretary, E. E. Esua, was invited to attend the International Labour Conference in Montreal in 1946.[20] These organizations mutually reinforced their shared militancy.

The NCNC's militant credentials grew even more after the war when the organization and its newspapers enthusiastically supported the unions that called for an increase in the cost-of-living allowance (COLA) and then a general strike in 1945. As Nigerian resources helped to support and then rebuild Britain, Nigerians remained trapped in the fiscal policies that sustained their deepening impoverishment. In the first two years of the war, the cost of living rose precipitously, so much so that by "1941 real wages had fallen to 68% of their 1939 level."[21] In 1941 and 1942, government workers in Lagos demanded a COLA increase and conducted a series of walkouts, demonstrations, and strikes as well as a march to the governor's residence. The government appointed a committee and ultimately accepted the committee's recommendation of a 50 percent increase in the COLA. While the strike appeared to be successful, its outcome was limited. Governor Bourdillon threatened that the awards would be subject to review. Moreover, officials also took advantage of the defense regulations to exile Michael Imoudu, head of the Railway Workers Union, who had led the march to Government House.[22]

Despite the 1942 COLA increase, real wages continued to decline from 1942 to 1945. The government ignored workers' continued complaints about the inadequacy of their salaries as well as the questions they raised about differences in the allowances accorded to European and African workers. On May 19, 1945, within days of the end of the war against Germany, "workers held a mass rally at Glover Memorial Hall in Lagos during which they adopted and forwarded a resolution to government that if their demands were not met by Thursday, June 21, 1945, they would go on strike."[23] Communication between the government and union representatives stalled, although acting governor G. C. Whiteley acceded to their demand for the release of Imoudu. Imoudu returned to Lagos on June 2 to a hero's welcome as well as a place on the executive of the NCNC. Robin Cohen characterizes Imoudu's release as a "grave political miscalculation," because Imoudu would ultimately take the lead in the decision to go out on strike on June 21 if the workers' demands remained unmet.[24] The government used a multipronged approach to break the strike. It created a skeletal crew of managers of prison laborers to maintain railway service. Officials threatened to forfeit the wages of striking workers while they ordered the arrest of several labor leaders suspected of being responsible for the derailment of a train. The government targeted the union's support base by banning the *West African Pilot* and the *Daily Comet* for their strident support of Imoudu and the strikers as well as for their equally strident criticism of the government.[25]

During the strike, the government and the union leadership remained deadlocked over a wage increase, with the government firmly maintaining that it would not increase wages because an increase would hurt the nonwage sectors of the economy. The deadlock essentially crumbled when the government issued an ultimatum stating that it would regard workers who did not return to their jobs by August 1 as dismissed.[26] Disunity among the union leaders and members led to some workers returning to their jobs after thirty-seven days while others stayed away for forty-four days. The unions officially called off the strike on August 4, while the government agreed not to victimize workers who had joined the strike and to withdraw legal proceedings against strike leaders. In time it also lifted the ban against the *West African Pilot* and the *Daily Comet*.[27] Discussions over wages continued, but they could not reach a resolution because the unions refused the government's offer of a 20 percent increase. Instead the union leaders opted to accept the government's proposal to create a commission of enquiry into the cost of living—the Tudor-Davies Commission—whose recommendations it would consider.

The commission, headed by Mr. W. Tudor-Davies and accompanied by a statistician and a nutritionist,[28] began its hearings on December 4, 1945, and met with representatives from twenty-four unions.[29] Wale Oyemakinde reports that L. M. E. Emejulu and J. M. Osindero of the Railway Workers Union and Felelis Ogunsheye of NUT did the background research for the lengthy memorandum that the Trade Union Congress (TUC) prepared of the meeting with the commission. Its research included a review of government memoranda and reports as well as texts such as *The Russian Peasant*.[30] In their memo to the commission, the trade unionists illustrated the hollowness of the government's claim that it kept wages low in order to prevent high inflation and to protect the non-wage-earning sections of the society. They were not engaged in an ideological debate about free markets, for they did not challenge the idea of the government exercising controls in the economy. In fact, Ogunsheye stated explicitly, "We do not believe in laisser-faire, so that if Government is going to be a real instrument for the promotion of welfare and raising the standard of living, it has to do its best to see that the workers get the most out of their wages."[31]

At the core of their critique, the unions challenged the ways in which the government chose to implement controls. They argued, for example, that it made no sense to keep the prices of foodstuffs low while the prices of imported goods went sky high. Furthermore, if the government wanted to exert control over the economy in a way that was fair to all sectors, "there should be control of agricultural products and imported goods, and . . . the prices of agricultural products must become fixed relatively to the prices of the imported goods. Proper consideration should be taken of the rise of the cost of living of the agricultural workers themselves, and the cost of production."[32] Members offered examples of the scenarios they faced because the prices on imports were not subject to control. S. B. Kuku of the Nigerian Civil Service Union visited a store to inquire about the cost of a piece of cloth he intended to purchase. The clerk told him that it was eighteen shillings a piece, but when he returned the next week the price had gone up to one pound. He continued, "When I expressed surprise, he said,

'You had better buy in time. If you come tomorrow it might be £1.5s. 6d.'"[33] The representatives offered their own rationale for the situation: "One of the reasons why Government will not control the prices of imported goods is that it stands in awe of the big firms and lacks the resolution to challenge their power."[34]

The discussion with the commission went beyond the cost of imports and the cost of living in Lagos. Representatives from provinces in the interior noted that there was an assumption that the cost of living only rose astronomically in Lagos. M. S. Sowole, of the Federal Union of Native Administration Staff and the All-Nigeria Government Technical and General Workers' Federation, who happened to live in Abeokuta, pointed out that cost of rents had risen substantially in Abeokuta. Moreover, L. L. Ike, the general secretary of the Supreme Council of Nigerian Workers, and the district secretary of the Plateau Postal Workers Union explained that workers in the provinces did not always get the full COLA increase because it was assumed that their costs were less. Workers in the provinces wanted equal COLA increases for everyone.[35] Commission members and union representatives expanded their discussion to diet and the nutritional value of foods, models of women's volunteer associations, education, and indebtedness.[36] The discussion of the Pullen market system, which imposed price freezes during the war, was quite revealing. M. A. Abosede, president of the Government Press Technical Workers' Union, raised questions about the basis on which prices for rice and gari were determined. He noted that the fixed price for rice actually decreased by fifty percent from 1942 to 1945, declining roughly fifty percent from three shillings in 1942 to 1/8d. in 1945.[37] The union representatives also challenged the veracity of the government's cost-of-living figures, charging that government based its index on the Pullen system and on what prices should be instead of the actual costs.[38]

Though armed with figures from the colonial government and the unions, the members of the commission chose not to rely on the provided data. They visited a number of cities, including Jos, Kaduna, Makurdi, Enugu, Calabar, Ibadan, and Abeokuta, and compiled their own cost-of-living indexes. They gathered prices for a range of food items (rice, yams, palm oil, tinned fish), clothing (prints, white shirting), rent, fuel (kerosene), and miscellaneous items such as matches, bicycles, and machetes. Using 1939 as their base of reference, they showed that the cost of living had increased over 200 percent in some parts of the country by 1945.[39] Table 5.1 provides a rough picture of what Nigerian consumers experienced.

TABLE 5.1. INCREASE IN COST OF LIVING

Town	Product	Cost in pence, 1939	% increase, 1942	% increase, 1945	% increase in cost of living, 1945
Calabar	Yams	1.200	66	400	287.37
Kaduna	Rice	1.017	75	191.6	288.61
Makurdi	Pepper	1.393	—	400	264.78

The Tudor-Davies Commission took six months to complete its report. Based on its calculations, the commission agreed with the unions' estimates and recommended a 50 percent increase in the COLA, retroactive to August 1, 1945. They did, however, discount the unions' suggestion that the COLA should be the same across the country rather than determined by local conditions. The report demonstrated that the commissioners discounted some of the government's arguments as well. For example, they rejected its claim that the increase in allowances would accentuate inflation, and they "regarded the Government's argument that it could make the allowance only by increasing taxation or postponing social and development work as irrelevant, as a reply to the unions' case."[40] The commission exercised a degree of autonomy that colonial officials did not expect.

While the unions celebrated the commission's recommendations, the governor of Nigeria, Arthur Richards, was beside himself. Noting his disappointment and embarrassment, Richards cast aspersions on the commission and its findings and recommended that the government not publish the commission's report. In a secret letter to secretary of state for the colonies, George Hall, Richards wrote, "I am now faced with conclusions and recommendations which appear to be based neither on logical argument nor on proved facts but which appear to represent the superficial opinion formed by three gentlemen, with no previous experience of Colonial conditions, after a short visit to Nigeria. I make so bold as to say, with great respect, that had I known that this was likely to be the outcome, I should have preferred to rely upon my own opinion and judgment."[41] The governor's attitude was not shared by all in the Colonial Office, for the report was published and made available to the public for 3/6d. through the British government's official publisher and booksellers.[42] An editorial in the magazine West Africa praised it as "the deepest probe yet into West Africa's Social Problems" and applauded the broad way in which Tudor-Davies interpreted the commission's terms of reference. The editorial's author enthusiastically endorsed the committee's recommendations and lauded its language of urgency.[43]

The successful outcome of this strike holds an important place in Nigerian labor history, but it was significant for additional reasons. It was the largest work stoppage Nigeria had ever experienced up to that time; given the role of the railway union, the strike extended into the provinces beyond Lagos; it had the support of people from a cross section of society; and, as Cohen suggests, it "raised the possibility of co-operation between the unions and the more populist-inclined politicians."[44] Imoudu's alliance with the NCNC deepened as he joined the organization's crusade against the new constitution imposed during Governor Richards's tenure.

AN EMERGENT NATIONAL POLITICS

The Richards Constitution built on administrative initiatives carried out by Richards's predecessor, Gov. Bernard Bourdillon. In 1939, Bourdillon received permission from the Colonial Office to subdivide the Southern Province into two regions. A series of political crises in the Yoruba provinces demonstrated that it was difficult for the chief commissioner to remain on top of developments in the western provinces from his eastern base in Enugu. While it would have been practical to consider subdividing the even larger region that constituted the Northern Province, I. M. Okonjo argues that Bourdillon did not consider doing so because of the well-known hostility of its political officers to any efforts to restructure the north's administrative structure or deepen central control over the region.[45] Thus, in March 1945, when Governor Richards submitted proposals for a new constitution, it largely enshrined the new administrative structure with three regions—North, West, and East. The proposals created a legislature in each of the three regions. Members of the legislatures would be elected from the native administrations, and the regional legislatures would in turn send representatives to a central Legislative Council. This proposal rankled Nigerian nationalists who wanted to see direct elections and responsible government rather than a structure that reinforced colonial control though undemocratic structures.[46] The legislature also passed four ordinances on land, minerals, and the position of chiefs that nationalists found objectionable.

In response to the constitutional proposals the NCNC began a campaign deriding the African members of the legislature who voted in favor of the ordinances and the constitution. They also decided to tour the country in order to get support for a delegation to visit London and present their objections to the Colonial Office. The tour did not begin until April 1946, but it benefited from the popular support of the Lagos general strike and Michael Imoudu's participation. The NCNC team toured the country for

eight months, received written mandates from 181 communities supporting its goals, and raised £13,500 to support the delegation's travel to Britain.

Abeokuta citizens contributed a total of £30 7s. 2d. to the campaign;
however, there was clear opposition to the NCNC's strategy of mass participation. The *Egba Bulletin* reported that approximately two hundred
adults and five hundred schoolboys attended a public meeting with
NCNC delegates, including Nnamdi Azikiwe, on December 23, 1946, at
Centenary Hall. Decorum devolved when some chiefs spoke out against
the fact that the mandate had not been presented to the alake and the
Egba Council. As Chief Emanuel Kinoshi, the seriki of the Egbas, condemned the proceedings as "an evil day for the country, whose affairs were
being handled by children and irresponsibles," the students in attendance
drowned out his speech with hooting. When several chiefs walked out
of the meeting, there was "yet more vigorous hooting of hooligans from
both sides of the gallery as well as . . . the Hall."[47] This episode is illumi-
nating because it revealed some of the fault lines in Abeokuta's political
landscape — chiefly along authority, generation, and education.

It is highly likely that Abeokuta's mixed reception of the NCNC tour
was not unique. Nonetheless, the written mandates they received undercut any charge by colonial officials that the NCNC did not have a representative voice. The members of the delegation to London also reflected
the country's ethnic and regional diversity. They included Chief Nyong
Essien (Ibibio), a member of the Legislative Council; Mallam Bukar Dipcharima (Kanuri), a businessman; Funmilayo Ransome-Kuti (Yoruba),
educator and founder and president of the Nigerian Women's Union;
Paul M. Kale (Bakweri, originally from British Cameroons), educator; and
the three elected members of the Legislative Council — Nnamdi Azikiwe,
president of the NCNC; Prince Adeleke Adedoyin (Ijebu), barrister and
president of the Nigerian Union of Young Democrats; and Dr. Abu Bakry
Ibiyinka Olorun-Nimbe (Lagos, Muslim), physician and leader of the
Lagos Ratepayers Association.[48]

The delegation met with a number of groups in London even before their meeting with the secretary of state for the colonies. Funmilayo Ransome-Kuti met on July 19 with the wife of Arthur Creech-Jones,
the secretary of state for the colonies, who made arrangements for her
to contact women's associations. She also visited and spoke at a factory
with a workforce of four thousand workers. The group met with members of the Communist Party of Great Britain on July 21 and informally
with members of the House of Commons as well as the Fabian Colonial Bureau on July 23. WASU arranged an interview for them with the

high commissioner for India and organized a grand dinner for them on July 30. The date of their official meeting with Arthur Creech-Jones was fixed for August 13.[49]

In preparation for their meeting with the secretary of state, the delegation submitted a detailed memorandum that characterized the current system of colonial rule as "static, unprogressive, and not in accordance with the democratic ideals for which our country contributed her share in man-power, money, and materials in World War II."[50] The memorandum also noted the six topics the delegation were empowered to discuss with the secretary of state: the Richards Constitution, repeal of four pieces of legislation, basic human rights, acts of maladministration, protectorate status, and self-government. The document offered more than a litany of complaints, for it included proposals to restructure the administrative apparatus in order to create something more democratic. For example, it proposed reconfiguring Nigeria and British Cameroons into eight protectorates that together would constitute the Commonwealth of Nigeria. The commonwealth would be headed by a governor general and a lieutenant governor, and they along with a cabinet of fifteen ministers would formulate policy.[51]

Two days after submitting the memorandum, the delegation met with Creech-Jones and members of the Colonial Office.[52] The discussion visited a range of topics as each member of the delegation highlighted issues specific to the region they represented. Dipcharima, for example, called attention to the power of the emirs, the absence of any form of democracy in the north, and the limited provision of education and social services. Adedoyin raised the question of the independence of the judiciary, while Ransome-Kuti spoke of the oppression created by the sole native authority system as well as the arbitrary nature of tax assessments.[53] At the conclusion of their presentations, Creech-Jones thanked the delegation, accepted that there were deficiencies in the education, medical, and social services in Nigeria, and promised to refer their concerns to the relevant officials. While claiming to be open to political criticism, he nonetheless rejected the charges made against the judiciary as well as the delegation's demand for constitutional reform. Instead, he "invited them to cooperate in trying to make the new constitution a success."[54]

Minutes of the delegation's meetings following their discussion with Creech-Jones reveal their disappointment. Some members wanted to return to Nigeria on the first available ship, but others wanted to remain in Britain and participate in a propaganda tour to educate the British and Irish public. Members of WASU as well as George Padmore, the Trinidadian activist, strongly encouraged them to stay and tour the country. In a lengthy letter, Padmore argued that appealing to Creech-Jones for constitutional changes was like "an appeal from Caesar to Caesar." He noted, "The constitution about which you so rightly complain was produced by Baron Richards in collaboration with two ex-governors of Nigeria; Sir Bernard Bourdillon and Sir Donald Cameron; vetted by Lord Hailey—Tory official adviser to the Colonial Office and blessed by Mr. Creech Jones himself, Labour Imperialist and head of the Colonial Office."[55] He argued that there were many people who wanted to retrieve "the honor and good name of their country" and would stand with them. In fact, the delegation had an obligation and a duty to put their cases before these people. He also encouraged them to hold a major press conference at the completion of the tour where they should issue a statement to the British and world press "summing up your mission and your future plan of action." The tour as well as the press conference would allow them to reframe the ways in which they had been characterized by some of the British papers. He concluded with additional suggestions of activities they should pursue when they returned to Nigeria.

The delegation ultimately accepted the advice to stay in the British Isles. From September 9 to September 22, they visited Manchester, Dublin, Glasgow, Edinburgh, Newcastle, Birmingham, Cardiff, Liverpool, and Sheffield, a tour they concluded with a press conference in Liverpool on September 23. By all accounts, the tour was extremely successful. In Scotland, they met local citizens and African students as well as political officials such as Jon Rankin, a Labour member of Parliament, and Oliver Brown, secretary of the Scottish Nationalist Party.[56] In Dublin, they were received by the lord mayor, Patrick J. Cahill, who assured them that they had the sympathy of the Irish people because the Irish had been under the yoke of English imperialism for over six hundred years.[57] In casting the tour as a goodwill mission, the delegation went a long way in tempering the accusations in some newspapers that Azikiwe was an agitator whose "purpose is to stir up feeling of the Empire's coloured citizens against what he calls British Imperialism"[58] and a "globe-trotter peddling racial hatred."[59] Some papers engaged the delegation's ideas thoughtfully, offering quotes from their speeches between detailed descriptions of their dress and regalia. Press coverage also revealed tremendous interest in Ransome-Kuti. She was asked to write an article for the *Daily Worker*, the British Communist Party newspaper,[60] and she was often quoted as the delegation traveled around Britain. Those quotes highlighted girls' education, taxation, and the vote.[61]

FIGURE 5.1. NCNC delegation to London with Funmilayo Ransome-Kuti on reporter John Parson's right. (From *Nigerian Chiefs Interview*, 1947, British Pathé Film Archive.)

Upon the delegation's return to Nigeria, the NCNC moved forward in cementing its organizational structure. In 1948, it rescinded its boycott of the Legislative Council and in April held its first national assembly in Kaduna where members adopted and refined the memorandum on constitutional reform that had been submitted to the secretary of state for the colonies and renamed it the NCNC Freedom Charter. During the convention, participants elected Azikiwe federal president for a three-year term and gave him the power to appoint all other officers of the NCNC. It appears that the only other elected position, federal auditor, went to O. N. Ojugun, manager of the African Continental Bank.[62] While Azikiwe appointed a federal cabinet that reflected the country's ethnic and regional diversity, he did not appoint any women to it. In spite of this auspicious beginning, the organization did not implement its freedom charter and according to James Coleman was virtually moribund from 1948 to 1951.[63]

NATIONAL POLITICS IN THE LOCAL ARENA

As we saw in chapter 3, nationalist organizations had roots in Abeokuta from the 1920s. The town had branches of the National Council of British

West Africa, the Nigerian Youth Movement, and the Nigerian National Democratic Party. Residents of the town, including the alake and both I. O. and Funmilayo Ransome-Kuti, actively supported WASU, and the Ransome-Kutis helped found the NCNC. Both Ransome-Kutis had national profiles. Reverend Ransome-Kuti's position as president of NUT ensured widespread recognition as branches of the union formed across the country. Funmilayo Ransome-Kuti enjoyed substantial name recognition from her participation on the NCNC delegation. In spite of their national platforms, both Ransome-Kutis were deeply engaged in local issues in Abeokuta. Their engagement increased significantly in the postwar period.

The 1945 general strike affected Abeokuta tangentially because wage-labor opportunities were limited in the town. The government's annual report noted that few of the government works and none of the Egba Native Administration employees joined the strike. Those workers who joined the strike included railway workers and the staff of the Post and Telegraph Department. Nonetheless, the strike did not create disruption within the town because strikers did not attempt to intimidate the emergency volunteer staff that replaced them.[64] Since agricultural production and trade dominated Abeokuta's economy, taxes, price freezes, commodity shortages, and the high price of imports affected its residents more significantly.

It is noteworthy that the same month workers in Lagos and across the country went on strike, June 1945, the government announced that tax rates would be increased 25 percent. According to the resident, the alake played a prominent role in the appeal, which led to a postponement in its implementation. However, before Egba officials received word that the postponement was granted, the alake had already agreed to an increase in the income tax assessment and the addition of new people to the tax rolls, measures that would allow the town to realize a 10 percent overall tax increase.[65] Although the poll tax increase was delayed, the announcement of the increase and its incremental application enhanced the sense of economic crisis and led to meetings between the alake and representatives of women's organizations.

On October 5, 1946, women's organizations sent a letter to the alake discussing the increase in the special assessment, poor economic conditions in the town, and the practice of conditional sales employed by the European trading companies.[66] The author of the letter appealed to the alake's self-presentation as the father of Abeokuta: "We, your children, entreat you respectfully and obediently kindly to consider the cases of women who have been specially assessed."[67] In this meeting with Funmilayo

Ransome-Kuti, the heads of market associations, and wealthy merchants such as Janet Ashabi, the alake discounted their complaint about poor profits and insisted that any financial difficulties they experienced was due to reckless trading. He suggested that Ransome-Kuti and the members of her society did not know trade or the women involved in trade. He recited the saga of the adire industry and reiterated that he had always tried to help women traders but they routinely ignored his advice. Ultimately, he argued, "the remedy was entirely in their own hands."[68] As he dismissed the complaints of women subject to the special assessment, he discounted the idea that the companies were doing anything that could affect trade negatively, and he made no mention at all of the price controls.

The alake's dismissal spurred what Cheryl Johnson-Odim and Nina Emma Mba argue was the beginning of the mass demonstration phase of the women's activism. In mid-October, Ransome-Kuti and nearly a thousand women marched to the Afin to protest the increase.[69] Some women also decided to contest their cases in court. Janet Ashabi, who had voiced support for the alake during the meeting, nonetheless filed an official complaint when her annual income was assessed at £150. The resident, E. N. Mylius, who heard the case refused to accept her figures and ordered assessment officials to increase her taxes further.[70] Like the resident, the alake's response appeared to be premised on the figures they were able to acquire from the firms. The alake, for example, telephoned the secretary of the Local Merchant Committee to obtain information about Ashabi. The information collected about her business dealings with European trading companies reveals that even in this time of economic crisis, some women traders were extremely wealthy, at least on paper. The secretary gathered information from the leading European firms about their business with Ashabi and sent it the alake:

U.A.C.	£3495
P. Z.	£2400
G. B. C.	Nil Does not deal with this firm
S.C.O.A.	£200 The Agent of this firm states that this lady was no longer a recognized customer of theirs as far back as 1938. She, however, buys occasionally from the shop for cash and this has been estimated at £200 P.A.
C.F.A.O.	£670
John Holt	£160 Started only trading with this firm in March 1946. £6925[71]

On their own, the figures do not provide much information. Ashabi clearly had a large inventory of goods, but these figures do not tell us how quickly she moved her inventory or how much profit she actually cleared. Moreover, it does not discount the reality of the vast majority of women and men who struggled financially with much less inventory or collateral. The pressure to enforce tax collection heightened tension for those women trading in commodities still under government price controls.

Rice remained under control prices in the postwar period, thus ensuring that conflicts around rice escalated rather than subsided. On September 11, 1945, the chief secretary to the government, George Beresford Stooke, wrote to the secretary of the western provinces about the poor collection results in Abeokuta. In thinly veiled language, he urged the secretary of the western provinces to apply pressure on the alake: "I am directed by His Excellency to request therefore that subject to His Honour's concurrence, the Alake should be informed that His Excellency hopes that he will use his personal influence to ensure that the maximum amount of rice is offered for sale to the Government buying agents."[72] Colonial officials put in place additional measures to obtain the rice. For example, police were given license to seize rice. In addition, a circular distributed on November 6, 1945, stated that any Egba Native Authority policeman on rice work would be held responsible for any district that failed to produce its quota of rice unless he is "prepared to give a detailed account of his activities to show that he has exerted all efforts and energy to get the particular district to produce its quota."[73] Officials also put pressure on truck owners. An order was put into effect on October 20, 1945, that compelled them to carry specific amounts of rice depending on the roads they traveled to reach Abeokuta. If they did not have the required amount of rice, the trucks would not be allowed to enter the town.[74] Meanwhile, the transport of rice outside of Abeokuta Province by anyone other than a licensed government contractor remained illegal.

The records are full of letters of complaint about rice during and after 1945. Letters came from women traders, farmers, and truck drivers about police confiscating rice without any compensation to the owner. Despite the order that only the police could seize rice, complainants identified private individuals who took their rice as well. In one complaint to the district officer, market women accused Mr. L. A. Alao, a military contractor who held the chiefly title *otun* of Ijaiye Obirinti, as a main culprit. They claimed that he and his assistants had taken more than five tons of rice from them.[75] In spite of the complaints, Alao continued to operate without censure. Some charged that Alao operated with impunity because he was the alake's agent. Moreover, traders reported to the Abeokuta Women's Union that the alake oversaw a brisk rice trade from his palace. Rice confiscated from traders was then sold at four shillings per *olodo* measure (approximately three pounds), even though the official price was about a quarter of that.[76]

In November 1945, the ENA issued an ordinance that revoked the rice production order that had been in place since 1943; however, this order did not end complaints about rice.[77] A letter to the *Daily Service* published on November 26, 1948, noted that quotas were still in place and farmers were prosecuted for not filling their quotas. The author, Omo Agbe (likely a pen-name) also acknowledged the work of the Abeokuta Ladies Club (ALC) in calling attention to the duress women traders of rice experienced. Not only was rice confiscated from traders—some farmers were forced to purchase rice above the control price and resell it to the government at the control price in order to avoid prosecution.[78] Agbe outlined a number of wrongs perpetrated on the farmers. For example, farmers insisted that they could not grow large quantities of rice for less than for 2s. 6d. per olodo, but the government imposed a price of 1s. 2d. Following this blow, the alake imposed a quota of eighteen hundred tons on several districts, without any consultation and "without reference to their ability, landed possessions, means of buying the necessary implements, food etc. . . . Many of those who were called upon to supply rice in their areas were not even farmers."[79] He also hinted that individuals associated with the rice purchase exercised a monopoly and were connected to the black market. The reporter expressed quite clearly that the colonial government and the alake acted against the best interest of the people of the town of Abeokuta.

The attacks on women traders galvanized them into action. They appealed to influential members of the community to advocate on their behalf. A group of thirty rice traders appealed to Rev. I. O. Ransome-Kuti to use his influence as principal of the Abeokuta Grammar School on their behalf because their rice had been confiscated and the alake had ignored them. The author of the letter, J. A. Ladipo, a school headmaster, used the imagery of the war to great effect, "I beg you to use your good influence for their freedom from want, freedom from fear, freedom of trade and freedom from exploitation for which we have fought the German Nazism, the Italian Fascism and the Japanese atrocity."[80] Women traders also appealed to Funmilayo Ransome-Kuti and the ALC. Johnson-Odim and Mba note that in September 1945, three members of the ALC and three members of NUT visited the assistant district officer to demand an end to the rice seizures. Funmilayo Ransome-Kuti also took their protests to the newspapers by holding a press conference. Although newspaper articles seemed to bring an end to rice seizures, it was only temporary, for in 1946 she reported in ALC minutes new complaints about seizures.[81]

Rice was not the only food item still entwined in control policies. In a letter to the district officer dated August 6, 1946, Lamide Olaniji complained that Mr. Alao, the military contractor, had taken maize from him sometime before and had not paid him. He specified that since maize was still being sold at the control price, he was due £3 18s. 6d. for the maize and an additional £1 for their bags. He also drew attention to his status as a taxpayer: "It is rather curious to see that my whole 10 bags maize were taken to Abeokuta from Ijoko Railway Shed in order to be sold at control price and nothing is paid for them while I am paying tax yearly, for this simple reason I crave for your honour's interference in this matter."[82] In a very curt letter, the district officer noted that he had spoken to Mr. Alao, who said that the maize was not fit for consumption and therefore unsalable. Since he had no reason to disbelieve Mr. Alao's word, he could do nothing more.[83]

Amusa Adeoshun and Kasabi Akanbi also wrote to the district officer for assistance. They had purchased seven bags of gari from Ikorodu and loaded it onto a truck traveling from Lagos to Ilorin. On their journey, they were stopped by ENA police who confiscated the gari. They subsequently learned that the gari was sold the following day. They asked for the district officer's assistance because jobs were not available and the profits of their trading venture was to pay their taxes as well as their wives' taxes.[84] In his response to the men, the district officer wrote, "I have to draw your attention to the fact that the export of gari from Abeokuta Province, except to Lagos, is strictly prohibited." In other words, the police acted lawfully; nonetheless, he advised that they speak to the senior assistant superintendent of police regarding the money.[85]

In addition to having their food items confiscated, owners could be summoned to court and fined ten shillings.[86] In a series of letters between B. O. Oshin Ayeye of Ibadan, the alake, and the district officer, the case of Mrs. Sabina Oshin provided information on how the system worked. Oshin, a draper, sold cloth on credit to someone in Agotuntun Ibadan District. The person was unable to pay her on the appointed day and offered to pay her in kind "one bag and two Sakasaka of Gari costing £1.12.0d." She agreed to accept the gari in exchange for the cloth. As the gari was being transported to Ibadan, an Egba Native Administration police officer in Ilugun stopped the truck and confiscated the gari. Given that the gari was neither produced in Abeokuta nor exported from Abeokuta, Oshin charged that the forfeiture was illegal.[87] When Oshin went to Ilugun to collect her gari, she was served with a summons to appear in court instead.[88]

The senior district officer subsequently ruled that the summons should be withdrawn and that Oshin should receive either the gari or the proceeds of the sale.[89] Instead of paying her the cost of the gari at the time it was confiscated, the court tried to pay her only fifteen shillings. In investigating the sale of the gari, the senior district officer learned that confiscated food items were put in a public auction and ostensibly sold to the first bidder. Dissatisfied with the responses from the police officer, S. O. Desile, who made the sale yet could not provide the name of the individual to whom the gari was sold, the senior district officer investigated further.[90] It was revealed that since November 23, 1946, Desile had sold seventy-three bags of gari by order of the court at ten shillings or under, even though a bag of gari garnered from twelve to eighteen during the period in question. As a result of Desile's actions, the government lost £21 from the sale of gari.

The senior district officer ultimately forced the court to restore the full amount that Oshin was due, but the particulars of this case illustrate the ordeal traders experienced if their goods were confiscated. This case dragged on for about ten months, indicating that the appeals process was extraordinarily slow. Even if traders were able to get the proceeds from the sale of their confiscated foodstuffs, they likely received less than the control price, if anything at all. Finally, these cases indicate that up to three years after the end of World War II, the economic landscape for traders and producers of food items remained difficult.

Consumers faced a dire situation as well. A report in the *Egba Bulletin* in March 1947 noted that the alake and the resident toured the rural districts for the first time since the middle of World War II to help prevent the food situation from worsening. They warned that "food was becoming scarce and prices were rising sharply . . . [and] where food was plentiful, it was being hoarded for transactions in the black market. . . . Gari which was the staple food of the people was being sold at prohibitive prices in almost all areas; in some places it was four times its pre-war price." In each locality they visited, the alake and the resident discussed the need to enforce newly enacted regulations that required "every able-bodied adult male, who had no whole-time occupation, to give attention to cultivate of foodstuffs — cassava, yams, maize, egusi, beans and the rest."[91] The alake also encouraged community members to report to the bale any male villagers who did not farm.[92]

Imported foodstuffs remained rationed as well. Correspondence between the Nigerian secretariat in Lagos and the deputy food controller in Abeokuta in May 1946 noted that butter, flour, whisky, milk, and beer were in short supply. As a result, the government ordered that they maintain strict control of ration cards: "The quota issued to the firms should not be exceeded which means that no ration cards (or bakers permits) should be issued to anyone who has not had a card before, other than new appointments from overseas."[93] Different factors accounted for the shortages. There was a worldwide shortage of flour, of which the United States was the source. Therefore, they planned to cut the ration by a third in order to stretch existing supplies until July. A sudden drop in butter production explained the shortage in 1946, but the situation did not seem to improve significantly, for in November 1947 they reduced the ration of butter to one pound.[94]

Availability of certain imports improved substantially by 1948, but it was in flux. In May, the food controller, R. E. Greswell, informed his deputies that "whisky imports will be severely reduced owing to the necessity of exporting larger quantities to the hard currency areas."[95] However, one month later, he urged his deputies to encourage firms to import Irish whisky to ration card holders and to "Clubs, Messes, Hotels and other institutions," for large quantities were available.[96] By September the government was able to begin relaxing control of other food items. For example, it quickly approved UAC's request to sell milk and flour off ration because the company held such large quantities in stock.[97] Clearly factors such as the rebuilding of production capacity around the world as well as Britain's weak economy shaped the availability of imported food items. This overview illuminates the larger set of national and international factors that contributed to the difficulties women traders experienced in the immediate postwar period. These factors also helped shape the increasingly strained relationship between the alake and a wide cross section of women in Abeokuta.

WOMEN'S POSTWAR ORGANIZING

Two years after the end of the war, as Europe rebuilt, women traders in Abeokuta still lived with economic austerity. Price controls remained in effect on certain commodities, and taxes increased. While nationalist leaders spoke of greater political responsibility and colonial officials insisted they were listening, women in Abeokuta faced a leadership that dismissed their concerns. This constellation of factors contributed to a new wave of political mobilization among women.

When the ALC held its first meeting on March 15, 1945, it listed its founders: F. Ransome-Kuti, S. F. Adeyinka, O. Akinwunmi, O. Sowunmi,

E. B. Majekodunmi, and E. Soyinka—and its patron, the alake. All of these women belonged to Abeokuta's Christian and/or economic elite. Eniola Soyinka was Reverend Ransome-Kuti's niece and the mother of Wole Soyinka, while E. B. Majekodunmi was the daughter of one of the largest African merchants in the town.[98] Meetings sometimes began with a short prayer and ended with tea and grace. Very little suggested that the ALC had any political intentions. During their second meeting, on June 1, 1945, the group passed several resolutions: catering charges for any society that requested their service, the creation of ALC auxiliaries for young women from the Gbagura and Ake Girls Schools who would be invited to join the group, plans for a social evening, and monetary contributions from men to support the social evening. Nonetheless, the organization wanted to raise the standard of womanhood in Abeokuta and put in place literacy classes for market women. Koye Ransome-Kuti and his cousin Wole Soyinka were among the tutors in the literacy classes.[99]

Minutes of their meeting on February 8, 1946, illustrated that rice seizures had not stopped. Funmilayo Ransome-Kuti "reported a case of seizure of rice at Isabo market by some N.A. policemen. She had taken steps to bring about the return of rice seized to their rightful owners." They discussed the need to draft rules and regulations for the club and planned a thanksgiving service and a picnic to mark the group's first anniversary on March 15, 1946. The discussion turned to politics as they decided to hold a special meeting on March 16 to pass resolutions, copies of which would be sent to the alake and the resident. Members suggested a range of issues to be included in the document: the need for more latrines and electric lights, daily removal of night soil, improvement of sanitary conditions in the town, proper drains, street sweepers, town planning, playgrounds, improved supply of water, school clinics, and adult education. Following this discussion, the group went on to plan a girls' meeting that would include a lesson in English cookery on February 16, a boys' meeting a fortnight later, and the design of a club badge. The badge would be a circular brooch bearing a "right hand with three fingers raised against Olumo Rock" and the inscription "Abeokuta Ladies Club—Service."[100]

The list of resolutions passed by the ALC in March 1946 contained most of the issues raised during their February meeting as well as two additional planks:

> There should be no increase of six pence on the taxation paid by women, as the majority of women in Abeokuta are very poor and can hardly afford what they are now paying. . . . There should

be free trade between Egba people and all other provinces, and that there should be no restriction as to what should be taken from one place to another except such restrictions is dictated by national necessities which must be determined by the judgment of the majority.[101]

The final list of resolutions submitted to the alake, the resident, and the literate members of the Egba Council clearly reflected the interest of poor women generally as well as market women, for they were the ones most affected by the continued restrictions on the movement of food after the war. Its political tone was equally self-evident, for the final plank sought to define national interest as limited to Nigeria and not the empire and stated that those interests could only be determined by majority rule. Originally imagined as a reformist document, the final list of resolutions included a radical thread.

A critical shift had occurred between the time of the original discussion and the creation of the final set of resolutions. The draft list of resolutions focused largely on social and environmental improvement. It mirrored the reformist agendas of elite women's organizations in Lagos. Nonetheless, as Abosede George reminds us, we cannot discount the activism expressed by these organizations because they demonstrated elite women's understanding of themselves as historical actors and creators of modernity. These women did not imagine themselves as disempowered colonial subjects. Instead, they assumed the right and the duty of their economic, social, and cultural privilege to participate in discussions about the quality of life in their community.[102] Whereas elite women's organizations in Lagos remained separate and distinct from market women's associations, the two types of associations formed a political and social alliance in Abeokuta.[103]

The sense of cultural privilege intimated in the ALC desire to raise the standard of womanhood did not stand in the way of creating a political alliance. Market women pursued an alliance because they, too, shared a desire to improve their livelihood and their condition in this evolving social and economic landscape. This was most clearly reflected in the importance they attached to literacy. The first thirty minutes of meetings were devoted to reading lessons.[104] Market women understood and valued the importance of literacy in trying to affect policy changes that impacted their livelihoods. In the 1930s, adire traders hired lawyers to represent them when they fought to overturn the bans on the use of caustic soda and synthetic dyes. The alliance with the ALC offered a new model for acquiring the political skills of literacy, for not only did these literate women advocate on their behalf—they democratized access to literacy. The ALC minutes illustrate the intentionality of this alliance-building. The minutes of the meeting on April 12, 1946, noted that the ALC would meet with all the *iya egbes* (leaders of women's organizations) on April 16 to make final arrangements for a social event—Women's Social Day. The program for Women's Social Day called for visits to the patrons of the club, including the alake and senior chiefs. However, the minutes from April 24, 1946, noted that the social day was postponed in part because women had to attend to court cases. In addition, the Egba Council planned to discuss the ALC's list of resolutions the following day, and all members needed to attend. The event eventually happened on July 5.[105]

By the time the heads of the market women's associations and the ALC met with the alake in October 1946 to discuss their petition against the increase in the special assessment, they were building on months of collaboration. The alake's lecture and "blame-the-victim" strategy unintentionally deepened the women's appreciation of Funmilayo Ransome-Kuti's advocacy on their behalf at home and abroad. She used her time in London with the NCNC delegation to highlight the plight of Nigerian women. The increasing estrangement between the alake and the majority of women in Abeokuta reached a new low following the publication of Ransome-Kuti's article in the *Daily Worker.* In the article titled "We Had Equality till Britain Came," she argued:

> With the advent of British rule, slavery was abolished, and Christianity introduced into many parts of the country, but instead of the women being educated and assisted to live like human beings their conditions deteriorated. The women of Nigeria are poverty-stricken, disease ridden, superstitious and badly nourished, although they are the main producers of their country's wealth. . . . Taxation of women is unknown in the Colony and Protectorate of Nigeria, with the singular exception of the Abeokuta and Ijebu Provinces of Western Nigeria. Here poll tax and income tax are forcibly demanded of women. The method of collecting and assessing taxes is abominable. Young girls are sometimes stripped naked in the street by the men officially designated collectors in order to ascertain whether they are mature enough to pay tax or not. Income tax is assessed arbitrarily. The members of the assessment committee work on commission basis: the more money they are able to collect, the greater their

commission, so they relentless extort money from those who can ill-afford to pay.[106]

Ransome-Kuti's scathing criticism as well as the publication of the article in England greatly embarrassed the colonial government. By the time she returned to Nigeria, a firestorm had erupted. Commentators in the Nigerian press condemned her position, while the alake and council held an extraordinary meeting on September 11, 1947, to discuss the allegations in the article. It was clear that Ransome-Kuti had hit a raw nerve, not only in Abeokuta but across Yorubaland. The alake noted that the paramount kings of Ife, Oyo, and Ijebu—the *oni*, the *alafin*, and the *awujale*, respectively—all had repudiated her assertions and claimed that in their provinces women were better off than men. The alake invited a small group of women to the council meeting who also expressed strong condemnation of Ransome-Kuti's article, especially her commentary on Jane McCotter, who had run the Child Welfare Center since 1929:

> Maternity and Child Welfare Services are still in their experimental stages where they exist at all. Child Welfare Centers are very few, poorly staffed and ill-organized. In one of the child welfare centres in Abeokuta . . . an old nurse, about 80 years of age, is in charge, with a few un-trained girls, straight from school to help her, without the help of a qualified medical practitioner. She is a Britisher of the type of Florence Nightingale or Mary Slessor. She prefers to die in Nigeria among the people she loves so well.[107]

The council voted unanimously to demand that Ransome-Kuti write a letter of apology to McCotter because she had allegedly diminished the important work performed by her and the 117 nurses and midwives she had trained. The alake's assertion that "the women today are prosperous" and the council's unanimous condemnation of Ransome-Kuti's allegations reflected the council's determined unwillingness to pay attention to the realities of women's lives in Abeokuta. Moreover, council members seemed to be most upset that Ransome-Kuti's statements suggested that Abeokuta as going backward instead of forward even though they grudgingly acknowledged that the health care Nurse McCotter provided was inadequate for its population.[108]

Determined to erase the sting of Ransome-Kuti's criticism, the alake and council recognized McCotter's contribution to women's health care at the next meeting, on October 30. McCotter and twelve of her trainees were invited to the meeting where the alake presented the trainees with their certificates for passing the Midwives Board Examination. Given an opportunity to address the council, McCotter discussed the success of the welfare centers. She had begun with one in Ijemo and noted that now there were two more in the town and eight in the districts, serving 1,450 women each day. To demonstrate the citizens' gratitude, the alake gave her a Yoruba name, Iya Olomowewe — Mother of Little Children.[109]

In response to the attacks on Ransome-Kuti, the AWU organized a welcome celebration when she returned to Abeokuta. It also passed a resolution that was sent to the authorities and the press. The resolution noted that over three thousand women had met on September 13, 1947, to affirm their support of Ransome-Kuti's article and implored her "to continue her good work for us as unto God and not unto men." They also challenged the women the alake had invited to the council meeting because they were not authorized to speak on the AWU's behalf.[110] The resolution and celebration accomplished two goals: these actions publicly refuted the alake's opinion of Ransome-Kuti's article, at the same time that this coalition of elite and market women acknowledged Ransome-Kuti as the person who spoke for the majority of women in Abeokuta and with their blessing.

At the end of World War II, Britain faced dire conditions. It was in debt, and it had to rebuild its manufacturing capacity as well as its political and financial capital, London. Political leaders and colonial officials took for granted that the empire would contribute to these objectives. Instead they confronted colonial subjects for whom the war was much more than an effort to assist the "mother country." The war helped crystalize new political organizations and identities built upon a nationalism coterminous with the colonial state. These new political organizations did not emerge fully formed or from the minds of nationalist leaders only. The NCNC reflected a multiplicity of organizations that came under its umbrella from different social, economic, and geographical locations. Furthermore, its delegates tried to reach the vast political constituency beneath the political authority of the chiefs and native authorities. In letters to newspapers, petitions, and resolutions, advocates demanded government attention to their grievances on the basis that they were taxpayers. They equated their taxpayer status and its entitlements to that of imperial citizens, not disenfranchised colonial subjects. Moreover, the war prioritized questions of democracy and sovereignty. Thus, as Nigerians invoked their status as taxpayers, they insisted that it also included the right to elect their rulers and determine their own economic and political priorities.

The ways in which critics claimed the mantle of taxpayer reflected a significant difference in the way in which colonial officials and Nigerians conceived of the status. In his study of rural society in the Belgian Congo, Osumaka Likaka argues that Belgian officials perceived the African taxpayer as an administrative category, specifically a healthy adult male who was a unit of labor and taxation.[111] British officials shared similar ideas. As we saw in chapter 1, they explained taxation as part of Africans' tutorial in civilization and a central part of revenue generation. They imposed this category assuming that Africans would appreciate its value without investing it with meaning or folding it into their political discourse. These invocations of citizenship and its entitlements and responsibilities were not unique to Nigeria. As Frederick Cooper demonstrated, similar political associations came to the foreground in France's African colonies as well.

As earlier chapters have shown, the citizens of Abeokuta participated in every phase of nationalist development in Nigeria. However, the postwar period is distinctive in that the austerity measures intended to rebuild Britain and the empire ultimately created the conditions that compelled women in Abeokuta to organize and challenge the faces and practice of colonialism locally and to assume a voice in the new narrative of a nation—Nigeria. The idea of Abeokuta as one constituency in the larger nation of Nigeria had taken root almost imperceptibly. When chiefs spoke out against the NCNC delegation's visit to Abeokuta, their concern focused on what they perceived to be the group's attempt to circumvent the alake and the council. They were not reconstructing the vision of an independent Abeokuta separate from Nigeria. By the postwar period, many understood Abeokuta as belonging to a Nigerian nation and that nation equal to Britain. Several factors contributed to this shift in perception: the mobilization of communities across the country to support the war, the spread of radio, the recruitment of soldiers from across the country, and the NCNC nationwide tour. The alake, who spoke so glowing of the desire for Egba independence during the centenary celebrations, closed out 1947 championing Nigerian independence. In a speech at the end of year, the alake noted,

> Yet another year is drawing to a close and I have been given the privilege once again to be at the microphone to convey to you my heartfelt congratulations on being spared to stand at the threshold of the year 1948. . . . To every one I say we have work to do for the nation—work in Council, in Committee, in the House of Assembly or the Central Parliament until we reach our goal which is the unity of tribes, and that of Nigeria as a single unit of Independence in the Commonwealth.[112]

6 ⌁ Daughters of Tinubu
Crisis and Confrontation in Abeokuta

JAMES C. SCOTT argues that modern states require more legibility of its subjects, terrain, and resources than premodern states. Consequently, they invest in surveys, maps, and censuses to create an inventory of land, people, incomes, occupations, and resources.[1] While these tools enable the legibility necessary to see its human and material resources, the state's vision is nonetheless narrow, for it ultimately captures "observations of aspects of social life that are of official interest."[2] Scott's formulation is extremely helpful for analyzing the Abeokuta tax revolt. What did colonial officials "see" as they confronted thousands of women parading through the streets or surrounding the alake's palace? It is equally important to ask the same question of the Abeokuta Women's Union as well as the Alake Ademola and the Egba Central Council. The escalating tension between these three groups suggests that each defined and diagnosed the problem in different ways. While there was consensus that a crisis had unfolded in Abeokuta, we cannot assume that each group understood "crisis" in the same way, for "crisis," as Janet Roitman argues, is a way to narrate history and to make a moral demand for a difference between the past and the future.[3] This chapter interrogates what the word meant for the colonial state, the alake and his council, and the AWU and contrasts their competing historical narratives of the crisis.

It mines official documents such as annual reports and minutes of council meetings as well as journals, newspapers, memoirs, biographies, and correspondence to capture the voices of these contending parties in the moment. The chapter also tries to paint the building tension in order to convey the sense of eminent danger that led one observer, the Reverend

FIGURE 6.1. Statue of Madam Tinubu, Ita-Iyalode, Owu, Abeokuta. (Photo by Joseph Ayodokun, 2014.)

G. A. Oke, to compare the events of 1948 to the Dahomean invasion of 1864. The good reverend was not alone, for even the resident, John Blair, who took over in April 1948, feared that Abeokuta was on the verge of another Adubi War, the 1918 tax revolt. Their references to past moments of cataclysmic disruption or threat alerts us to the real sense of fear that pervaded the town.

The chapter also explores the centrality of Madam Tinubu, who became a national hero in the wake of her support during the 1864 Dahomean invasion, to the symbolic landscape of the women's tax revolt. Drawing on the insights of Wale Adebanwi, it considers the ways in which Tinubu exemplified how the dead can be used symbolically for political mobilization and be made to contribute to collective integrity and group solidarity.[4] As this chapter moves through these layers of narration and symbolism, it documents the importance of this tax revolt to the anticolonial struggle as well as the larger nationalist project. As these women critiqued the colonial state and its agents, they also helped to define the contours of the emerging postcolonial state.

ENVISIONING THE CRISIS

The 1948 annual report of the senior district officer, J. M. Beeley, provided a brief overview of the events that together created the sense of dread that enveloped the town. The overview was produced by a cadet, F. Ratcliffe, and incorporated into Beeley's report:

> Political opposition to the sole rule of the Alake which had started as far back as 1927, had grown during 1947 into a formidable campaign. In the middle of 1947, Mrs Kuti had started an agitation for the abolition of poll tax on women and this campaign appears to receive an ever growing measure of support from all classes. She had founded her Egba Women's Union and her husband . . . presided over the strongest political party in Egbaland, called the Majeobaje [Let Us Improve It] Society.[5] The Majeobaje Society gave general support to Mrs Kuti's campaign. Grave allegations of corruption were leveled against the Alake and demands were made for a more efficient and democratic administration. The abolition of women's poll tax was made the first demand and the main plank on the political platform of the opposition parties. But even during 1947 demands were made that the Alake should abandon his status as Sole Native Authority and should act on the guidance of his council. During November and December, 1947, there were unruly and unlawful demonstrations in the town, and 1948 commenced in a highly strained political atmosphere. In February, and again in April, there were major demonstrations by the Egba women, in the first instance, outside the Afin, in an attempt to bring pressure upon the Alake, and in the second, throughout the town generally when Mrs Kuti was summoned for non-payment of income tax. In April, 1948 there was a probability of a major demonstration

by the women's union and the Majeobaje Society outside the Magistrate's court and the Prison when Mrs Kuti's income tax case was due to be heard. This crisis however passed off without serious incident because, at the last moment, Mrs Kuti's tax was paid by some person unknown.[6]

Ratcliffe's overview framed the conflict largely as a political struggle between the alake and the Ransome-Kutis. While he acknowledged the critique of the alake's dominant position as sole native authority, he discounted taxation by characterizing it as a campaign issue on which the Ransome-Kutis settled and then used to create their respective organizations. Absent from his overview is an appreciation of the organic groundswell that put the issue of women's taxation on the agenda. The Ransome-Kutis helped articulate and direct that groundswell into organizations that could ameliorate the women's immediate economic distress and work toward long-term political solutions—democracy and independence. Ratcliffe's schematic overview did not convey the deep interlocking relationship between democracy and taxation that lay at the core of the protests.

Before the first major protest in November, discussion about ending taxation for women had been circulating throughout Abeokuta. Funmilayo Ransome-Kuti pushed the discussion further by refusing to pay taxes in April 1947, and her case ended up in court. On the day of the trial, five thousand women demonstrated at the courthouse to support her. She was found guilty and given the choice of a £3 fine or one month's imprisonment. In order to participate in the NCNC trip to England, she paid the fine.[7]

Commentators used the newspapers to weigh in on the debate. In a letter to the editor of the *Egba Bulletin* in June 1947, Detunji Dedeke addressed the rumors that women may seek an exemption from income tax. He noted that women in the districts were contemplating contributing to the antitax campaign, but he felt that "the illiterate women who are the majority in the camp of Mrs. Kuti must have mis-interpreted her." Though he did not condemn Ransome-Kuti—he in fact praised her "laudable efforts among the Egba women to educate them in the right way"— Deleke argued that it would be "both an impossibility and ruinous to the Egba Native Administration for the women to be exempted entirely from tax payment."[8] Moreover, he claimed that the majority of Egba women were financially healthier than Egba men. He suggested that "90% of the women have something to do to gain their living, whereas 40% of the men in Abeokuta are parasites and jobless folks with little or no income, and yet of necessity they must pay income tax double that of the women." He then offered estimates of women's incomes, though never revealing the sources of his evidence. He suggested that the poorest women in the districts earned eight shillings per week, while wives of farmers with economic trees—for example, palm and cocoa—earned about ten to twelve shillings per week, or about £20 per year. The wealthiest women in the rural areas were those traders selling cloth, enamel basins, and hardware and who made the rounds of approximately eight markets and earned about £24 per year. He offered calculations for women in the town as well. The poorest—carriers, importers of foodstuffs, hawkers—earned about eight shillings per week; the second group, venders of food and cooking ingredients, earned about £26 per year; while the wealthiest group—dealers in quantity of adire clothes, hardware, exporters of palm oil, and direct dealers with European firms—were worth from £100 to £200 per year.[9]

To further strengthen his argument, Dedeke provided estimates of men's incomes. The poorest men, who did not own but rented land to farm, may have no income for six to fifteen months but still had to pay seven shillings in taxes. Middle-rank farmers—about 20 percent of farmers, who owned land with economic trees, cassava, and rice—have an income of roughly £24, but £20 went to feeding their families. Big farmers, who only made up about 5 percent, had incomes from £50 to £200. Finally, the population of women exceeded that of men. He questioned how the revenue would be replaced if women did not pay income tax. He also argued that the rural districts paid a greater share of the revenue but received fewer amenities—health care, transportation, schools—and fewer representatives on the council.

Dedeke's letter is revealing in a number of interesting ways. Tax reports supported his contention that Abeokuta's gender ratio skewed toward women and that the rural districts produced a greater share of the revenue but received fewer amenities. His rather lengthy letter revolved around issues of fairness to men with heavy family obligations as well as heavier tax burdens, if financially solvent women were exempt from paying taxes. In constructing this scenario, he conflated elements of Yoruba and British gender ideology, for he championed Egba women's economic engagement while folding it into the model of the male breadwinner. Thus, he created an argument in which financially solvent women should be made to pay taxes to support the state as well as financially overburdened men caught between taxes and family obligations. In Dedeke's universe, women's social and economic responsibilities to their children were erased, and they were untouched by the larger economic crisis.

Minutes of Egba Central Council meetings illustrate similar ideas among its members. During its meeting on June 6, 1947, its Assessment Committee discussed the question of women paying taxes, and the alake invited opinions from the full council during its meeting on June 26. The majority of members of the council strongly favored continued taxation on women. They argued that Egba women were as industrious as Egba men and had paid taxes from 1918 when they were first imposed. Council members refuted reports that Egba women were poor. However, several suggested that women should be given representation in the council "to enable them to have a voice in the Administration of the country and on matters affecting their general welfare." The alake noted that the council was open to women if any township would send female representatives, and it was in the process of resuscitating women's general chieftaincies, such as the iyalode of the Egbas, that had been vacant since Madam Jojolola died in 1932.[10] The council's discussion framed women once again as untouched by the broader economic crisis and lacking any economic obligations that would challenge their ability to pay taxes. As they refused to give women's claims any credibility, the alake and the council explored options to improve tax collection.

The alake noted with frustration in the October 30 council meeting that tax collection was not going well and, though he had delayed prosecuting defaulters for a month, that would end. The district officer also advised him to increase the fines and consider returning to the old practice of imposing fines on township heads when their people failed to pay their taxes on time.[11] The suggested restoration of more onerous collection strategies in part related to the financial crisis facing all native administrations in the colony. Native administrations were expected to become financially self-sufficient; however, this was unfolding at the same time that the colonial government planned to withdraw certain financial supports and the creation of the Western House of Assembly required contributions from all native administrations in the region. Financing the Western House of Assembly meant that in 1948 the Egba Native Administration would have to pay six pence per taxpayer. The ENA would also be responsible for paying the cost-of-living increases proposed by the Harragin Commission, for the government planned to stop paying cost-of-living increases granted to native administration employees.[12] Given the financial crisis facing the ENA, revisiting more coercive tax-collection strategies appeared reasonable in part because they had been successful in the past. The district officer, the alake, and council members justified their consideration of coercive methods because they began with the premise that taxpayers had money that they simply withheld from the government or did not understand their role as taxpayers. The district officer articulated these ideas:

> Nobody wished that anyone should be assessed above his income or pay more than he ought to pay but it was absolutely necessary that everybody should pay to the last penny what he ought to pay. . . . Many people thought that the flat rate tax was what everybody ought to pay and that only a very few of the richest people should have to pay anything more in the way of income tax. That was quite wrong. The flat rate tax was meant to be the very lowest rate of tax which was to be paid only by the very poorest people. Anybody who is richer than the very poorest should pay more in the form of income tax in proportion to his riches, even though he was only a very little richer.[13]

In this scenario no one was exempt from paying taxes, and only the destitute should pay the flat tax. For the district officer, those who supported the abolition of taxes on women or who paid the flat rate when they were not absolutely destitute were manufacturing an economic crisis that threatened the local native administration as well as the reforms of the postwar colonial state. Equally important, this scenario did not acknowledge the material conditions of those supporting the antitax campaign.

Even those who did not support the agitation against the alake, such as editorial writers of the *New Times of Nigeria*, acknowledged the depressed economic conditions of the town. The author of an editorial on March 10, 1948, blamed the inhabitants of Abeokuta of "resting on their oars." Nonetheless, he noted,

> Owing to a combination of circumstances, Abeokuta began to lose its pre-eminence. There was a slump in the produce trade, the Ijebu-Ibadan road was opened, and other Yoruba sons began to compete in the professions which in Nigeria gave honour and prestige, phenomenal rise of Ibadan, with her government offices, commercial houses and educational institutions has not only helped in the decline of Abeokuta, but serves also as an object which must make Egbas feel their present state with something near poignancy of defeat.[14]

Some of this economic picture is reflected in the Egba Division's annual report. Due to low rainfall, "yields on annual crops were disappointing." Weather also "prevented any large scale distribution of budded citrus trees and selected oil palm seedling." Cocoa, however, was not affected by the weather, and there was a slight increase in tonnage as well as an improvement in the quality.[15] Women traders who largely dealt in food crops would have been greatly affected by the low yields in annual crops. Yet colonial officials and the Egba Council maintained a conscious disconnect between economic conditions and taxes.

The rhetorical strategies used by officials in Abeokuta were identical to those used during the interwar depression and reflected a long-standing practice in which officials deliberately limited their vision by separating taxation from the cost of social reproduction.[16] In 1928, C. C. Adeniyi-Jones, a member of the Nigerian Legislative Council, gave an address to the West African Students' Union in London in which he critiqued the Income Tax Ordinance and the Native Revenue Ordinance imposed on Lagos Colony in 1927. Adeniyi-Jones questioned the real purpose of the income tax since it was intended to raise £50,000, yet most of it, £33,000, would go toward the maintenance of the European staff, and only £17,000 would go into the Treasury. He also charged that the ordinance did not make any distinction between

> "gross income," "statutory income," "earned income," and "taxable income"; nor . . . [make] any allowances for wife and number of children in the family. All that it does is merely to deduct from the gross income the expenses of earning the income, and then assess the above. And what is more, the limit of exemption is placed so low as to cover only those earning the starvation wage of under £30 per annum; although £100 is the lowest limit a man may earn which will entitle him, if he is of sound mind to enjoy the privilege of the franchise.[17]

Adeniyi-Jones was incensed that these ordinances were imposed at a time of high unemployment, did not make allowances for social reproduction, and enmeshed the vast majority of men who lacked representation, for they did not meet the financial bar to qualify to vote.[18]

The rhetorical strategy of disconnecting taxation from the cost of social reproduction was evident in the postwar period as well. The strategy had added benefits, for it also allowed colonial officials to discount the women's complaints about the alake's role in the economy. The alake was a wealthy individual. He had substantial land holdings and owned buildings in Abeokuta as well in Marina, the main commercial district in Lagos.[19] His salary reached £6,000 by the 1940s; however, the alake confided to Resident Blair that "his official salary was only a small part of his real income. A much larger part came from the 'dashes' (or presents) that Yoruba custom demanded should be given to any chief or person in authority by anyone who came before him with a request. What came from his many business ventures I have no idea but it was reported to be a great deal."[20] It was precisely those business dealings that generated the greatest complaints. In a memorandum submitted to Resident Blair in May 1948, the AWU characterized the alake as a voracious trader. They charged that he traded with all the firms in almost every line of their goods, business that he conducted under different names and by way of a network of people selling on his behalf. That network included his wives, who were pressured into selling his goods. The memo itemized a long list of misdeeds in connection with a range of goods: salt, caustic soda, indigo dye, gari, rice, and illicit gin. He stood accused of taking people's properties at very low prices. Moreover, he was a very avid moneylender, and as a result many of the houses in Abeokuta belonged to him. Beyond the charges of misdeeds, the AWU argued that he used his prerogative as a king to dominate in trade and compete unfairly with women in the markets, even though he was not economically reliant on trade because he received a salary as the head of a government organized on modern lines.[21] In the AWU's estimation, the alake's economic activities were in the pursuit of individual wealth, which disturbed women's efforts at economic survival.

PROTEST UNLEASHED

On Saturday, November 29, 1947, the AWU launched a protest at the Afin following its regular meeting. Wole Soyinka beautifully captured the dramatic tension of that protest in his memoir Aké. He reports that during the AWU meeting, an old woman relayed the distressing story of barely surviving as she, her thirteen grandchildren, and her late son's wives continued to cultivate her late son's farm and use the proceeds to pay for the children's schooling. The Assessment Committee had imposed a special assessment on her because she had a large farm, "but they say nothing about the thirteen children and four women who depend on the farm for gari, no."[22] Although the women's decision to go to the palace appeared to be a spontaneous act in response to the elderly woman's story, it was largely a response to the local government's refusal to take into account women's social and economic circumstances as it created the tax bill and the futility of the women's efforts to appeal through the proper channels. Soyinka tells us that the women "rose in a body. Hands flew to heads and off came the head-ties, unfurling in the air like hundreds of banners."[23]

When the women arrived at the palace demanding immediate abolition of the payment of tax by women, the alake told them that he was not
"prepared to deal with any matter in the face of such a demonstration."
If anybody had any complaints, they should present them to the council,
and the complaint would be discussed at the next council meeting. The
women would not accept Ademola's attempt to dismiss them, and he was
forced to address them a second time.[24] Soyinka suggests that the alake
tried to reason with the women by noting both the need for revenue and
his inability to make such an important decision by himself. Despite his
efforts, the women insisted that he, not the council, was the government,
and therefore he could make the decision to end the situation. Tensions in
the Afin grew as both Funmilayo Ransome-Kuti and the district officer arrived. Women levied insults at the district officer, who ultimately shouted
to Ransome-Kuti, "Shut up your women!" To which she replied, "You may
have been born, you were not bred. Could you speak to your mother like
that?" Several women who heard this exchange called on the alake to "get
rid of the insolent white man at once, within minutes. If he was not out,
they would come in, cut off his genitals and post them to this mother."[25]
The threat to emasculate a colonial official may not have been made in
earnest, but it reflected a critical shift in the tenor of the discussion and the
mood of the women in attendance.

The tension did not lessen as ogboni chiefs filtered into the palace
courtyard. The balogun of the Egbas ordered the women to go home,
mind their kitchens, and feed their children because they knew nothing about running state affairs. As he moved to demonstrate the kick he
claimed they needed in their rump, his leg gave out, and he collapsed on
the spot. He had to be carried away by his retainers. The women then set
upon the other ogboni chiefs, stripping them of their wrappers and symbols of power—shawls, fans, office staffs, caps—and used the items to
beat them. The chiefs were forced to flee into the palace or back home
in their underpants. In a final insult to the powerful ogboni, the women
usurped the chiefs' symbolic power by declaring that they were going to
perform oro.

> Oro o, a fe s'oro
> Oro o, a fe s'oro
> E ti'lekun mo'kunrin
> A fe s'oro
> (Òrò-o, we are about to perform òrò. Lock up all the
> men, we are bringing out òrò.)[26]

In the precolonial era, ogboni chiefs exercised tremendous political power. Their enforcer, the human manifestation of the spirit Oro, could impose curfews, sanction those accused of witchcraft and execute criminals. Oro, symbolically represented the collective male dead, thus its appearance reinforced male authority. As we saw in chapter 1, whenever it was announced that Oro would be out on the streets, women had to go indoors and stay away from windows and doorways, for any women who looked at Oro would be killed. The cultural significance of stripping ogboni chiefs of their clothes, performing oro and calling for men to be locked up cannot be underestimated, for this symbolized an overthrow of male privilege and chiefly authority.[27]

The women decided to occupy the palace grounds until their demands were satisfied. The decision was conveyed throughout the town and the districts, markets were closed, and thousands of women converged on the palace. Some brought food and water, fires were lit, and the women settled in. Possibly due to the excitement of the day, one woman went into labor, and before she could be taken to a hospital or clinic, her baby—a girl—arrived. Soyinka suggests that the mood transformed over the course of the day and that by the time the baby arrived, the gathering was festive. They sang outwardly religious songs inspired by orisa, Islam, or Christianity.[28] Reports on the number of women present differed considerably. The newspapers estimated ten thousand, while the *Egba Bulletin* estimated fifteen hundred to two thousand.[29] Even the *Bulletin*'s lower estimate still acknowledges that a sizeable group of women from across the town and districts mutually agreed that the time to be heard had arrived.

On the following day, twelve representatives from the AWU, including Ransome-Kuti and Soyinka's mother, Eniola, met with the Egba Council to discuss the protest. The minutes of this meeting are especially helpful for they reveal the women's narration of the crisis. They identified three critical factors: the unresponsiveness of the alake and colonial officials, Abeokuta women's indebtedness and impoverishment, and the arbitrary nature of the tax structure. They noted, for example, that a year had passed since they had forwarded a petition about taxation to the alake, the resident, and the chief commissioner for the western provinces. Furthermore, they accused the council of treating their petition with contempt. Ransome-Kuti elaborated on the bureaucratic runaround that many women experienced when they sought redress:

> Whenever they had any complaint and had come to the Alake
> he would tell them to go to the township collectors, when they

got to the township collectors they would tell them to go and see the Alake, the Assessment Committee would also tell them to go to the Alake. In the long run the complainants would be sued without finding any responsible person before whom they could obtain redress for their grievances. If they appeared before the Tax Court and wished to state their complaints the president would tell them his duty was not to hear complaints but to try the defaulters for failing to pay their tax. He would also tell them that if they any complaint they should go to the Alake.[30]

Given that all roads for redress led back to the alake, it was not unreasonable for the women to insist that only the alake could address their grievances.

While the bureaucratic shell game was distressing, the depressed economic conditions and the arbitrary nature of the tax structure had the women "groaning in poverty," as Eniola Soyinka argued.[31] Traders were selling goods at a loss in the market, and many had taken out loans and were heavily in debt. Nonetheless, Madam Ogunye of Kemta stated that "she was annually being specially assessed on increasing scale and every year she had appealed to the Alake. If reduction was made in one year in the next year the assessment would be increased by about a £ [one pound]."[32] Moreover, the women charged that tax collectors earned a commission on the amount they collected.[33] They reported it was common for collectors in the rural districts to demand 3s. 1d. from each woman before issuing the tax receipt, suggesting that women paid this sum in addition to their tax. The women noted that they were also subjected to arbitrary monetary demands from the police for birth certificates. Birth certificates were supposed to be free, and families were constantly encouraged to register births, but when rural women, in particular, tried to obtain birth certificates, the police charged them one shilling per year of the child's age.[34] The ENA refuted the charge that tax collectors received commissions. In a letter to the editor of the *Daily Service*, ENA secretary C. A. A. Titcombe explained that the administration did not pay commission on taxes collected by the Assessment Committee; however, due to the distances they traveled, they received an allowance.[35] His carefully crafted letter did not discount the possibility that tax collectors operated independently of the law.

Many chiefs claimed to be unaware of the women's grievances. However, they promised to consider them carefully, and the women agreed to leave the Afin and be patient. In spite of the promise, the alake and council members did not inform the women that a tax increase was already planned for the next year. On November 29, while the women protested outside the palace, the alake and council were meeting to discuss tax collection. Tax collection in the town was disappointing compared to that in the districts, so the alake urged the chiefs and councillors to "comb up their respective townships for defaulters."[36] In addition, he promised to have bell ringers remind people to carry their tax receipts with them when going about. He informed the council that in the "next year there would be an increase in tax for men and women, and in the Forestry, Court and Slaughter fees. The increase was necessary not only because of the increased salaries to employees of the Administration but also for general development and maintenance. Councillors' salaries would be slightly increased."[37] The tenor of the discussion reflected the state's determination to view taxation as simply a matter of extracting money from the town's inhabitants. A chief from Ake quarter, the *base*, suggested that "defaulters as well as the evaders should be prosecuted whenever they could be found. The period of collection should be extended to six months, and collectors should be paid salaries as in Lagos. There should be no respect of person in enforcing the law and collectors should be backed up by the Authorities."[38]

On December 2, the council members met to strategize for their meeting with the women the next day. They unanimously reaffirmed their support for the alake, with Titcombe declaring that "the Alake was an embodiment of true democracy."[39] They also agreed that financially the administration could not afford to abolish taxes on women, but they disagreed on how to handle the women. Some suggested pacifying them by deception—for example, telling the women that their grievances would be addressed in the next two months or would be considered against the next year's tax.[40] They debated the forces behind the protests, for "women never started trouble on their own." One council member suggested the men engineered it. Another thought the alake had offended the Ransome-Kutis, and they were "looking for a chance to wreak vengeance on him." A third member suggested it must have been connected to Ransome-Kuti's trip to the United Kingdom because before she went she "never opposed payment of tax by women."[41] They recounted the stories of individual women whose special assessment had been reduced by the alake, such as Eniola Soyinka and Madam Ogunye, who had over £1,000 worth of goods in her shop, yet both had participated in the protest.

Council members were also perplexed by the large number of men who supported the protests as well as the role of "wives of clergymen and teachers," and they devoted a substantial part of their discussion to gender relations. The otun of the Egbas stated that "a man must not allow a woman or child to frighten him" and reinforced his point by adding, "*Obirin ko ni oro*" (Women do not have oro); therefore they cannot frighten men. One member lamented that husbands could not control their wives because their wives were richer demonstrated by the fact that they had multistory houses "built upstairs . . . [and] many had to feed their husbands." But council members fully recognized that their political authority was also being challenged and they had to respond because "the authority of women cannot be made to override the authority of their own."[42] These statements make clear that the AWU had upset the political and cultural universe in Abeokuta. For the alake and chiefs, the protests represented an upheaval of gender relations that was as significant as the threat to their political authority. Reminding each other that the women did not have oro reaffirmed male privilege and chiefly authority.

The council's discussion is also revealing for its silences. Only one member brought up economic conditions. The balogun of Itoku noted that before the war his own trade was valued at £1,000; however, he experienced great losses due to conditional sales. Councillors also gave short shrift to how assessment occurred. It appears that assessors did not have a systematic way of determining the incomes of those who were not salaried workers. One of their oldest strategies was to look for visible signs of expenditure. In an Assessment Committee meeting a decade earlier, it was pointed out "in a place like Abeokuta unless people built storey-houses [multilevel dwellings] or used their money in doing some great thing thereby people could assess their financial strength, it was difficult to know who was rich."[43] In addition to paying attention to those who had big houses, the Assessment Committee gathered information from the large trading companies about women who held accounts with them. They also gathered information about those who should be exempt from township collectors and chiefs, who in theory knew the specific conditions of those in their communities. There was no discussion about how they gathered income data for the vast majority of people who did not have accounts with the trading companies or multilevel homes. In addition, there was no discussion about the tax collectors. Since collectors did not receive salaries, they had incentive to demand taxes from people regardless of their ability to pay.[44] The greatest silence revolved around the groups that did not pay taxes—European, Syrian, or African businesses based in Abeokuta. At no point was the question of imposing taxes on firms ever considered, though the question would be raised eventually in the Western House of Assembly by Egbas based in Lagos and by the AWU.[45]

During the meeting with the AWU the following day, it was clear that the council and the women were talking past each other. The women's representatives reiterated the role that the lack of jobs and trade played in the unrest around taxes. Both Funmilayo Ransome-Kuti and Eniola Soyinka clarified their positions on taxation, insisting that they were not opposed to income tax. They opposed the flat tax precisely because it asked the poorest people to pay taxes. The council, on the other hand, gave the women a detailed report on tax collection and reaffirmed that the town's administration and infrastructure could not continue if women did not pay taxes. The meeting ended with the council promising to suspend taxation on women pending further investigation, and the women agreeing to be patient while ignorant of the fact that taxes would be increased again in 1948 to five shillings for women and ten shillings for men.[46]

The brief calm that followed the meeting on December 3 would be overtaken by the decision to prosecute and imprison seven women who had not paid their taxes. A week later, on December 8, women lay siege to the palace again when the alake informed them that he could not release the women. Police prevented the large crowd from entering the Afin, so it gathered outside where it sang abusive songs to the alake as well as funeral dirges and spent the night. The following morning, small groups of supporters wandered throughout the town, and there were reports of vandalism. The windows of the house belonging to the wealthy merchant and alake supporter Janet Ashabi were smashed.[47] Supporters of the AWU assaulted people in the "public streets by stripping them into nakedness and ridiculing them."[48] Some opponents were also beaten. Chief E. B. Sorunke, a former member of the Majeobaje, recalled a set of young male supporters whom he characterized as thugs, for they attacked "not only Ogboni . . . all Egba chiefs, stoning and damaging their property."[49] Ministers of several churches complained about the "obscene language of the dancing women about the town in connection with the Women's Demonstration."[50] Nonetheless, they did not condemn the women protesters or the men's mass meeting that Reverend Ransome-Kuti organized on December 10 at Sapon market in support of the women. The ministers of the Protestant churches passed a resolution condemning the ways in which the *Nigerian Daily Times* characterized the men's meeting—mob demonstration, a rabble—and encouraged the alake and council to address the women's grievances "sympathetically and arrive at a peaceful settlement as early as possible."[51]

The women finally left the Afin on December 10 when all those who were arrested on tax evasion were released. However, this protest proved even more unsettling to the town's power structure. In council discussions, the alake branded Funmilayo Ransome-Kuti's behavior deplorable and the protests unprecedented and argued "that in olden days no woman who had caused such an incident could have escaped without forfeiting her life, but they were Christians."[52] Since the officials could not kill Ransome-Kuti, they tried to rein her in as well as the AWU. She was banned from the Afin, and they promulgated orders to restrict gatherings. For example, one order claimed that it went against custom for ordinary individuals to ring bells to summon others to political meetings. Another order specified that "any procession of more than 10 persons formed before during or after this meeting and any public meeting of more than 10 persons would be illegal" without written permission of the alake or his representative.[53] The alake also tried to get in front of the opposition by announcing plans to appoint two women councillors as members of the Egba Central Council to serve the 1948–51 term. One would represent Egba Alake (the town's quarter where the Afin was located), and the other would rotate among the other three quarters.[54]

Despite efforts to limit the size of gatherings, over a thousand women met on December 27. Funmilayo Ransome-Kuti thanked the women for their unity and emphasized that they did not commit a wrong in taking their grievances to the alake. Nonetheless, she laid out guidelines for future marches. For example, she advised against carrying a cudgel or anything that could be construed as a weapon, for it could incur the use of tear gas. She also declared that singing abusive songs or taking people's goods were forbidden by the union. Ultimately, she said, these activities detracted from "the greater task in front of them." Ransome-Kuti repeated the organization's main position—abolition of tax on women, specifically the flat tax, and a special assessment on women with an income of £200 per year. She rallied the women, insisting there were "many ways of demonstration" and that what they had done was "only one of them and only a start." Ransome-Kuti essentially declared that the efforts to intimidate and dismiss the women's grievances would not work.[55]

The year 1948 began very tense and strained. Things blew up again in February, when the alake invited representatives from the AWU to attend a meeting in the Afin but stipulated that Ransome-Kuti could not attend. Although she went to the Afin with the group, the alake refused to allow her inside because she had not offered an apology for the previous year's demonstration. An altercation subsequently developed between the members of the AWU, Ransome-Kuti, the district officer, and the resident. The women blocked the exits so that the district officer and resident could not leave the palace grounds, and it was reported that Ransome-Kuti held on to "the steering wheel of the D.O.'s car until he pried her hand loose."[56]

In spite of Resident Mylius's threat to prosecute the leaders of the protests, the women's campaign continued.[57] They tried to circumvent the restrictions on demonstrations by calling them picnics or festivals, they continued to write letters to the editors of newspapers as well as petitions to colonial authorities, and they amassed information about the alake's financial activities. During these gatherings they sometimes went to the grave site of Madam Tinubu "to invoke her spirit in support of the protest."[58] Ransome-Kuti refused to pay her tax again, initiating another court case and a fine. Rumors circulated that Ransome-Kuti did not intend to pay the fine because she wanted to be arrested. Once she was arrested, the AWU "would head a mass march to the Native Administration prison, rescue Mrs. Kuti and, some thought, carry her in triumph to the afin and dispose of the Alake."[59] It is not clear if the authorities tried to ascertain if there was any veracity to the rumors, but John Blair, who had recently returned to Abeokuta as resident, and the alake planned countermeasures. The alake wanted to reinforce the police or call out the troops. However, Blair vetoed these ideas, suggesting instead that someone pay her court fines anonymously because that would deescalate the situation and forestall another protest. He assumed the alake arranged for the payment of her fines, so that night (April 24) on a radio broadcast, Blair announced that Ransome-Kuti's fines had been paid.[60] The alake also appointed a committee to investigate the AWU's grievances, suspended the tax on women, agreed to women members on the Egba Central Council, and left town for a short vacation.[61]

Council minutes suggest that the alake's decision to act resulted in part from the broad base of support for the AWU. In a meeting on April 23, 1948, members of the council continued to reaffirm their support for the alake and declare over and over that the women had brought shame to Abeokuta. Rev. Adeola Delumo, a member of the council, reported that when he visited Kaduna and other parts of the country, he learned that Abeokuta had become notorious due to the actions of the women. As the council members lamented the shameful actions of the women, the alake pointed out that the protestors included their wives, children, and relatives. One member advised his colleagues to "go to their respective townships and sections to warn their wives and children to put a stop to going in the bad company of women who were demonstrating."[62] With their own family members in the streets, council members could not ignore the agitation, so they expressed ever greater support for the alake.

Resident Blair's return to Abeokuta following the retirement of Resident Mylius proved critical during this tense period. He introduced a complete about-face in administration policy as he invited representatives from both the AWU and the Majeobaje Society to meet with him. In his letter to the alake informing him of the meetings, Blair outlined the two goals confronting them:

(a)   That you, as Native Authority, and I, as representing the Nigerian Government, should find out for sure what are the real underlying grievances which made it possible for an agitation to obtain a wide measure of support;

(b)   That our genuine desire to ascertain the real grievances, and to remedy them, shall be made so well-known by our actions that it cannot be denied by any ill-wisher.[63]

Blair tried to rewrite the script of the tax revolt by shifting the state's position from one of dismissal of the women's grievances to one of concern and acceptance.

The resident's new tone was also in line with a larger effort from London to be perceived as a kinder, gentler imperial power. On April 4, 1948, a parliamentary subcommittee of the Select Committee on Estimates headed by Sir Ralph Glyn visited Abeokuta and enjoyed lunch with the alake. According to Glyn, "It was the first time in the history of Parliament . . . that a select Committee of the House of Commons had visited a Colony." They had come to see what had been done for Nigeria with the money granted under the Colonial Development and Welfare Act. The committee's stated purpose did not square with the reality. The alake noted that nothing definite or appreciable had been done in Abeokuta, and Glyn concurred, stating,

> The Sub-Committee were well aware that the scheme under the Act had not gone forward as fast as they had hoped and that much disappointment had been caused. The reason was that there was a great shortage of materials and skilled men not only in Nigeria but throughout the British Empire, not least in the United Kingdom. The United Kingdom had suffered great losses in the war and was extremely short of steel and a great many other things as well. The Sub-Committee wanted to help him and other Africans to take their full share in the enormous tasks which needed to be done.[64]

Given the political upheaval in Abeokuta, this visit to see nothing had great symbolic meaning. It affirmed the government's support of the alake and signaled its intent to protect the postwar empire from the demands of radical nationalists. It also provided an opportunity for committee members to assess how Nigeria would be able to help rebuild the empire.

Two months after the visit of the parliamentary committee, the new governor, John Stuart Macpherson, and Lady Macpherson visited Abeokuta on June 2. In his speech to welcome the governor, the alake praised the long happy relationship the people of Abeokuta had enjoyed with the British. Ademola gave a fairly lengthy account of the development that his administration hoped to bring to Abeokuta with the support of Colonial Welfare and Development funds: expansion of electricity and water, roads, health and sanitation services (especially to the rural areas), and industrialization, such as expansion of the fruit juice industry and revitalization of adire production. He did not avoid the political protest; he acknowledged the upheaval in Abeokuta but attributed it to a misunderstanding of those in authority.[65]

In response, Macpherson offered important policy points. He affirmed the alake's position on economic development, noting that the colonial government had also decided to prioritize economic development over social expenditure. "Without economic development and a resulting increase in the national income—and in the taxable capacity of the country—we shall not be able to carry the cost of the social services that our people are entitled to demand." He noted that governments everywhere were playing a great role in the economic lives of their people, but he cautioned that they should not expect too much. The colonial government planned to concentrate its resources in "basic services and public utilities which are essential for economic development—light, water, power, transportation, telecommunications—and securing stable markets and prices for the country's exports." The government also planned to attract private enterprise through the Colonial Development Corporation, "which combines all that is best in Government and private enterprise." He suggested that Africans who participated in these enterprises would gain managerial and technical skills.[66] Macpherson's formula for economic development was in line with what became the dominant development model in the postwar era—industrialization by invitation. The governor clearly articulated the colonial government's support of the alake and cast him as the political authority who would oversee this process from Abeokuta.

THE END OF A SOLE NATIVE AUTHORITY

During the inauguration of the fourth session of the Egba Central Council on May 28, 1948, the alake declared that the disorders had died down and the committee he appointed to resolve the tax issue was hard at work.

He called attention to the fact that no women were nominated to sit on either the sectional or central councils, even though he had announced widely that he did not object to women candidates. He also offered the council a brief history lesson on the sole native authority system:

> A certain section of the populace placed undue emphasis on the power with which the Alake has been clothed from time immemorial as Sole Native Authority. That aspect of the power of the Alake is as old as Abeokuta or the foundation of Egbaland in the homesteads. Neither in war or peace has the Sole Authority of the Alake ever been challenged nor can a single instance of its misuse then or now be pointed at. But in the exercise of this prerogative care has been taken to use it as a last resort only. . . . The Sole Native Authority in Egbaland exists only in name — nothing is done without the advice of my Council.[67]

Ademola used the inauguration of this new council to rewrite the history of the alakeship and his tenure in the position. As we saw in the early chapters of this study, historically alakes were weak kings and often challenged by powerful military chiefs or merchants. The colonial government in Lagos created the conditions that allowed Ademola and his predecessor, Gbadebo I, to consolidate power over the other kings, wealthy chiefs, and power brokers. While extending the idea of an all-powerful alake back in time, Ademola also claimed to have been judicious in the use of this power and attributed a strong role to the council in the town's governance.

The resident also addressed the issue of sole native authority but offered a perspective that differed in tone and scope. For example, the resident did not give a preamble beginning with time immemorial. Instead he stated,

> The Alake is the Sole Native Authority and this Council is responsible for advising him as to the manner in which he should exercise his authority. I have the Alake's assurance that he will not exercise his authority contrary to the advice of this Council — and indeed in the past he has not done so — except for very weighty reasons and with the approval of the Governments. . . . I do not think it would be going too far to say that the advice of the Council would not be over-ruled unless it were contrary to natural justice and humanity or it affected Nigeria beyond the bounds of the Egba Division and was thus ultra vires.[68]

The resident's comments are riddled with ambivalence since he makes it clear that he would be operating on the alake's assurance going forward.

The resident spent most of his speech discussing the role of the council. He emphasized the council members' pivotal role between the government and their communities, which was to gather grievances and issues from the communities and relay them to the alake and the resident during council meetings "honestly and fearlessly." In addition, they were to report to their communities the council's discussions and decisions. In reiterating the responsibilities of the council members, Blair hoped to strengthen the council as an active participant within the structure of government and in relation to the alake. Blair also announced that he was engaged in meetings with different societies in the town, but he did not know "whether their words are the words of the Egba people or of themselves alone. Only from you, the elected members of this Council, can the opinions of the whole Egba people be learnt."[69] In short, the council was the only official voice of the people that colonial officials recognized. As he tried to build the confidence of the members of the council in order to reorient their relationship with the alake, Blair simultaneously reaffirmed the colonial government's distrust of educated elites such as the Ransome-Kutis and the state's determination to rely on bodies like this council, composed largely of members who held traditional chieftaincies.

Both the resident and the alake hoped that the momentary calm would hold indefinitely, and the alake went to Jos to help things cool down. Nonetheless, the situation continued to devolve as the AWU and their supporters expanded their demands to include an end of the sole native authority system. The system had been created through a series of ordinances that tried to define the relationship between the colonial state, indigenous authorities, and their communities. Olufemi Vaughn argues that as an important part of the vehicle for indirect rule, the sole native authority structure "disrupted the balance of power between political actors and local authorities." Prior to Abeokuta's absorption into the protectorate, Oyo Province provided one of the best examples of the ways in which indirect rule disrupted the local balances of power. Colonial officials expanded the territorial jurisdiction of the alafin of Oyo, essentially giving him power over communities that had asserted their independence in the nineteenth century as well as dominance over the Oyo Mesi, the council in Oyo's political structure, that operated as a check on monarchal power. In 1901, Sir William MacGregor, the governor of Lagos, revised the Native Council Ordinance, reducing the role of the British residents and augmenting that of the paramount chiefs. The resident would no longer serve as an executive on the governing council; his role became strictly advisory.[70] While the resident became an adviser, the alafin was appointed

a paramount ruler and executive president, cementing a "hierarchal struc-
ture of local administration under the authority of a traditional ruler." In
Oyo Province, this structure reached its zenith under Capt. William A.
Ross, who served as resident in Oyo from 1914 to 1931.[71]

When Abeokuta was brought into the protectorate, the alake was
designated a sole native authority. As we saw in chapter 2, the council
expanded in the 1920s and in 1926 established three-year terms. By the
end of the decade, the council had thirty members, including two literate chiefs who represented the Abeokuta Educated Elements, M. Kuforiji
and Z. I. Renner. The Abeokuta Educated Elements was a part of a larger
organization, the Abeokuta Society of Union and Progress, which comprised educated Egbas in Abeokuta and Lagos. The members of the Abeokuta Educated Elements came from all sections of the town and reflected
Abeokuta's religions diversity—"Moslems, Christians and Pagans."[72] At
different points the Egba authorities sought the advice of the Educated
Elements on issues, but it also offered unsolicited advice, especially on the
structure of local government. In the 1930s, in the wake of the Women's
War in eastern Nigeria, the colonial government was forced to reinvent
local governing bodies. Blair argues that the Women's War "opened our
eyes to our past mistakes in judging the nature of African chieftainships,
and we had, since that time, devoted an enormous amount of energy
to producing 'Intelligence Reports,' which recommended new forms of
government that would better fit the needs of the various tribes for the
future."[73] When Blair gathered information for the Abeokuta intelligence
report, he, too, consulted the Educated Elements.

Between intelligence reports and amendments to the Native Authority ordinance, the colonial government attempted to rein in the autocratic
features of the position. For example, the 1933 Native Authority Ordinance
"required that paramount rulers consult a council of chiefs and elders on
all matters affecting the welfare of the people under their jurisdiction.
While they still retained their executive powers under the supervision of
the residents and the district officers, paramount rulers would now have
to recognize the council's advisory and consultative roles."[74] These reforms theoretically reconfigured the relationship between the oba and the
council, making the king "oba-in-council." In 1936, the Abeokuta Society of Union and Progress offered proposals for a more radical restructuring of local government. It wanted a separation of the Native Authority
from the council, election of all councillors instead of life membership
(which some still enjoyed), and representation by class instead of sectarian identities. The alake would remain in a ceremonial capacity, but the

government would be run by an educated staff experienced in administration.[75] That effort to weaken the alake's position led to a split within the Educated Elements along geographical lines. Several members from Ake Township, including the representatives of the Educated Elements on the council, tried to create an alternative group.[76] Many of them had business dealings with the alake or were beholden to him in some way.[77] Clearly, Ademola had critical support to maintain the status quo from those who perceived or received benefits from his rule.

In spite of the rhetoric from the central administration, colonial officials were fully aware that Ademola dominated the council. Furthermore, Blair suggests that Ademola tried to have his way with colonial officials as well. Blair recounted Ademola as dignified and stately, but

> nobody could be in the place very long without being aware of his existence, for in normal time he was often to be seen about his royal occasions, driving in his silver Rolls Royce with the hood rolled back, and an attendant holding a State umbrella over him, and a trumpeter sitting on each running board making the air hideous with their fanfares. . . . Like the Oba of Benin and the Alafin of Oyo, he was reckoned a paramount chief with the privilege of direct access to the Resident, and he sometimes gained his ends by playing the Resident and the D.O. off against each other. He was the sole native authority, his council was only advisory, and he sometimes browbeat them into giving the advice which he wished to receive. If, as rarely happened, this failed, he could lawfully reject their advice and go his own way.[78]

Ademola in many ways symbolized the autocratic nature of colonial rule, and Blair's 1938 intelligence report presented yet another opportunity to, in theory, democratize indirect rule.

Blair's recommendations led to a reorganization of the Egba government. The council over which the alake presided became the Egba Central Council, each section of the town—Owu, Gbagura, Oke-Ona— had its own council, and each township within each section also created a council that met at regular intervals. Minutes from the sectional councils were to be forwarded to the central council for discussion and decision.[79] The new Egba Central Council was inaugurated in 1941 to much fanfare. People lined the streets, and Centenary Hall's gallery filled with councillors and spectators as the chief commissioner of the western provinces, G. C. Whiteley, the resident of the province, and district officers appeared in full uniform to help mark the occasion.[80] The commissioner acknowledged that the previous "body had ceased to reflect fully the public opinion of all classes in Abeokuta . . . and fuller representation was desirable." He hoped that the new council would represent "a decisive step forward in the evolution of good government in Egbaland, . . . government for the people by representatives of the people under the wise leadership of the Alake."[81]

From the beginning, a steady stream of criticism appeared in the newspapers. Critics noted that the government had created a selection process even though there was unanimous support for an election of council members.[82] While some saw the council as a great step forward, others noted that although the council was to be fully representative, literate councillors were in the minority. One observer described the council as "almost ninety-nine per cent . . . chiefs of various grades and almost all of them . . . advanced in years with antiquated ideas."[83] Contrary to this commentator's portrayal of the council as full of old men, the alake suggested a more diverse age range: "We have now built something on the lines of the models operating in civilized countries. Young or adult males rub shoulders or sit side by side with their grandsires and what is more each Councillor has been chosen freely and by the will of the people of the particular township."[84] The portrayal of the council as an exclusively male space was so naturalized it did not raise any discussion or questions in the press.

The pages of the *Egbaland Echo* reveal strong differences of opinion about the relationship between the different councils and what democracy looked like in practice. There was a rancorous debate about the role of the township councils in selecting members to the central council.[85] There were numerous instances when decisions taken by the central council were vetoed by the alake or the commissioner, and the council had no recourse. As the chief commissioner was drawn into these disputes, he upheld the alake's authority as sole native authority and his right to veto decisions by the council. The commissioner also withdrew support of a plan to add literate members to the Financial Advisory Committee and declared that only members of the central council could serve on the committee.[86] In his memoir, Blair concurred that the reorganization of the Egba Council did not lead to the political changes he had envisioned. He had recommended that the alake be made a constitutional monarch "presiding in person or preferably by a deputy over a Council, the authority being vested in the Alake in council." However, his "recommendations were kept officially confidential but their tenor soon leaked out. The Alake opposed them strongly and the government decided to suppress them and leave matters as they were during his lifetime."[87] The promises of democratization and decentralization had already been forfeited before the fanfare of the inauguration of the new, reorganized council in 1941. From 1941 to 1948, residents of Abeokuta were struggling against an alake who had not lost any power despite the grand reorganization. The absolute failure to reform the sole native authority system, the alake's continued misdeeds, and his general disregard for the women's grievances helped ensure that his vacation did not serve as a cooling-down period.

While the alake was out of town, planning and strategizing continued. Reverend Ransome-Kuti met with ogboni chiefs to persuade them to withdraw their support from the alake. On July 4, several members broke rank with the alake and passed a resolution in which they repudiated him as king and stated their rejection of the sole native authority system because it was "not in accordance with native law and custom." They also accused him of corruption and usurping powers not rightfully his and called for the abolition of taxes on women. When the alake returned from his vacation, the ogboni greeted him by "sounding a bell and beating drums, the traditional method of rejecting a king."[88] They also sent him the symbol that meant they wanted him to commit suicide, the customary practice when a community rejected its oba.[89] Ademola accepted the terms of the July 4 resolutions but rejected their effort to remove him as king.

In response, many council members boycotted central council meetings, essentially shutting down the government. The AWU held mass demonstrations on July 7 and 8, escalating the pressure on him. The resident observed the women's actions, capturing the inherent drama: "She [Ransome-Kuti] organized not only the siege of the Afin, but also monster marches of ten thousand or more women, many with their babies on their backs. We watched them from the Residency hill going by in serried ranks all wearing white head ties, the token of her Women's Union, and singing dirges to indicate to the Alake that they wished to be rid of him."[90] On July 26, Ademola finally resigned as sole native authority, in exchange for the position as chair of the Egba Central Council and retention of his title as alake. Women took to the streets again on July 27 and 28 to register their dissatisfaction. The alake's son, Adegbola, who had to walk through the crowd of women on his way to and from school, recalled that thousands of women camped out in front of the palace, shouting and abusing his father. He knew the situation was very serious and the possibility of bloodshed existed because soldiers had been put on alert. Given the tension, Adegbola argues that his father decided to leave because he did not want the troops or colonial powers to intervene as they had, most notably, in 1914.[91] On July 29, a fleet of trucks commandeered by the resident transported

Ademola, his wives, and family from Abeokuta to Oshogbo in Oyo Province. On January 3, 1949, he abdicated as alake.

Adegbola Ademola's recollection of the seriousness of the period is accurate. However, his father's decision to leave was more complex than a desire to forestall armed intervention. John Blair suggests that the alake was not against intervention, because "a wealthy business man, who was closely connected with the Alake, once came to the Residency and in a roundabout way intimated to me that I could have twenty thousand pounds or as much more as I like to ask, to be paid into a Swiss bank, if I would take the Alake's side and put down the opposition with a strong hand."[92] Blair made it clear that he could not be bribed. Instead, he tried to encourage the alake to give up his position as the sole native authority, but the alake adamantly refused, declaring, "Over my dead body."[93] The resident was caught between the movement against the alake and the alake's intransigence. Blair's situation was further complicated by the fact that he had a trigger-happy superintendent of police who wanted to fire on protesters, and he received little support from his superiors. On multiple occasions, the superintendent of police requested permission "to fire on a rioting mob." He was forced to defuse these moments by "walking through a row of policemen already on one knee with rifle pointing at the mob, and harangue the crowd, telling them to disperse and bring any complaint" to him in the morning.[94] He attempted to contact the governor through the chief secretary for guidance as he weighed giving in to the demands of the opposition groups or calling in the troops to buttress the alake's authority but never received a reply to his question.

The tension in Abeokuta was not restricted to the province. Blair noted, "There was hardly a day when Abeokuta, the Alake and I were not in the headlines in the Lagos press. The whole of Abeokuta and Ijebu, the next door province, were simmering and parts of Oyo and Ondo were ready to catch fire."[95] He called in the Second Battalion of the Nigeria Regiment, led by Lt. Col. Philip Lane-Joynt, and based it at Aro, on the outskirts of the town, for two months. Twice Blair had it mobilized for action, but luckily he was able to rescind the orders. He feared that "if he had allowed a single shot to be fired there would immediately be a conflagration comparable with the Egba rising of 1918." Furthermore, he did not know if the government had enough troops in Nigeria to counter an uprising of that scale, for they had sent Nigerian troops to the Gold Coast to assist with protests there.[96] The pressure clearly got to him as it had the district officer. Blair reported that the district officer was "knocked off his rocker by the situation and resorted to the bottle." Furthermore, the district officer was so prejudiced against the reformers that Blair could not accept his judgment.[97] The resident was not unsympathetic to the district officer's condition, for he wrote,

> We lived in a state of constant strain for we never knew when the pot would boil over. There must have been respites, but looking back on it now it seems as if the crises occurred almost daily, when I had to decide how they could be met without seeming to yield to mob violence, but without offer any provocation to violent response by police or military. . . . When the tension was at its worst . . . I got quite ill and the doctors sent me to hospital in Lagos. I was sure that what I was suffering from was merely nervous exhaustion, but the doctors maintained that it was malaria and that they had found the parasites in my blood. The Egbas were all convinced that it was a juju that some ill wisher had put on me, or possibly just poison. Whatever the diagnosis, it gave me a few days rest.[98]

Things came to a head when Blair traveled to Lagos to attend a session of the Legislative Council. He was forced to turn around immediately and return to Abeokuta because crowds were coursing through the town, overturning cars and burning houses belonging to the alake and his supporters. In addition, the police were using tear gas in an attempt to restore order. He was at least able to speak with the chief commissioner, who authorized his plan—"whisking the Alake out at dead of night through the sleeping besiegers, and conveying him and his wives and family to Oshogbo in Oyo Province, and appointing an interim council to run the place until a permanent reformed constitution could be agreed on."[99] Thus, the alake's decision to leave was conditioned by the escalating violence and the clear loss of support from the administration.

Blair had been told by the chief secretary "there was a revolution going on in Abeokuta, and that it was believed I was the only man who might be able to deal with it."[100] On the night the alake was secretly whisked out of town, it was clear that a revolution had happened. It was unimaginable that the alake, who, in Blair's estimation, was "more lionized than any of the other . . . potentates" when he visited England, could be removed from office. It was also a shock to the alake. He confided to Blair that he contemplated following the ogboni's instruction that he commit suicide, the customary measure for removing a king. Moreover, the alake's son, Adetokunbo, gave Blair his father's .45-caliber revolver for safekeeping for fear that his father would use it to kill himself.[101] Administration officials were not speaking in hyperbole when they declared the situation in Abeokuta a revolution.

THANKSGIVING, TINUBU, AND THE CRISIS OF SIMILARITY

From July 29 to August 2, 1948, the AWU organized a number of thanksgiving events. They included dancing throughout the town, a service at St. John's Church (Igbein), and a picnic at the grave of Madam Tinubu as well as a lecture by the deputy director of education for the western provinces.[102] The main event—"Celebration of Egba Freedom," organized by the AWU and the Majeobaje Society—occurred from August 21 to September 5. The extensiveness of the program was reminiscent of that organized to recognize the town's centenary eighteen years earlier. The program read:

21st August, 1948	Drumming in all Ogboni's Houses from 5 p.m. to 6 p.m. Firing of guns by hunters in all townships from 6 p.m. WORO Dance from 4 p.m. to 5 p.m.
22nd August, 1948	Thanksgiving Service at the Centenary Hall, Ake at 11 a.m.
27th "	United Prayer at Central Mosque, Iporo
28th "	Opera by the Members of the Church
31st "	Picnic at Ita Iyalode Tinubu, Ago-Owu from 10 a.m. to 4 p.m.
1st Sept. 1948	Maje 'O Baje's [Majeobaje's] Day of Prayer in all Churches and Mosques in the town and districts of Egbaland
2nd "	Public Holiday in Egbaland
	Dance and merriment in the Town
	WORO DANCE by members of Maje 'O Baje
4th "	African Dance in its various forms—Entrance fees 6d. commencing from 11 a.m. to 4 p.m. at Alake's Square
4th "	GRAND DANCE IN THE ABEOKUTA AFRICAN RECREATIVE CLUB'S HALL at 8 p.m.
5th "	THANKSGIVING SERVICE IN THE CHURCH OF THE LORD at 9 a.m.[103]

The schedule of events reflected the religious and cultural diversity in Abeokuta as well as the broad cross section of groups that supported the AWU. Following the extensive celebrations and speeches, the AWU published a pamphlet that documented some of the speeches and photographs of events. The cover had a picture of Ademola next to the title *The Fall of a Ruler or the Freedom of Egbaland.*[104] The pamphlet, edited by Abiodun Aloba, a journalist who wrote for the *Comet*, the *West African Pilot* (1946–47), and other newspapers over the course of his career,[105] was in many ways the women's narration of the crisis.

Through the selection of text, speeches, quotes, and photographs, readers were presented with the historical antecedents that supported their revolutionary movement—individuals who stepped forward to save their community from threats—as well as the immediate factors that generated it—the alake's abuse of power and the political marginalization and impoverishment of women. All of these were brought together in the speech given by Rev. Superintendent G. A. Oke during the thanksgiving service in Centenary Hall on August 22, which he began with a discussion of Madam Tinubu:

> What happened in the time of Pharaoh might have been repeated in Egbaland but for the mercy of God. For this we have cause to thank God as the Egba Women's Union and others are now doing this morning in the Hall through the leadership of Mrs. F. Ransome-Kuti, popularly known as Woman Leader No. 1 of Egbaland, although I would rather call her Woman Leader No. 2 in view of the fact that she is only following the footsteps of her predecessor and compatriot, Madam Tinubu, the Iyalode of the Egba people during a crisis similar to what we are experienced today. . . .
>
> Of Lisabi we can only exclaim, "Greater love hath no man than this that a man lay down his life his friends." Madam Tinubu, the Iyalode of the Egba people—the Women Leader No. 1 of Egbaland, through her bravery and patriotism contributed her own share to the safety and freedom of Egbaland during the invasion of this your father-land.[106]

It is important to step back and explore the critical historical and cultural work embedded in this foregrounding of Madam Tinubu. Tinubu was both an economic and political powerhouse in the nineteenth century. Although she settled in Abeokuta after the British forced her to leave Lagos, her power extended beyond Abeokuta.[107] When she received the

title "iyalode of the Egbas" following the successful repulsion of the Dahomean army in 1864, she was catapulted to the level of national hero like
Lisabi, who liberated the Egbas from Oyo imperialism, and Sodeke, who
led them to Olumo Rock. This newly incorporated title into the Egbas'
political structure carved out important political space for Tinubu indi-
vidually and for women generally. This was not a township title—it was
a national title—thus it brought official recognition of her activism on
behalf of and for the nation. The title also conferred on her the position of
women's representative to the central administration. The circumstances
under which this title was awarded also suggests recognition that women
had a space and belonged in the mobilization around national issues, including war. Thus, the recognition of Tinubu's critical role in the national
politics of the 1860s stand in stark contrast to her erasure during the centenary celebrations in 1930. In invoking Tinubu as the predecessor/ancestor
of Funmilayo Ransome-Kuti, Reverend Oke legitimized Ransome-Kuti's
leadership and the actions of the AWU, which did, in "less than twenty-
four months, what wavering men had failed to do in twenty-eight years," as
well as their engagement in "national" politics.[108]

In the post–World War II period in Nigeria, there was no threat of invasion comparable to that of Dahomey's in the nineteenth century. However, there was a palpable fear of bloodshed in Abeokuta, and Resident
Blair made clear that the threat of force was very seriously considered on
multiple occasions. Blair's fear of a comparable Adubi uprising suggests
that the similarities Reverend Oke drew between 1864 and 1948 were not
figurative—they were much more literal than many appreciated. In casting these periods as similar, Oke captured the heightened fear, tension,
and brinksmanship that marked this historical moment. In this battle
against an internal form of tyranny, Ransome-Kuti was a liberator in the
footsteps of Lisabi and Tinubu.

The AWU relied on other political actors and thinkers to legitimate
its activism. The first page of the pamphlet showed a picture of Funmilayo
and beside it three quotes of varying lengths. The first came from Thomas
Jefferson and the Declaration of American Independence:

> We hold these truths to be self-evident: that all men are created
> equal; that they are endowed by their Creator with certain un-
> alienable rights; that among these are life, liberty and the pursuit
> of happiness that whenever any form of government becomes
> destructive of these ends, it is the right of the people to alter or
> to abolish it and to institute a new government. . . . Prudence,

indeed, will dictate that government long established should not be changed for light and transient causes. But when a long train of abuses usurpations, pursuing invariable the same object evinces a design to reduce them under absolute despotism, it is their duty to throw off such government.[109]

It was followed by:

What is the end of government? Certainly the happiness of the governed. What are we to think of a government whose good fortune is supposed to spring from the calamites of its subjects, whose aggrandizement grows out of the miseries of mankind. (Charles James Fox)[110]

And:

Power always corrupts: absolute power corrupts absolutely. (Lord Acton)[111]

The available records do not reveal the process through which these quotes were selected. However, they were not random. The quotes expressed the political ideals that guided the actions of the AWU as well as their underlying conceptualization of state-society relations. Through these quotes, the AWU argued that the purpose of government was to secure the well-being of the governed. Since that expectation had not been met, they had an obligation to challenge the alake's monopoly of power as well as his abuse of that power. The quotes justified the women's mass rallies and vigils and demonstrated their commitment to the ideals articulated by some of the most venerated theorists of secular liberal democracy. The composers of this pamphlet were no doubt aware that the authors quoted did not in theory or practice include women in their theories of democracy. Nonetheless, in using these quotes the AWU signaled that they intended for women to regain and surpass the political rights they had lost.

&

By the time Ademola left office in 1948, the Egba Central Council had expanded to ninety members. Twenty more had been added in 1945 to represent people in the rural districts. The alake lauded the expansion of the council in his inaugural speech of the central council in 1945, at the same time taking credit for the changes:

Up to 1926 all members of council were life members, but later I found that the system of representation in the Council of State was not constitutionally democratic enough as several Chiefs who were useful citizens were anxious to come forward to assist the affairs of the country. Consequently in March 1926, this triennial appointment, which gave entire satisfaction to the Public, was started with 28 members.

He also took credit for the expansion in the 1940s:

> A few years ago it occurred to me that the district village heads should be given the responsibilities of collecting tax in their areas. When that arrangement was effected and put into operation I was very pleased that the Bales had justified my expectation by collecting the tax more readily. . . . In view of this fact it is of paramount importance that the district should be represented in the Council. . . . In having representatives in Council they will be in position to voice out the minds of their constituents on democratic principles and we shall be in a better position to know their feelings and needs.[112]

As Ademola recounted the expansion of the council, he painted himself as a champion of expansion and democratic practice. His self-presentation did not square with either his political or economic practice. Thus, the AWU's protests and mobilization against him grew out of a determination to hold Ademola as well as the system that supported him accountable.

In Lagos, across Nigeria, and in London, people followed events in Abeokuta. The removal of the alake created a yawning hole in the fabric of indirect rule, but it was welcomed by nationalists such as Ladipo Solanke. He saw the struggle in Abeokuta as essential to the unraveling of colonial rule and foundational to the establishment of elected government. In a letter to the Ransome-Kutis, he specified:

> This is the last and best opportunity of effecting every reform which is both necessary and sound, and we have to bear in mind that whatever be the conclusion and results, other Native Authority Areas in not only Nigeria but also other parts of West Africa will have to copy it useful, helpful and beneficial to the interests of the masses or common people. . . .
>
> I like to impress upon you once more that effective abolition of "Sole Native Authority" is at the bottom of the whole problem. It is upon this that all other problems hang. We need to draft a special Memorandum in high legal terms on this particular subject to be submitted to the Government for approval

and support. If this is agreed upon and approved by the Government, then the whole running of the Administration in Egbaland will be transferred completely to the Egba Central Council with the Alake (or whoever be the President) as a mere figure head. This is really the first and about the last thing we want in effecting necessary reforms. As soon as we get this all other necessary reforms become quite easy to be effected.[113]

Solanke encouraged the Ransome-Kutis to work closely with all parties in Abeokuta to get rid of the sole native authority system, which he called "that West African Type of Fascism of British Product." He envisioned a structure similar to that of Britain's, where the alake, like the king of England, would be a figurehead. That would address the question of abdication, while the state would "be run entirely by our Central Council as England is run by Parliament."[114] Ademola's departure and abdication had created a scenario that few had anticipated, especially the colonial government, for it did not have a plan for a local government structure without a Native Administration. The government had been forced to improvise.

The tax revolt created concrete and existential crises for the colonial state. Where it had only wanted to see taxpayers who had not mastered the moral understanding of the benefits of taxation, it was now confronted by colonial subjects who used the language of tyranny and democracy to challenge the political and ideological foundation of colonial rule. The tax revolt also challenged Yoruba and British models of patriarchy. As the wives, sisters, and daughters of teachers, ministers, chiefs, and traders took to the streets and claimed the right to perform oro, they stepped outside the boundaries of appropriate female behavior. Their appeal to Madam Tinubu legitimated their actions and provided a cultural and historical mantle to shield them. She, too, had transgressed gender expectations but was rewarded because she helped save the town from destruction. She proved herself a national hero, and her reward included the iyalode title, honorary male status, and a state funeral.

Tinubu's fearlessness as she challenged the British and the Dahomeans was symbolically important in the iconography of Abeokuta/Egba womanhood. Her qualities allowed all women in Abeokuta—regardless of religion, occupation, social class, and ethnicity—to imagine themselves represented by this woman, an illiterate, slave-owning merchant and orisa devotee, who helped make and unmake kings. The comparisons to Tinubu and the references to other national heroes in the narratives created during and after the tax revolt effectively constructed a new narrative of the nation in which women took center stage. Like the centenary celebrations in 1930, the thanksgiving ceremony of 1948 was also a highpoint of nation-making. Whereas the centenary celebrated the male monopoly of political space and the alake as the center of political power, the thanksgiving ceremony following the tax revolt marked women as nation-makers who ended colonial tyranny and brought democracy to Abeokuta. In this new narrative, Funmilayo Ransome-Kuti assumed the role of Tinubu and galvanized women from all quarters of Abeokuta to save the town from the alake's corrupt rule. Informed by the spirit and history of Tinubu, Ransome-Kuti and the AWU created a great upheaval that reached beyond Abeokuta as women across Nigeria paid great attention to its success.

CODA

When Ademola left Abeokuta in July 1948, he had not yet abdicated. While the AWU and the Majeobaje Society continued to call for his abdication, officials went about creating an interim government. An Egba Interim Council replaced the Egba Native Administration. The interim council included four appointed women, including Ransome-Kuti, as well as four men from the Majeobaje Society. Their first official acts included the abolition of the tax on women, including the water rate tax, and an increase in the flat-rate tax on men. To offset the impact on the budget, the colonial government agreed to cut the salaries of council employees, increase the fees for certain licenses, and decrease capital expenditures.[115] In 1949, Abeokuta held its first free election. At the inauguration of the Egba Central Council on June 30, 1949, the resident declared,

> Today is a momentous occasion in the history of Egbaland for this is the first time that an Egba Central Council consisting of representatives properly elected by the people has met together. In the past some have said that the Egba Native Authority contained persons who were not chosen by the units they were supposed to represent and it has not always been easy to refute such statements. But no one can level such an accusation at the present Council.[116]

The resident also lauded the fact that four women were elected and not nominated as before. He hoped that the number of women on the council would increase and warned that "no community which tries to leave its women out of the picture will progress far."

By all accounts the elections went smoothly. All taxpayers—men and women—had the right to vote. Townships nominated candidates well

before election day at township meetings. Administrative officers monitored the proceedings in the town and the districts. People were encouraged to vote for the person they thought would best report to them on
discussions at every council meeting. They voted enthusiastically, for
many recognized this was an important experiment.[117] These elections
were a significant political development in Abeokuta, especially when
coupled with the removal of the alake, because they portended a severe
blow to the existing Native Authority system.

In its first few months, the council carried out a number of important
tasks. It had to select a chair of the central council, and it chose the agura
since he was the most senior oba by status. It established a committee to
write a new constitution for the Abeokuta Native Authority. It passed an
order restricting the length of oro performance, "thus removing a virtual
restriction on the movements of women during the hours of darkness."[118]
The council began to explore ways to increase the presence of women
across the government when Ransome-Kuti raised the question of allow-
ing female assessors to sit on the native courts. The council also discussed
proposals to increase the presence of literate individuals. The issue was discussed at the provincial conference, and the resident sought the Executive
Committee's opinion on requiring literacy of the presidents of the native
courts and the gradual replacement of illiterate court members by literate members.[119] While there was strong support for requiring that court
presidents be literate, there was strong protest against replacing illiterate
court members. The Owu sectional council, for example, argued in favor
of maintaining illiterate members on the courts because the majority of
the people were also illiterate.[120] The council also had to wrestle with the
issue of revenue, and it agreed to raise taxes on men to fifteen shillings and
the water rate to five shillings. Resident Blair complimented the Executive Committee as he prepared to leave in March 1949, noting that it had
faced its heavy responsibility "bravely and without shirking." Since the
committee had shown such a sense of responsibility, he encouraged it to
begin improving the public services, especially in the rural areas, "so that
the people might see tangible return for the increased taxation."[121]

Although the Native Authority was able to accomplish its work, Ademola's absence and subsequent abdication did not send his supporters into
the background. On the day the resident read out the alake's instrument of
abdication to the council, January 3, 1949, members of the newly formed
organization Egbe Atunluse and supporting ogboni presented themselves
to the council and their plan to fight for Ademola's recall. The meeting
was tense as Atunluse members charged the Majeobaje Society with being

"a menace to the future of Egbaland" and claimed that the council was unrepresentative of "the great mass of Egba public opinion." In response, a Mr. Soetan, a newly elected member of the Legislative Council based in Lagos, suggested that those demanding the return of the alake were "not right in the head." Although the Egbe Atunluse called for the alake's return, even it did not suggest that he return as a sole native authority. They wanted him to be a constitutional monarch "whose power and prerogatives . . . [would] be severely limited by a new constitution, which, they hoped, would largely vest power in the hands of the Ogbonis, the Oloruguns and the Parakoyis."[122] While their proposal seemed a retreat from the electoral politics of the new council, it was clear that the new constitution overturned the power that the alakeship had gained since the days of the Egba United Government. Ademola's supporters recognized that the alakeship would be less powerful going forward; nonetheless, they also hoped to check the increasing influence of literate members in the council.

Egbe Atunluse would spend the next twenty-two months agitating for the alake's return. On November 30, 1950, the Egba Central Council voted twenty-nine to nineteen in favor of recalling Ademola. Since the voting showed that a significant number did not want Ademola to return, the resident also approved a proposal to create a Peace Committee to help reconcile the opposing views.[123] Escorted by ogboni and the ENA police, Ademola returned to Abeokuta on December 3 the same way he had left—secretly and under the cover of darkness.[124]

Conclusion

FOR MANY people outside Nigeria, Wole Soyinka's memoir, Aké: The Years of Childhood, was their introduction to the Abeokuta women's tax revolt. As he described the gathering of market women at the palace, readers were transfixed by the dramatic and evocative prose that conveyed the sights, sounds, and smells of the moment. The story was also powerfully represented in the Tony Award–winning musical Fela! Built around the life of Fela Kuti, Funmilayo Ransome-Kuti's third child, the brief discussion of the tax revolt portrayed the organic nature of Fela's radicalism and the especially strong relationship he shared with his mother. The play introduced entirely new audiences to this story as it traveled from off Broadway to Broadway, London, Lagos, and many other places.[1]

Though formative to the political and cultural consciousness of these highly creative sons of Abeokuta, the tax revolt was ultimately a footnote in their lives. The Great Upheaval benefited from the attention given to the tax revolt, but its goal has been to provide a fuller appreciation of the significance of this event to the larger history of colonialism, nationalism, and decolonization in Nigeria. Moreover, in placing women and gender at the center of this inquiry, this book has offered new insights and revealed new lines of inquiry as it sought to enlarge our understanding of the late colonial era and the consequences of this period on the postcolonial state.

TOWARD A WOMEN'S MOVEMENT

At its core, The Great Upheaval is about women, activism, and politics in colonial Nigeria. It challenges the notion by recent scholars that women in Nigeria were averse to political engagement. To argue that "politics by nature and definition in Nigeria is a militant activity and women are not interested and involved in militant activity" and that "they are more located within the caring professions" mischaracterizes Nigerian women's history.[2] The tax revolt is one among multiple examples of moments during which women challenged colonial policies, political structures, and distribution of resources. Their marginalization from the institutions of power did not mean an absence of political engagement. That engagement took many forms, from social uplift programs designed to disprove racist ideas and improve the lives of women to Ransome-Kuti's political work on behalf of market women. Ultimately, Ransome-Kuti was one among many women who functioned as community leaders and organizers.[3] In this era of nationalist mobilization, Ransome-Kuti and other women leaders assumed their engagement would ensure a place for them in the new institutions of governance that were emerging.

The Great Upheaval has contextualized the factors that gave rise to this distinctive political moment in Abeokuta. Some of Ransome-Kuti's detractors suggested that it was just the outcome of a personal falling-out between the alake and her and her husband. As a result, Ransome-Kuti used her substantial influence among the market women to trick them into supporting her activities. Others intimated that her challenge to the alake was connected to the slave past of her family—that as a descendant of this group, she did not have a right to say anything about matters in the town.[4] Such claims overlooked the vast systemic debate embedded in the actions carried out by the Abeokuta Women's Union that ultimately undermined Ademola, the sole native authority structure, and colonial rule in Abeokuta.

As this study has shown, the women's tax revolt brought together multiple historical debates that attempted to define Abeokuta's political community, the exercise of power, and the role, rights, and duties of women within its institutions. These debates had their antecedents in the nineteenth century as Egba and Owu refugees constructed this new polity under Olumo Rock. It did not take the path of Ibadan, the former military encampment, which completely eliminated the monarchy as it grew into a regional power. Instead, the Egbas and the Owus maintained the monarchy while establishing a decentralized political structure that incorporated men, women, and different religious communities as the town consolidated and expanded.

Colonialism changed the context in which these debates continued, and colonial priorities informed their outcomes. Colonial officials helped create the infrastructure that invested alakes with much more power through the Native Authority system and empowered them to facilitate the integration of their communities into the international economy and the adoption of new social and cultural mores. These transformations created an ambivalent situation for many women in Abeokuta. Women's long history in trade and other economic activities furthered the town's integration into the international economy and helped to satisfy the colonial state's demand for revenue. However, women could no longer transform their economic gain into political capital, and their recognition as a political constituency faded. Women's political marginalization fomented increasing tension as their economic conditions deteriorated during the Depression and World War II, and it became clear that they had little impact on policies.

Contrasting the town's centenary celebration and the thanksgiving celebration after the tax revolt reveals the depth of women's marginalization and well as their agency in reclaiming their place. Their thanksgiving celebration inscribed a new national history in Abeokuta that highlighted the heroic qualities of Madam Tinubu and Ransome-Kuti. They created a women-centric narrative of saving the nation in which Ransome-Kuti, like Madam Tinubu, rescued the Egba nation. This time, however, the nation had to be saved from the alake's tyranny. This narrative foregrounded the central role of women to the practice of politics and the distribution of power and resources. The AWU's narrative minimized the role of political geography in determining membership on the council and led to the establishment of an electoral process in the town. Equally important, the protests' success became the foundation for a different dynamic in the evolving political landscape—one in which Ransome-Kuti argued women should think of "forming themselves into one big and powerful unit."[5]

These local developments made Abeokuta a powerful example to women across Nigeria. Its timing was equally important, for it allowed the women to reassess the political losses they experienced during the early colonial decades and anticipate the corrective measures they could bring to the nationalist movement. It was also important that political parties had not yet developed and the National Council of Nigeria and the Cameroons had lost momentum. This relatively quiescent period provided fertile ground for women to mobilize.

Letters to Ransome-Kuti attested to the inspiration women across Nigeria took from this event. Alhaji Abubaharu from Kano learned of Ransome-Kuti and the AWU during a visit to Ibadan in March 1948. On his return to Kano, he shared this information with many Hausa women:

"I explained to them about your endeavor to open the eyes of Nigerian women and to make a great union becoming the same nation." By May, he sent Ransome-Kuti a note on behalf of women in Kano: "We women of Kano want permission to make a union."[6] Women in Zaria expressed similar excitement. A letter from the Etsako Women Democratic Movement there conveyed the significance of the Abeokuta protests:

> We are following your foot prints and we are this day appealing to you to give us courage. We want to know if we are destined to be kitchen slaves. We want to know if the woman is not the mother and pride of a nation. Are we not having rights of our own? Are women not having pants to play in the political up lift of a country? But we think it had been proved from what we saw at the demonstration of Abeokuta women.[7]

Etsako women had first attempted to form their union in 1943, but it failed. A visit from labor leader Michael Imoudu led them to rekindle their efforts, but they met strong resistance from Etsako men, who claimed that "unions composed of women are nothing but schools or institutions where women are trained to be classical harlots." This charge directly challenged the respectability of the members of the union who were "mostly . . . married women and ladies and girls out of schools." They needed courage to continue their struggle, thus they asked Ransome-Kuti to send them a few words publicly through the *West African Pilot*.[8] Another letter writer, Elizabeth Adekogba from Ibadan, offered cooperation to Ransome-Kuti because she was "our mother in the field of politics" and they were fighting for a common cause—"the emancipation of Nigerian women."[9]

The files are full of letters from women across northern, eastern, and western Nigeria who wanted to create a union or attach an existing organization to the AWU. Thus, the impetus to create the Nigerian Women's Union in 1949 emerged organically as women in different parts of the country learned about the successful protests in Abeokuta. The letters also reveal the issues that motivated women to create or join a women's union. The Tax Payers Movement in Gbelle-Okpekpe wanted assistance to establish a branch of the NWU in order to bring more facilities into the community, specifically a maternity home and schools.[10] Ika women of Agbor also wanted a list of very specific items: a permanent garage for cars and trucks, daily markets in several towns, an adequate number of stalls for market women, education for women, a stationary medical officer in Agbor General Hospital or the shared services of the rural medical officer in a neighboring village, and a midwife.[11] These local issues all had larger ramifications because they went beyond the resources of local councils. They required policy decisions from different levels of government.

Women were not the only group inspired by the AWU. Communities in other parts of western Nigeria also called into question the Native Authority system and the tax structure. Councils in Ijebu Remo and Ijebu Igbo followed Abeokuta's example and ended taxes on women. The events also forced the colonial government to take note of the inconsistences in tax policy. In a confidential memo from Governor Macpherson to the secretary of state for the colonies, he acknowledged that the taxation of women in Abeokuta and Ijebu was an anomaly.[12] As his memo circulated, officials came to agree that the discussion could not reside only with the Native Authority of Abeokuta. One official suggested "that we draw attention to this semi-officially and ask whether the Governor has considered an investigation of the general question at Government rather than Native Authority level, so as to insure a co-ordinated solution of the present anomalies."[13] The Abeokuta tax revolt became a local issue with national implications for both nationalists and colonial officials.

The success of the Abeokuta protests contributed to the spread of branches of the Majeobaje Society. In fact, Obafemi Awolowo entered local politics in Remo by accepting the invitation to become secretary of the Majeobaje Society. This provided the base from which he was elected to the town council. The Majeobaje Society appealed to educated young men who were often denied access to Native Authority councils, but local politics determined the nature of their mobilization. Awolowo accepted the Majeobaje Society's offer on the condition that it abandon its complaints about the tax increase and the oba's authoritarian control over local funds. Insa Nolte suggests that Awolowo's positions drew on beliefs that lay at the center of his political thought: paying taxes was a civic duty to be expected of all who were able to pay, and traditional kings could play a central role in the formation of a nation.[14] Awolowo would later support Ademola's return to Abeokuta in 1951 as a constitutional monarch and in the process earn the ire of a segment of the Ake ogboni chiefs.[15] In a show of gratitude, Ademola tried to confer a title on Awolowo, aro of Ijeun, but he respectfully declined.[16]

The success of the tax revolt helped propel nationwide discussions on women's economic, political, and social positions as ideas for the new nation evolved. Carving out organizational spaces locally and nationally assumed greater significance after the colonial government revised the maligned Richards Constitution early and replaced it with the Macpherson Constitution. The latter, crafted with input from across Nigeria, laid the groundwork for the development of self-government but preserved the three large administrative regions—North, East, and West. These developments combined to accelerate the emergence of regionally and ethnically based political parties.

WOMEN AND POLITICS IN THE AGE OF PARTIES

The NCNC largely devolved from a pan-Nigerian organization into the party that would be dominated by Igbos. In the Western Region, the Action Group, led by Obafemi Awolowo, primarily represented the Yorubas, while in the Northern Region, the Northern People's Congress was dominated by Hausas. The creation of political parties changed the landscape for women activists because the parties were collectively threatened by independent women's organization. Awolowo actively discouraged women in Ikare who were trying to organize a branch of the NWU. In a letter to Funmilayo Ransome-Kuti, Shefiatu Olubaka reported, "Last time I got ten people excluding myself but when Awolowo came he said that women meeting is not so good, therefore many of them ran away."[17] The NCNC pressured Ransome-Kuti to bring the NWU into the NCNC, claiming that any organization not under the Azikiwe's leadership would fail. When Ransome-Kuti proved resistant to this pressure, the NCNC forced women in the east to choose between the NCNC and the NWU. One of the most prominent leaders in the east, Margaret Ekpo, in time resigned from the NWU after insisting that she could not be in an organization that was independent of the NCNC and declared her willingness to die for the NCNC.[18]

Ekpo's exaggerated declarations epitomized the gender dynamics that would ultimately define the nationalist period. While the parties claimed to represent all Nigerians, they did not stand for gender equity, especially in the political arena. They wanted women in the parties, but they did not support women as candidates or exercising an independent political voice. Nigerian men's ambivalence toward women's political organizations was not unique. In French Cameroon, the Union of the Peoples of Cameroon felt compelled to express concern about its women's wing, the Democratic Union of Cameroonian Women, and to remind it that women "best address nationalistic issues that dealt with maternity, markets, public water pumps and other activities outside male domains."[19]

As women continued to organize independent political spaces and mobilize with one eye toward local issues and the other toward national issues, some men supported these efforts. Others, however, resisted. In a letter drafted to the editor of the *African Echo*, Ransome-Kuti acknowledged that "some of the few long trousers Ogboni who are tied hand and feet with the chains of debit sheets . . . want to eliminate women from Egba politics, because they know that Egba women stand for truthfulness, justice, uprightness, and equity."[20] Ransome-Kuti's response suggests that women brought more than their bodies to politics—they brought a critical set of values that were missing in Nigerian politics of the day.

In spite of the desire to remove women from politics in Abeokuta, women's political engagement continued to expand beyond the town. In 1953, the NWU hosted a two-day conference in Abeokuta, which Ransome-Kuti described as "a parliament of the women of Nigeria." During this gathering, comprising four hundred delegates from fifteen provinces, women belonging to the NWU and a host of other women's organizations created the Federation of Nigerian Women's Societies (FNWS). The leadership explicitly noted that membership in the FNWS did not preclude membership in other organizations. The parliament of women did not see ethnicity, region, or religion in a zero-sum battle with gender. It assumed that women could hold membership in multiple political communities and still advance a collective set of ideals. These ideas were advanced in some of Ransome-Kuti's speeches. In a speech on citizenship, for example, she defined citizens as individuals who contributed to the welfare and progress of their communities. She did not define "citizen" by any other affiliation.[21] Her writings expressed concern about religion-based schools because they had the potential to undermine the creation of a national community. Most importantly, she believed that women, by their training to manage households, already practiced the skills necessary to be involved in politics.[22]

In fact, the FNWS encouraged women to actively participate in multiple forms of political work. For example, participants passed resolutions declaring that women should be represented in all local councils, one-third of the seats in all legislative houses should be allocated to women, and women should select their own candidates. They also called for more facilities for girls' education, universal adult suffrage, and consultation with the FNWS when new bills were introduced. Ultimately, they wanted to raise the status of Nigerian women and to create equal opportunities for both men and women.[23] Although they recognized the importance of membership in the political parties, belonging to the parties challenged women's political organizations in ways that were unanticipated given the rhetoric of unity.

In a 1953 meeting of the Executive Committee of the FNWS in Benin City, the first topic on the agenda was "The Role of Women in the revised constitution." There, Ransome-Kuti raised concerns about ongoing constitutional discussions: "You will all notice that practically nothing was said about women during the London Conference for the amendment of the Macpherson Constitution, so we shall have to demand our right. And then we must talk about 'Adult Suffrage.'"[24] Other women shared her assessment. For example, Elizabeth Adekogba wanted women nationalists to demand universal adult suffrage, direct elections, and an end to the Macpherson Constitution.[25]

It was already clear to Ransome-Kuti and members of the FNWS that women had to make their voices heard, otherwise they would lose out when the terms and resources of citizenship were being decided. They stressed the language of adult suffrage because in Britain the concept guaranteed both men and women above the age of twenty-one had the right to vote. Therefore, adult suffrage had to become the starting point for all discussions about voting. The committee also discussed the creation of a newspaper that someone proposed they name *Woman*. Ransome-Kuti argued, "I don't think the world will know what we are doing unless we have our own press or our own newspaper."[26] Newspapers, among other forms of print media, were critical to the creation of the nation. Wale Adebanwi argues that they "constitute one of the most powerful means of constructing, mobilizing, and contesting meaning in the service of power." In Nigeria, where certain newspapers were aligned with certain political parties, the press helped create a grand narrative about a unifying nation though the newspapers could not mask the disunity and fragmentation that characterized their attacks on each other.[27] The most salient feature of their grand narrative was the naturalization of male political domination. Their narrative was similar to that created by Abeokuta's centenary planners in 1930, for they, too, attempted to naturalize men's political dominance. Only by creating their own press could women hope to be heard above the din. For a brief period the FNWS published its own newspaper, the *Nigerian Sunshine*.[28]

Women of the AWU, the NWU, and the FNWS promoted a politics of inclusion. Some men supported and welcomed these discussions that placed women at the center of deliberations about nation, citizenship, and rights. Some, however, vehemently resisted. This resistance was reflected most in the agreement by all major political parties and the colonial government to deny the vote to women in the north. The colonial government enshrined this compromise in the 1954 Lyttleton Constitution, which stipulated that the country "did not have to have a uniform system of electoral regulations based on universal adult suffrage."[29] In 1958,

Awolowo admitted "with solemn remorse, that we have committed a griev-
ous wrong," but he felt duty-bound to honor the agreement.[30] As a result,
only women in the Eastern and Western Regions gained the right to vote
at independence.

The Great Upheaval amplifies the evolution of the AWU into a political
movement and grounds it in changes in the larger political economy. In the
local arena, women linked issues of economic and political marginalization
to one of representation and successfully gained a place in local government. In the 1950s, they tried to take their achievement national, but we
have a very incomplete picture of the outcome. Many more questions need
to be asked about women and politics during the 1950s. Scholars must craft
a more detailed understanding of the relationship between local women's
social movements and the nationalist parties. In many ways, Abeokuta con-
forms to Nolte's argument that local divisions and politics determined to a
great extent where and how the nationalist parties become incorporated in
specific communities. At a general level, the Action Group appeared more
conservative, given its strong reliance on traditional rulers, in contrast to the
NCNC, which primarily focused on mobilizing groups—educated elites,
migrants, and trading populations—associated with what Nolte suggests
were distinctly modern ambitions. Nonetheless, the AG was able to mobilize some support in the Eastern Region, and the NCNC had support in
the Western Region. In the 1951 elections, the NCNC had significant support in parts of Remo and Awolowo's hometown of Ikenne.[31] The NCNC
also bested the AG in Abeokuta, in part because market women supported
Ransome-Kuti, who had remained a member of the NCNC.

We also need a much better understanding of the changing landscape as the parties developed women's wings. Some women challenged
the political parties as they consolidated power, but others succumbed to
the allure of these sections. Who were these women? What did women
of different social classes gain from this model of political engagement?
How did the structure of women's wings differ across political parties?
Did women in the Northern Elements Progressive Union exercise greater
political engagement since the party's leader, Aminu Kano, supported
women's education and emancipation? Similarly, we need a much fuller
picture of parties launched by women, such as the Common People's
Party, established by Ransome-Kuti after she left the NCNC, and the Nigerian Commoners's Party, created by Adunni Oluwole, an opponent of
self-government.[32]

We need a much more nuanced understanding of how women's organizations, such as the FNWS, tried to bridge ethnic, religious, cultural,

and regional divisions and demarcate and define collective goals in the climate of ethnic politics. When these collective efforts failed, what form did failure assume at the national, regional, and local levels? What aspects of their efforts survived? Having a better picture of the forms of women's mobilization during the 1950s will help us overcome the dead zone in Nigerian women's political history. We get very little sense of the continuities between the 1950s and the postcolonial period or the discontinuities that resulted from changes in the large social context and political economy. Much of the literature on women and politics in Nigeria provides names of the handful of women who were in government after 1960 but without larger social context. Or it focuses on the period after universal franchise was established in the 1970s.[33] While women's activism and their representation in government is linked, they cannot be conflated. Thus, we need more social histories of women's activism that also examine the relationship between activists on the ground and women who entered government.

RETHINKING TAXES

Tax revolts in colonial Nigeria were not unique. In eastern Nigeria, according to Ben Naanen, there were very pronounced tax revolts in the Ikigwe and Bende Divisions of Owerri Province from November 1938 to January 1939. In Calabar Province, especially in Ogoniland, tax incidents were common throughout the 1930s.[34] There were also numerous protests led by women. In Ijebu, women actively protested tax increases in the early 1930s, and in December 1940, Lagos market women closed the markets and marched to the residences of the commissioner and the governor to protest two new wartime taxes.[35] Most of these have not been examined, while, according to Naanen, the Igbo Women's War has been elevated to a cult status.[36] The significance accorded to the Igbo Women's War in part derives from the convergence of feminist and Africanist historiographies in the 1960s as scholars sought to represent African women as historical actors transformed by but also transforming colonialism.[37] This study has built on the foundation established by scholars of the Igbo Women's War and suggests important and distinctive features that differentiate the anti-tax movement in postwar Abeokuta.

Indirect rule in Nigeria over the course of its multiple iterations came to rely increasingly on direct taxation. Anthony I. Nwabughuogu argues that officials became more doctrinaire about applying indirect rule, and by extension direct taxation, by the mid-1920s.[38] Officials' willingness to expand direct taxation was a direct outcome of the interwar depression.

Similarly, the economic crises during and after World War II ensured that tax collection remained a top priority. Given the economic circumstances, taxes drew heightened concern as African producers, traders, and merchants navigated tax increases or more zealous collection regimes. For the market women who formed the core of the AWU, tax levels in that economic environment threatened their social and economic reproduction. Whereas rumors about the intention to tax women instigated the Igbo Women's War, women in Abeokuta had been taxpayers for several decades and more deeply embedded in the networks of fiscal extraction.

The protests revealed multiple relationships to taxes. At the same time that people complained about tax rates or zealous collection, they also made demands on the state based on their status as long-standing taxpayers. They wanted protection from robbers, corrupt state employees, and the alake, who competed unfairly with them. They equated paying taxes with a form of imperial citizenship that entitled them to have the resources of the colonial state used to safeguard their interests.

Taxes also formed the core of the debate about the sole native authority system because women paid taxes, but they lacked direct representation on the council. Historically their representation was subsumed under the geographical, sectarian, or class interests that shaped council membership, since women resided in the townships and villages and belonged to the Christian and Muslim communities as well as the Educated Elements. The AWU in essence insisted that women by virtue of being taxpayers had earned the right to be recognized as a political constituency on the council. They used history and custom—Madam Tinubu and her position as iyalode—to justify this demand. The AWU was not a conservative keeper of custom, for, as we saw, it was willing to circumscribe or challenge customs, such as oro. Nonetheless, the inclusion of women advocating on behalf of women's interests mattered precisely because the council made numerous decisions that affected their social and economic lives, yet they had no input in these decisions. Furthermore, seeking redress often meant challenging the alake.

In the same way that representation held competing meanings, notions of democracy differed. Naomi Chazan argues that the concept of democracy that developed during the anticolonial phase of decolonization was of an abstract, aggregate sort. It became "the password for the enfranchisement of broad social communities."[39] While this may capture democracy at the larger level, notions of democracy were shaped by the very specific contours of the local colonial state. The colonial state, as she argues, lacked a popular component, for it created a very authoritarian and vertical relationship between ruler and ruled. The challenge for colonial officials was how to create something that looked democratic but did not jeopardize the state's control. Sir Arthur Richards believed that a form of democratic government could be created in the colonies that, while not the Westminster model, still operated on the principles behind it.[40] Neither he nor Sir Bernard Bourdillon, who coauthored an article discussing the Richards Constitution, believed in direct elections for Nigerians. Bourdillon wrote, "The ballot box is certainly not the immediate solution. Nor need it necessarily be the ultimate aim." He believed that some form of indirect election would fit the bill for years to come and working through indigenous local authorities was the best solution.[41]

For Ladipo Solanke and other Egba nationalists, the Westminster model was, in fact, the appropriate model. However, the realities on the ground forced them to experiment with yet a third model—a governing council without a constitutional monarch. In the years while the alake was in exile Abeokuta's political structure was indeed unique. Taxpayers voted for their representatives on the council; women were among the elected representatives, though Ransome-Kuti admitted that "most of the men are not happy about this."[42] In 1950, the Egba Council became the Abeokuta Urban District Council (AUDC). In many ways the AUDC prefigured the Local Government Law passed in 1954. The law acknowledged that the Native Authority Ordinance no longer met the needs of the region and empowered communities that seemed the most progressive to create local government structures that removed titleholders from the business of government. Under the law, councils were no longer subordinate to Native Authorities, for all councils now derived their power directly from the Regional Authority. The bill also changed the nomenclature of the councils to (a) divisional councils, (b) urban district councils and rural district councils, and (c) local councils.[43] In many ways, the women's tax revolt and the forced exile of the alake allowed the town to put in place for a brief period the sort of local government council that the nationalist government created under self-rule.

As this book demonstrated, the Abeokuta women's tax revolt was the outcome of a very specific historical moment—a moment in which economic crisis, new political vistas, dynamic leadership, and an overreaching ruler aligned. That alignment allowed women to present themselves as an overwhelming force for change in state-society relations. While many women came together in those powerful waves that the resident, John Blair, described, they were still a very diverse group. Some women were willing to work within the ideology of women's dependency and argued that women should not pay taxes at all.[44] Some, like Ransome-Kuti, believed women should pay taxes but supported only an income tax, not a flat tax. Therefore, only men and women with incomes over a certain level should pay taxes. The NWU would come to realize by the 1950s that in wedding taxes and voting rights, they created a conundrum—a restrictive political exercise that hinged on financial resources. Under this formulation, residents who did not pay taxes forfeited their political participation. This became most apparent during the elections in 1949 when residents had to show their tax receipts at the polls.

Taxation and voting became national issues as constitutional discussions unfolded. By 1952, Ransome-Kuti would argue that "voting should not be limited to women who pay some sort of rate and a minimum of tax at all."[45] Even though taxes were not on the agenda of the NWU's executive committee meeting in Benin City the following year, the issue arose because of newspaper accounts that suggestively tied taxation to a denial of resources and rights. The *Daily Times* published a letter on September 12, 1953, in which the reader stated "unless they [women] are prepared to pay for what they ask they cannot get them." Ransome-Kuti explained to the committee that the reader "meant that women should pay tax before they will be allowed to vote." She saw this as a scare tactic that men intended to use to frighten women into accepting either payment of taxes or limited voting rights.[46] However, the implications went beyond voting or paying taxes, for the statement seems to suggest that the women's demands only benefited them and not the entire society. It lacked any sense of support for a set of common goods that required the investment of all members of society, not just those with the means to pay. The larger political implications, such as who defined the needs and goals of a society or how would resources be allocated, underscored the critical need for multiple women's organization engaged in all levels of politics. The AWU and its successor organizations tried through their deliberations, protests, letters, and petitions to shape a new nation that would formulate and lead to what political scientist Thomas Hodgkin termed "a new philosophy of life"— the discovery of the institutions required "to live humanly and sociably" in the world.[47] Although the women of Ransome-Kuti's generation did not succeed in many ways, we can still see evidence of the resilience of their questions, demands, ideas, and strategies in the political work carried out by nongovernmental and community-based organizations across Nigeria today and among the women who moved beyond protests and joined insurgencies in the oil-rich Niger Delta region.[48]

Notes

INTRODUCTION

1 Alake Ladapo Ademola II, Message to the Egba People When He Abdicated the Egba Throne, box 45, file 2, Ransome-Kuti Papers, Kenneth Dike Memorial Library, University of Ibadan (hereafter cited as KDML).

2 Oshogbo, the capital of Osun State, is approximately 128 miles northeast of Abeokuta. The British restructured the political relationship between indigenous political leaders and their communities through Native Authority ordinances. Leaders designated sole native authority enjoyed expanded privileges as paramount chiefs. They sat at the pinnacle of a hierarchical structure. They enjoyed direct access to the British residents and only received advice from the councils that formed part of the local government. See Olufemi Vaughan, *Nigerian Chiefs: Traditional Power in Modern Politics, 1890s–1990s* (Rochester, NY: University of Rochester Press, 2000): 25–26; and, John Blair, *Juju and Justice* (Perth, Australia: P & B Press, 1991), 231.

3 Wole Soyinka, *Aké: The Years of Childhood* (New York: Random House, 1981), 181.

4 Nina Mba, *Nigerian Women Mobilized: Women's Political Activity in Southern Nigeria, 1900–1965* (Berkeley: Institute of International Studies, University of California, 1982), 166.

5 Partha Chatterjee, *The Nation and Its Fragments: Colonial and Postcolonial Histories* (Princeton, NJ: Princeton University Press, 1993), 5.

6 Chatterjee, *Nation and Its Fragments*, 156. For equally important discussions along similar lines, see also Kelly M. Askew, *Performing the Nation: Swahili Music and Cultural Politics in Tanzania* (Chicago: University of Chicago Press, 2002); Anthony D. Smith, *The Ethnic Origins of Nations* (Oxford: Basil Blackwell, 1988); and Prasenjit Duara, "Historicizing National Identity, or Who Imagines What and When," in *Becoming National: A Reader*, ed. Geoff Eley and Ronald Grigor Suny (New York: Oxford University Press, 1996), 151–78.

7 Prasenjit Duara, *Rescuing History from the Nation: Questioning Narratives of Modern China* (Chicago: University of Chicago Press, 1995), 10.

8 Marissa J. Moorman, *Intonations: A Social History of Music and Nation in Luanda, Angola, from 1945 to Recent Times* (Athens: Ohio University

Press, 2008), 11; Askew, *Performing the Nation*; and Thomas Turino, *Nationalists, Cosmopolitans, and Popular Music in Zimbabwe* (Chicago: University of Chicago Press, 2000).

9 Geoff Eley and Ronald Grigor Suny, "Introduction: From the Moment of Social History to the Work of Cultural Representation," in *Becoming National: A Reader*, ed. Geoff Eley and Ronald Grigor Suny (New York: Oxford University Press, 1996), 7.

10 Eley and Suny, "Introduction," 7.

11 Akin L. Mabogunje, "Some Comments on Land Tenure in Egba Division, Western Nigeria," *Africa: Journal of the International African Institute* 3, no. 3 (1961): 260.

12 Saburi O. Biobaku, *The Egba and Their Neighbors, 1842–1872* (Oxford: Clarendon Press, 1965), 5–7.

13 N. A. Fadipe, *The Sociology of the Yoruba* (Ibadan: Ibadan University Press, 1970), 97–100; P. C. Lloyd, *Yoruba Land Law* (London: Oxford University Press, 1962), 231–32; J. S. Eades, *Strangers and Traders: Yoruba Migrants, Markets and the State in Northern Ghana* (Trenton, NJ: Africa World Press, 1984), 47.

14 Robin Law, "The Heritage of Oduduwa: Traditional History and Political Propaganda among the Yoruba," *Journal of African History* 14, no. 2 (1973): 208.

15 J. D. Y. Peel, *Religious Encounter and the Making of the Yoruba* (Bloomington: Indiana University Press, 2000), 284.

16 J. Lorand Matory, "The English Professors of Brazil: On the Diasporic Roots of the Yoruba Nation," *Comparative Studies in Society and History* 41, no. 1 (1999): 85.

17 Peel, *Religious Encounter*, 283–84.

18 Peel, 281.

19 Peel, 281.

20 Peel, 282. For more on Johnson, see Emmanuel A. Ayandele, *Holy Johnson, Pioneer of African Nationalism, 1836–1917* (London: Cass, 1970).

21 Peel, *Religious Encounter*, 282. See also "Henry Venn on Nationality and Native Churches," in *Origins of West African Nationalism*, ed. Henry S. Wilson (London: St. Martin's, 1969), 131–35.

22 Antoinette M. Burton, *Burdens of History: British Feminists, Indian Women, and Imperial Culture, 1865–1915* (Chapel Hill: University of North Carolina Press, 1994), 12.

23 For an important discussion on the differences between Yoruba and Christian marriage, see Kristin Mann, *Marrying Well: Marriage, Status and Social Change among the Educated Elite in Colonial Lagos* (New York: Cambridge University Press, 1985), 35–52.

24 Robin Law, "Early Yoruba Historiography," *History in Africa* 3 (1976): 71.

25 Law, "Early Yoruba Historiography," 77–78.

26 Law, 78.

27 Michel Doortmont, "The Invention of the Yorubas: Regional and Pan-African Nationalism versus Ethnic Provincialism," in *Self-Assertion and Brokerage: Early Cultural Nationalism in West Africa*, ed. P. F. de Moraes Farias and Karin Barber (Birmingham: Centre of West African Studies, University of Birmingham, 1990), 105.

28 Law, "Early Yoruba Historiography," 78; Doortmont, "Invention of the Yorubas," 106.

29 Law, "Early Yoruba Historiography," 73.

30 Doortmont, "Invention of the Yorubas," 106.

31 Michel Doortmont, "Recapturing the Past: Samuel Johnson and the Construction of Yoruba History" (PhD thesis, Eramus Universiteit, Rotterdam, 1994), 53, cited in Adrian Montrell Deese, "Making Sense of the Past: Ajayi Kolawole Ajisafe and the (Re)making of Modern Abeokuta" (MPS thesis, Cornell University 2013), xvii.

32 Deese, "Making Sense of the Past," 21–42.

33 For a fuller discussion on the subversive qualities of Johnson's *History of the Yoruba*, see Andrew Apter, *Black Critics and Kings: The Hermeneutics of Power in Yoruba Society* (Chicago: University of Chicago Press, 1992), 193–211.

34 Chatterjee, *Nation and Its Fragments*, 6.

35 Philip S. Zachernuk, *Colonial Subjects: An African Intelligentsia and Atlantic Ideas* (Charlottesville: University of Virginia Press, 2000), 19.

36 Zachernuk, *Colonial Subjects*, 26–29.

37 Zachernuk, 34–36.

38 For example, see St. Clair Drake, *Black Folk Here and There: An Essay in History and Anthropology*, vol. 2 (Los Angeles: Center for Afro-American Studies, University of California, 1990); Wilson Jeremiah Moses, *Afrotopia: The Roots of African American Popular History* (New York: Cambridge University Press, 1998); and Patrick Bryan, *The Jamaican People, 1880–1902: Race, Class and Social Control* (London: Macmillan Caribbean, 1991).

39 Zachernuk, *Colonial Subjects*, 59.

40 See Emmanuel A. Ayandele, *The Missionary Impact on Modern Nigeria, 1842–1914: A Political and Social Analysis* (Harlow, UK: Longman, 1966); Titiola Euba, "Dress and Status in 19th Century Lagos," in *History of the Peoples of Lagos State*, ed. Ade Adefuye et al. (Ikeja, Lagos: Lantern Books, 1987), 142–63; and Leo Spitzer, *The Creoles of Sierra Leone: Responses to Colonialism, 1870–1945* (Madison: University of Wisconsin Press, 1974).

41 Law, "Early Yoruba Historiography," 76.

42 Karin Barber, "Introduction: Hidden Innovators in Africa," in *Africa's Hidden Histories: Everyday Literacy and Making the Self*, ed. Karin Barber (Bloomington: Indiana University Press, 2006), 8–9, 13, 16–17.

43 Karin Barber, "Experiments with Genre in Yoruba Newspapers of the 1920s," in *African Print Cultures: Newspapers and Their Publics in the*

Twentieth Century, ed. Derek Peterson, Emma Hunter, and Stephanie Newell (Ann Arbor: University of Michigan Press, 2016), 158–64, 173.

44 Andrew Apter, *Black Critics and Kings: The Hermeneutics of Power in Yoruba Society* (Chicago: University of Chicago Press, 1992), 19.

45 Apter, *Black Critics and Kings,* 25.

46 Wale Adebanwi, "Death, National Memory and the Social Construction of Heroism," *Journal of African History* 49 (2008): 420.

47 Anne McClintock, "'No Longer in a Future Heaven': Nationalism, Gender, and Race," in *Becoming National: A Reader,* ed. Geoff Eley and Ronald Grigor Suny (New York: Oxford University Press, 1996), 273.

48 Adebanwi, "Death, National Memory," 421.

49 Ọladipọ Yemitan, *Madame Tinubu: Merchant and King-Maker* (Ibadan: University Press 1987), 71–72.

50 Lloyd Kramer, "Historical Narratives and the Meaning of Nationalism," *Journal of the History of Ideas* 58, no. 3 (1997): 536.

51 Homi Bhabha, "Introduction: Narrating the Nation," in *Nation and Narration,* ed. Homi Bhabha (New York: Routledge, 1990), 1.

52 Wale Adebanwi, *Nation as Grand Narrative: The Nigerian Press and the Politics of Meaning* (Rochester, NY: University of Rochester Press, 2016), 13–18, 20.

53 Adebanwi, *Nation as Grand Narrative,* 72.

54 Chatterjee, *Nation and Its Fragments,* 136.

55 Anne McClintock, *Imperial Leather: Race, Gender and Sexuality in the Colonial Contest* (New York: Routledge, 1995), 355–56. See also Catherine Hall, "Gender, Nations and Nationalisms," in *People, Nation and State: The Meaning of Ethnicity and Nationalism,* ed. Edward Mortimer (New York: I. B. Tauris, 1999), 45–55, and Ruth Roach Pierson and Nupur Chaudhuri, eds., *Nation, Empire, Colony: Historicizing Gender and Race* (Bloomington: Indiana University Press, 1998).

56 McClintock, *Imperial Leather,* 354.

57 Beth Baron, *Egypt as a Woman: Nationalism, Gender, and Politics* (Berkeley: University of California Press, 2005). See also Suruchi Thapar, "Women as Activists; Women as Symbols: A Study of the Indian Nationalist Movement," *Feminist Review,* no. 44 (Summer 1993): 81–96.

58 Zahia Smail Salhi, "The Algerian Feminist Movement between Nationalism, Patriarchy and Islamism," *Women's Studies International Forum* 33, no. 2 (2010): 115.

59 Elizabeth Schmidt, *Mobilizing the Masses: Gender, Ethnicity, and Class in the Nationalist Movement in Guinea, 1939–1958* (Portsmouth, NH: Heinemann, 2005), 114–43.

60 Meredith Terretta, *Petitioning for Our Rights, Fighting for Our Nation: The History of the Democratic Union of Cameroonian Women, 1949–1960* (Bamenda, Cameroon: Langaa Research and Publishing Common

Initiative Group, 2013), 8. From its inception in 1948, the UPC earned the government's disfavor since it advocated independence and reunification of French and British Cameroon. In response to the government's decision to ban the party in 1955, some of its leadership fled to British Cameroon, but Ruben Um Nyobé, the UPC secretary-general, remained in the French territory and launched a guerrilla struggle. A French military patrol ambushed and killed Nyobé in 1958. Meredith Terretta, "'God of Independence, God of Peace': Village Politics and Nationalism in the *Maquis* of Cameroon, 1957–71," *Journal of African History* 46, no. 1 (2005): 79.

61   Abosede A. George, *Making Modern Girls: A History of Girlhood, Labor, and Social Development in Colonial Lagos* (Athens: Ohio University Press, 2014); Saheed Aderinto, *When Sex Threatened the State: Illicit Sexuality, Nationalism, and Politics in Colonial Nigeria, 1900–1958* (Urbana: University of Illinois Press, 2014).

62   Timothy Scarnecchia, "Poor Women and Nationalist Politics: Alliances and Fissures in the Formation of a Nationalist Political Movement in Salisbury, Rhodesia, 1950–6," *Journal of African History* 37, no. 2 (1996): 284. See also Timothy Scarnecchia, *The Urban Roots of Democracy and Political Violence in Zimbabwe: Harare and Highfield, 1940–1964* (Rochester, NY: University of Rochester Press, 2008).

63   Joane Nagel, "Masculinity and Nationalism: Gender and Sexuality in the Making of Nations," *Ethnic and Racial Studies* 21, no. 2 (1998): 242–69.

64   Insa Nolte, *Obafemi Awolowo and the Making of Remo: The Local Politics of a Nigerian Nationalist* (Trenton, NJ: Africa World Press, 2010), 156. Hannah played a public political role during his absence—during his imprisonment and after his death.

65   Thembisa Waetjen, "The Limits of Gender Rhetoric for Nationalism: A Case Study from Southern Africa," *Theory and Society* 30, no. 1 (February 2001): 124.

66   Waetjen, "Limits of Gender Rhetoric," 126.

67   Susan Z. Andrade, *The Nation Writ Small: African Fictions and Feminisms, 1958–1988* (Durham, NC: Duke University Press, 2011), 8, 20–21. For a discussion on the critical role of novels in nation-building and the trope of family in constructing the nation, see Doris Sommer, "Irresistible Romance: The Foundational Fictions of Latin America," in *Nation and Narration*, ed. Homi Bhabha (New York: Routledge, 1990), 71–98, and Doris Sommer, *Foundational Fictions: The National Romances of Latin America* (Berkeley: University of California Press, 1991).

68   Lloyd S. Kramer, "Nations as Texts: Literary Theory and the History of Nationalism," *Maryland Historian* 24, no. 1 (1993): 78.

69   James S. Coleman, *Nigeria: Background to Nationalism* (Berkeley: University of California Press, 1971), 79.

70   Coleman, *Nigeria*, 89.

71 Coleman, 115.

72 Coleman, 291.

73 Coleman, 86.

74 Richard L. Sklar, *Nigerian Political Parties: Power in an Emergent African Nation* (1963; repr., Trenton, NJ: Africa World Press, 2004), 402.

75 Thomas Hodgkin, *Nationalism in Colonial Africa* (1957; repr., New York: New York University Press, 1971), 89–92.

76 Hodgkin, *Nationalism in Colonial Africa*, 90–91.

77 Hodgkin, 91.

78 Hodgkin, 91–92. The original quote is taken from John Lawrence Le Breton Hammond and Barbara Bradby Hammond, *The Age of the Chartists, 1832–1854: A Study of Discontent* (London: Longmans, Green, 1930).

79 Jane I. Guyer, "Representation without Taxation: An Essay on Democracy in Rural Nigeria, 1952–1990," *African Studies Review* 35, no. 1 (April 1992): 42.

80 Franklin wrote the phrase in a letter to the French scientist Jean-Baptiste Leroy on November 13, 1789. "Almanac," Associated Press, *Telegraph Herald* (Dubuque, IA), November 13, 2014, 2.

81 John Brewer, *The Sinews of Power: War, Money and the English State, 1688–1783* (Cambridge, MA: Harvard University Press, 1988), 92.

82 Guyer, "Representation without Taxation," 42–43.

83 Guyer, 41.

84 A. G. Adebayo, "Jangali: Fulani Pastoralists and Colonial Taxation in Northern Nigeria," *International Journal of African Historical Studies* 28, no. 1 (1995): 117.

85 For examples, see Ben Naanen, "'You Are Demanding Tax from the Dead': The Introduction of Direct Taxation and Its Aftermath in South-Eastern Nigeria, 1928–39," *African Economic History*, no. 34 (2006): 69–102; Paul E. Lovejoy and Jan S. Hogendorn, *Slow Death for Slavery: The Course of Abolition in Northern Nigeria, 1897–1936* (Cambridge: Cambridge University Press, 1993); Colin Newbury, "Accounting for Power in Northern Nigeria," *Journal of African History* 45 (2004): 257–77; and Philip J. Havik, "Colonial Administration, Public Accounts and Fiscal Extraction: Policies and Revenues in Portuguese Africa (1900–1960)," *African Economic History* 41 (2013): 159–221.

86 See Nancy Rose Hunt, "Noise over Camouflaged Polygamy, Colonial Morality Taxation, and a Woman-Naming Crisis in Belgian Africa," *Journal of African History* 32, no. 3 (1991): 471–94, and Sean Redding, "Legal Minors and Social Children: Rural African Women and Taxation in the Transkei, South Africa," *African Studies Review* 36, no. 3 (1993): 49–74.

87 A. G. Hopkins, "Back to the Future: From National History to Imperial History," *Past and Present* 164, no. 1 (1999): 229.

88 Moses E. Ochonu, *Colonial Meltdown: Northern Nigeria in the Great Depression* (Athens: Ohio University Press, 2009).

89 Barbara Bush and Josephine Maltby, "Taxation in West Africa: Transforming the Colonial Subject into the 'Governable Person,'" *Critical Perspectives on Accounting* 15, no. 1 (2004): 7.

90 Bush and Maltby, "Taxation in West Africa," 15.

91 Janet Roitman, *Fiscal Disobedience: An Anthropology of Economic Regulation in Central Africa* (Princeton, NJ: Princeton University Press, 2005), 60.

92 Roitman, *Fiscal Disobedience*, 60.

93 Dean Neu and Monica Heincke, "The Subaltern Speaks: Financial Relations and the Limits of Governmentality," *Critical Perspectives on Accounting* 15, no. 1 (2004): 182–84.

94 Bush and Maltby, "Taxation in West Africa," 26.

95 Roitman, *Fiscal Disobedience*, 53–56.

CHAPTER 1: THE BIRTH AND DEMISE OF A NATION

1 Olúfémi Táíwò, *How Colonialism Preempted Modernity in Africa* (Bloomington: Indiana University Press, 2010), 103.

2 Lord Lugard first crafted the principles that became the foundation of indirect rule in the treaty he concluded with the kabaka in 1892. His subsequent experiences in Nigeria further convinced him that British imperial success was best assured by ruling through indigenous political elites. I. M. Okonjo, *British Administration in Nigeria 1900–1950: A Nigerian View* (New York: NOK, 1974), 25. See also Elliott Green, "Ethnicity and Nationhood in Precolonial Africa: The Case of Buganda," *Nationalism and Ethnic Politics* 16, no. 1 (2010): 11–14.

3 William MacGregor, "Lagos, Abeokuta and the Alake," *Journal of the Royal African Society* 3, no. 12 (July 1904): 481.

4 MacGregor, "Lagos, Abeokuta and the Alake," 475.

5 MacGregor, 475.

6 Returnees to Yorubaland included groups from different regions of what some scholars now call the Yoruba diaspora. Especially in Lagos, one could find returnees of Yoruba ancestry from Brazil, Cuba, Sierra Leone, and the United States. West Indians, though not necessarily of Yoruba ancestry, also settled in Lagos in the nineteenth century. For a fuller discussion, see the pioneering study by Jean Herskovits Koyptoff, *A Preface to Modern Nigeria: The "Sierra Leonians" in Yoruba, 1830–1890* (Madison: University of Wisconsin Press, 1965), as well as Kristin Mann, *Slavery and the Birth of an African City: Lagos, 1760–1900* (Bloomington: Indiana University Press, 2007); Lisa Lindsay, *Atlantic Bonds: A Nineteenth-Century Odyssey from America to Africa* (Chapel Hill: University of North Carolina Press, 2017); and Toyin Falola and Matt D. Childs, eds., *The Yoruba Diaspora in the Atlantic World* (Bloomington: Indiana University Press, 2004).

7 Emmanuel A. Ayandele, *The Missionary Impact on Modern Nigeria, 1842–1914: A Political and Social Analysis* (Harlow, UK: Longman, 1966), 7.

8   Ayandele, *Missionary Impact*, 11.

9   Agneta Pallinder-Law, "Aborted Modernization in West Africa? The Case of Abeokuta," *Journal of African History* 15, no. 1 (1974): 68.

10 Ayandele, *Missionary Impact*, 11.

11 Ayandele, 13–15. Egba mistrust of Europeans grew exponentially after Lagos was annexed in 1861. By 1867, as the Egba relationship with the British became more strained, rage at the British manifested in the destruction of property belonging to white missionaries. The immediate spark for the uprising against the missionaries, the Ifole, was the decision by the Lagos government to post constables in areas on the mainland that the Egbas considered to be under their jurisdiction. The EUBM ordered the closure of churches and chapels in Abeokuta, which seemed to be the impetus for the destruction of mission stations and converts' homes.

12 Robert W. July, *The Origins of Modern African Thought: Its Development in West Africa during the Nineteenth and Twentieth Centuries* (New York: Frederick A. Praeger, 1967), 197. Johnson was invited to England by Prince Alfred in 1860 after the prince heard him play the flute in Freetown during a visit.

13 Pallinder-Law, "Aborted Modernization," 69–70.

14 Pallinder-Law, 70.

15 July, *Origins of Modern African Thought*, 207.

16 Ayandele, *Missionary Impact*, 49.

17 Pallinder-Law, "Aborted Modernization," 71.

18 S. O. Biobaku, "The Egba Council, 1899–1918," in *Odù: A Journal of Yoruba and Related Studies*, vol. 2, ed. S. O. Biobaku, H. U. Beier, and L. Levi (Ibadan: Western Region Literature Committee; Edinburgh: Thomas Nelson and Sons, 1955), 16.

19 Biobaku, "Egba Council," 17–18.

20 Táíwò, *How Colonialism Preempted Modernity in Africa*, 226.

21 Koyptoff, *Preface to Modern Nigeria*, 178.

22 Ayandele, *Missionary Impact*, 45.

23 Ajayi Kọlawọlẹ Ajiṣafẹ, *History of Abeokuta*, 3rd ed. (Lagos: Kash and Klare Bookshop, 1948), 75.

24 Pallinder-Law, "Aborted Modernization," 71.

25 Ayandele, *Missionary Impact*, 46.

26 "A Political Commotion at Abeokuta," *Lagos Times*, August 24, 1881.

27 Ajiṣafẹ, *History of Abeokuta*, 77–78. Townsend tried to return in 1871 but was refused entry. The Egba chiefs refused entry to all Europeans, largely due to their suspicions of the Lagos government. Townsend and his wife did not return to Abeokuta until 1875.

28 Ajiṣafẹ, 79.

29 Adebesin Folarin, *The Ogboni and Other Chieftaincies in Abeokuta: Their Purports and Meanings* (Itoko, Abeokuta: E.N.A. Press, 1934), 22–24. For more on these deities, see Nouréini Tidjani-Serpos, "The

Postcolonial Condition: The Archaeology of African Knowledge: From the Feat of Ogun and Sango to the Postcolonial Creativity of Obatala," *Research in African Literatures* 27, no. 1 (1996): 3–16, and William R. Bascom, "The Sanctions of Ifa Divination," *Journal of the Royal Anthropological Institute of Great Britain and Ireland* 71, nos. 1/2 (1941): 43–54.

30 "The Mighty Is Fallen," *Lagos Times,* October 25, 1882.

31 "The Mighty Is Fallen."

32 Koyptoff, *Preface to Modern Nigeria,* 233.

33 Oladipo Yemitan, *Madame Tinubu, Merchant and King-Maker* (Ibadan: University Press, 1987), 14–27, 47–49. Tinubu played host to a number of important visitors to the town, including Benjamin Campbell, the British consul in Lagos, and the African American journalist Martin Robinson Delany.

34 Ayandele, *Missionary Impact,* 194.

35 Ayandele, 116.

36 Ayandele, 194.

37 Ayandele, 196.

38 Ayandele, 46.

39 "Chief Ogundipe of Abeokuta," *Lagos Times,* May 10, 1882.

40 Ayandele, *Missionary Impact,* 47.

41 Emmanuel A. Ayandele, *Holy Johnson, Pioneer of African Nationalism, 1836–1917* (London: Cass, 1970), 124.

42 Ayandele, *Holy Johnson,* 115.

43 James Johnson to H. Wright, September 18, 1879, CA2/o56, Church Missionary Society (hereafter CMS).

44 James Johnson to H. Wright.

45 James Johnson, "The Debate on the European Marriage Custom, Friday, November 2, 1888, at the Breadfruit Schoolroom, Lagos, at the Call of the Lagos Young Men's Christian Association," CA2/o56, CMS, microfilm available through the Center for Research Libraries.

46 Anna Hinderer, *Seventeen Years in the Yoruba Country* (London: Seeley, Jackson and Halliday, 1873), 5. For more examples of missionary households, see R. H. Stone, *In Africa's Forest and Jungle or Six Years among the Yorubas* (Edinburgh: Anderson and Ferrier, 1900).

47 Hinderer, *Seventeen Years,* 103.

48 Hinderer, 70.

49 Hinderer, 91.

50 Hinderer, 126.

51 Hinderer, 101.

52 Hinderer, 111.

53 Hinderer, 110. "These Yoruba people have some very nice arrangements about their form of government. I found out that there was an 'Iyalode' or mother of the town, to whom all the women's palavers (disputes) are taken. . . . She is, in fact, a sort of queen, a person of much influence, and looked up to with much respect."

54 Ernest Fry, "Letter from Mr. Ernest Fry (No. IX)," Abeokuta, May 1902, 4, CMS.

55 Phillis Fry, "Letter No. 20 (Mrs. Fry)," Abeokuta, August 1, 1908, 2, CMS.

56 J. White to Venn, June 6, 1867, quoted in J. D. Y. Peel, "Gender in Yoruba Religious Change," *Journal of Religion in Africa* 32, fasc. 2 (May 2002): 161.

57 Peel, "Gender in Yoruba Religious Change," 161.

58 N. A. Fadipe, *The Sociology of the Yoruba* (Ibadan: Ibadan University Press, 1970), 88.

59 Mann, *Marrying Well: Marriage, Status, and Social Change among the Educated Elite in Colonial Lagos* (New York: Cambridge University Press, 1985), 40. These practices were shaped to varying degrees by the type of marriage one entered—dowry, gift, or slave—and the status of each spouse.

60 Mann, *Marrying Well*, 88–91.

61 James Johnson to H. Wright, August 2, 1879, 5, CA2/o56, CMS. Johnson estimated that fifty strings of cowries were equivalent to one shilling. He thought owners were unconscionable for demanding such payments from their slaves while opposing efforts to raise church dues to seven and a half strings per week.

62 Johnson to Wright.

63 Johnson to Wright. Mary Coker was an especially important trader, and two of her three sons went on to hold important titles. Isaac became a parakoyi chief in 1904, and Samuel became an assistant Christian balogun, while Robert became a catechist for the CMS in Abeokuta. E. A. Oroge, "The Institution of Slavery in Yorubaland with Particular Reference to the Nineteenth Century" (PhD thesis, University of Birmingham, 1971), 257.

64 J. D. Y. Peel, *Religious Encounter and the Making of the Yoruba* (Bloomington: Indiana University Press, 2000), 234.

65 Hinderer, *Seventeen Years*, 131–36.

66 Peel, *Religious Encounter*, 235.

67 Peel, "Gender in Yoruba Religious Change," 158.

68 "Chief Ogudipe of Abeokuta," *Lagos Times*, May 10, 1882.

69 J. B. Kenny, letter to the editor, *Lagos Standard*, July 29, 1896.

70 An Eye Witness, "The Coronation of Alake Gbadebo, Present King of the Kingdom of Abeokuta," *Lagos Standard*, September 7, 1898. Gbadebo's father was the first alake of Abeokuta. Though born into the aristocracy, he was not wealthy. He was a canoe-man, transporting passengers across the Ogun river, before his installation.

71 Governor G. T. Carter to the Marquis of Ripon, January 18, 1893, in *British Policy towards West Africa: Select Documents, 1875–1914*, comp. C. W. Newbury (Oxford: Clarendon Press, 1971), 131. See also Agneta Pallinder-Law, "Government in Abeokuta, 1830–1914: With Special

Reference to the Egba United Government, 1898–1914" (PhD diss., University of Gothenburg, 1973), 59. The treaty, however, forced Abeokuta to relinquish control of several towns near Lagos. See Harry A. Gailey, *Lugard and the Abeokuta Uprising: The Demise of Egba Independence* (London: Frank Cass, 1982), 28.

72 Samuel Johnson, *The History of the Yorubas: From the Earliest Times to the Beginning of the British Protectorate* (1921; repr., London: Routledge and Kegan Paul, 1973), 651.

73 Gailey, *Lugard and the Abeokuta Uprising*, 31.

74 Pallinder-Law, "Government in Abeokuta," 65. Pallinder-Law argues that this was the most novel feature of the reorganization. For various religious reasons, obas were not allowed to meet previously.

75 An Eye Witness, "Coronation of Alake Gbadebo."

76 Cyril Punch, "A Report on the Native Law of Egbaland, 1906," MSS Afr.s.1913, Rhodes House Library, Oxford University.

77 Akin Mabogunje, "The Evolution of Rural Settlement in Egba Division, Nigeria," *Journal of Tropical Agriculture* 13 (1959): 72.

78 Urbanization is a long-standing feature of Yoruba culture. Towns are made of up of quarters comprising compounds belonging to different lineage groups. In Abeokuta, lineage groups staked out farmlands as far as thirty miles away, and farmers established hamlets near them because it was too great a distance to walk daily. However, festivals were held in Abeokuta, and it was the custom for every Egba to be buried in the section of town to which he or she belonged. See Akinjide Osuntokun, *Nigeria in the First World War* (Atlantic Highlands, NJ: Humanities Press, 1979), 103, and P. C. Lloyd, *Yoruba Land Law* (London: Oxford University Press, 1962), 54–59. See also Jeremy S. Eades, *The Yoruba Today* (London: Cambridge University Press, 1980).

79 Julian Clarke, "Households and the Political Economy of Small-Scale Cash Crop Production in South-Western Nigeria," *Africa* 51, no. 4 (1981): 819–20. See also Daryll Forde, "The Rural Economies," in *The Native Economies of Nigeria*, ed. Margery Perham (London: Faber and Faber, 1946), 98–99. Forde estimated that women constituted 50 percent of these traders, who were called pan, or basket, buyers.

80 His obituary identified Blaize as a generous donor to the Africa Society, a member of its council, and "a strong Imperialist in his belief that the British empire was on the whole the best agency in knitting together the white, black, and yellows races of the world in a league of peace and commerce." "Mr. Richard B. Blaize," *Journal of the Royal African Society* 4, no. 13 (1904): 150.

81 Ajiṣafẹ, *History of Abeokuta*, 100.

82 Agneta Pallinder-Law, "Adegboyega Edun: Black Englishman and Yoruba Cultural Patriot," in *Self-Assertion and Brokerage: Early Cultural Nationalism in West Africa*, ed. P. F. de Moraes Farias and Karin Barber

(Birmingham: Centre of West African Studies, University of Birmingham, 1990), 17.

83   *Westminster Gazette,* April 24, 1904, quoted in Pallinder-Law, "Adegboyega Edun," 17. Interestingly, Pallinder-Law argues that it is doubtful that he considered himself to be a cultural nationalist. He wore Yoruba robes on only two occasions—his two trips to London. In Lagos and Abeokuta, he always wore suits.

84   Fred I. A. Omu, *Press and Politics in Nigeria, 1880–1937* (Atlantic Highlands, NJ: Humanities Press, 1978), 26.

85   *Lagos Standard,* February 23, 1898, and *Lagos Weekly Record,* March 22, 1913, cited in Omu, *Press and Politics,* 216.

86   Ernest Fry, Letter from Mr. Ernest Fry (No. 4), Abeokuta, April 1900, 3, CMS.

87   Ernest Fry, Letter from Mr. Ernest Fry (No. 2), Abeokuta, October 1899, 4, CMS.

88   Cheryl Johnson-Odim and Nina Emma Mba, *For Women and the Nation: Funmilayo Ransome-Kuti of Nigeria* (Urbana: University of Illinois Press, 1997), 24. See also Judith A. Byfield, "In Her Own Words: Funmilayo Ransome-Kuti and the Auto/biography of an Archive," *Palimpsest: A Journal on Women, Gender, and the Black International* 5, no. 2 (2016): 107–27.

89   Pallinder-Law, "Aborted Modernization," 74.

90   Ajiṣafẹ, *History of Abeokuta,* 99. Sokunbi had attended Lagos Grammar School. Ajiṣafẹ noted, "All the intelligent persons in Abeokuta also took and recognized him as their own King, and not the King of Oke Ona people alone."

91   Pallinder-Law, "Aborted Modernization," 75.

92   Pallinder-Law, 76.

93   "Presentation to Hon. A. Edun, Appreciation by Young Abeokuta," *Lagos Weekly Record,* November 1, 1913. The delegation with members from other British colonies went to London to speak against the West African Lands Committee proposal to give the Crown control of peasant lands. More than likely, the Reverend Ransome-Kuti in attendance would have been the father-in-law (J. J. Ransome-Kuti) of Funmilayo. Her husband, Rev. I. O. Ransome-Kuti, was in Sierra Leone at Fourah Bay College from January 1913 to the end of 1916. See Tunde Adeyanju, *The Rev. Israel Oludotun Ransome-Kuti: Teacher and Nation Builder* (Abeokuta: Litany Nigeria, 1993), 4.

94   Ayandele, *Holy Johnson,* 120.

95   Omu, *Press and Politics,* 29–30.

96   Ayandele, *Holy Johnson,* 95–97.

97   Ajiṣafẹ, *History of Abeokuta,* 104.

98   Ayandele, *Holy Johnson,* 95–97.

99   Ernest Fry, Letter from Mr. Ernest Fry (No. 9), Abeokuta, May 1902, CMS.

100 Quoted in Pallinder-Law, "Adegboyega Edun," 24–25.

101 Ernest Fry, Letter from Mr. Ernest Fry (No. 5), Abeokuta, July 1900, 3, CMS.

102 Ayandele, *Missionary Impact*, 290.

103 Phillis Fry, Letter from Mrs. Ernest Fry (No. 23), Abeokuta, February 1, 1910, 1, CMS.

104 Ernest Fry, Letter from Mr. Ernest Fry (No. X), Abeokuta, August 1902, 2, CMS.

105 "The Health of Abeokuta," *Lagos Weekly Record*, April 6, 1913.

106 Letter from Frederick Lugard to the Secretary of State, January 17, 1913, CO 520/122 157387, National Archives, Kew Gardens (hereafter cited as TNA). The information was gathered for the West African Lands Committee.

107 Notes on Interview of the Alake with Representatives of the Christian Bodies, June 12, 1914, Miscellaneous Record Book, Egba Council Records (hereafter ECR) 1/1/9, National Archives of Nigeria, Abeokuta (hereafter NAN Abeokuta). The obituary of John Okenla, the Christian balogun, noted that during periods of insecurity he called "his important friends together and advised them to subscribe toward procuring more ammunitions for the defence of Abeokuta against the attack of enemies." See "Mighty Is Fallen."

108 Ajiṣafẹ, *History of Abeokuta*, 116.

109 Clarke, "Households and the Political Economy," 819.

110 Isaac O. Delano, *The Singing Minister of Nigeria: The Life of Canon J. J. Ransome-Kuti* (London: United Society for Christian Literature, 1942), 27.

111 From Our Own Correspondent, "Captain Denton's Mission to Abeokuta," *Lagos Standard*, September 1, 1897.

112 Ernest Fry, Letter from Mr. Ernest Fry (No. XIV), Abeokuta, November 1903, 1, CMS. He also noted that the town had several other health practitioners—two or three qualified native dispensers who opened druggist shops and a government doctor at the railway station.

113 C. Partridge, "Native Law and Custom in Egbaland," *Journal of the Royal African Society* 10, no. 40 (1911): 423–24.

114 "The Social Disruption Going on in the Hinterland," *Lagos Weekly Record*, July 8, 1911.

115 Fadipe, *Sociology of the Yoruba*, 91.

116 Committee on the Currency of the West African Colonies, Minutes of Evidence, November 17, 1899, 13, CSO 520/4, TNA.

117 In 1899, George Denton, the acting governor of Lagos, effectively forced the Egbas to cede two hundred yards on both sidesof the railway line to the British government in a ninety-nine-year lease. In addition, the EUG ceded judicial control over matters pertaining to the railway and its substantial number of employees (eight thousand). Pallinder-Law, "Government in Abeokuta," 73.

118   Ernest Fry, Letter from Mr. Ernest Fry (No. XIV), Abeokuta, November 1903, 2, CMS.

119   Editorial, *Lagos Standard*, January 31, 1900. A young woman in third or fourth standard would be in the American equivalent of elementary school. For a fuller discussion of the role of dress in this discussion, see Judith Byfield, "'Unwrapping' Nationalism: Dress, Gender and Nationalist Discourse in Colonial Lagos" (discussion paper, African Humanities Program, no. 30, 2000, African Studies Center, Boston University), 1–21.

120   G. O. Oguntomisin, "Political Change and Adaptation in Yorubaland in the Nineteenth Century," *Canadian Journal of African Studies* 15, no. 2 (1981): 229.

121   Pallinder-Law, "Government in Abeokuta," 178–79.

122   Gailey, *Lugard and the Abeokuta Uprising*, 58.

123   Pallinder-Law, "Government in Abeokuta," 117. In fact, the oluwo of Ijemo was only invited to sit on the EUG council in April 1907 in response to agitation that began in December 1906. His election was "so that he may be improved and tamed."

124   Osuntokun, *Nigeria in the First World War*, 104–5.

125   Adebesin Folarin, *The Demise of the Independence of Egba-Land: The Ijemo Trouble*, pt. 1 (Lagos: Tika-Tore Printing Works, 1916), 4–6.

126   Gailey, *Lugard and the Abeokuta Uprising*, 62.

127   Gailey, 63.

128   Gailey, 61.

129   Gailey, 63. Sir Hugh Clifford, who became governor of Nigeria in 1919, later suggested that Young had misled Moorhouse and not informed him of the real reason that sparked the insurrection against the EUG, the death of Ponlade. Clifford read all the reports on the 1914 and 1918 uprisings in Abeokuta before assuming his office in Nigeria and offered rather scathing criticisms of Governor Lugard and several members of his administration. See Confidential Despatch, Governor Hugh Clifford to Viscount Alfred Milner, Secretary of State for the Colonies, para. 11, August 29, 1919, CO 583/77, TNA. Clifford's criticisms raised a furor at the Colonial Office, and his argument was rebutted by the senior member of the Colonial Office staff, J. E. Clauson, who "intimated that Clifford was motivated by a sense of rancour and jealousy of Lugard." Gailey, *Lugard and the Abeokuta Uprising*, 115.

130   Saburi O. Biobaku, *The Egba and Their Neighbors, 1842–1872* (Oxford: Clarendon Press, 1965), 6. See also Peter Morton-Williams, "An Outline of the Cosmology and Cult Organization of the Oyo Yoruba," *Africa: Journal of the International African Institute* 34, no. 3 (1964): 256, and John Thabiti Willis, *Masquerading Politics: Kinship, Gender, and Ethnicity in a Yoruba Town* (Bloomington: Indiana University Press, 2018), 111.

131 Folarin argues that the person who held the title of oluwo was acknowledged as the civil and political head of their township. See Adebesin Folarin, *The Ogboni and Other Chieftaincies in Abeokuta: Their Purports
and Meaning* (Itoko, Abeokuta: E.N.A. Press, 1934), 9.

132 Gailey, *Lugard and the Abeokuta Uprising*, 64.

133 For the first figure, see Perlham Vernon Young, Report of Commission of
Enquiry into the 1914 Killings in Abeokuta, Abe Prof 7/2, NAN Ibadan.
For the second figure, see Israel Aladegbami, *Report of Commission of
Enquiry into the 1914 Killings in Abeokuta*, Abe Prof 7/2, NAN Ibadan.
Aladegbami, a gardener at the Ake church in Abeokuta, claimed that
the dead included five children and a pregnant woman.

134 Belo Bida, *Report of the Commission of Enquiry into the 1914 Killing in
Abeokuta*, Abe Prof 7/2, NAN Ibadan.

135 August Anthony Martins, *Report of Commission of Enquiry into the 1914
Killings in Abeokuta*, Abe Prof 7/2, NAN Ibadan. Martins, the acting
commandant of police, was in charge of prisoners. Martins reported
that prisoners were commanded to set the dynamite charges.

136 Gailey, *Lugard and the Abeokuta Uprising*, 64.

137 Folarin, *Demise of the Independence of Egba-Land*, 12.

138 Lugard had instructed his staff to encourage the alake to accept military
assistance from the Lagos government whenever there was a political
crisis so that he could be pressured into surrendering the town's independence. See Clifford to Milner, para. 13, August 29, 1919, CO 583/77,
TNA.

139 Clifford to Milner, para. 19, August 29, 1919, CO 583/77, Public Records
Office, TNA. Clifford quoted a letter from the alake after his meeting
with Moorhouse, who encouraged him to call for assistance. The alake
wrote, "I have laid the whole matter before the Members of my Council, and I am pleased to say that I have their unanimous opinion that
the one remedy possible is the assistance of the British Government *if
the independence of the Egba Government in matters of internal administration is not to be entirely destroyed* [emphasis in original]." He also
accused Moorhouse of withholding from the alake that accepting his
advice would in fact abrogate the 1893 treaty.

140 Gailey, *Lugard and the Abeokuta Uprising*, 66.

141 Clifford also raised doubts about the decision to abrogate the treaty. He
noted that the EUG was not allowed to arm its police forces, thus making
it impossible for the government to defend itself in the face of insurrection. Clifford to Milner, para. 6, August 29, 1919, CO 583/77, TNA.

142 "The Fate of Abeokuta," *Lagos Weekly Record*, September 19, 1914.

143 Editorial, "The Lagos Native Councils and Forest Ordinances," *Lagos
Weekly Record*, December 6, 1902.

144 The Native Authority Ordinance and the administrative structure Lord
Lugard created retained its nomenclature, but his successors, beginning

with Governor Clifford, altered the structure. This contributed to the multiple terms used to identify Abeokuta's government—Egba Native Authority and Egba Native Administration. This was reflected in the name of the government bulletin as well. The Egba United Government published a monthly gazette, the *Egba Government Gazette*, from March 1904 until the loss of independence in 1914. Publication resumed in the 1920s as the *Egba Administration Bulletin*, but in the 1930s the gazette was renamed the *Egba Bulletin*. For more on the *Egba Government Gazette*, see Pallinder-Law, "Government in Abeokuta," 113–14.

145 Gailey, *Lugard and the Abeokuta Uprising*, 74.

146 Oluwatoyin Oduntan, *Power, Culture and Modernity in Nigeria: Beyond the Colony* (New York: Routledge, 2018), 109. Oduntan argues that earlier studies of the Adubi War ignore the importance of questions of identity and assimilation to the tensions between Owu chiefs and the ENA. Owu settlers looked upon the creation of new titles to oversee the tax plan as further evidence of their political marginalization.

147 Jane I. Guyer, "Representation without Taxation: An Essay on Democracy in Rural Nigeria, 1952–1990," *African Studies Review* 35, no. 1 (April 1992): 42–43.

148 Janet Roitman, *Fiscal Disobedience: An Anthropology of Economic Regulation in Central Africa* (Princeton, NJ: Princeton University Press, 2005), 60.

149 Nancy Rose Hunt, "Noise over Camouflaged Polygamy, Colonial Morality Taxation, and a Woman-Naming Crisis in Belgian Africa," *Journal of African History* 32, no. 3 (November 1991): 474.

150 Sean Redding, "Legal Minors and Social Children: Rural African Women and Taxation in the Transkei, South Africa," *African Studies Review* 36, no. 3 (December 1993): 62–63.

151 Alfred Harding, August 12, 1914, CO 583/17–82393, TNA.

152 Andrew E. Barnes, *Making Headway: The Introduction of Western Civilization in Colonial Northern Nigeria* (Rochester, NY: University of Rochester Press, 2009), 71. The jihad led by Usman Dan Fodio, a Muslim reformer of Fulani descent, paved the way for the Fulani to conquer the Hausa city-states of northern Nigeria and create the Sokoto Caliphate. Their attempt to push south finally ended with the conquest of the most northern Yoruba state, Ilorin. Although presented as a fully developed administrative model, indirect rule emerged from pragmatic needs and concessions as the British established dominance through the institutions, structures, and practices created by the Hausa-Fulani leadership of the caliphate. The British effectively reinforced the caliphate's control of much of the territory it conquered because caliphate officials served as proxy rulers for the colonial state. See Moses E. Ochonu, *Colonialism by Proxy: Hausa Imperial Agents and Middle Belt Consciousness in Nigeria* (Bloomington: Indiana University Press, 2014), 13.

153 Secret Letter from H. R. Palmer to Governor Lugard, December 19, 1914, MSS Lugard 58/6, Rhodes House Library, Oxford University. It appears that Palmer's tour began sometime in 1913. In the last half of 1914 after the Ijemo massacre, he was sent secretly to Abeokuta.

154 Secret Letter from Palmer to Lugard.

155 Governor-General Lugard Frederick Lugard to Lewis Harcourt, Secretary of State for the Colonies, August 10, 1914, CO 583/17–82393, TNA.

156 Minute on file, Direct Taxation, CO 583/17–82393, TNA.

157 A. Olorunfemi, "The Liquor Traffic Dilemma in British West Africa: The Southern Nigerian Example, 1895–1918," *International Journal of African Historical Studies* 17, no. 2 (1984): 237.

158 Olorunfemi, "Liquor Traffic," 238. Olorunfemi provides a chart that shows the amount of duty collected on spirits each year, the amount collected on other goods, and the percentage the spirits duty represented out of the total custom revenues.

159 Olorunfemi, 241.

160 *Report of the Commission of Enquiry into the Disturbances in Abeokuta Province*, 1918, 6, MSS AFR.S.1481, Rhodes House Library, Oxford University.

161 See A. Bonar-Law to Gov. Lugard, August, 12, 1916, CO583/45–158048, and Alfred Harding, May 17, 1916, CO583/45–158048, TNA. For more on the capture of Cameroon from Germany, see Osuntokun, *Nigeria in the First World War*, 169–205.

162 Confidential Letter from Alake Gbadebo to Sir Frederick Lugard, December 14, 1915, Ake 1/4, box II–5/1/7. The commission of enquiry report suggested that these discussions in fact began in 1913. *Report of Commission of Enquiry into Disturbances*, 11.

163 See "Annexure B—Report of Public Meeting, Ake Square Abeokuta 6 September, 1917," in Extracts from a Report by Mr. W. C. Syer, Resident Abeokuta Province, on the Introduction of Direct Taxation into the Egba Territory, March 18, 1918, CO583/66/157716, TNA.

164 Osuntokun, *Nigeria in the First World War*, 127. See also John L. Ausman, "The Disturbances in Abeokuta in 1918," *Canadian Journal of African Studies* 5, no. 1 (1971): 45–60.

165 Extracts from a Report by Syer, March 18, 1918, annex C, para. E.

166 H. R. Palmer, Report on a Tour in the Southern Provinces, Nigeria 1914, appendix C, 87, MSS Lugard 58/7, Rhodes House Library, Oxford University.

167 In order to understand the tax structure in the north, Edun toured Kano and Zaria. See Fred I. A. Omu, *Press and Politics in Nigeria, 1880–1937* (Atlantic Highlands, NJ: Humanities Press, 1978), 217.

168 Letter from C. T. Lawrence, Acting Secretary, Southern Provinces, to F. Adams, Resident, Abeokuta Province, March 11, 1927, CSO 26/19855, NAN Ibadan.

169 Letter from F. Adams, Resident Abeokuta Province to Secretary, Southern Provinces, April 11, 1927, C.S.O. 26/19855, NAN Ibadan.

170 Letter from Adams, 2.

171 *Report of Commission of Enquiry into Disturbances*, 17–18.

172 Gailey, *Lugard and the Abeokuta Uprising*, 87, 91; Osuntokun, *Nigeria in the First World War*, 128. For more on Nigeria's colonial army, see John Barrett, "The Rank and File of the Colonial Army in Nigeria, 1914–18," *Journal of Modern African Studies* 15, no. 1 (1977): 105–15.

173 Extracts from a Report by Syer, March 18, 1918, 2.

174 *Report of Commission of Enquiry into Disturbances*, 19–20.

175 *Testimony to the Commission of Enquiry into the Disturbances into Abeokuta Province*, November 8, 1918, 129, CSO 16/120 C92/1918, NAN Ibadan.

176 W. Folarin Sosan, Report of the Clerk of Council on the Visit of the Alake and Other Members of Council to Oba to Arrange for Labour for the Construction of Abeokuta-Ijebu-Ode Road, 3, Abe Prof 2/3–239/15, NAN Ibadan.

177 J. H. Balfour de Montmorency, Acting District Officer, Egba Division, Road Report 10/3/1917, Abe Prof 2/3–239/15, NAN Ibadan.

178 Letter from the Resident to the Alake, May 8, 1917, ECR 3/1/12, NAN Ibadan.

179 Extracts from a Report by Syer, March 18, 1918, 4.

180 Letter from Resident to Alake, June 21, 1917, ECR 3/1/12, NAN Ibadan.

181 *Report of Commission of Enquiry into Disturbances*, 20.

182 *Testimony to Commission of Enquiry into Disturbances*, October 30, 1918, 27.

183 *Testimony to Commission of Enquiry into Disturbances*, November 30, 1918, 130.

184 *Testimony to Commission of Enquiry into Disturbances*, November 8, 1918, 8–9.

185 *Testimony to Commission of Enquiry into Disturbances*, November 8, 1918, 17.

186 *Report of Commission of Enquiry into Disturbances*, 22.

187 Extracts from a Report by Syer, March 18, 1918, annex C, para. E, TNA.

188 *Report of Commission of Enquiry into Disturbances*, 12.

189 Samuel Fury Childs Daly, "From Crime to Coercion: Policing Dissent in Abeokuta, Nigeria, 1900–1940," *Journal of Imperial and Commonwealth History* 47, no. 3 (2019): 483.

190 Confidential Memo from Hugh Clifford to Viscount Milner, August 29, 1919, CO 583/77, 118, TNA. Several witnesses to the commission of enquiry testified that Syer instructed the presidents of the native courts at one of their monthly meetings to increase the fines and charge costs. *Report of Commission of Enquiry into Disturbances*, 18.

191 *Report of Commission of Enquiry into Disturbances*, 17.

192 *Testimony to Commission of Enquiry into Disturbances*, November 8, 1918, 131.

193 *Report of Commission of Enquiry into Disturbances*, 18.

194 *Report of Commission of Enquiry into Disturbances*, 18.

195 Ajisafe, *History of Abeokuta*, 117.

196 *Report of Commission of Enquiry into Disturbances*, 18.

197 *Report of Commission of Enquiry into Disturbances*, 18.

198 *Report of Commission of Enquiry into Disturbances*, 5, 27.

199 Letter from Hugh Clifford to Alfred Harding, July 28, 1919, CO 583/76/158043, TNA.

200 Mabogunje, "Evolution of Rural Settlement," 66.

201 Mabogunje, 72.

202 *Testimony to Commission of Enquiry into Disturbances*, November 8, 1918, 18.

203 *Testimony to Commission of Enquiry into Disturbances*, November 8, 1918, 14.

204 *Testimony to Commission of Enquiry into Disturbances*, November 11, 1918, 212.

205 This stands in contrast to the Igbo Women's War in 1929, in which Igbo men and women challenged the social and moral efficacy of taxing women. See Nina Mba, *Nigerian Women Mobilized: Women's Political Activity in Southern Nigeria, 1900–1965* (Berkeley: Institute of International Studies, University of California, 1982), 76.

206 As Emma Hunter points out, most colonial regimes across the continent justified forced labor on the basis of the public good. Emma Hunter, "Voluntarism, Virtuous Citizenship, and Nation-Building in Late Colonial and Early Postcolonial Tanzania," *African Studies Review* 58, no. 2 (2015): 50.

207 "Adebesin Folarin," Open Library, https://openlibrary.org/authors/OL874631A/Adebesin_Folarin.

208 Adebesin Folarin, *England and the English: Personal Impressions during a Three Years' Sojourn* (London: John Taylor, n.d.), 47–48.

209 Mba, *Nigerian Women Mobilized*, 76.

210 Benedict Anderson, *Imagined Communities: Reflections on the Origin and Spread of Nationalism*, rev. ed. (New York: Verso, 1991), 7.

211 Gailey, *Lugard and the Abeokuta Uprising*, 106.

CHAPTER 2: ABEOKUTA'S CENTENARY

1 Anne McClintock, "'No Longer in a Future Heaven': Nationalism, Gender, and Race," in *Becoming National: A Reader*, ed. Geoff Eley and Ronald Grigor Suny (New York: Oxford University Press, 1996), 273. See also J. Alton Templin, "The Ideology of a Chosen People: Afrikaner Nationalism and the Ossewa Trek, 1938," *Nations and Nationalism* 5, no. 3 (1999): 397–417.

2 Srirupa Roy, *Beyond Belief: India and the Politics of Postcolonial Nationalism* (Durham, NC: Duke University Press, 2007), 66, cited in

Carola Lentz, "Celebrating Independence Jubilees and the Millennium: National Days in Africa," *Nations and Nationalism* 19, no. 2 (2013): 208–9.

3   Lentz, 209–10. Postapartheid South Africa's commemoration of the centenary of the Boer War offers one of the best examples of the challenges when using commemorations to perform nation-building. The event raised questions about the use of Black boys and girls to represent the Boers and debates about the degree to which Blacks suffered during this conflict that had been constructed as a war between the British and the Boers. See Albert Grundlingh, "Reframing Remembrance: The Politics of the Centenary Commemoration of the South African War of 1899–1902," *Journal of Southern African Studies* 39, no. 2 (2004): 359–75.

4   See Andrew Apter, *The Pan-African Nation: Oil and the Spectacle of Culture in Nigeria* (Chicago: University of Chicago Press, 2005), 167–93, and Wendy Griswold and Muhammed Bhadmus, "The Kano Durbar: Political Aesthetics in the Bowel of the Elephant," *American Journal of Cultural Sociology* 1, no. 1 (2013): 125–51. Lord Lugard first staged a durbar in Nigeria to mark the takeover of the Royal Niger Company's charter. It was a contrived spectacle imported from India by British officials to represent indirect rule. In contrast, the Odwira festival (the celebration of the new yams) over time became the central mechanism for reaffirming the proper relationship between the ancestors and the living as well as the loyalty of political leaders to the *asantehene* (the Asante king). See T. C. McCaskie, *State and Society in Pre-Colonial Asante* (Cambridge: Cambridge University Press, 1995), 144–242, and Janet Berry Hess, *Art and Architecture in Postcolonial Africa* (Jefferson, NC: McFarland, 2006), 46–48.

5   Partha Chatterjee, *The Nation and Its Fragments: Colonial and Postcolonial Histories* (Princeton, NJ: Princeton University Press, 1993), 120.

6   Judith A. Byfield, *The Bluest Hands: A Social and Economic History of Women Dyers in Abeokuta (Nigeria), 1890–1940* (Portsmouth, NH: Heinemann, 2002), 128.

7   Byfield, *Bluest Hands*, 136–37.

8   Moses E. Ochonu, *Colonial Meltdown: Northern Nigeria in the Great Depression* (Athens: Ohio University Press, 2009), 49.

9   Ochonu, *Colonial Meltdown*, 28–29.

10 Ochonu, 29.

11 Bellmen traveled to the different parts of Abeokuta to inform townspeople about pronouncements from the alake. Minutes Egba Council Meeting, May 5, 1930, ECR 1/1/45, vol. 2, NAN Abeokuta.

12 C. W. Alexander, Annual Report 1930, Abeokuta Province, CSO 26/2–11875, 8:9, NAN Ibadan.

13 Adebesin Folarin, *A Short Historical Review of the Life of the Egbas from 1829 to 1930* (Abeokuta: E. N. K. Press, 1931), 123.

14   Saburi O. Biobaku, *When We Were Young* (Ibadan: University Press, 1992), 33.

15   John Lonsdale, "Writing Competitive Patriotisms in Eastern Africa," in *Recasting the Past: History Writing and Political Work in Modern Africa*, ed. Derek R. Peterson and Giacomo Macola (Athens: Ohio University Press, 2009), 252.

16   Alexander, Annual Report 1930—Abeokuta Province, 1–2. CSO 26/2 11875 Vol. VIII (NAI).

17   Alexander, Annual Report 1930, 2. Hetherington argues that after 1920, the architects and supporters of indirect rule emphasized the British genius for government "both in the creation of superior institutions at home, and also in the administration of colonial peoples abroad." See Penelope Hetherington, *British Paternalism and Africa 1920–1940* (London: Frank Cass, 1978), 49.

18   Alexander, Annual Report 1930, 7.

19   Andrew E. Barnes, *Making Headway: The Introduction of Western Civilization in Colonial Northern Nigeria* (Rochester, NY: University of Rochester Press, 2009), 56. Barnes argues that the British revolutionized the Fulani aristocracy in Northern Nigeria in order to create what they considered the correct approach to aristocratic rule.

20   E. A. Brackenbury, Abeokuta Province Annual Report for the Year 1926, CSO 26/2–11875, 4:7, NAN Ibadan. The thirteen council members in office at the time of the revision were allowed to hold their membership for three years, and only eight new members were brought on through elections.

21   F. B. Adams, Annual Report for 1929—Abeokuta Province, part 2, CSO 26/2 11875, 7:12, NAN Ibadan.

22   F. B. Adams, Annual Report for 1931, CSO 26/2 11875, 8:9, NAN Ibadan.

23   E. A. Brackenbury, Abeokuta Province Annual Report 1924, CSO 26/2 11875, 2:10, NAN Ibadan.

24   Alexander, Annual Report 1930, 8.

25   Byfield, *Bluest Hands*, 173–74. See also Minutes Book of Interest, ENA Minutes of Egba Council Meeting, April 22, 1920, ECR 1/1/10, NAN Abeokuta.

26   Minutes of the Egba Council, September 18, 1930, ECR 1/1/45, vol. 2, NAN Abeokuta. They requested that each section submit names of candidates from which they would appoint the titleholder.

27   Minutes of the Abeokuta Women Centenary Celebration Committee, June 9, 1930, ECR, 1/1/49, NAN Abeokuta.

28   Minutes of the Abeokuta Women Centenary Celebration Committee, July 7, 1930, ECR, 1/1/49, NAN Abeokuta.

29   Brackenbury, Annual Report 1924, 2:14–15, NAN Ibadan.

30   E. A. Brackenbury, Abeokuta Province Annual Report for the Year 1925, CSO 26/2–11875, 3:3–4, NAN Ibadan.

31   Adedamola was accused of raping a young woman and infecting her with a sexually transmitted disease that caused her fetus to abort. Coker

alleged that the charges were false because, when tested by a European doctor, Adedamola tested negative, and the woman's husband was found to have an STD. See J. K. Coker to Adegbite Sobo, Esqr, September 30, 1926, 5, Coker Papers, Church Affairs, 4/1/34, NAN Ibadan.

32 Alexander, Annual Report 1930, 7.

33 Adams, Annual Report 1929, 6.

34 Adams, part 1, 1. For more on Nurse McCotter, see O. O. Thompson, S. A. Afolabi, and O. G. F. Nwaorgu, "Sweeter with Age: The Enigmatic Miss Jane McCotter in the Colonial Services of the Egba Native Administration in Abeokuta, Nigeria, 1929–1955," *Journal of International Women's Studies* 20, no. 7 (2019): 334–48.

35 E. J. G. Kelly, Resident, Native Administration Affairs, Abeokuta Province Annual Report, 1934, CSO 26/2 11875, 11:5, NAN Ibadan.

36 Brackenbury, Abeokuta Province Annual Report for the Year 1925, 3:10.

37 Folarin, *Short Historical Review*, 154.

38 Donald Cameron, "Native Administration in Tanganyika and Nigeria," *Journal of the Royal African Society* 36, no. 145 (1937): 5–6. While Cameron championed indirect rule, he introduced a new theoretical underpinning to it that differed substantially from that originally conceptualized and practiced by Lord Lugard and colonial officials in Northern Nigeria. See I. M. Okonjo, *British Administration in Nigeria, 1900–1950: A Nigerian View* (New York: NOK, 1974), 211–41.

39 Cameron, "Native Administration, 20.

40 The informant reported that Gbadebo was actually recovering from a first dose of poison when a second dose was administered. They suspected the involvement of one of his wives as well as a wealthy Muslim trader, Subuola, and her father, Alfa Egberongbe. C. W. Alexander, Confidential Memorandum, Addendum to Political Report on Egba Division, contained in the Abeokuta Province Report, January 1, 1920–March 31, 1921, CSO 21/309, 2, NAN Ibadan.

41 Alexander, Confidential Memorandum, 1.

42 Alexander, 2.

43 Alexander, 3–4.

44 The fear of communist influence, especially among overseas students and labor leaders, and the castigation of critics of colonial rule as communists would become much stronger in the 1930s and the postwar period. See Nike Edun Adebiyi, "Radical Nationalism in British West Africa, 1945–1960" (PhD diss., University of Michigan, 2008), 53–81.

45 Alexander, Confidential Memorandum, 4.

46 Copy of letter dated June 26, 1920, with spaces for signatures of Ladapo Ademola, Alake Elect, and J. K. Coker, president, Lagos Egba Society. Alexander, Confidential Memorandum.

47 Alexander, Confidential Memorandum, 6.

48 C. W. Alexander, Annual Report Abeokuta Province for the Year 1921, CSO 21/309, 2, NAN Ibadan.

49   Alexander, Confidential Memorandum, 8.
50   Annual Report of Abeokuta Province for Period 1st January 1920–31st March 1921, 8, CSO 21/309, NAN Ibadan.
51   Alexander, Confidential Memorandum. In amplification of the heading "Political & Administrative" Egba Division, Annual Report, Abeokuta Province for 1922, CSO26/1 /09104, 1, NAN Ibadan.
52   They assumed that Ademola had contacted Macaulay and Shyngle in relation to the court case because it involved a relative, Madam Subuola, whom the resident characterized as unscrupulous. Shyngle had tried land cases before the Privy Council in London on behalf of Lagos chiefs, including the Amodu Tijani case, which established the principle that the British administration had to recognize "native" land rights. See Bonny Ibhawoh, *Imperial Justice: Africans in Empire's Court* (Oxford: Oxford University Press, 2013), 40, 133.
53   Alexander, Confidential Memorandum. In amplification of the heading "Political & Administrative" Egba Division, Annual Report, Abeokuta Province for 1922, 3.
54   C. W. Alexander, Annual Report Abeokuta Province, 1921, CSO 21/309, 1, NAN Ibadan.
55   Brackenbury, Annual Report Abeokuta Province 1924, 8:3–4.
56   Folarin, *Short Historical Review*, 35–37.
57   Folarin, 44–45.
58   Oluwatoyin Oduntan, *Power, Culture and Modernity in Nigeria: Beyond the Colony* (New York: Routledge, 2018), 96–120.
59   The struggle around the ENA in many ways resonates with the efforts of educated Zulus to shape the Zulu kingship in the early twentieth century. See Nicholas Cope, *To Bind the Nation: Solomon kaDinuzulu and Zulu Nationalism: 1913–1933* (Pietermaritzburg, South Africa: University of Natal Press, 1993).
60   Alexander claimed that Subuola was a relative of the Alake and a frequent visitor to his house. The charges against her were considered so serious that the case was moved from Abeokuta to the Supreme Court in Lagos. Alexander, Confidential Memorandum. In amplification of heading "Political and Administrative," Annual Report, Abeokuta Province for 1922, 1–3. Ademola also had a strong relationship with other members of the Egberongbe family. Oduntan, *Power, Culture and Modernity in Nigeria*, 109.
61   Letter from Alake Ademola to A. E. F. Murray, Resident of Abeokuta, August 3, 1934, ECR 4/1/1, NAN Abeokuta. Ogboni regalia included a wrapper, hat, staff, *itagbe* (special cloth), and an umbrella. Brackenbury was not the first European to be given an ogboni title. Several European missionaries had joined the ogbonis—the Reverends Henry Townsend, J. B. Wood, Valentine Faulkner—and in 1934 a title was be given to Resident Murray. See Christopher Slogar, "Carved Ogboni Figures from Abeokuta, Nigeria," *African Arts* 35, no. 4 (2002): 14–27, 91–92; R. E.

Dennett, "The Ogboni and Other Secret Societies in Nigeria," *Journal of the Royal African Society* 16, no. 61 (1916): 16–29; Peter Morton-Williams, "The Yoruba Ogboni Cult," *Africa: Journal of the International African Institute* 30, no. 4 (1960): 362–74; and Babatunde Lawal, "À Yà Gbó, À Yà Tó: New Perspectives on Edan Ògbóni," *African Arts* 28, no. 1 (1995): 36–49, 98–100.

62   E. A. Brackenbury, Abeokuta Province Annual Report for the Year 1926, CSO 26/2 11875, 4:8.

63   F. B. Adams, Abeokuta Province Annual Report for the year 1927, CSO 26/2 11875, 5:3–4, NAN Ibadan.

64   Brackenbury, Annual Report 1926, 9.

65   Adams, Annual Report 1927, 5.

66   Minutes of Council, November 27, 1927, ECR 1/1/38, Minutes of Council 1927, 2:11, NAN Abeoktua.

67   Minutes of Council, 12–17.

68   Oduntan, *Power, Culture and Modernity*, 99.

69   Oduntan, 113–14. In 1917, when the Owu quarter selected a new olowu, Adesina, and crowned him without Alake Gbadebo's knowledge or consent, Gbadebo refused to accept him and sent in troops to seize the paraphernalia associated with his office. Gbadebo ultimately recognized Adesina after the Owu people apologized to him.

70   F. B. Adams, Annual Report for 1929 Abeokuta Province, Part 1, Organization, CSO 26/211875, 7:1, NAN Ibadan.

71   Adams, Annual Report 1927, 9.

72   Brackenbury, Annual Report 1924, 2.

73   Adams, Annual Report 1927, 6.

74   Anthony I. Nwabughuogu, "The Role of Propaganda in the Development of Indirect Rule in Nigeria, 1890–1929," *International Journal of African Historical Studies* 14, no. 1 (1981): 90.

75   Adams, Annual Report 1927, 9.

76   Adebesin Folarin, *The Ogboni and Other Chieftaincies in Abeokuta: Their Purports and Meanings* (Itoko, Abeokuta: E.N.A., Press 1934), 17.

77   Oduntan, *Power, Culture and Modernity*, 101. For a comparative analysis of the texts produced by Ajisafe, Folarin, and Solanke, see Jenna K. Germaine, "Integrating Egba Epistemologies: Writing Historical Knowledge in Colonial Nigeria" (MA thesis, Dalhousie University, 2007).

78   Adams, Annual Report 1927, 7.

79   Saburi O. Biobaku, *The Egba and Their Neighbors, 1842–1872* (Oxford: Clarendon Press, 1965), 8; Oduntan, *Power, Culture and Modernity*, 28.

80   Adams, Annual Report 1927, 8. Oduntan argues that in fact there is little mention of Lisabi in nineteenth-century discussions of Abeokuta. He suggests that Lisabi first appeared in Ajisafe's *History of Abeokuta*. Oduntan, *Power, Culture and Modernity*, 28.

81   Folarin, *Short Historical Review*, 13–14.
82   Folarin, 12.
83   Oduntan, *Power, Culture and Modernity*, 28, 32.
84   Folarin, *Short Historical Review*, 13.
85   Folarin, 35.
86   Folarin, 34–51.
87   Folarin, 52.
88   Folarin, 12–13. Council records show that the alake leased stores and land to firms such as John Holt and Companie du Lobi for £30 to £60 per year. See Minutes of Egba Council Meeting, October 23, 1930, and December 11, 1930, ECR 1/1/45, vol. 2, NAN Abeokuta.
89   Allister MacMillan, *The Red Book of West Africa: Historical and Descriptive Commercial and Industrial Facts, Figures and Resources* (London: Frank Cass, 1968), 102.
90   Folarin, *Short Historical Review*, 86.
91   Folarin, 87.
92   Ladipo Solanke, *The Egba-Yoruba Constitutional Law and Its Historical Development* (Lagos: Asaoku Printing Press, 1931), preface.
93   Solanke, *Egba-Yoruba Constitutional Law*, 4–5.
94   Solanke, 7.
95   Solanke, 8.
96   Solanke, 10.
97   Philip Zachernuk, "The Lagos Intelligentsia and the Idea of Progress, ca. 1860–1960," in *Yoruba Historiography*, ed. Toyin Falola (Madison: University of Wisconsin Press, 1991), 156–57.
98   Solanke, *Egba-Yoruba Constitutional Law*, 11.
99   Solanke, 15, 18 (italics in original). The first olowu in Abeokuta was crowned in 1855, the first agura in 1863, and the first osile in 1897.
100 Zachernuk, "Lagos Intelligentsia," 157.
101 Solanke, *Egba-Yoruba Constitutional Law*, 16 (italics in original).
102 Solanke, 26.
103 Solanke, 32.
104 Solanke, 42–43.
105 Solanke, 43.
106 Solanke, 43–45. The alake also created a school in the palace, the Afin School. He paid the cost to run it, £100, as well as the salary of the principal, a Mrs. Abiodun, who had trained in Sierra Leone. Poor children attended the school free of charge. Minutes of Egba Council Meeting, February 6, 1936, ECR 1/1/74, vol. 1, NAN Abeokuta.
107 Solanke, *Egba-Yoruba Constitutional Law*, 47–48.
108 They received a letter of regret from the shehu and a letter of acknowledgement from King Fuad. Ake 2/1—Centenary Hall, 1943, NAN Abeokuta.
109 Ladapo Ademola, "Alake's Open Letter to All Egbas at Home and Abroad," *Akede Eko*, September 27, 1930.

110 See Minutes of the Abeokuta Women Centenary Celebration Committee, July 30, 1930, and Minutes of the Abeokuta Women Centenary Celebration Committee, September 24, 1930, ECR 1/1/49, NAN Abeokuta.

111 "Abeokuta Centenary Celebrations, Official Programme of Events," *Akede Eko*, October 25, 1930, NAN Abeokuta.

112 Ojumito [I Was There], "The News of the Centenary Anniversary of Abeokuta," *Akede Eko*, November 1, 1930.

113 Anonymous, "The Abeokuta Centenary Celebration, a Great National Event," *West African Nationhood*, October 27, 1930; Folarin, *Short Historical Review*, 120.

114 Ojumito, "News of the Centenary Anniversary," 11.

115 Special Correspondent, "The Abeokuta Centenary Celebrations: A Message from the King to the Alake — Tributes to Bygone Personalities — Missions, Commerce and Politics," *West Africa*, November 29, 1930, 1691.

116 Folarin, *Short Historical Review*, 121.

117 Folarin, 122.

118 *West Africa* also carried a photograph of the state drums with a caption that noted the quality of their workmanship: "These State drums, centuries old, had not been used for several generations before the present ceremonies. The wooden parts of the drums are wonderfully carved." "Abeokuta Centenary Celebrations: First Pictures from Our Own Photographer, Mr. Reginald Silk," *West Africa*, December 6, 1930, 1744.

119 "Abeokuta Centenary Celebrations, Official Programme of Events," 18. See also Minutes of the Sub-Committee of the Abeokuta Centenary Celebration, June 23, 1930, 3–4, ECR 1/1/39, NAN Abeokuta.

120 Anonymous, "The Abeokuta Centenary Celebrations," *West Africa*, October 25, 1930, 1490.

121 Folarin, *Short Historical Review*, 118–24.

122 Minutes of the Abeokuta Women Centenary Celebration Committee, September 24, 1930. See also T. M. Akinwumi, "Art and Political Leadership: The Example of the Alake," *Journal of Cultural Studies* 4, no. 1 (2002): 190–94.

123 Biobaku, *When We Were Young*, 33–34.

124 Minutes of the Abeokuta Women Centenary Celebration Committee, June 23, 1930, ECR 1/1/49, NAN Abeokuta.

125 John Collins, *Fela: Kalakuta Notes* (Middletown, CT: Wesleyan University Press, 2015), 3. Although Canon Ransome-Kuti is credited with composing the song, Oluwatoyin Oduntan argues that there were other national anthems before it, and there has been no consensus on an anthem. Moreover, some suggest that Ransome-Kuti's song may have originated as a CMS grammar school anthem. Personal communication, Oluwatoyin Oduntan, July 6, 2020.

126 T. K. E. Phillips joined the committee for one of its meetings to discuss the copyright of the anthem. He gave it the right to use the anthem for

the celebrations with the understanding that it would return the manuscript to him afterward. Minutes of the Abeokuta Centenary Celebration Committee, August 25, 1930, ECR 1/1/39, NAN Abeokuta. See also Minutes of the Abeokuta Centenary Celebration Committee, August 11, 1930, ECR 1/1/39, NAN Abeokuta.

127   Alake Ademola II, *The Alake's Centenary Message to the Egba People* (Abeokuta: E.K.A. Press, 1930), 2, box 45, Ransome-Kuti Papers, Kenneth Dike Memorial Library, University of Ibadan (hereafter cited as KDML).

128   Alake Ademola II, *Alake's Centenary Message*, 3.

129   Alake Ademola II, 1.

130   Alake Ademola II, 3.

131   Alake Ademola II, 9.

132   Alake Ademola II, 4. This providential pronouncement also appears in A. K. Ajisafe's *History of Abeokuta*. For a fuller discussion of the ways in which providentialism shaped this important text, see Adrian M. Deese, "Making Sense of the Past: Ajayi Kolawole Ajisafe and the (Re)Making of Modern Abeokuta (Nigeria)" (MA thesis, Cornell University, 2013).

133   Alake Ademola II, *Alake's Centenary Message*, 13.

134   Alake Ademola II, 14.

135   Alake Ademola II, 124–25.

136   Special Correspondent, "Abeokuta Centenary Celebrations," 1691.

137   Special Correspondent, 1691.

138   Special Correspondent.

139   *West Africa*, December 6, 1930, 1741.

140   Egba Omo-Lisabi, "Abeokuta the City of the Egba," *Akede Eko*, September 27, 1930.

141   A. K. Ajisafe, "Abeokuta Is Now 100 Years Old," *Akede Eko*, August 9, 1930.

142   A. K. Ajisafe, *Abeokuta Centenary and Its Celebrations* (Lagos: Ife-Olu Printing, 1931), 6–8.

143   Ajisafe, *Abeokuta Centenary*, 13–14.

144   Ajisafe, 22.

145   Ajisafe, 31–32.

146   In a recent study of aso ebi in Lagos, Okechukwu Nwafor found that servers were instructed not to serve food to guests not wearing aso ebi. See Okechukwu Nwafor, "The Fabric of Friendship: Aso Ebi and the Moral Economy of Amity in Nigeria," *African Studies* 72, no. 1 (2013): 6–10.

147   Ajisafe, *Abeokuta Centenary and Its Celebrations*, 37.

148   Folarin, *Short Historical Review*, 126–57.

149   Griswold and Bhadmus, "Kano Durbar," 126.

150   Mikael Karlström, "On the Aesthetics and Dialogics of Power in the Postcolony," *Africa: Journal of the International African Institute* 73, no. 1 (2003): 66.

151　See Minutes of Centenary Celebration Committee, March 14, 1927, ECR 1/1/39, NAN Abeokuta, and Minutes of Centenary Celebration Committee, June 9, 1930, ECR 1/1/39, NAN Abeokuta.

CHAPTER 3: RACE, NATION, AND
POLITICS IN THE INTERWAR PERIOD

1　Steven Feierman, *Peasant Intellectuals: Anthropology and History in Northern Tanzania* (Madison: University of Wisconsin Press, 1990), 3. See also Thomas Spear, "Neo-Traditionalism and the Limits of Invention in British Colonial Africa," *Journal of African History* 44, no. 1 (2003): 3–27.

2　Oluwatoyin Oduntan, *Power, Culture and Modernity in Nigeria: Beyond the Colony* (New York: Routledge, 2018), 164.

3　Prasenjit Duara, "Historicizing National Identity, or Who Imagines What and When," in *Becoming National: A Reader*, ed. Geoff Eley and Ronal Grigor Suny (New York: Oxford University Press, 1996), 165.

4　Karin Barber, "Experiments with Genre in Yoruba Newspapers of the 1920s," in *African Print Cultures: Newspapers and Their Publics in the Twentieth Century*, ed. Derek Peterson, Emma Hunter, and Stephanie Newell (Ann Arbor: University of Michigan Press, 2017), 154–55.

5　Philip Zachernuk, *Colonial Subjects: An African Intelligentsia and Atlantic Ideas* (Charlottesville: University of Virginia Press, 2000), 87.

6　Rina Okonkwo, "A Jamaican Export to Nigeria! The Life of Amos Stanley Wynter Shackleford," *Caribbean Quarterly* 30, no. 2 (1984): 50, 54. Amos Shackleford arrived in Nigeria in 1913 to work for the railway department and subsequently tried other ventures before entering the baking trade in 1921. He founded Shackleford's Bakeries in Nigeria and is credited with two major innovations that launched Nigeria's modern baking industry. He also extended his baking company into Ghana. Peter Kilby, *African Enterprise: The Nigerian Bread Industry* (Stanford, CA: Hoover Institution, Stanford University, 1965), 7–8. After his death, his wife, Gwendolyn, was general manager of Kingsway Electric Bakery Ltd. *The Diplomatic Press Directory of the Republic of Ghana* (London: Diplomatic Press and Publishing, 1959), 204.

7　Mustafa Abdelwahid, ed., *Dusé Mohamed Ali (1866–1945): The Autobiography of a Pioneer Pan African and Afro-Asian Activist* (Trenton, NJ: Red Sea Press, 2011), 2–27.

8　Abdelwahid, *Dusé Mohamed Ali*, 28.

9　J. Ayodele Langley, *Pan-Africanism and Nationalism in West Africa 1900–1945: A Study in Ideology and Social Classes* (Oxford, UK: Clarendon Press, 1973), 114.

10　Langley, *Pan-Africanism*, 124–25.

11　G. I. C. Eluwa, "Background to the Emergence of the National Congress of British West Africa," *African Studies Review* 14, no. 2 (1971): 206.

12　Langley, *Pan-Africanism and Nationalism*, 127.

13　Langley, 128.

14 Langley, 128.
15 C. W. Alexander, Annual Report of Abeokuta Province for the Year 1921, Political and Administrative: Egba Division, 11–12, CSO 21/309, NAN Ibadan.
16 Confidential Memo Secretary of the Southern Provinces to C. W. Alexander, Resident Abeokuta Province, 2, Annual Report of Abeokuta Province for the Year 1921, CSO 21/309, NAN Ibadan.
17 Oduntan, *Power, Culture and Modernity in Nigeria*, 102.
18 Tekena N. Tamuno, "The Role of the Legislative Council in the Administration of Lagos, 1886–1913," *Journal of the Historical Society of Nigeria* 4, no. 4 (1969): 556–58.
19 Michael Crowder, *The Story of Nigeria* (London: Faber and Faber, 1962), 228. The election rules further restricted voting rights for at least twelve months and to adult men resident in Lagos having a gross income of £100 pounds per year.
20 Patrick Cole, *Modern and Traditional Elites in the Politics of Lagos* (New York: Cambridge University Press, 1975), 136–37.
21 Cole, *Modern and Traditional Elites*, 152.
22 Raymond J. Smyke, "A History of the Nigeria Union of Teachers," *West African Journal of Education* 16, no. 3 (1972): 396–97.
23 Smyke, "History of Nigeria Union of Teachers," 397.
24 Raymond J. Smyke and Denis C. Storer, *Nigerian Union of Teachers: An Official History* (Ibadan: Oxford University Press, 1974), 28.
25 Smyke and Storer, *Nigerian Union of Teachers*, 32–33.
26 Smyke and Storer, 36–37. NUT was estimated to have 1,130 members by 1942.
27 Smyke and Storer, 46–52.
28 *West Africa*, January 2, 1932. Several women in Lagos also belonged to WASU. Solanke referred to them as his WASU sisters—Ibidun Doherty, Mijoke Cole, Sade Agbebi—and encouraged them to establish a women's branch of WASU in Lagos. Letter from Ladipo Solanke to Miss Ibidun Doherty, March 26, 1935, Egba Affairs, vol. 2, no. 1, 1935, Record Pen or Pencil Carbon Duplicate Book, Warden's Correspondence, Solanke Papers, Special Collections, University of Lagos Library.
29 Smyke and Storer, *Nigerian Union of Teachers*, 65–66.
30 F. O. E. Okafor, *The Nigerian Youth Movement, 1934–44: A Re-Appraisal of the Historiography* (Onitsha, Nigeria: Etukokwu Press, 1989), 22. See also Richard L. Sklar, *Nigerian Political Parties: Power in an Emergent African Nation* (1963; repr., Trenton, NJ: Africa World Press, 2004), 48–55, and Pieter Boele van Hensbroek, *Political Discourses in African Thought: 1860 to the Present* (Westport, CT: Praeger, 1999), 78–84.
31 Okafor, *Nigerian Youth Movement*, 40–43.
32 A. G. Hopkins, "Economic Aspects of Political Movements in Nigeria and in the Gold Coast 1918–1939," *Journal of African History* 7, no. 1 (1966): 150.

33 Zachernuk, *Colonial Subjects*, 86.
34 "The Nigerian National Democratic Party, Abeokuta Branch," *Egbaland Echo*, August 22–29, 1941.
35 Report of the Inauguration of the Nigerian National Democratic Party, Abeokuta Branch, May 15, 1943, at the Centenary Hall, 3, ECR, Ake 2/1, file 54, NAN Abeokuta.
36 Barber, "Experiments with Genre," 154.
37 Chidi Oguamanam and W. Wesley Pue, "Lawyers' Professionalism, Colonialism, State Formation, and National Life in Nigeria, 1900–1960: 'The Fighting Brigade of the People,'" *Social Identities* 13, no. 6 (2007): 780.
38 Bonny Ibhawoh, *Imperial Justice: Africans in Empire's Court* (Oxford: Oxford University Press, 2013), 140.
39 Ibhawoh, *Imperial Justice*, 144.
40 Barber, "Experiments with Genre," 155.
41 Cole, *Modern and Traditional Elites*, 136–37.
42 Letter from Acting Financial Secretary, C. W. Marlow, to Mesdames Alimotu Pelewura and Barikisu, January 7, 1941, Herbert Macaulay Papers, KDML.
43 Nina Mba, *Nigerian Women Mobilized: Women's Political Activity in Southern Nigeria, 1900–1965* (Berkeley: Institute of International Studies, University of California, 1982), 196.
44 Abosede A. George, *Making Modern Girls: A History of Girlhood, Labor, and Social Development in Colonial Lagos* (Athens: University of Ohio Press, 2014), 39–43.
45 Quoted in George, *Making Modern Girls*, 45.
46 George, 116.
47 Saheed Aderinto, *When Sex Threatened the State: Illicit Sexuality, Nationalism, and Politics in Colonial Nigeria, 1900–1958* (Urbana: University of Illinois Press, 2015), 33, 156–59.
48 George, *Making Modern Girls*, 114–33.
49 Aderinto, *When Sex Threatened the State*, 41.
50 Benedict Naanen, "'Itinerant Gold Mines': Prostitution in the Cross River Basin of Nigeria, 1930–1950," *African Studies Review* 34, no. 2 (1991): 68–69.
51 Aderinto, *When Sex Threatened the State*, 157.
52 Mba, *Nigerian Women Mobilized*, 226. During the war, the colonial government established a wage freeze and fixed prices on the sale and purchase of local foodstuffs. In Lagos, Captain Pullen organized the system, and his name became attached to it. See chapter 4.
53 Toyin Falola and Adam Paddock, *The Women's War of 1929: A History of Anti-Colonial Resistance in Eastern Nigeria* (Durham, NC: Carolina Academic Press, 2011), 23.
54 Susan Martin, *Palm Oil and Protest: An Economic History of the Ngwa Region, South-Eastern Nigeria, 1800–1980* (New York: Cambridge University Press, 1988), 106–18.

55   Caroline Ifeka-Moller, "Female Militancy and Colonial Revolt: The Women's War of 1929, Eastern Nigeria," in *Perceiving Women*, ed. Shirley Ardener (London: Malaby Press, 1975), 127–57; Nancy Rose Hunt, "Placing African Women's History and Locating Gender," *Social History* 14, no. 3 (1989): 363–64; Temma Kaplan, "Naked Mothers and Maternal Sexuality: Some Reactions to the Aba Women's War," in *The Politics of Motherhood: Activist Voices from Left to Right*, ed. Annelise Orleck, Diana Taylor, and Alexis Jetter (Hanover, NH: University Press of New England, 1997), 209–22.

56   Misty L. Bastian, "'Vultures of the Marketplace': Southeastern Nigerian Women and Discourses of the *Ogu Umunwaanyi* (Women's War) of 1929," in *Women in Colonial African History*, ed. Jean Allman, Susan Geiger, and Nakanyike Musisi (Bloomington: Indiana University Press, 2002), 260–81; Misty Bastian, "Dancing Women and Colonial Men: The Nwaobiala of 1925," in *"Wicked" Women and the Reconfiguration of Gender in Africa*, ed. Dorothy Hodgson and Sheryl McCurdy (Portsmouth, NH: Heinemann, 2001), 109–29. See also Gloria Chuku, *Igbo Women and Economic Transformation in Southeastern Nigeria, 1900–1960* (New York: Routledge, 2005).

57   Caustic soda and synthetic dyes allowed dyers to lower their cost of production to match declining consumer incomes. However, many did not know how to use the products properly, and consumers complained to the alake about the poor quality of the cloths they purchased. See Judith Byfield, *The Bluest Hands: A Social and Economic History of Women Dyers in Abeokuta (Nigeria), 1890–1940* (Portsmouth, NH: Heinemann, 2002), 157–68.

58   Byfield, *Bluest Hands*, 168–78.

59   S. K. B. Asante, "The Catholic Missions, British West African Nationalists, and the Italian Invasion of Ethiopia," *African Affairs* 73, no. 291 (1974): 204–16; George Baer, "Sanctions and Security: The League of Nations and the Italian-Ethiopian War, 1935–1936," *International Organization* 27, no. 2 (1973): 165–79.

60   S. K. B. Asante, *Pan-African Protest: West Africa and the Ethiopian Crisis, 1934–1941* (London: Longman, 1977); Fikru Gebrekidan, "In Defense of Ethiopia: A Comparative Assessment of Caribbean and African American Anti-Fascist Protests, 1935–1941," *Northeast African Studies* 2, no. 1 (New Series, 1995): 145–73; Joseph E. Harris, *African-American Reactions to War in Ethiopia 1936–1941* (Baton Rouge: Louisiana State University, 1994); G. O. Olusanya, *The Second World War and Politics in Nigeria, 1939–1953* (London: Evans Bros. for the University of Lagos, 1973); William Shack, *Harlem in Montmartre: A Paris Jazz Story between the Great Wars* (Berkeley: University of California Press, 2001); William R. Scott, *The Sons of Sheba's Race: African-Americans and the Italo-Ethiopian War, 1935–1941*, 2nd ed. (Hollywood, CA: Tsehai Publishers, 2006); Robert Weisbord, "British West Indian Reaction to

the Italian-Ethiopian War: An Episode in Pan-Africanism," *Caribbean Studies* 10, no. 1 (1970): 34–41.

61 Anthony Mockler, *Haile Selassie's War: The Italian-Ethiopian Campaign, 1935–1941* (New York: Olive Branch, 2003), 151, 399.

62 Princess Tsaha of Abyssinia, "Appeal to All Women of the World," Ake 2/1, file 29, NAN Abeokuta.

63 Asante, *Pan-African Protest*, 149.

64 Asante, 60. Selassie argued that Ethiopians were a mixed Hamito-Semitic people. His predecessor, Menelik, claimed that Ethiopians were Caucasians.

65 Robert Hill, ed., *The Marcus Garvey Papers*, vol. 7 (Berkeley: University of California Press, 1990), 682–85, 687–92.

66 See Hailu Habtu and Judith Byfield, "Fighting Fascism: Ethiopian Women Patriots 1935–1941," in *Africa and World War II*, ed. Judith A. Byfield, Carolyn A. Brown, Timothy Parsons, and Ahmad Sikainga (New York: Cambridge University Press, 2015), 383–400.

67 Scott, *Sons of Sheba's Race*, 12.

68 Hakim Adi, *Pan-Africanism and Communism: The Communist International Africa and the Diaspora, 1919–1939* (Trenton, NJ: Africa World Press, 2013), 246.

69 Scott, *Sons of Sheba's Race*, 7, 150.

70 Scott, 175–77.

71 Fikru Negash Gebrekidan, *Bond without Blood: A History of Ethiopian and New World Black Relations, 1896–1991* (Trenton, NJ: Africa World Press, 2005), 51.

72 Marc Matera, *Black London: The Imperial Metropolis and Decolonization in the Twentieth Century* (Oakland: University of California Press, 2015), 69. James would become one of the leading Marxist intellectuals in London. Ashwood Garvey, the first wife of Marcus Garvey, was also a leading pan-African activist.

73 Asante, *Pan-African Protest*, 48.

74 Asante, 50.

75 Matera, *Black London*, 70.

76 Gebrekidan, *Bond without Blood*, 51, 105, 112.

77 Metasebia Woldermariam, "Alternative Representations of War in Africa: New Times and Ethiopia News Coverage of the 1935–41 Italian-Ethiopian War," in *Narrating War and Peace in Africa*, ed. Toyin Falola and Hetty ter Haar (Rochester, NY: Rochester University Press, 2010), 50, 53.

78 Asante, *Pan-African Protest*, 148–49. For more on Shackleford, see LaRay Denzer, "Intersections: Nigerian Episodes in the Careers of Three West Indian Women," in *Gendering the African Diaspora: Women, Culture and Historical Change in the Caribbean and Nigerian Hinterland*, ed. Judith Byfield, LaRay Denzer, and Anthea Morrison (Bloomington: Indiana University Press, 2010), 257.

79   Asante, *Pan-African Protest*, 149. See also Abdelwahid, *Dusé Mohamed Ali*, 27–30.

80   S. K. B. Asante, "The Italo-Ethiopian Conflict: A Case Study in British West African Response to Crisis Diplomacy in the 1930s," *Journal of African History* 15, no. 2 (1974): 295–96. The Shacklefords, originally from Jamaica, played a prominent role in the local branch of Marcus Garvey's UNIA.

81   Letter from G. Shackleford, June 10, 1936, Ake 2/1, file 29, National Archives of Nigeria, Abeokuta (hereafter cited as NAN Abeokuta). According to Asante, "Mrs. Shackleford made the following moving appeal in the name of the Empress of Ethiopia," but it is clear from the letter that Shackleford credits Princess Tsaha with writing the statement. Asante, *Pan-African Protest*, 148.

82   "Iyalode" was the highest title given to women in precolonial Abeokuta. It was one of multiple traditional titles later adopted by members of the Christian community.

83   Programme, Women's Meeting on the Abyssinian Question, Ake 2/2, file 29, NAN Abeokuta. The subscription list of the women who donated money is dated June 16, 1936, suggesting that the meeting occurred on that date.

84   The documents do not define African churches. Aladura and Seraphim are independent Yoruba Christian churches not affiliated with missionaries.

85   Asante, *Pan-African Protest*, 127.

86   Letter from Gwendolyn Shackleford to His Highness Ademola II, June 16, 1936, Ake 2/1, file 29, NAN Abeokkuta.

87   Kristin Mann, *Marrying Well: Marriage, Status and Social Change among the Educated Elite in Colonial Lagos* (New York: Cambridge University Press, 1985); LaRay Denzer, "Yoruba Women: A Historiographical Study," *International Journal of African Historical Studies* 27, no. 1 (1994): 1–39; Abosede A. George, *Making Modern Girls: A History of Girlhood, Labor, and Social Development in Colonial Lagos* (Athens: Ohio University Press, 2014).

88   Asante, "Italo-Ethiopian Conflict," 297.

89   "Abeokuta," *West African Pilot*, September 15, 1938.

90   "Abeokuta Public Hold Meeting against Project of Transfer," *West African Pilot*, November 22, 1938.

91   Alake Ademola, "Rumour of Nigeria Being Transferred to Germany, 1938," November 17, 1938, ECR 1/1/89, NAN Abeokuta

92   Asante, "Italo-Ethiopian Conflict," 296.

93   "Ourselves and Ethiopia," *Egba Administration Bulletin: Extraordinary*, January 1943, 7, NAN Ibadan.

94   June Purvis, "Past Papers, Future Thinking: Sylvia Pankhurst (1882–1960), Suffragette, Political Activist, Artist and Writer," *Gender and Education* 20, no. 1 (2008): 84. A portion of the proceeds for the

hospital also came from the trust Haile Selassie had established for the princess. See Horder, "Princess Tsahai Memorial Fund," *British Medical Journal* 2, no. 4375 (November 11, 1944): 644, and Gebrekidan, *Bond without Blood*, 123.

CHAPTER 4: WOMEN, RICE, AND WAR

1 Timothy Parsons, "The Military Experiences of Ordinary Africans in World War II," in *Africa and World War II*, ed. Judith A. Byfield, Carolyn A. Brown, Timothy Parsons, and Ahmad Alawad Sikainga (New York: Cambridge University Press, 2015), 3.

2 See, for example, Judith A. Byfield, "Producing for the War," in Byfield et al., *Africa and World War II*, 24–42; William G. Clarence-Smith, "Africa's 'Battle for Rubber' in the Second World War," in Byfield et al., *Africa and World War II*, 166–82; and Emad A. Helal, "Egypt's Overlooked Contribution to World War II," in *The World in World Wars: Experiences, Perceptions and Perspectives from Africa and Asia*, ed. Heike Liebau, Katrin Bromber, Katharina Lange, Dyala Hamzah, and Ravi Ahuja (Boston: Brill, 2010), 217–47.

3 Ayodeji Olukoju, "'Buy British, Sell Foreign': External Trade Control Policies in Nigeria during World War II and Its Aftermath, 1939–1950," *International Journal of African Historical Studies* 35, no. 2/3 (2002): 364–65.

4 A. Olorunfemi, "Effects of War-Time Trade Controls on Nigerian Cocoa Traders and Producers, 1939–45: A Case-Study of the Hazards of a Dependent Economy," *International Journal of African Historical Studies* 13, no. 4 (1980): 676.

5 Olukoju, "'Buy British, Sell Foreign,'" 366–67.

6 Toyin Falola, "'Salt Is Gold': The Management of Salt Scarcity in Nigeria during World War II," *Canadian Journal of African Studies* 26, no. 3 (1992): 415–16. For example, firms had to obtain a license from the Nigerian Supply Board to import salt. Towns and villages were limited to varying amounts of salt based on a formula of six ounces per person per month.

7 Circular Telegram No. 82, Secretary of State for the Colonies (SSC), London, to Governor, Lagos, June 5, 1940, Abe Prof 1/1, ABP 1631, NAN Ibadan.

8 Antony Beevor, *The Second World War* (New York: Little, Brown, 2012), 126.

9 "Rice," Letter from Deputy Chairman, West African Governors' Conference, Lagos, to the Chief Secretary (CS), Lagos, August 23, 1941, Department of Commerce and Industries (hereafter cited as DCI), 1/1 4041/S.20, NAN Ibadan; Draft Minutes of Second Meeting of Committee of Supply Center Held at Accra, June 10–11, 1942, 1–2, Chief Secretary's Office (hereafter cited as CSO) 26/38717, NAN Ibadan.

10 Draft Minutes of Second Meeting of Committee of Supply Center Held at Accra, June, 10–11, 1942, 3; Letter about "Food Supplies to Other Colonies" from Chief Marketing Officer to Food Controller, July 14,

1942, CSO 26/38717, NAN Ibadan. Nigeria promised to provide three hundred tons of salt to Sierra Leone each month. Egusi oil is made from the seed of the egusi melon, ghee is made from clarified butter, and gari is processed cassava.

11 Annual Report, Abeokuta Province, 1941, 9–10, CSO 26/2/11875, vol. 15, NAN Ibadan.

12 Savingram from the Resident, Abeokuta Province, to the Secretary, Western Provinces, April 15, 1944, ABP 1401/23, NAN Ibadan.

13 Annual Report, Abeokuta Province, 1944, 11, CSO 26/2/11875, vol. 15, NAN Ibadan.

14 Annual Report, Abeokuta Province, 1945, 11, CSO 26/2/11875, vol. 15, NAN Ibadan.

15 Robert Pearce, "The Colonial Economy: Nigeria and the Second World War," in *Development Studies and Colonial Policy*, ed. Barbara Ingham and Colin Simmons (London: Frank Cass, 1987), 272.

16 Pearce, "Colonial Economy," 272. See also Olukoju, "'Buy British, Sell Foreign,'" 367.

17 The phony war refers to the period after the occupation of Poland and before the invasion of France when life in England and France seemed to go back to normal. Beevor, *Second World War*, 40.

18 David Anderson and David Throup, "Africans and Agriculture in Colonial Kenya: The Myth of the War as a Watershed," *Journal of African History* 26, no. 4 (1985): 335.

19 Annual Report, Abeokuta Province, 1940, 1, CSO 26/2/11875, vol. 15, NAN Ibadan.

20 Nancy E. Lawler, *Soldiers, Airmen, Spies, and Whisperers: The Gold Coast in World War II* (Athens: Ohio University Press, 2002), 19.

21 Annual Report, Abeokuta Province, 1942, 2, Abeokuta Provincial Office Papers (hereafter cited as Abe Prof) 1/ABP 1543, vol. 4, NAN Ibadan; Annual Report, Abeokuta Province, 1943, 2, CSO 26/2/11875, vol. 15, NAN Ibadan.

22 Siân Nicholas, "'Brushing Up Your Empire': Dominion and Colonial Propaganda on the BBC's Home Services, 1939–45," *Journal of Imperial and Commonwealth History* 31, no. 2 (2003): 214.

23 M. Fortes, "The Impact of the War on British West Africa," *International Affairs* 21, no. 2 (1945): 213.

24 Ronke Doherty, interview by author, October 3 and November 12, 1988, Abeokuta. "Ronke" was a nickname; she was christened Augusta Modupe Bolande Williams.

25 Dolu Ransome-Kuti, interview by the author, September 7, 1988, Abeokuta.

26 Saburi O. Biobaku, *When We Were Young* (Ibadan: University Press, 1992), 107.

27 Prince Adegbola Ademola, interview by the author, August 25, 2003, Lagos.

28 Mrs. Ronke Doherty, interview by the author, November 12, 1988, Abeokuta.

29 Justice Adewale Thompson, interview by the author, August 14, 2003, Jericho, Ibadan.

30 Chief Emanuel Sorunke, interview by the author, August 19, 2003, Abeokuta.

31 Christopher Ajboola Ajao, interview by the author, September 22, 2003, Ibadan.

32 M. S. Ogunbisi to the resident, Abeokuta Province, March 22, 1948, ABP 1497E, Prof 2, 2nd Accession, NAN Ibadan. Ogunbisi was single when he first received his ration card, but he had recently married and needed a new card increasing the amount of milk, sugar, flour, and butter he could buy from the firms.

33 Annual Report, Abeokuta Province, 1940, 4, CSO 26/2/11875, vol. 15, NAN Ibadan.

34 Soyinka, *Aké: The Years of Childhood* (New York: Random House), 109.

35 Soyinka, *Aké*, 112.

36 Justice Thompson, interview by the author, August 14, 2003, Jericho, Ibadan.

37 Pa Michael Adeyinka, interview by Victoria Ayodokun, August 7, 2003, Totoro, Abeokuta.

38 Isaiah Oladele Adebayo, interview by the author, July 2003, Abeokuta.

39 Soyinka, *Aké*, 123.

40 General Woolner, 81(West Africa) Division Report, MSS Afr.S.1734 (403), 7, Bodleian Library, Oxford,

41 A. F. Giles, "West African Way," 4, MSS Afr.S.1734, 150, Bodleian Library, Oxford.

42 Annual Report, Abeokuta Province, 1940, 3, CSO 26/2/11875, vol. 15, NAN Ibadan.

43 Annual Report, Abeokuta Province, 1943, 13, CSO 26/2/11875, vol. 15, NAN Ibadan.

44 Annual Report, Abeokuta Province, 1946, 9, CSO 26/2/11875, vol. 15, NAN Ibadan.

45 Annual Report, Abeokuta Province, 1944, 11, CSO 26/2/11875, vol. 15, NAN Ibadan.

46 "To the Chiefs and People of the Western Provinces of Nigeria," *Yoruba News*, August 11, 1942.

47 "Clothes," *Yoruba News*, November 3–December 15, 1942, 1.

48 Oladipo Somoye to President Roosevelt and Mr. Winston Churchill, August 26, 1943, Abe Prof 1/1 APB 1631—War General Correspondence, NAN Ibadan.

49 Annual Report, Abeokuta Province, 1940, 3–4, CSO 26/2/11875, vol. 15, NAN Ibadan.

50 *Egba Administration Bulletin*, January 1943, 11.

51 Ademola II, Alake of Abeokuta, to Mrs. Winston Churchill, June 18, 1942, *Egba Administration Bulletin*, January 1943, 4.

52   Secretary, Western Provinces, to Resident, Abeokuta Province, February 3, 1942, Abeokuta Provincial Papers 1631, NAN Ibadan.

53   *Yoruba News*, July–August 1940. The information was gathered from a telegram from the secretary of state for the colonies thanking the governor of Nigeria, on July 3, 1940.

54   Annual Report, Abeokuta Province, 1943, 1, CSO 26/2/11875, vol. 15, NAN Ibadan.

55   Annual Report, Abeokuta Province, 1944, 2, CSO 26/2/11875, vol. 15, NAN Ibadan.

56   "Burglars at Large in Abeokuta," *Egbaland Echo*, August 15, 1941; "Scarcity of Policemen in Abeokuta," *Egbaland Echo*, August 15, 1941.

57   Judith A. Byfield, "Producing for the War," in Byfield et al., *Africa and World War II*, 28.

58   Minutes of Egba Council Meeting, September 4, 1939, ECR 1/1/97, vol. 1, NAN Abeokuta.

59   Annual Report 1940, ECR 1/1/12, vol. 2; also Minutes of Extraordinary Meeting of Egba Council, January 8, 1940, ECR 1/1/97, vol. 2, NAN Abeokuta.

60   Carol Summers, "Ugandan Politics and World War II (1939–1949)," in Byfield et al., *Africa and World War II*, 480–98.

61   For a fuller discussion of tax collection during the depression, see Judith A. Byfield, *The Bluest Hands: A Social and Economic History of Women Dyers in Abeokuta (Nigeria), 1890–1940* (Portsmouth, NH: Heinemann Press, 2002), 137.

62   Minutes of Egba Council Meeting, June 30, 1932, ECR 1/1/55, vol. 1, NAN Abeokuta; Minutes of Egba Council Meeting, July 7, 1932, ECR 1/1/55, vol. 1, NAN Abeokuta.

63   I. W. E. Dods, Report on Tax Collection in the Egba Division for the Year 1938–39, 1–2, ECR 1/1/12, vol. 1, NAN Abeokuta.

64   Dods, Report on Tax Collection in the Egba Division, 3.

65   Dods, 6.

66   Dods, 9.

67   I. W. E. Dods, Supplementary Report on Tax Collection in the Egba Division, 5, NAN Abeokuta

68   Annual Report 1939, pt. 2—Egba Division Native Administration Affairs, ECR 1/1/12, vol. 1, NAN Abeokuta.

69   Minutes of Egba Council Meeting, August 31, 1939, ECR 1/1/97, vol. 1, NAN Abeokuta.

70   Annual Report 1939, pt. 2—Egba Division Native Administration Affairs, CSO 26/2/11875, vol. 14, NAN Ibadan.

71   Minutes of Egba Council Meeting, October 26, 1939, ECR 1/1/97, vol. 1, NAN Abeokuta.

72   Minutes of Egba Council Meeting, April 7, 1941, ECR 1/1/101, NAN Abeokuta. See also Annual Report, Abeokuta Province, 1941, 4, CSO 26/2/11875, vol. 15, NAN Ibadan.

73 The district officer argued that the surplus resulted in part from delayed road improvements. Annual Report Egba Division 1943, 4, Abe Prof 1/1 ABP 1543, vol. 4.

74 Annual Report, Abeokuta Province, 4–5, CSO 26/2/11875, vol. 15, NAN Ibadan.

75 Ake Grade "B" Criminal Court, vol. 17, January 29, 1940, Obafemi Awolowo University Library, Ile Ife.

76 Ake Grade "B" Criminal Court, vol. 17, January 26, 1940, Obafemi Awolowo University Library, Ile Ife.

77 Ake Grade "A" Criminal Court, vol. 17, February 8, 1942, 136, Obafemi Awolowo University Library, Ile Ife.

78 Ake Grade "A" Criminal Court, vol. 17, February 26, 1943, Obafemi Awolowo University Library, Ile Ife.

79 Speech by Oba Alaiyeluwa the Alake, Ademola II, CBE, at the Inauguration of the Egba Central Council, May 10, 1945, 2, Oba Ademola's Speeches and Replies vol. 3, Ake 2/2, NAN Abeokuta.

80 Dods, Report on Tax Collection in the Egba Division, 8.

81 Minutes of Egba Council Meeting, April 4, 1940; Minutes of Egba Council Meeting, April 25, 1940, 5; both in ECR 1/1/98, NAN Abeokuta.

82 *Comet* (Lagos), June 29, 1940.

83 Minutes of Egba Council Meeting, April 25, 1940, ECR 1/1/98, NAN Abeokuta.

84 Minutes of Egba Council Meeting, July 25, 1940, ECR 1/1/98, NAN Abeokuta.

85 Minutes of Egba Council Meeting, June 27, 1940, ECR 1/1/98, NAN Abeokuta.

86 Annual Report, Abeokuta Province, 1943, 4, CSO 26/2/11875, vol. 15, NAN Ibadan.

87 Oladipo Shomoye (Dansaki), "As I View It, Systematic Impoverishment of Egba Market Union," *Egbaland Echo*, May 16, 1941.

88 See Julian Clarke, "Households and the Political Economy of Small-Scale Cash Crop Production in South-Western Nigeria," *Africa* 51, no. 4 (1981): 807–23.

89 See Byfield, *Bluest Hands*, 141–44.

90 Olorunfemi, "Effects of War-Time Trade Controls," 676, 683–84; Olukoju, "'Buy British, Sell Foreign,'" 367, 369.

91 Olorunfemi, "Effects of War-Time Trade Controls," 684.

92 Annual Report 1940, CSO 26/2/11875, vol. 15, NAN Ibadan; Olorunfemi, "Effects of War-Time Trade Controls," 684.

93 Allister E. Hinds, "Government Policy and the Nigerian Palm Oil Export Industry, 1939–49," *Journal of African History* 38, no. 3 (1997): 452.

94 Olukoju, "'Buy British, Sell Foreign,'" 370.

95 Starch was used to make industrial adhesives as well as in the preparation of dextrin, a product used for stiffening cloth goods, thickening colors in calico prints, and in the making of surgical bandages. For more

information, see Nyerhovwo John Tonukari, "Cassava and the Future of Starch," *Electronic Journal of Biotechnology* 7, no. 1 (2004), DOI: 10.2225/vol7-issue1-fulltext-io2.

96 Annual Report, Abeokuta Province, 1940, 18–19, CSO 26/2/11875, vol. 15, NAN Ibadan.

97 Toyin Falola, "Cassava Starch for Export in Nigeria during the Second World War," *African Economic History*, no. 18 (1989): 76, 78, 92. In other regions, starch was a food staple. It was a food item among the Isoko, Urhobo, and Itshekiri of Benin and Warri Provinces.

98 ENA v. Feyisitan, May 4, 1944, Ake Native Court, Grade "A," Criminal Record Book, vol. 61, 1944, 174, Obafemi Awolowo University Library, Ile-Ife.

99 Letter to district officer, August 13, 1944, Abe Prof 1/1 ABP 1497B, vol. 3, NAN Ibadan.

100 The Women's Union Grievances presented to Mr. J. H. Blair, Resident Abeokuta Province, May 31, 1948, Ransome-Kuti Papers, box 45, file 8, KDML.

101 A. E. V. Walwyn, Acting Deputy Chairman, to the Chief Secretary, Lagos, January 29, 1942, 1, CSO 26/37909/S.14, NAN Ibadan.

102 A. E. V. Walwyn to Chief Secretary, August 23, 1941, DCI 1/1 4041/S.20, NAN Ibadan.

103 Savingram from Government of Nigeria to Resident Minister, Achimota, Accra, Gold Coast, June 1, 1945, 1, CSO 26/37909/S.14, vol. 2, NAN Ibadan.

104 Director of Supplies, Lagos, "Grain Bulk Purchase: Maize from Ilaro Division, Abeokuta Province," No. 37/405, November 20, 1943, continuation sheet 16, case file (1) Abeokuta Province Correspondence Maize Purchases (2) Smuggling from Abeokuta to Dahomey, DCI 1/1, NAN Ibadan.

105 Annual Report, Abeokuta Province, 1942, 2–3, Abe Prof 1/ABP 1543, vol. 4, NAN Ibadan; Annual Report, Abeokuta Province, 1942, 2, Abe Prof 1/ABP 1543, vol. 4, NAN Ibadan; Annual Report, Abeokuta Province, 1943, 2, CSO 26/2/11875, vol. 15, NAN Ibadan.

106 Egba Division Report, 1943, 12, Abe Dist1 ED 32, NAN Ibadan.

107 Dr. G. Bryce (Director, Agriculture Department), "War Organisation Production of Rice," September 13, 1939, 1, 6, CSO 26/36378/S.10, vol. 1, NAN Ibadan.

108 Annual Report, Abeokuta Province, 1940, 15, CSO 26/2/11875, vol. 15, NAN Ibadan.

109 Annual Report, Abeokuta Province, 1943, 9, CSO 26/2/11875, vol. 15, NAN Ibadan.

110 Annual Report, Egba Division, 1943, 7, Abe Prof 1/ABP 1543, vol. 4, NAN Ibadan.

111 Report on Food Production and Supply, October 1941–March 1942, 3, CSO 26/36378/S.24, vol. 2, NAN Ibadan.

112   Annual Report, Abeokuta Province, 1941, 10, Abe Prof 1/ABP 1543, vol. 4, NAN Ibadan.

113   Acting Secretary, Western Provinces, to Chief Secretary, November 11, 1943, DCI 1/1/4041/S.20/C1, NAN Ibadan.

114   Memo from Deputy Food Controller A. Pullen to Chief Secretary, October 15, 1943, 5–6, DCI 1/1/4041/S.20/C1, NAN Ibadan; extract from letter from P. F. Brandt to the Director of Supplies, January 12, 1944, 65, DCI 1/1/4041/S.20/C1, NAN Ibadan.

115   Wale Oyemakinde, "The Pullen Marketing Scheme: A Trial in Food Price Control in Nigeria, 1941–1947," *Journal of the Historical Society of Nigeria* 6, no. 4 (1973): 416.

116   Continuation sheet 3, October 8, 1943, DCI 1/1/4041/S.20/C1, NAN Ibadan.

117   A. M. Salami to District Officer, Abeokuta, September 1, 1945, Abe Prof 1/ABP 2060, NAN Ibadan.

118   Annual Report, Abeokuta Province, 1941, 6, CSO 26/2/11875, vol. 15, NAN Ibadan.

119   Annual Report, Abeokuta Province, 1943, 5, CSO 26/2/11875, vol. 15, NAN Ibadan.

120   Acting Chief Secretary to Secretary, Western Provinces, October 16, 1943, 7, DCI 1/1/4041/S.20/C2, NAN Ibadan.

121   "Sympathy for Farmers," *Daily Service* (Lagos), May 20, 1944, DCI 1/1/4041/S.20/C1, NAN Ibadan.

122   Axel Harneit-Sievers, "African Business, 'Economic Nationalism,' and British Colonial Policy: Southern Nigeria, 1935–1954," *African Economic History*, no. 23 (1995): 102.

123   Confidential letter from J. C. Graham to AWAM delegate, Lagos, November 25, 1943, DCI 1/1/4041/S.20/C1, NAN Ibadan.

124   Continuation sheet 41, November 23, 1943, DCI 1/1/4041/S.20/C1, NAN Ibadan.

125   J. F. Winter to Mr. Booth, November 27, 1943, DCI 1/1/4041/S.20/C1, NAN Ibadan.

126   Continuation sheet 21, DCI 1/1/4041/S.20/C1, NAN Ibadan.

127   Letter to resident, July 3, 1943, APB 1497B, vol. 3, NAN Ibadan.

128   Acting Chief Secretary of Government to Secretary, Western Provinces, October 16, 1943, DCI 1/1/4041/S.20/C1, NAN Ibadan.

129   Acting Secretary, Western Provinces, to Chief Secretary of Government, November 16, 1943, DCI 1/1/4041/S.20/C1, NAN Ibadan.

130   Continuation sheet 69, March 17, 1944, DCI 1/1/4041/S.20/C1, NAN Ibadan.

131   M. L. Crapp, "Jungle Commando: The Story of the West African Expeditionary Force's First Campaign in Burma," 4–5, MSS Afr.S.1734, 108, Bodleian Library, Oxford. Wingate split his forces into mobile units that harried the enemy and destroyed their lines of communication. According to Crapp, Wingate tried his theories first in Palestine and perfected them in Abyssinia.

132 Annual Report, Abeokuta Province, 1945, 11, CSO 26/2/11875, vol. 15, NAN Ibadan.

133 Investiture of Oba Alaiyeluwa Ademola II, C.M.G., C.B.E., the Alake of Abeokuta by His Excellency Sir Arthur Richards, the Governor and Commander-in-Chief of Nigeria, November 27, 1945, at 10 a.m. in the Centenary Hall, Ake, Ake Palace Papers, 2/1/51, NAN Abeokuta.

134 Barbara Bush and Josephine Maltby, "Taxation in West Africa: Transforming the Colonial Subject into the 'Governable Person,'" *Critical Perspectives on Accounting* 15, no. 1 (2004): 22.

CHAPTER 5: "FREEDOM FROM WANT"

1 Tim Rooth, "Economic Tensions and Conflict in the Commonwealth, 1945–c. 1951," *Twentieth Century British History* 13, no. 2 (2002): 123.

2 Michael Crowder, "The Second World War: Prelude to Decolonisation," in *The Cambridge History of Africa*, ed. Michael Crowder, vol. 8, *c. 1940–c. 1975* (Cambridge: Cambridge University Press, 1984), 24.

3 Crowder, "Second World War," 25. The fund set aside by the 1945 act represented a significant improvement over the paltry sum of £5 million annually stipulated in the bill's precursor, the Colonial Development and Welfare Act of 1940. Nonetheless, given the vastness of the British Empire, £12 million per year remained an abysmally small amount.

4 Allister E. Hinds, "Sterling and Imperial Policy, 1945–1951," *Journal of Imperial and Commonwealth History* 15, no. 2 (1987): 149.

5 Hinds, "Sterling and Imperial Policy," 149.

6 Hinds, 150.

7 Hinds, 155.

8 Hinds, 155.

9 Hinds, 160.

10 *West African Pilot*, November 8, 1947, quoted in Hinds, "Sterling and Imperial Policy," 160.

11 Rooth, "Economic Tensions and Conflict," 133–35.

12 Investiture of Oba Alaiyeluwa Ademola II, C.M.G., C.B.E., the Alake of Abeokuta by His Excellency Sir Arthur Richards, the Governor and Commander-in-Chief of Nigeria on Tuesday, November 27, 1945, at 10 a.m. in the Centenary Hall, Ake, 1, Ake 2/1/51, NAN Ibadan.

13 Richard L. Sklar, *Nigerian Political Parties: Power in an Emergent African Nation* (1963; repr., Trenton, NJ: Africa World Press, 2004), 56.

14 Sklar, *Nigerian Political Parties*, 53–54. NUS was organized by students at the Abeokuta Grammar School at the encouragement of Reverend Ransome-Kuti.

15 *West African Pilot*, August 28, 1944, quoted in Sklar, *Nigerian Political Parties*, 57.

16 G. O. Olusanya, *The Second World War and Politics in Nigeria, 1939–1953* (London: Evans Bros. for the University of Lagos, 1973), 17.

17   The *West African Pilot* played an especially important role during the nationalist era because it was the first newspaper to have a significant circulation beyond Lagos. Its circulation extended beyond Nigeria as well. In 1937 when the paper was launched, it had a daily print run of six thousand copies. By 1950, it produced more than ten thousand copies daily. See Sam O. Idemili, "What the *West African Pilot* Did in the Movement for Nigerian Nationalism between 1937 and 1957," *Black American Literature Forum* 12, no. 3 (1978): 86.

18   Raymond J. Smyke, "A History of the Nigeria Union of Teachers," *West African Journal of Education* 16, no. 3 (1972): 396–97.

19   Smyke, "History of Nigeria Union of Teachers," 399.

20   See Confidential Report, NUT Executive, May 25, 1946, 2, and Minutes Emergency Meeting of the Executive, July 3, 1946, Ransome-Kuti Papers, box 43, folder 3, KDML. Ransome-Kuti exchanged letters with Dr. Rita Hinden, the secretary of the Fabian Colonial Bureau. See letter to Rev. Ransome-Kuti from Rita Hinden, November 16, 1946, Ransome-Kuti Papers, box 4, folder H, KDML.

21   Robin Cohen, "Michael Imoudu and the Nigerian Labour Movement," *Race and Class* 18, no. 4 (1977): 350.

22   Imoudu was exiled to Auchi, a region in midwestern Nigeria, hundreds of miles away from Lagos, and he would remain there until 1945. Cohen, "Michael Imoudu," 351.

23   Wale Oyemakinde, "The Nigerian General Strike of 1945," *Journal of the Historical Society of Nigeria* 7, no. 4 (1975): 696.

24   Cohen, "Michael Imoudu," 354.

25   Cohen, 355–56.

26   Oyemakinde, "Nigerian General Strike of 1945," 705.

27   Cohen, "Michael Imoudu," 356; Oyemakinde, "Nigerian General Strike," 707.

28   *West Africa*, October 26, 1946, 987, CO 583/30647/6A, TNA. The other committee members were F. W. Dalley and G. F. W. Lamb, the chief statistical officer of the Colonial Office.

29   Although Imoudu participated in the meeting, Cohen suggests that this group was dominated by the moderates in the trade union movement. Cohen, "Michael Imoudu," 357.

30   Commission of Enquiry into the Cost of Living and the Control of the Cost of Living in the Colony and Protectorate of Nigeria, Glover Memorial Hall, December 5, 1945, 18, CO 583/276/30647/6B, TNA. In a fascinating exchange, Ogunsheye noted that they quoted from *The Russian Peasant* in the TUC memorandum and asked the commissioner, Tudor-Davies, if he had read the book. The commissioner replied that he had read it carefully. *The Russian Peasant and Other Studies* by Sir John Maynard was considered one of the best studies of the Russian peasantry. Maynard, who was fluent in Russian and well versed in Russian history written in English and Russian, began visiting the country in 1895.

His book provided one of the most comprehensive studies of the Russian peasant from the tsarist period to the creation of collective farms in 1936. Maynard's discussion of the improving living conditions for Russia's peasantry when they were not "producing for an unsympathetic market" like that controlled by the colonial state likely resonated with the TUC. See E. John Russell, "Sir John Maynard and His Studies of the Russian Peasant," *Slavonic and East European Review* 24, no. 63 (1946): 64.

31   Commission of Enquiry, December 5, 1945, 22.
32   Commission of Enquiry, December 5, 1945, 18.
33   Commission of Enquiry, December 5, 1945, 20.
34   Commission of Enquiry, December 5, 1945, 22.
35   Commission of Enquiry, December 5, 1945, 32.
36   Commission of Enquiry into the Cost of Living and the Control of the Cost of Living in the Colony and Protectorate of Nigeria, Glover Memorial Hall, December 6, 1945, 2–32, CO 583/276/30647/6B, TNA.
37   Commission of Enquiry into the Cost of Living and the Control of the Cost of Living in the Colony and Protectorate of Nigeria, Glover Memorial Hall, December 7, 1945, 17, CO 583/276/30647/6B, TNA.
38   Commission of Enquiry, December 7, 18.
39   Commission of Enquiry into the Cost of Living and the Control of the Cost of Living in the Colony and Protectorate of Nigeria, Cost of Living Index—Calabar, CO 583/30647/ Rc/4627, TNA; Commission of Enquiry into the Cost of Living and the Control of the Cost of Living in the Colony and Protectorate of Nigeria, Cost of Living Index—Kaduna, CO 583/30647/ Rp/0602, TNA; Commission of Enquiry into the Cost of Living and the Control of the Cost of Living in the Colony and Protectorate of Nigeria, Cost of Living Index—Makurdi, CO 583/30647/ Rc/4627, TNA. The cost indices were part of the commission's report submitted to Governor Richards on May 3, 1946.
40   *West Africa*, October 26, 1946, 991.
41   Governor Richards to Secretary of State for the Colonies, George Hall, May 25, 1946, 1, CO 583/30647/6A, TNA.
42   *West Africa*, October 26, 1946, 989.
43   *West Africa*, October 26, 1946, 987–91.
44   Cohen, "Michael Imoudu," 356.
45   I. M. Okonjo, *British Administration in Nigeria, 1900–1950: A Nigerian View* (New York: NOK, 1974), 313–16.
46   Sklar, *Nigerian Political Parties*, 58–60.
47   "The N.C.N.C. Meeting at Abeokuta," *Egba Bulletin*, February 1947 (reprinted from the *Daily Times*, December 23, 1946).
48   Sklar, *Nigerian Political Parties*, 61–62. Of the 153 mandates, 24 came from communities in the north, 48 in the west, and 81 in the east as well as the Oba District of Lagos.
49   "NCNC Delegates Give Account of Their Stewardship," *Daily Comet*, October 11, 1947.

50 Memorandum Submitted by the Delegation of the National Council of Nigeria and the Cameroons to the Secretary of State for the Colonies on August 11, 1947, 1, Ransome-Kuti Papers, box 75, KDML.

51 Memorandum Submitted, August 11, 1947, 7. Ransome-Kuti notes that the memorandum was drafted and signed by Azikiwe alone and not circulated among the members of the committee before it was submitted to the Colonial Office. There were tensions among the members of the delegation; nonetheless, it appears that they were able to put them aside in order to carry out their tasks. See Funmilayo Ransome-Kuti's observations of the NCNC delegation to London in a meeting held at Kristen Hall on October 17, 1947, Ransome-Kuti Papers, box 75, file 5, KDML.

52 Notes of a meeting with the National Council for Nigeria and the Cameroons and secretary of state for the colonies, held on August 13, 1947, at the Colonial Office. Ransome-Kuti Papers, box 75, KDML. The other participants in the meeting were Sir Thomas Lloyd, permanent undersecretary of state, Colonial Office; A. B. Cohen, assistant undersecretary, African Division, Colonial Office; K. W. Blackburne, director of information services; and K. E. Robinson and A. Emanuel, West African Department, Colonial Office.

53 Meeting with the NCNC and the secretary of state for the colonies held on August 13, 1947, at the Colonial Office, 4–7, Ransome-Kuti Papers, box 75, KDML.

54 Meeting with the NCNC and the secretary of state for the colonies, 12.

55 George Padmore, An Open Letter to the Nigerian Delegation, Paris, August 20, 1947, Ransome-Kuti Papers, box 75, KDML. Trinidadian-born Padmore was a journalist and active in the Communist International and the pan-African movement. See *George Padmore: Pan-African Revolutionary*, ed. Fitzroy André Baptiste and Rupert Lewis (Kingston, Jamaica: Ian Randle, 2009).

56 Press release, Nigerian Goodwill Mission to Scotland, September 20, 1947, Ransome-Kuti Papers, box 75, file 5, KDML.

57 Press release, Nigerian Goodwill Mission to Ireland, September 12, 1947, Ransome-Kuti Papers, box 75, file 5, KDML.

58 *Scottish Daily Express*, July 12, 1947, in National Council of Nigeria and the Cameroons, What the British Press Says: July 3 to August 2, 1947, Ransome-Kuti Papers, box 75, file 5, KDML.

59 *Daily Mail*, July 3, 1947, in National Council of Nigeria and the Cameroons, What the British Press Says: July 3 to August 2, 1947, Ransome-Kuti Papers, box 75, file 5, KDML.

60 Minutes of Meeting of the Delegation held at 20 Bentinck Street, London, August 5, 1947, Ransome-Kuti Papers, box 75, file 5, KDML.

61 *Irish Times*, September 12, 1947, in National Council of Nigeria and the Cameroons, What the British Press Says: July 3 to August 2, 1947, Ransome-Kuti Papers, box 75, file 5, KDML.

62 Sklar, *Nigerian Political Parties*, 63. For the names of appointees to the national cabinet appointed by Azikiwe, see p. 63n68.

63 Cited in Sklar, 64.

64 Annual Report, Abeokuta Province, 1945, 2, CSO 26/2 11875, vol. 15, NAN Ibadan.

65 Annual Report, Abeokuta Province, 1945, 5.

66 Conditional sales effectively extended credit to African traders, for it allowed them to take goods from the European trading companies with the expectation that the debt would be paid at a specified date. During the Depression, many European firms ceased conditional sales or shortened the length of the repayment period. For more on conditional sales, see Byfield, *Bluest Hands*, 107.

67 F. Ransome-Kuti, S. F. Adeyinka, El. Soyinka, F. W. Fagbemi, M. S. Oluwole, Alice Ayeyinka, On Behalf of All Women's Societies in Abeokuta, to Oba Alaiyeluwa Ademola II, October 5, 1946, ECR 1/1/114, NAN Abeokuta.

68 Ransome-Kuti et al., On Behalf. See also Titcombe to All Women's Societies of Abeokuta, October 8, 1946, Ransome-Kuti Papers, box 45, file 5, KDML.

69 Cheryl Johnson-Odim and Nina Emma Mba, *For Women and the Nation: Funmilayo Ransome-Kuti of Nigeria* (Urbana: University of Illinois Press, 1997), 79.

70 Johnson-Odim and Mba, *For Women and the Nation*, 80.

71 Secretary, Local Merchant Committee, to Alake of Abeokuta, October 19, 1946, ECR 1/1/114, NAN Abeokuta.

72 G. Beresford Stooke to the Secretary, Western Province, September 11, 1945, Abe Prof 1/ABP 2060, NAN Ibadan.

73 Re: Seizure of Rice, Instructions, from Officer i/c ENA Police, No. EP 87/101, September 24, 1945, Abe Prof 1/ABP 2060, NAN Ibadan; Circular from Officer i/c, ENA Police, no. EP 87/111/ANC, November 6, 1945, Abe Prof 1/ABP 2060, NAN Ibadan.

74 S. A. Fajembola, Secretary, Local Merchants Committee, to Managers, United Africa Company, Ltd., and Patterson Zochonis, Ltd., Abe Prof 1/ABP 2060, NAN Ibadan. The district officer shared this information with Fajembola the day before the order went into effect. Trucks entering Abeokuta on the Ijebu Ode road had to carry ten bags of rice, while those along the Asha road had to carry three bags of rice.

75 Eleti Ofe to District Officer, Abeokuta, September 19, 1945, Abe Prof 1/ABP 2060, NAN Ibadan. See also Lamide Olaniji to District Officer, August 6, 1946, Abe Prof 1/1, ABP 1875/1. Olaniji identified Alao as a military contractor.

76 The Women's Union Grievances, presented to Mr. J. H. Blair, Resident Abeokuta Province, May 31, 1948, Ransome-Kuti Papers, box 45, file 8, KDML.

77 The Native Authority Rice Production Revocation Order (1945), issued by the Alake of Abeokuta, November 20, 1945, Abe Prof 1/ABP 2060, NAN Ibadan.

78 Omo Agbe, "More about Rice Trouble in Abeokuta," *Daily Service* (Lagos), November 26, 1948. Omo Agbe appears to be a pen name adopted by the author. It has multiple meanings, including "child of a farmer" and "child of a beggar."

79 Agbe, "More about Rice Trouble." Traders use the five-ounce evaporated milk can as a measuring cup. The most common olodo measure used to apportion yam flour, rice, and other small grains was twelve milk cans. Joseph Ayodokun, email to author, September 30, 2013.

80 J. A. Ladipo, Headmaster, Oke-Ona United School, to Rev. I. O. Ransome-Kuti, Principal, Abeokuta Grammar School, September 19, 1945, Ransome-Kuti Papers, box "Reign of Oba Ademola," KDML. Police seized rice from both Ladipo and his sister, a rice trader. He also claimed that the police who seized the rice were Alao's messengers.

81 Johnson-Odim and Mba, *For Women and the Nation*, 65–66; Minutes of the Abeokuta Ladies Club, February 8, 1946, Ransome-Kuti Papers, box 87/1, KDML.

82 Olaniji to District Officer, Abeokuta, August 6, 1946.

83 District Officer, Egba Division, to Mr. Lamidi Olaniji, October 24, 1946, Abe Prof 1/1, ABP 1875/1, NAN Ibadan.

84 Anonymous to District Officer, Egba Division, Abeokuta, July 23, 1946, Abe Prof 1/1, ABP 1875/1, NAN Ibadan.

85 District Officer, Egba Division, to Mr. Amusa O. Adeoshun and Others, July 23, 1946, Abe Prof 1/1, ABP 1875/1, NAN Ibadan.

86 See Mesdames Mojisola of Apena Village, Wuraola of Bada Village, and Adetutu of Ikeiyi, Opeji, to Senior District Officer, Abeokuta, June 23, 1947, Abe Prof 1/1, ABP 1875/1, NAN Ibadan.

87 B. O. Oshin Ayeye to His Highness the Alake of Abeokuta, December 18, 1946, Abe Prof 1/1, ABP 1875/1, NAN Ibadan.

88 B. O. Oshin to Assistant Food Controller, Abeokuta, February 3, 1947, Prof 1/1, ABP 1875/1, NAN Ibadan.

89 C. J. Gunton, Senior District Officer, Egba Division, to President, Native Court Ake 'A,' February 21, 1947, Abe Prof 1/1, ABP 1875/1, NAN Ibadan.

90 Senior District Officer, Egba Division, to Alake of Abeokuta, July 28, 1947, Abe Prof 1/1, ABP 1875/1, NAN Ibadan.

91 Adsec, "Resident and Alake Tour Districts," *Egba Bulletin*, March 1947, 3, NAN Ibadan.

92 Detunji Dedeke, letter to the editor, *Egba Bulletin*, March 1947, 4. NAN Ibadan. Dedeke reported on the alake and resident's visit to Owode District.

93 Nigerian Secretariat to Deputy Food Controller, Abeokuta Province, May 11, 1946, Abe Prof 1/1, ABP 1497, NAN Ibadan.

94   C. J. Gunton, District Officer, Egba Division, to the Agents of P. Z. & Co, S.C.O.A., C.F.A.O., G.B. Ollivant, John Holt, and the Manager of U.A.C. in Abeokuta, October 24, 1947, Abe Prof 1/1, ABP 1497, NAN Ibadan.

95   R. E. Greswell, Food Controller, to Deputy Food Controllers, Yola, Bauchi, Makurdi, Maiduguri, Ilorin, Lokoja, Kano, Katsina, Minna, Jos, Sokoto, Zaria, Calabar, Buea, Ogoja, Onitsha, Port Harcourt, Abeokuta, Benin, Ijebu-Ode, Akure, Oyo, Warri, Com/Col., Lagos, May 13, 1948, Abe Prof 1/1, ABP 1497, NAN Ibadan.

96   Greswell to Deputy Food Controllers.

97   See Manager of United Africa Company to Assistant Food Controller, Abeokuta, September 14, 1948.

98   Minutes of Egba Women's Union, December 27, 1947, 6, ECR 1/1/114, NAN Abeokuta. J. B. Majekodunmi was a member of the Egba Council as well as one of the leading African merchants in Abeokuta. His four wives were also wealthy traders in their own right. Chief Adura Majekodunmi, interview by the author, June 21, 1988, Abeokuta.

99   Johnson-Odim and Mba, *For Women and the Nation*, 64. See also Wole Soyinka, *Aké: The Years of Childhood* (New York: Random House, 1981).

100 Minutes of the Abeokuta Ladies Club, Ransome-Kuti Papers, box 87, KDML.

101 Abeokuta Ladies Club Resolution, March 15, 1946, Ransome-Kuti Papers, box 87, file 1, KDML.

102 Abosede A. George, *Making Modern Girls: A History of Girlhood, Labor, and Social Development in Colonial Lagos* (Athens: Ohio University Press, 2014).

103 Marjorie McIntosh argues that only in Ijebu and Abeokuta did market women and educated women cooperate on the struggle around taxation. She credits the National Council of Women's Societies in 1957 with bringing women of all ranks from multiple places under one institutional umbrella. Marjorie Keniston McIntosh, *Yoruba Women, Work, and Social Change* (Bloomington: Indiana University Press, 2009), 231.

104 Johnson-Odim and Mba, *For Women and the Nation*, 75; Soyinka, *Aké*, 180–81.

105 Johnson-Odim and Mba, *For Women and the Nation*, 78.

106 Funmilayo Ransome-Kuti, "We Had Equality till Britain Came," *Daily Worker*, August 18, 1947, reprinted in *Feminist Writings from Ancient Times to the Modern World: A Global Sourcebook and History*, vol. 2, ed. Tiffany K. Wayne (Santa Barbara, CA: Greenwood, 2011), 544–45.

107 Ransome-Kuti, "We Had Equality," 545.

108 "Egba Council Meeting, September 11, 1947," *Egba Bulletin*, November 1947, Abe Dist 1—ED 267A, NAN Ibadan.

109 "Egba Council Meeting, October 30, 1947," *Egba Bulletin*, December 1947, Abe Dist 1—ED 267A, NAN Ibadan.

110 E. Soyinka (Acting President) and F. W. Fagbemi (Secretary), Mrs. F. Ransome-Kuti, and the Egba Central Council Resolution Passed by the Women's Union, Abeokuta, on September 13, 1947, ECR 1/1/114, NAN Abeokuta. The name, AWU, was adopted in the latter part of 1946.

111 Osumaka Likaka, *Rural Society and Cotton in Colonial Zaire* (Madison: University of Wisconsin Press, 1997), 27, 107.

112 Address by Ademola II, 1 & 2, Ake 2/2—Oba Ademola's Important Addresses and Reply, vol. 2, NAN Abeokuta.

CHAPTER 6: DAUGHTERS OF TINUBU

1 James C. Scott, *Seeing Like a State: How Certain Schemes to Improve the Human Condition Have Failed* (New Haven, CT: Yale University Press, 1998), 51.

2 Scott, *Seeing Like a State*, 80.

3 Janet Roitman, *Anti-Crisis* (Durham, NC: Duke University Press, 2014), 8.

4 Wale Adebanwi, "Death, National Memory and the Social Construction of Heroism," *Journal of African History* 49 (2008): 421–22.

5 Nina Mba suggests that the Majeobaje Society formed in early 1947, but the women had to pressure it to publicly support the AWU protests. The group claimed a membership of nine thousand men, which included Christians and Muslims, and Reverend Ransome-Kuti was its first president. Like the AWU, the Majeobaje Society also crafted resolutions and memos detailing its complaints about Ademola and supporting calls for his resignation. See Nina Mba, *Nigerian Women Mobilized: Women's Political Activity in Southern Nigeria, 1900–1965* (Berkeley: Institute of International Studies, University of California, 1982), 156. See also Resolution from the Majeobaje Society to the Egba Interim Council, August 7, 1948, Ransome-Kuti Papers, box 50, file 9, KDML.

6 Cadet F. Ratcliffe, quoted in J. M. Beeley, Snr. District Officer, Annual Report, 1948—Egba Division, 2, Abe Dist 1, ED 32, NAN Ibadan.

7 Cheryl Johnson-Odim and Nina Emma Mba, *For Women and the Nation: Funmilayo Ransome-Kuti of Nigeria* (Urbana: University of Illinois Press, 1997), 80.

8 Detunji Deleke, letter to the editor, *Egba Bulletin*, June 1947.

9 Deleke, letter.

10 "Egba Council Meeting, June 20th, 1947," *Egba Bulletin*, August 1947, Abe Dist 1—ED 267A, NAN Ibadan.

11 "Egba Council Meeting, October 30th, 1947," *Egba Bulletin*, December 1947, Abe Dist 1—ED 267A, NAN Ibadan.

12 "Egba Council Meeting, October 30th, 1947." The Harragin Commission's report established the government's Africanization policy in 1947 when it mandated the replacement of British civil servants with African candidates. See Stephanie Decker, "Africanization in British

Multinationals in Ghana and Nigeria, 1945–1970," *Business History Review* 92 (2018): 707.

13   "Egba Council Meeting, October 30th, 1947."

14   "The Abeokuta Affairs," *New Times of Nigeria*, March 10, 1948, ERC 1/1/114, NAN Ibadan.

15   Annual Report 1948 Egba Division, 20, Abe Dist 1, ED 32, NAN Ibadan.

16   For a fuller discussion of what Moses E. Ochonu calls the economic propaganda around tax collection, see Moses E. Ochonu, *Colonial Meltdown: Northern Nigeria in the Great Depression* (Athens: Ohio University Press, 2009), 100–120.

17   Dr. the Hon. C. C. Adeniyi-Jones, Political and Administrative Problems of Nigeria, 23, 31, Solanke Collection, WASU, box 48, Special Collections, University of Lagos Library.

18   These ordinances lay at the roots of the Igbo Women's War in 1929 when it appeared that officials intended to extend the tax to women. There is an extensive literature on this important women's tax revolt. See Judith Van Allen, "'Aba Riots' or Igbo 'Women's War'? Ideology, Stratification, and the Invisibility of Women," in *Women in Africa: Studies in Social and Economic Change*, ed. Nancy J. Hafkin and Edna G. Bay (Palo Alto, CA: Stanford University Press, 1976); Misty L. Bastian, "'Vultures of the Marketplace': Southeastern Nigerian Women and Discourses of the *Ogu Umunwaanyi* (Women's War) of 1929," in *Women in African Colonial Histories*, ed. Jean Allman, Susan Geiger, and Nakanyike Musisi (Bloomington: Indiana University Press, 2002); Toyin Falola, *Colonialism and Violence in Nigeria* (Bloomington: Indiana University Press, 2009); Marc Matera, Misty Bastian, and Susan Kingsley Kent, *The Women's War of 1929: Gender and Violence in Colonial Nigeria* (New York: Palgrave, 2012); and Robin Chapdelaine, "A History of Child Trafficking in Southeastern Nigeria, 1900–1930s" (PhD diss., Rutgers University, 2014).

19   Kunle Ademola, the alake's grandson, recalled helping out on the farm, harvesting palm kernels. He noted the family still owned a lot of land but that by the 1980s they were beginning to dispose of some of it because people were encroaching on it. Interview by the author, August 11, 2003. Kunle's parents were Kofo Ademola and Adetokunbo Ademola, the former chief justice of Supreme Court of Nigeria.

20   John Blair, *Juju and Justice* (Perth, Australia: P & B Press, 1991), 231–32.

21   The Women's Union Grievances, May 31, 1948, Presented to J. H. Blair, Resident Abeokuta Province, Ransome-Kuti Papers, box 45, file 8, KDML.

22   Wole Soyinka, *Aké: The Years of Childhood* (New York: Random House, 1981), 201.

23   Soyinka, *Aké*, 201.

24   E. A. A. Fadayiro, "Abeokuta Monthly Newsletter," *Egba Bulletin*, January 1948, Abe Dist 1 — ED 267A, NAN Ibadan.

25 Soyinka, *Aké*, 211.

26 Soyinka, 213.

27 For more examples of the songs performed during the protests, see Nina Mba, *Nigerian Women Mobilized: Women's Political Activity in Southern Nigeria, 1900–1965* (Berkeley: Institute of International Studies, University of California, 1982), 150; Johnson-Odim and Mba, *For Women and the Nation*, 82–83; and Stephanie Shonekan, "Fela's Foundation: Examining the Revolutionary Songs of Funmilayo Ransome-Kuti and the Abeokuta Market Women's Movement in 1940s Western Nigeria," *Black Music Research Journal* 29, no. 1 (2009): 127–44. For more on the political significance of dress and undress during the protests see, Judith Byfield "Dress and Politics in Post–World War II Abeokuta (Western Nigeria)," in *Fashioning Africa: Power and the Politics of Dress*, ed. Jean Allman (Bloomington: Indiana University Press, 2004), 31–49.

28 Soyinka, *Aké*, 216–17.

29 Fadayiro, "Abeokuta Monthly Newsletter," *Egba Bulletin*, January 1948.

30 Minutes of Meeting to Discuss Grievances of Abeokuta Women's Union, November 30, 1947, in the Afin, 4, ECR 1/1/114, NAN Abeokuta.

31 Minutes of Meeting, November 30, 1947, 1.

32 Minutes of Meeting, November 30, 1947, 2.

33 Minutes of Meeting, November 30, 1947, 1, 3. Eniola Soyinka claimed that the commission was 2s. per pound, while Ransome-Kuti claimed they received 2s. or 1s. 6d.

34 Minutes of Meeting, November 30, 1947, 2.

35 Letter from ENA Secretary C. A. A. Titcombe to the Editor, *Daily Service*, November 20, 1946, ECR 1/3, NAN Abeokuta.

36 G. A. Adedayo, Clerk of Council, "Egba Council Meeting," *Egba Bulletin*, February 1948, Abe Dist 1—ED 267A, NAN Ibadan.

37 Adedayo, "Egba Council Meeting."

38 Adedayo, "Egba Council Meeting."

39 Informal Meeting of Councillors held on Tuesday 2nd December, 1947 to Consider Abeokuta Women's Union Grievances, 8, ECR 1/1/114, NAN Abeokuta.

40 Informal Meeting of Councillors, 4–5.

41 Informal Meeting of Councillors, 2, 3, 5.

42 Informal Meeting of Councillors, 3, 7.

43 Minutes of First Meeting of the Assessment Committee, Thursday, June 23rd, 1938, 3. Abe Prof 1/1 ABP 1208, NAN Ibadan.

44 Informal Meeting of Councillors, 7.

45 Letter from C. A. A. Titcombe, Secretary, Egba Native Administration, to Akitoye Tejuoso, Secretary, Executive Committee of Egbas Resident in Lagos, February 20, 1948, ECR 1/1/114, NAN Abeokuta. This group wrote to Titcombe requesting detailed information about revenue sources, taxes, and fees collected and to whom they were paid—the

central government or the Egba Native Authority. See also Johnson-Odim and Mba, *For Women and the Nation*, 73. Titcombe's response did not provide any details about the African businesses. It is possible that these enterprises were owned by Nigerians from other parts of the country or by individuals from other African countries.

46 Johnson-Odim and Mba, *For Women and the Nation*, 84; Adedayo, "Egba Council Meeting," *Egba Bulletin*, February 1948.

47 Fadayiro, "Abeokuta Monthly Newsletter," *Egba Bulletin*, January 1948.

48 Looting and Damage of Atupa's Parlour House, Letter to the Secretary of the Native Administration February 26, 1951, Egba Council Records, Ake 2/1, file 41, NAN Abeokuta.

49 Chief Sorunke, interview by the author, August 19, 2003, Keesi, Abeokuta.

50 Resolution passed by a meeting of the ministers of the Protestant churches in Abeokuta in connection with the recent women's demonstration at Canon Green's Hall, Ake, Abeokuta, on December 16, 1947, ECR 1/1/114, NAN Abeokuta. The resolution was signed by representatives from the Anglican, Methodist, and Baptist churches as well as the Salvation Army.

51 Resolution passed by meeting of ministers.

52 Adedayo, "Egba Council Meeting," *Egba Bulletin*, February 1948.

53 Letter from Representative of the Native Authority, C. A. A. Titcombe, to Mrs. F. Ransome-Kuti, December 12, 1947, ECR 1/1/114, NAN Abeokuta.

54 Adedayo, "Egba Council Meeting," *Egba Bulletin*, February 1948.

55 Meeting of Egba Women Union on December 27, 1947, 1–2, ECR 1/1/114, NAN Abeokuta. The minutes noted that the alake had "arranged for certain gas which he wanted to be used to drive them away in case of further demonstration." Johnson-Odim and Mba learned Funmilayo Ransome-Kuti held training sessions to instruct the women on how to cover their eyes, noses, and mouths with cloth when tear gas was thrown and how to pick up the canisters and throw them back at the policemen. Johnson-Odim and Mba, *For Women and the Nation*, 81.

56 Johnson-Odim and Mba, *For Women and the Nation*, 85.

57 Minutes of Combined Sectional Council Meeting, February 27, 1948, ECR 1/1/114, NAN Abeokuta. The resident, E. N. Mylius, also published an announcement in the *Egba Bulletin*, April 1948.

58 Pa Akinola Sho, interview by the author and Abiola Tope Oladunjoye, 2003, Quarry, Abeokuta.

59 Blair, *Juju and Justice*, 236.

60 Ransome-Kuti was in Lagos and did not hear the broadcast. She was told about it when she returned to Abeokuta the following day and promptly wrote to Blair complaining that this was done without her permission. Letter to J. H. Blair, Resident, from F. Ransome-Kuti, April 25, 1948, Ransome-Kuti Papers, box 45, file 5, KDML. A letter was also

sent to Ransome-Kuti the same day notifying her that the tax case was withdrawn. Letter to Mrs. F. Ransome-Kuti from Secretary, Egba Native Administration, April 25, 1948, Ransome-Kuti Papers, box 45, file 5, KDML.

61 Johnson-Odim and Mba, *For Women and the Nation*, 86–87.

62 Minutes of a Combined Meeting of the Egba Alake, Oke-Ona, Gbagure, and Owu Sectional Councils, April 23, 1948, 1–2, ECR 1/1/114, NAN Abeokuta.

63 Letter from Resident to Alake of Abeokuta, May, 1948, ECR 1/1/114, NAN Abeokuta.

64 "British Parliamentary Committee at Abeokuta Entertained by the Alake," *Egba Bulletin*, May 1948.

65 Oba Alaiyeluwa Ademola II, Alake of Abeokuta, "An Address of Welcome Presented to His Excellency the Governor and Lady Macpherson," *Egba Bulletin*, July 1948.

66 Governor Macpherson, "His Excellency's Speech at Abeokuta June 2, 1948," *Egba Bulletin*, July 1948.

67 "The Alake and the Resident's Speeches at the Inaugural Meeting of the 4th Session of the Egba Central Council Held on Friday, 28th May, 1948: Alake's Speech," *Egba Bulletin*, July 1948.

68 "Alake and Resident's Speeches."

69 "Alake and Resident's Speeches."

70 Olufemi Vaughan, *Nigerian Chiefs: Traditional Power in Modern Politics, 1890s–1990s* (Rochester, NY: University of Rochester Press, 2000), 25.

71 Vaughan, *Nigerian Chiefs*, 25–26.

72 J. A. Cashmann, General Secretary, Educated Elements, to the District Officer, Egba Division, August 10, 1938, 1, 3, Ake 2/1/43, NAN Abeokuta. The Educated Elements published their constitution and bylaws in 1938. Ake 2/1/3, Educated Elements in Abeokuta, 1938–1941, NAN Abeokuta.

73 Blair, *Juju and Justice*, 237.

74 Vaughan, *Nigerian Chiefs*, 34.

75 Oduntan, "Elite Identity and Power: A Study of Social Change and Leadership among the Egba of Western Nigeria 1860–1950" (PhD diss., Dalhousie University, 2010), 304–5.

76 Cashmann, General Secretary, Educated Elements, 4.

77 Notes about the Chiefs Who Are Fomenting Troubles, Ake 2/1/43, Educated Elements 1940, NAN Abeokuta. I. A. Shodipo, an ogboni title holder, the *bagbimo* of Iporo in Egba Alake section, played a significant role in the effort to recall the alake. The notes suggest that he functioned as Ademola's agent in an enterprise known as Shodipo and Company. Although the business carried Shodipo's name, Ademola guaranteed a two thousand pounds overdraft obtained from the Bank of British West Africa. As we saw in chapter 4, Shodipo was deeply implicated in rice

purchasing during World War II and many linked the alake to Shodipo's activities.

78 Blair, *Juju and Justice*, 231.
79 "The New Great Egba Central Council," *Egbaland Echo*, January 17, 1941.
80 J. O. K., "Inauguration of Egba Central Council," *Egbaland Echo*, March 7, 1941.
81 "Address by His Honour the Chief Commissioner Western Provinces at the Inauguration of the Egba Central Council," *Egbaland Echo*, March 7, 1941.
82 Filikaja, "The Egba Central Council: Some Observations," *Egbaland Echo*, February 28, 1941.
83 "The Inauguration of the Egba Central Council," *Egbaland Echo*, March 7, 1948.
84 "Opening of New Council 1941: Alake's Speech," *Egbaland Echo*, March 14, 1941.
85 It was initially understood that the township councils would select six representatives for the sectional council and from that group select one to represent them on the central council. However, the alake disputed this claim, suggesting he had incorrectly implied this during his inaugural address. In short, only the sectional council could appoint members to the central council. See "Alake's Announcement," *Egbaland Echo*, April 25, 1941.
86 An Egba, "The Egba Central Council," *Egbaland Echo*, April 18, 1941.
87 Blair, *Juju and Justice*, 237.
88 Johnson-Odim and Mba, *For Women and the Nation*, 87
89 Blair, *Juju and Justice*, 239.
90 Blair, 238.
91 Adegbola Ademola, interview by the author, August 25, 2003, Lagos.
92 Blair, *Juju and Justice*, 239.
93 Blair, 241.
94 Blair, 240.
95 Blair, 241.
96 Blair, 242.
97 Blair, 240.
98 Blair, 242–43.
99 Blair, 243.
100 Blair, 235.
101 Blair, 232, 240.
102 Johnson-Odim and Mba, *For Women and the Nation*, 88.
103 The Egba Women's Union and the Majeobaje Society Welcome You All to Free Egbaland, 3, Ransome-Kuti Papers, box 45, file 1, KDML. The Lisabi Mills Orchestra, led by internationally known saxophonist Ezekiel Akpata, played for the dance program. The opera, *The Reign of Terror, Baptism of Fire*, characterized as a grand comic opera, was

produced by Josie A Olajide, a young comedian. Unfortunately, a recording of the opera could not be located.

104   Abiodun Aloba, ed., *The Fall of a Ruler or the Freedom of Egbaland* (Ake, Abeokuta: Egba Women's Union, ca. 1949).

105   See "Abiodun Aloba," Nigerian Wiki, http://nigerianwiki.com/Abiodun_Aloba. Aloba worked at the United Africa Company before taking a job at the *Mercantile Guardian* and the *Nigerian Advocate* in 1945 and the *West African Pilot* the following year.

106   Rev. Superintendent G. A. Oke, "Sermon Delivered at the Centenary Hall, August 22, 1946," in Aloba, *Fall of a Ruler*, 14. The date of the speech in the pamphlet should be 1948, although it is listed as 1946.

107   For example, she supported Ijaiye during the Ibadan-Ijaiye War in 1860 by sending arms to Ijaiye's leader, Aare Kurunmi. She supplied arms to the Egba soldiers during their battle with Ijebu Makun in 1862 and during the Dahomean invasion in 1864. See Ọladipọ Yemitan, *Madame Tinubu, Merchant and King-Maker* (Ibadan: University Press, 1987), 42–48.

108   Abiodun Aloba, "The Freedom of Egbaland," in Aloba, *Fall of a Ruler*, 2.

109   Jan Lewis and Peter Onuf, "American Synecdoche: Thomas Jefferson as Image, Icon, Character and Self," *American Historical Review* 103, no. 1 (1998): 125–36; Gary Wills, *Inventing America: Jefferson's Declaration of Independence* (Garden City, NY: Doubleday, 1978); Francis Cogliano, *Thomas Jefferson: Reputation and Legacy* (Charlottesville: University of Virginia Press, 2006).

110   Charles James Fox served in the British Parliament for over thirty years. For most of his time in government, he was in the Opposition, for he supported issues such as fiscal and administrative reforms and abolition of the slave trade. Penelope Corfield, Edmond Green, and Charles Harvey argue that despite few legislative successes, he was continually reelected to Parliament because his constituency viewed him as a "man of the people." Penelope Corfield, Edmond Green, and Charles Harvey, "Westminster Man: Charles James Fox and His Electorate, 1780–1806," *Parliamentary History* 20, pt. 2 (2001): 160–61.

111   Acton, an English Catholic historian, politician, and writer, was a strong supporter of individual freedoms and the separation of church and state. He argued that both had the potential to become absolutist and tyrannical. He supported the Confederacy during the American Civil War because of the absolutism he associated with the abolitionists. J. M. Vella, "Acton's Political Trajectory," *Modern Age* 46, no. 3 (2004): 256–58.

112   Speech by Oba Alaiyeluwa the Alake, Ademola II, C.B.E., at the Inauguration of the Egba Central Council on Thursday, 10th May, 1945 at 10 a.m. in the Centenary Hall, 2–3, Ake 2/2 Oba Ademola's Speeches and Replies, vol. 2, NAN Abeokuta.

113   Letter from Ladipo Solanke to Funmi and Dotun Ransome-Kuti, September 25, 1948, Ransome-Kuti Papers, box 87, KDML.

114 Letter from Ladipo Solanke to the Revd. Dotun and Funmi Ransome-Kuti, n.d., Ransome-Kuti Papers, box 1, file 1, KDML. He also encouraged the Ransome-Kutis to forward to the leading newspapers in West Africa the text of his old lecture "Sole Native Authority" under a new heading, "Sole Native Authority Must Go."

115 Johnson-Odim and Mba, *For Women and the Nation*, 88.

116 Acting Resident, "The Newly Elected Egba Central Council," *Egba Bulletin*, June 1949.

117 "Democratic Election in Abeokuta," *Egba Bulletin*, June 1949.

118 "Egba Central Council," *Egba Bulletin*, October 1949.

119 Extract from Minutes of Executive Committee Meeting, No. 8/1948, Held on December 2, 1948, Ake 2/2, NAN Abeokuta. The provincial conference brought together residents, district officers, and assistant district offers who served in the group of provinces headed by the lieutenant governor. See I. M. Okonjo, *British Administration in Nigeria: 1900–1950: A Nigerian View* (New York: NOK, 1974), 243.

120 Extract from the Minutes of the Owu Sectional Council Meeting of Friday, December 31, 1948, Ake 2/2, NAN Abeokuta.

121 Minutes Executive Committee, March 7, 1949, 71, ECR 1/1/130, NAN Abeokuta.

122 "Thus My Egbaland," *Egba Bulletin*, January 1949.

123 Letter from District Officer, Egba Division, to the Secretary, Egba Native Authority, December 1, 1950, Ake 2/1, file 41, NAN Abeokuta.

124 Johnson-Odim and Mba, *For Women and the Nation*, 90.

CONCLUSION

1 Francesca T. Royster, "*Fela!* Fela Kuti, Bill T. Jones, and the Marketing of Black Masculine Excess on Broadway," *Biography* 34, no. 3 (2011): 492.

2 R. I. Aboribo and E. Oguoe, "Nigerian Women and Effective Participation in Politics," *Political Science Review* 4, no. 1 (2007): 29–40, cited in Daniel Gberevbie and Faith Osasumwen Oviasogie, "Women in Governance and Sustainable Democracy in Nigeria, 1999–2012," *Economics and Sociology* 6, no. 1 (2013): 101.

3 Timothy Scarnecchia, *The Urban Roots of Democracy and Political Violence in Zimbabwe: Harare and Highfield, 1940–1964* (Rochester, NY: University of Rochester Press, 2008), 3. See also Teresa Barnes, "*We Women Worked So Hard*": *Gender, Urbanization, and Social Reproduction in Colonial Harare, 1930–1956* (Portsmouth, NH: Heinemann, 1999).

4 Letter to Funmilayo Kuti from K. B. Adebesin Agboju, Oluwo Ifa of Itoko, Abeokuta. September 8, 1949, Ransome-Kuti Papers, box 59, file 5, KDML. The letter writer was also outraged that many women referred to her as "Iyalode."

5 Judith A Byfield, "In Her Own Words: Funmilayo Ransome-Kuti and the Auto/biography of an Archive," *Palimpsest: A Journal on Women, Gender and the Black International* 5, no. 2 (2016): 118.

6 Letters to Mrs. Ransome Kuti from Alhaji Abubaharu, March 2, March 6, and May 4, 1948, Ransome-Kuti Papers, box 89, file 6, KDML.

7 Letter to Mrs. Kuti from M. A. Deke, Founder of the Etsako Women Democratic Movement, November 27, 1948, Ransome-Kuti Papers, box 89, file 1, KDML.

8 Letter to Kuti from Deke.

9 Letter from Elizabeth Adekogboa to Mrs. Kuti, April 2, 1953, Ransome-Kuti Papers, box 89, file 3, KDML.

10 Letter from Yusufu Ibrahim, Tax Payers' Movement, December 16, 1957, Ransome-Kuti Papers, box 89, file 4, KDML.

11 The Demands of the Women of Ika Nation, Agbor, July 27, 1954, Ransome-Kuti Papers, box 89, file 7, KDML.

12 Confidential Savingram no. 1670, December 30, 1947, from Sir J. Macpherson to Secretary of State of Colonies, CO 5832-293/1-122014, TNA.

13 L. H. Gorsuch to H. M. Foot, June 11, 1948, CO 5832-293/1-122014, TNA.

14 Insa Nolte, *Obafemi Awolowo and the Making of Remo: The Local Politics of a Nigerian Nationalist* (Trenton, NJ: Africa World Press, 2010), 131–32, 134.

15 See letter from S. K. Adenekan to Obafemi Awolowo, June 5, 1950, with attachment "Resolution from Ake Ogboni House, Ake Abeokuta June 1, 1950," Awolowo Papers, #1022, Sopolu Research Library, Olabisi Onabanjo University, Ikenne, Ogun State (hereafter SRL).

16 Letter from Alake Ademola II to Obafemi Awolowo, Minister of Local Government, June 4, 1952, and letter from Awolowo to Ademola, September 11, 1952, Awolowo Papers, #1707, SRL.

17 Letter from Shefiatu Olubaka to Mrs. Kuti, November 30, 1953, Ransome-Kuti Papers, box 89, file 3, KDML.

18 Judith A. Byfield, "Gender, Justice, and the Environment: Connecting the Dots," *African Studies Review* 55, no. 1 (2012): 3.

19 Meredith Terretta, *Petitioning for Our Rights, Fighting for Our Nation: The History of the Democratic Union of Cameroonian Women, 1949–1960* (Bamenda, Cameroon: Langaa Research and Publishing Common Initiative Group, 2013), 42–43.

20 Letter to the Editor of the *African Echo*. Although the date is not on the draft, it was likely prepared in 1949 because it referenced discussion of the 1948–49 tax collection. Ransome Kuti Papers, box 89, file 2, KDML.

21 Judith A. Byfield, "From Ladies to Women: Funmilayo Ransome-Kuti and Women's Political Activism in Post–World War II Nigeria," in *Toward an Intellectual History of Black Women*, ed. Mia Bay, Farah J. Griffin, Martha S. Jones, and Barbara D. Savage (Chapel Hill: University of North Carolina Press, 2015), 205.

22 Byfield, "In Her Own Words," 118.

23 Nina Mba, *Nigerian Women Mobilized: Women's Political Activity in Southern Nigeria, 1900–1965* (Berkeley: Institute of International Studies, University of California, 1982), 173–74.

24 Minutes, Executive Committee of the Federation of All Nigeria Women's Organizations, September 30, 1953, Benin City, Ransome-Kuti Papers, box 89, file 4, KDML.

25 Minutes, Executive Committee.

26 Minutes, Executive Committee.

27 Wale Adebanwi, *Nation as Grand Narrative: The Nigerian Press and the Politics of Meaning* (Rochester, NY: University of Rochester Press, 2016), 25, 80.

28 Although the newspaper is discussed among the Ransome-Kuti Papers in KDML, a copy could not be located.

29 Richard L. Sklar, *Nigerian Political Parties: Power in an Emergent African Nation* (1963; repr., Trenton, NJ: Africa World Press, 2004), 133n103.

30 Sklar, *Nigerian Political Parties*, 274n97.

31 Nolte, *Obafemi Awolowo and the Making of Remo*, 138–52.

32 Mba, *Nigerian Women Mobilized*, 280–88.

33 For examples, see Daniel Gberevbie and Faith Osasumwen Oviasogie, "Women in Governance and Sustainable Democracy in Nigeria, 1999–2012," *Economics and Sociology* 6, no. 1 (2013): 89–107; Ayesha Imam, "The Dynamics of WINing: An Analysis of Women in Nigeria (WIN)," in *Feminist Genealogies, Colonial Legacies, Democratic Futures*, ed. M. Jacqui Alexander and Chandra Mohanty (New York: Routledge, 1997), 230–307; Barbara J. Callaway, "Women and Political Participation in Kano City," *Comparative Politics* 19, no. 4 (1987): 379–93; and Gloria Chuku, "Igbo Women and Political Participation in Nigeria, 1800–2005," *International Journal of African Historical Studies* 42, no. 1 (2009): 81–103.

34 Ben Naanen, "'You Are Demanding Tax from the Dead': The Introduction of Direct Taxation and Its Aftermath in South-Eastern Nigeria, 1928–39," *African Economic History*, no. 34 (2006): 80–81.

35 McIntosh, *Yoruba Women, Work and Social Change*, 230–31.

36 Naanen, "'You Are Demanding Tax from the Dead,'" 82.

37 Marc Matera, Misty Bastian, and Susan Kingsley Kent, *The Women's War of 1929: Gender and Violence in Colonial Nigeria* (New York: Palgrave, 2012), 5.

38 Anthony I. Nwabughuogu, "The Role of Propaganda in the Development of Indirect Rule in Nigeria, 1890–1929," *International Journal of African Historical Studies* 14, no. 1 (1981): 90.

39 S. N. Eisenstadt, ed. *Democracy and Modernity* (Leiden: Brill, 1992). See also Oluwatoyin B. Oduntan, "Elite Identity and Power: A Study of Social Change and Leadership among the Egba of Western Nigeria, 1860–1950" (PhD diss., Dalhousie University, 2010), 310–15.

40 Bernard Bourdillon and Richmond Palmer, "Nigerian Constitutional Proposals," *African Affairs* 44, no. 176 (1945): 120.

41 Bourdillon and Palmer, "Nigerian Constitutional Proposals," 122. Bourdillon completely dismissed extending the experiment with adult

suffrage in Ceylon to Nigeria but suggested extending the Nigerian model to places outside of Africa.

42 Letter from Funmilayo Ransome-Kuti to Ladipo Solanke, November 18, 1948, Solanke Papers, box 48, Special Collections Library, University of Lagos.

43 Given Ransome-Kuti's experience on the Egba Central Council and her commitment to greater women's political participation, she followed the evolution of the local government law closely. She sent Solanke a copy of a proposal highlighting the main features of the new law and asked him to comment on it. See Letter from Funmilayo Ransome-Kuti to Ladipo Solanke, July 2, 1952, Solanke Papers, box 21, file 9, Special Collections Library, University of Lagos.

44 Susan Martin identified competing ideologies of womanhood in the Igbo case as well. See Susan Martin, *Palm Oil and Protest: An Economic History of the Nwga Region, South-Eastern Nigeria, 1800–1980* (New York: Cambridge University Press, 1988), 116.

45 Letter from Funmilayo Ransome-Kuti to Ladipo Solanke, July 2, 1952, 2, Solanke Papers, box 21, file 9, Special Collections Library, University of Lagos.

46 Minutes, Executive Committee.

47 Thomas Hodgkin, *Nationalism in Colonial Africa* (New York: New York University Press, 1971), 91–92.

48 Temitope Oriola, "'I Acted Like a Man': Exploring Female Ex-Insurgents' Narratives on Nigeria's Oil Insurgency," *Review of African Political Economy* 43, no. 149 (2016): 451–69. There is tremendous resonance between the demands of the AWU and those of female combatants in eastern Nigeria today. Factors that informed women's decision to join groups such as the Movement for the Emancipation of the Niger Delta include state repression, marginalization of the oil-rich region, desire for development, and a concern for the welfare of others, particularly children. See also Adryan Wallace, "Influencing the Political Agenda from the Outside: A Comparative Study of Hausa Women's NGOs and CBOs in Kano, Nigeria," *National Political Science Review* (2014): 67–80.

Bibliography

ARCHIVES

Africana Collections, Kenneth Dike Memorial Library (KDML), University of Ibadan, specifically the Herbert Macaulay Papers and Ransome-Kuti Papers.

Church Missionary Society (CMS), Abeokuta, Southern Nigeria, West Africa, specifically CMS CA2/056.

National Archives of Nigeria, Abeokuta (NAN Abeokuta).

National Archives of Nigeria, Ibadan (NAN Ibadan).

New Bodleian Library, Oxford University.

Sopolu Research Library, Olabisi Onabanjo University. Ikenne, Ogun State, specifically Obafemi Awolowo Papers.

Special Collections, Gandhi Library, University Library, University of Lagos, specifically Ladipo Solanke Papers.

Special Collections, Obafemi Awolowo University Library, Ife, specifically the Criminal Court Records.

The National Archives (TNA), Kew, United Kingdom.

NEWSPAPERS

Daily Service
Egba Administrative Bulletin
Egbaland Echo
Lagos Standard
Lagos Times
Lagos Weekly Record
West African Pilot
Westminster Gazette
Yoruba News

INTERVIEWS

Adebayo, Madam Adepeju. Interview by Victoria Ayodokun, October 10, 2006. Oniyanma Village, Ifo.

Adebayo, Pa Isaiah Oladele. Interview by Victoria Ayodokun. August 9, 2003. Itoko, Abeokuta.

Adebiyi, Pa Hezekiah Oluwole. Interview by Victoria Ayodokun, November 3, 2006. Oniyanmo Town, Ifo.

Adedayo, Pa Amosu Israel. Interview by Victoria Ayodokun, April 30, 2004. Abule Egbensere Ikopa, Abeokuta.

Ademola, Kunle. Interview by author, August 11, 2003. Ikoye, Lagos.

Ademola, Prince Adegbola. Interview by author, August 25, 2003. Ikoyi, Lagos.

Adeniji, Alhaji and Alahaja Idowu. Interview by Victoria Ayodokun and Judith Byfield, August 23, 2008. Akomojo, Lagos.

Adeyinka, Pa Michael. Interview by Victoria Ayodokun, August 7, 2003. Owu, Abeokuta.

Ajao, Christopher Agboola. Interview by author, September 22, 2003. Jericho, Ibadan.

Akeju, Eng. Timothy. Interview by author, October 17, 2003. Yaba, Lagos.

Amosu, Madam Emily Olufunmike. Interview by Victoria Ayodokun, January 12, 2007. Olorulekan Ikopa Village, Abeokuta.

Amosu, Pa Isola. Interview by Victoria Ayodokun, February 8, 2007. Olorulekan Egbensere Ikopa, Abeokuta.

Anigbedu, Chief Fasheun. Interview by Victoria Ayodokun, April 30, 2007. Gbabura Amigbedu Village, Abeokuta.

Atkinson, Michael. Interview by author, November 6, 2004. Winchester, UK.

Bradney, Robert. Interview by author, August 29, 2006. London.

Doherty, Agusta Modupe (Ronke). Interview by author, October 3 and November 12, 1988. Ibara, Abeokuta.

Elemide, Chief Tunde. Interview by author; August 13, 2008. Ake, Abeokuta.

Jinadu, Madam Falilatu. Interview by Victoria Ayodokun, September 26, 2006. Oniyanmo Village, Abeokuta.

Kareem, Alhaja Sidiju, iyaloja of Lafenwa. Interview by Victoria Ayodokun, October 6, 2003. Lafenwa, Abeokuta.

Lawson, Mrs. Alaba Oluwaseun, iyalode of Egbaland. Interview by author, June 6, 2004. Ibara, Abeokuta.

Macauley, Babatunde. Interview by author, August 7, 2002. Bodija, Ibadan.

Majekodunmi, Chief Adura. Interviewed by author, June 21, 1988. Ikereku, Abeokuta.

Makinde, Chief Fustus Oluwole. Interview by author, October 10, 2003. Ibara, Abeokuta.

Ogunwulu, Alhaji Chief Liakeem. Interview by Bola Sowemimo, August 30, 2003. Abeokuta.

Oladunjoye, Pa Stephen. Interview by Victoria Ayodokun, August 2, 2006. Okoko Ojo, Lagos.

Omitogun, Pa Simeon. Interview by Victoria Ayodokun, September 26, 2006. Oniyanmo Town, Abeokuta.

Oyenekan, Chief Oses Olusoji. Interview by Bola Sowemimo, August, 2003. Ake, Abeokuta.

Pratt, Eric Windston. Interview by author, October 6, 2004. London.

Ransome-Kuti, Beko. Interview by author, October 17, 2003. Ikoyi, Lagos.

Ransome-Kuti, Dolupo. Interview by author, September 7, 1988, and October 9, 2003. Isabo, Abeokuta.

Sho, Pa Akinola. Interview by the author and Victoria Ayodokun, August 2003, Quarry, Abeokuta.

Sorunke, Chief Emanuel. Interview by author, August 19, 2003. Abeokuta.

Thompson, Justice Adewale. Interview by author, August 14, 2003 Jericho, Ibadan

UNPUBLISHED THESES AND DISSERTATIONS

Adebiyi, Nike Edun. "Radical Nationalism in British West Africa, 1945–1960." PhD diss., University of Michigan, 2008.

Chapdelaine, Robin. "A History of Child Trafficking in Southeastern Nigeria, 1900–1930s." PhD diss., Rutgers University, 2014.

Deese, Adrian M. "Making Sense of the Past: Ajayi Kolawole Ajisafe and the (Re)Making of Modern Abeokuta (Nigeria)." Master's thesis, Cornell University, 2013.

Germaine, Jenna K. "Integrating Egba Epistemologies: Writing Historical Knowledge in Colonial Nigeria." Master's thesis, Dalhousie University, 2007.

Oduntan, Oluwatoyin B. "Elite Identity and Power: A Study of Social Change and Leadership among the Egba of Western Nigeria, 1860–1950." PhD diss., Dalhousie University, 2010.

Oroge, E. A. "The Institution of Slavery in Yorubaland with Particular Reference to the Nineteenth Century." PhD thesis, University of Birmingham, 1971.

Pallinder-Law, Agneta. "Government in Abeokuta, 1830–1914: With Special Reference to the Egba United Government, 1898–1914." PhD diss., University of Gothenburg, 1973.

PRIMARY SOURCES

Ademola II. *The Alake's Centenary Message to the Egba People*. Abeokuta: E. K. A. Press, 1930.

Ajiṣafẹ, Ajayi Kọlawọlẹ. *Abeokuta Centenary and Its Celebrations*. Lagos: Ebute Metta, 1931.

———. *History of Abeokuta*. 3rd ed. Lagos: Kash and Klare Bookshop, 1948.

Aloba, Abiodun, ed. *The Fall of a Ruler or the Freedom of Egbaland*. Ake, Abeokuta: Egba Women's Union, ca. 1949.

Biobaku, Saburi O. *When We Were Young*. Ibadan: University Press, 1992.

Blair, John. *Juju and Justice* (Perth, Australia: P & B Press, 1991).

Cameron, Donald. "Native Administration in Tanganyika and Nigeria." *Journal of the Royal African Society* 36, no. 145 (1937): 3–29.

Crapp, M. L. "Jungle Commando: The Story of the West African Expeditionary Force's First Campaign in Burma." MS Afr.S.1734. Bodleian Library, Oxford.

Folarin, Adebesin. *The Demise of the Independence of Egba-Land: The Ijemo Trouble*. Pt. 1. Lagos: Tika-Tore Printing Works, 1916.

——. *The Ogboni and Other Chieftaincies in Abeokuta: Their Purports and Meanings*. Itoko, Abeokuta: E.N.A. Press, 1934.

——. *A Short Historical Review of the Life of the Egbas from 1829 to 1930*. Abeokuta: N.p., 1931.

Giles, A. F. "West African Way." MS Afr.S.1734. Bodleian Library, Oxford.

Hinderer, Anna. *Seventeen Years in the Yoruba Country*. London: Seeley, Jackson and Halliday, 1873.

Ransome-Kuti, Funmilayo. "We Had Equality till Britain Came." In *Feminist Writings from Ancient Times to the Modern World: A Global Sourcebook and History*, edited by Tiffany K. Wayne, 2:544–45. Santa Barbara, CA: Greenwood, 2011.

Solanke, Ladipo. *The Egba-Yoruba Constitutional Law and Its Historical Development*. Lagos: Asaoku Printing Press, 1931.

Stone, R. H. *In Africa's Forest and Jungle or Six Years among the Yorubas*. Edinburgh: Anderson and Ferrier, 1900.

Venn, Henry. "Henry Venn on Nationality and Native Churches." In *Origins of West African Nationalism*, edited by Henry S. Wilson, 131–35. London: St. Martin's, 1969.

Woolner, Maj.-Gen. Christopher. "81 (West Africa) Division Report, 7." MS. Afr.S.1734 (403). Bodleian Library, Oxford.

SELECTED PUBLISHED SOURCES

Abdelwahid, Mustafa, ed. *Dusé Mohamed Ali (1866–1945): The Autobiography of a Pioneer Pan African and Afro-Asian Activist*. Trenton, NJ: Red Sea Press, 2011.

Adebanwi, Wale. "Death, National Memory and the Social Construction of Heroism." *Journal of African History* 49 (2008): 491–44.

——. *Nation as Grand Narrative: The Nigerian Press and the Politics of Meaning*. Rochester, NY: University of Rochester Press, 2016.

Adebayo, A. G. "Jangali: Fulani Pastoralists and Colonial Taxation in Northern Nigeria." *International Journal of African Historical Studies* 28, no. 1 (1995): 113–50.

Aderinto, Saheed. *When Sex Threatened the State: Illicit Sexuality, Nationalism, and Politics in Colonial Nigeria, 1900–1958*. Urbana: University of Illinois Press, 2014.

Adeyanju, Tunde. *The Rev. Israel Oludotun Ransome-Kuti: Teacher and Nation Builder*. Abeokuta: Litany Nigeria, 1993.

Adi, Hakim. *Pan-Africanism and Communism: The Communist International Africa and the Diaspora, 1919–1939*. Trenton, NJ: Africa World Press, 2013.

Akinwumi, T. M. "Art and Political Leadership: The Example of the Alake." *Journal of Cultural Studies* 4, no.1 (2002): 185–214.

Anderson, Benedict. *Imagined Communities: Reflections on the Origin and Spread of Nationalism*. Rev. ed. New York: Verso, 1991.

Anderson, David, and David Throup. "Africans and Agriculture in Colonial

Kenya: The Myth of the War as a Watershed." *Journal of African History* 26, no. 4 (1985): 327–45.

Andrade, Susan Z. *The Nation Writ Small: African Fictions and Feminisms, 1958–1988.* Durham, NC: Duke University Press, 2011.

Apter, Andrew. *Black Critics and Kings: The Hermeneutics of Power in Yoruba Society.* Chicago: University of Chicago Press, 1992.

——. "The Embodiment of Paradox: Yoruba Kingship and Female Power." *Cultural Anthropology* 6, no. 2 (1991): 212–29.

——. *The Pan-African Nation: Oil and the Spectacle of Culture in Nigeria.* Chicago: University of Chicago Press, 2005.

Asante, S. K. B. "The Catholic Missions, British West African Nationalists, and the Italian Invasion of Ethiopia." *African Affairs* 73, no. 291 (1974): 204–16.

——. "The Italo-Ethiopian Conflict: A Case Study in British West African Response to Crisis Diplomacy in the 1930s." *Journal of African History* 15, no. 2 (1974): 291–302.

——. *Pan-African Protest: West Africa and the Ethiopian Crisis, 1934–1941.* London: Longman, 1977.

Askew, Kelly M. *Performing the Nation: Swahili Music and Cultural Politics in Tanzania.* Chicago: University of Chicago Press, 2002.

Ayandele, Emmanuel A. *Holy Johnson, Pioneer of African Nationalism, 1836–1917.* London: Cass, 1970.

——. *The Missionary Impact on Modern Nigeria, 1842–1914: A Political and Social Analysis.* Harlow, UK: Longman, 1966.

Ayele, N. "The Horn of Africa and Eastern Africa in the World War Decade (1935–45)." In UNESCO, *Africa and the Second World War: Reports and Papers of the Symposium,* 77–90. Paris: UNESCO, 1985.

Baptiste, Fitzroy André, and Rupert Lewis, eds. *George Padmore: Pan-African Revolutionary.* Kingston, Jamaica: Ian Randle, 2009.

Barber, Karin. "Experiments with Genre in Yoruba Newspapers of the 1920s." In *African Print Cultures: Newspapers and Their Publics in the Twentieth Century,* edited by Derek Peterson, Emma Hunter, and Stephanie Newell, 151–78. Ann Arbor: University of Michigan Press, 2016.

——. "Introduction: Hidden Innovators in Africa." In *Africa's Hidden Histories: Everyday Literacy and Making the Self,* edited by Karin Barber, 1–24. Bloomington: Indiana University Press, 2006.

Baer, George. "Sanctions and Security: The League of Nations and the Italian-Ethiopian War, 1935–1936." *International Organization* 27, no. 2 (1973): 165–79.

Barnes, Andrew E. *Making Headway: The Introduction of Western Civilization in Colonial Northern Nigeria.* Rochester, NY: University of Rochester Press, 2009.

Barnes, Teresa. *"We Women Worked So Hard": Gender, Urbanization, and Social Reproduction in Colonial Harare, 1930–1956.* Portsmouth, NH: Heinemann, 1999.

Baron, Beth. *Egypt as a Woman: Nationalism, Gender, and Politics.* Berkeley: University of California Press, 2005.

Barrett, John. "The Rank and File of the Colonial Army in Nigeria, 1914–18." *Journal of Modern African Studies* 15, no. 1 (1977): 105–15.

Bascom, William R. "The Sanctions of Ifa Divination" *Journal of the Royal Anthropological Institute of Great Britain and Ireland* 71, no. 1/2 (1941): 43–54.

Bastian, Misty. "Dancing Women and Colonial Men: The Nwaobiala of 1925." In *"Wicked" Women and the Reconfiguration of Gender in Africa,* edited by Dorothy Hodgson and Sheryl McCurdy, 109–29. Portsmouth, NH: Heinemann, 2001.

———. "'Vultures of the Marketplace': Southeastern Nigerian Women and Discourses of the *Ogu Umunwaanyi* (Women's War) of 1929." In *Women in African Colonial Histories,* edited by Jean Allman, Susan Geiger, and Nakanyike Musisi, 260–81. Bloomington: Indiana University Press, 2002.

Beevor, Antony. *The Second World War.* New York: Little, Brown, 2012.

Bhabha, Homi, ed. *Nation and Narration.* New York: Routledge, 1990.

Biobaku, Saburi O. "The Egba Council, 1899–1918." In *Odù: A Journal of Yoruba and Related Studies,* vol. 2, edited by S. O. Biobaku, H. U. Beier, and L. Levi, 14–20. Ibadan, Nigeria: Western Region Literature Committee; Edinburgh: Thomas Nelson and Sons, 1955.

———. *The Egba and Their Neighbors, 1842–1872.* Oxford: Clarendon Press, 1965.

Bourdillon, Bernard, and Richmond Palmer. "Nigerian Constitutional Proposals." *African Affairs* 44, no. 176 (1945): 120–24.

Brewer, John. *The Sinews of Power: War, Money and the English State, 1688–1783.* Cambridge, MA: Harvard University Press, 1988.

Bryan, Patrick. *The Jamaican People, 1880–1902: Race, Class and Social Control.* London: Macmillan Caribbean, 1991.

Burton, Antoinette M. *Burdens of History: British Feminists, Indian Women, and Imperial Culture, 1865–1915.* Chapel Hill: University of North Carolina Press, 1994.

Bush, Barbara, and Josephine Maltby. "Taxation in West Africa: Transforming the Colonial Subject into the 'Governable Person.'" *Critical Perspectives on Accounting* 15, no. 1 (2004): 5–34.

Byfield, Judith A. *The Bluest Hands: A Social and Economic History of Women Dyers in Abeokuta (Nigeria), 1890–1940.* Portsmouth, NH: Heinemann, 2002.

———. "Dress and Politics in Post–World War II Abeokuta (Western Nigeria)." In *Fashioning Africa: Power and the Politics of Dress,* edited by Jean Allman, 31–49. Bloomington: Indiana University Press, 2004.

———. "From Ladies to Women: Funmilayo Ransome-Kuti and Women's Political Activism in Post–World War II Nigeria." In *Toward an Intellectual History of Black Women,* edited by Mia Bay, Farah J. Griffin, Martha S.

Jones, and Barbara D. Savage, 197–211. Chapel Hill: University of North Carolina Press, 2015.

———. "Gender, Justice, and the Environment: Connecting the Dots." *African Studies Review* 55, no. 1 (2012): 1–12.

———. "In Her Own Words: Funmilayo Ransome-Kuti and the Auto/biography of an Archive." *Palimpsest: A Journal on Women, Gender, and the Black International* 5, no. 2 (2016): 107–27.

———. "Producing for the War." In Byfield et al., *Africa and World War II*, 24–42.

———. "'Unwrapping' Nationalism: Dress, Gender and Nationalist Discourse in Colonial Lagos." Discussion paper no. 30 in the African Humanities Program. Boston: African Studies Center, Boston University, 2000.

Byfield, Judith A., Carolyn A. Brown, Timothy Parsons, and Ahmad Alawad Sikainga, eds. *Africa and World War II*. New York: Cambridge University Press, 2015.

Callaway, Barbara J. "Women and Political Participation in Kano City." *Comparative Politics* 19, no. 4 (1987): 379–93.

Chatterjee, Partha. *Nationalist Thought and the Colonial World: A Derivative Discourse*. Minneapolis: University of Minnesota Press, 1986.

———. *The Nation and Its Fragments: Colonial and Postcolonial Histories*. Princeton, NJ: Princeton University Press, 1993.

Chuku, Gloria. *Igbo Women and Economic Transformation in Southeastern Nigeria, 1900–1960*. New York: Routledge, 2005.

———. "Igbo Women and Political Participation in Nigeria, 1800–2005." *International Journal of African Historical Studies* 42, no. 1 (2009): 81–103.

Clarence-Smith, William G. "Africa's 'Battle for Rubber' in the Second World War." In Byfield et al., *Africa and World War II*, 166–82.

Clarke, Julian. "Households and the Political Economy of Small-Scale Cash Crop Production in South-Western Nigeria." *Africa* 51, no. 4 (1981): 807–23.

Cogliano, Francis. *Thomas Jefferson: Reputation and Legacy*. Charlottesville: University of Virginia Press, 2006.

Cohen, Robin. "Michael Imoudu and the Nigerian Labour Movement." *Race and Class* 18, no. 4 (1977): 345–62.

Cole, Patrick. *Modern and Traditional Elites in the Politics of Lagos*. New York: Cambridge University Press, 1975.

Coleman, James S. *Nigeria: Background to Nationalism*. Berkeley: University of California Press, 1971.

Collins, John. *Fela: Kalakuta Notes*. Middletown, CT: Wesleyan University Press, 2015.

Cooper, Frederick. *Citizenship between Empire and Nation: Remaking France and French Africa, 1945–1960*. Princeton, NJ: Princeton University Press, 2014.

———. "Conflict and Connection: Rethinking Colonial African History." *American Historical Review* 99, no. 5 (1994): 1516–45.

Cope, Nicholas. *To Bind the Nation: Solomon kaDinuzulu and Zulu Nationalism, 1913–1933*. Pietermaritzburg, South Africa: University of Natal Press, 1993.

Corfield, Penelope, Edmond Green, and Charles Harvey. "Westminster Man: Charles James Fox and His Electorate, 1780–1806." *Parliamentary History* 20, pt. 2 (2001): 157–85.

Crowder, Michael. "The Second World War: Prelude to Decolonisation." In *The Cambridge History of Africa*: Vol. 8, *c. 1940–c. 1975*, edited by Michael Crowder, 8–51. Cambridge: Cambridge University Press, 1984.

———. *The Story of Nigeria*. London: Faber and Faber, 1962.

Daly, Samuel Fury Childs. "From Crime to Coercion: Policing Dissent in Abeokuta, Nigeria, 1900–1940." *Journal of Imperial and Commonwealth History* 47, no. 3 (2019): 474–89.

Decker, Stephanie. "Africanization in British Multinationals in Ghana and Nigeria, 1945–1970." *Business History Review* 92 (2018): 691–718.

Delano, Isaac O. *Oba Ademola II: A Great Alake of Egba*. Ibadan: Oxford University Press, 1969.

———. *The Singing Minister of Nigeria: The Life of Canon J. J. Ransome-Kuti*. London: United Society for Christian Literature, 1942.

de Moraes Farias, P. F., and Karin Barber, eds. *Self-Assertion and Brokerage: Early Cultural Nationalism in West Africa*. Birmingham, UK: Centre of West African Studies, University of Birmingham, 1990.

Dennett, R. E. "The Ogboni and Other Secret Societies in Nigeria." *Journal of the Royal African Society* 16, no. 61 (1916): 16–29.

Denzer, LaRay. "Intersections: Nigerian Episodes in the Careers of Three West Indian Women." In *Gendering the African Diaspora: Women, Culture and Historical Change in the Caribbean and Nigerian Hinterland*, edited by Judith Byfield, LaRay Denzer, and Anthea Morrison, 245–84. Bloomington: Indiana University Press, 2010.

Doortmont, Michel. "The Invention of the Yorubas: Regional and Pan-African Nationalism versus Ethnic Provincialism." In de Moraes Farias and Barber, *Self-Assertion and Brokerage*, 101–8.

Drake, St. Clair. *Black Folk Here and There: An Essay in History and Anthropology*. Vol. 2. Los Angeles: Center for Afro-American Studies, University of California, 1990.

Duara, Prasenjit. "Historicizing National Identity, or Who Imagines What and When." In Eley and Suny, *Becoming National*, 151–78.

Eades, J. S. *Strangers and Traders: Yoruba Migrants, Markets and the State in Northern Ghana*. Trenton, NJ: Africa World Press, 1984.

———. *The Yoruba Today*. London: Cambridge University Press, 1980.

Eisenstadt, S. N., ed. *Democracy and Modernity*. Leiden: E. J. Brill, 1992.

Eley, Geoff, and Ronald Grigor Suny, eds. *Becoming National: A Reader*. New York: Oxford University Press, 1996.

———. "Introduction: From the Moment of Social History to the Work of Cultural Representation." In Eley and Suny, *Becoming National*, 3–37.

Eluwa, G. I. C. "Background to the Emergence of the National Congress of British West Africa." *African Studies Review* 14, no. 2 (1971): 205–18.

Euba, Titiola. "Dress and Status in 19th Century Lagos." In *History of the Peoples of Lagos State*, edited by Ade Adefuye, Babatunde Agiri, and Jide Osuntokun, 142–63. Ikeja, Lagos: Lantern Books, 1987.

Fadipe, N. A. *The Sociology of the Yoruba*. Ibadan: Ibadan University Press, 1970.

Falola, Toyin. "Cassava Starch for Export in Nigeria during the Second World War." *African Economic History*, no. 18 (1989): 73–98.

———. *Colonialism and Violence in Nigeria*. Bloomington: Indiana University Press, 2009.

———. *Pioneer, Patriot and Patriarch: Samuel Johnson and the Yoruba People*. Madison: University of Wisconsin Press, 1993.

———. "'Salt Is Gold': The Management of Salt Scarcity in Nigeria during World War II." *Canadian Journal of African Studies* 26, no. 3 (1992): 412–36.

Falola, Toyin, and Adam Paddock. *The Women's War of 1929: A History of Anti-Colonial Resistance in Eastern Nigeria*. Durham, NC: Carolina Academic Press, 2011.

Forde, Daryll. "The Rural Economies." In *The Native Economies of Nigeria*, edited by Margery Perham, 119–79. London: Faber and Faber, 1946.

Fortes, M. "The Impact of the War on British West Africa." *International Affairs* 21, no. 2 (1945): 206–19.

Gailey, Harry A. *Lugard and the Abeokuta Uprising: The Demise of Egba Independence*. London: Frank Cass, 1982.

Gberevbie, Daniel, and Faith Osasumwen Oviasogie. "Women in Governance and Sustainable Democracy in Nigeria, 1999–2012." *Economics and Sociology* 6, no. 1 (2013): 89–107.

Gebrekidan, Fikru Negash. *Bond without Blood: A History of Ethiopian and New World Black Relations, 1896–1991*. Trenton, NJ: Africa World Press, 2005.

———. "In Defense of Ethiopia: A Comparative Assessment of Caribbean and African American Anti-Fascist Protests, 1935–1941." *Northeast African Studies* 2, no. 1 (New Series, 1995): 145–73.

George, Abosede A. *Making Modern Girls: A History of Girlhood, Labor, and Social Development in Colonial Lagos*. Athens: Ohio University Press, 2014.

Green, Elliott. "Ethnicity and Nationhood in Precolonial Africa: The Case of Buganda." *Nationalism and Ethnic Politics* 16, no. 1 (2010): 1–20.

Griswold, Wendy, and Muhammed Bhadmus. "The Kano Durbar: Political Aesthetics in the Bowel of the Elephant." *American Journal of Cultural Sociology* 1, no. 1 (2013): 125–51.

Guyer, Jane I. "Representation without Taxation: An Essay on Democracy in Rural Nigeria, 1952–1990." *African Studies Review* 35, no. 1 (April 1992): 41–79.

Habtu, Hailu, and Judith Byfield. "Fighting Fascism: Ethiopian Women Patriots 1935–1941." In Byfield et al., *Africa and World War II*, 383–400.

Hall, Catherine. "Gender, Nations and Nationalisms." In *People, Nation and State: The Meaning of Ethnicity and Nationalism*, edited by Edward Mortimer, 45–55. New York: I. B. Tauris, 1999.

Harneit-Sievers, Axel. "African Business, 'Economic Nationalism,' and British Colonial Policy: Southern Nigeria, 1935–1954." *African Economic History*, no. 23 (1995): 79–128.

Harris, Joseph E. *African-American Reactions to War in Ethiopia 1936–1941*. Baton Rouge: Louisiana State University, 1994.

Havik, Philip J. "Colonial Administration, Public Accounts and Fiscal Extraction: Policies and Revenues in Portuguese Africa (1900–1960)." *African Economic History* 41 (2013): 159–221.

Helal, Emad A. "Egypt's Overlooked Contribution to World War II." In *The World in World Wars: Experiences, Perceptions and Perspectives from Africa and Asia*, edited by Heike Liebau, Katrin Bromber, Katharina Lange, Dyala Hamzah, and Ravi Ahuja, 217–47. Boston: Brill, 2010.

Hess, Janet Berry. *Art and Architecture in Postcolonial Africa*. Jefferson, NC: McFarland, 2006.

Hetherington, Penelope. *British Paternalism and Africa, 1920–1940*. London: Frank Cass, 1978.

Hinds, Allister E. "Government Policy and the Nigerian Palm Oil Export Industry, 1939–49." *Journal of African History* 38, no. 3 (1997): 459–78.

———. "Sterling and Imperial Policy, 1945–1951." *Journal of Imperial and Commonwealth History* 15, no. 2 (1987): 148–69.

Hodgkin, Thomas. *Nationalism in Colonial Africa*. New York: New York University Press, 1971.

Hopkins, A. G. "Back to the Future: From National History to Imperial History." *Past and Present* 164, no. 1 (1999): 198–243.

———. "Economic Aspects of Political Movements in Nigeria and in the Gold Coast 1918–1939." *Journal of African History* 7, no. 1 (1966): 133–52.

Horder. "Princess Tsahai Memorial Fund." *British Medical Journal* 2, no. 4375 (November 11, 1944): 644.

Hunt, Nancy Rose. "Noise over Camouflaged Polygamy, Colonial Morality Taxation, and a Woman-Naming Crisis in Belgian Africa." *Journal of African History* 32, no. 3 (November 1991): 471–94.

———. "Placing African Women's History and Locating Gender." *Social History* 14, no. 3 (1989): 359–73.

Ibhawoh, Bonny. *Imperial Justice: Africans in Empire's Court*. Oxford: Oxford University Press, 2013.

Idemili, Sam O. "What the *West African Pilot* Did in the Movement for Nigerian Nationalism between 1937 and 1957." *Black American Literature Forum* 12, no. 3 (1978): 84–91.

Ifeka-Moller, Caroline. "Female Militancy and Colonial Revolt: The Women's War of 1929, Eastern Nigeria." In *Perceiving Women*, edited by Shirley Ardener, 127–57. London: Malaby Press, 1975.

Imam, Ayesha. "The Dynamics of WINing: An Analysis of Women in Nigeria (WIN)." In *Feminist Genealogies, Colonial Legacies, Democratic Futures*, edited by M. Jacqui Alexander and Chandra Mohanty, 230–307. New York: Routledge, 1997.

Johnson, Samuel. *The History of the Yorubas: From the Earliest Times to the Beginning of the British Protectorate*. 1921. Reprint, London: Routledge and Kegan Paul, 1973.

Johnson-Odim, Cheryl, and Nina Emma Mba. *For Women and the Nation: Funmilayo Ransome-Kuti of Nigeria*. Urbana: University of Illinois Press, 1997.

July, Robert W. *The Origins of Modern African Thought: Its Development in West Africa during the Nineteenth and Twentieth Centuries*. New York: Frederick A. Praeger, 1967.

Kaplan, Temma. "Naked Mothers and Maternal Sexuality: Some Reactions to the Aba Women's War." In *The Politics of Motherhood: Activist Voices from Left to Right*, edited by Annelise Orleck, Diana Taylor, and Alexis Jetter, 209–22. Hanover, NH: University Press of New England, 1997.

Karlström, Mikael. "On the Aesthetics and Dialogics of Power in the Postcolony." *Africa: Journal of the International African Institute* 73, no. 1 (2003): 57–76.

Kilby, Peter. *African Enterprise: The Nigerian Bread Industry*. Stanford, CA: Hoover Institute, Stanford University, 1965.

Koyptoff, Jean Herskovits. *A Preface to Modern Nigeria: The "Sierra Leonians" in Yoruba, 1830–1890*. Madison: University of Wisconsin Press, 1965.

Kramer, Lloyd S. "Nations as Texts: Literary Theory and the History of Nationalism." *Maryland Historian* 24, no. 1 (1993): 71–82.

Langley, J. Ayodele. *Pan-Africanism and Nationalism in West Africa 1900–1945: A Study in Ideology and Social Classes*. Oxford, UK: Clarendon Press, 1973.

Law, Robin. "Early Yoruba Historiography." *History in Africa* 3 (1976): 69–89.

———. "The Heritage of Oduduwa: Traditional History and Political Propaganda among the Yoruba." *Journal of African History* 14, no. 2 (1973): 207–22.

Lawal, Babatunde. "À Yà Gbó, À Yà Tó: New Perspectives on Edan Ògbóni." *African Arts* 28, no. 1 (1995): 36–49, 98–100.

Lawler, Nancy E. *Soldiers, Airmen, Spies, and Whisperers: The Gold Coast in World War II*. Athens: Ohio University Press, 2002.

Lentz, Carola. "Celebrating Independence Jubilees and the Millennium: National Days in Africa." *Nations and Nationalism* 19, no. 2 (2013): 208–16.

Lewis, Jan, and Peter Onuf. "American Synecdoche: Thomas Jefferson as Image, Icon, Character and Self." *American Historical Review* 103, no. 1 (1998): 125–36.

Likaka, Osumaka. *Rural Society and Cotton in Colonial Zaire*. Madison: University of Wisconsin Press, 1997.

Lloyd, P. C. *Yoruba Land Law*. London: Oxford University Press, 1962.

Lonsdale, John. "Writing Competitive Patriotisms in Eastern Africa." In *Recasting the Past: History Writing and Political Work in Modern Africa*, edited by Derek R. Peterson and Giacomo Macola, 251–67. Athens: Ohio University Press, 2009.

Lovejoy, Paul E., and Jan S. Hogendorn. *Slow Death for Slavery: The Course of Abolition in Northern Nigeria, 1897–1936*. Cambridge: Cambridge University Press, 1993.

MacGregor, William. "Lagos, Abeokuta and the Alake." *Journal of the Royal African Society* 3, no. 12 (July 1904): 464–81.

MacMillan, Allister. *The Red Book of West Africa: Historical and Descriptive, Commercial and Industrial, Facts, Figures and Resources*. London: Frank Cass, 1968.

Martin, Susan. *Palm Oil and Protest: An Economic History of the Ngwa Region, South-Eastern Nigeria, 1800–1980*. New York: Cambridge University Press, 1988.

Matera, Marc. *Black London: The Imperial Metropolis and Decolonization in the Twentieth Century*. Oakland: University of California Press, 2015.

Matera, Marc, Misty Bastian, and Susan Kingsley Kent. *The Women's War of 1929: Gender and Violence in Colonial Nigeria*. New York: Palgrave, 2012.

Matory, J. Lorand. "The English Professors of Brazil: On the Diasporic Roots of the Yoruba Nation." *Comparative Studies in Society and History* 41, no. 1 (1999): 72–103.

Mba, Nina. *Nigerian Women Mobilized: Women's Political Activity in Southern Nigeria, 1900–1965*. Berkeley: Institute of International Studies, University of California, 1982.

McCaskie, T. C. *State and Society in Pre-Colonial Asante*. Cambridge: Cambridge University Press, 1995.

McClintock, Anne. *Imperial Leather: Race, Gender and Sexuality in the Colonial Contest*. New York: Routledge, 1995.

——. "'No Longer in a Future Heaven': Nationalism, Gender, and Race." In Eley and Suny, *Becoming National*, 260–85.

McIntosh, Marjorie Keniston. *Yoruba Women, Work, and Social Change*. Bloomington: Indiana University Press, 2009.

Mockler, Anthony. *Haile Selassie's War: The Italian-Ethiopian Campaign, 1935–1941*. New York: Olive Branch, 2003.

Moorman, Marissa J. *Intonations: A Social History of Music and Nation in Luanda, Angola, from 1945 to Recent Times*. Athens: Ohio University Press, 2008.

Morton-Williams, Peter. "An Outline of the Cosmology and Cult Organization of the Oyo Yoruba." *Africa: Journal of the International African Institute* 34, no. 3 (1964): 243–60.

———. "The Yoruba Ogboni Cult." *Africa: Journal of the International African Institute* 30, no. 4 (1960): 362–74.

Moses, Wilson Jeremiah. *Afrotopia: The Roots of African American Popular History*. New York: Cambridge University Press, 1998.

"Mr. Richard B. Blaize." *Journal of the Royal African Society* 4, no. 13 (1904): 149–50.

Naanen, Benedict. "'Itinerant Gold Mines': Prostitution in the Cross River Basin of Nigeria, 1930–1950." *African Studies Review* 34, no. 2 (1991): 68–69.

———. "'You Are Demanding Tax from the Dead': The Introduction of Direct Taxation and Its Aftermath in South-Eastern Nigeria, 1928–39." *African Economic History*, no. 34 (2006): 69–102.

Nagel, Joane. "Masculinity and Nationalism: Gender and Sexuality in the Making of Nations." *Ethnic and Racial Studies* 21, no. 2 (1998): 242–69.

Neu, Dean, and Monica Heincke. "The Subaltern Speaks: Financial Relations and the Limits of Governmentality." *Critical Perspectives on Accounting* 15, no. 1 (2004): 179–206.

Newbury, C. W., comp. *British Policy towards West Africa: Select Documents, 1875–1914*. Oxford: Clarendon Press, 1971.

Newbury, Colin. "Accounting for Power in Northern Nigeria." *Journal of African History* 45 (2004): 257–77.

Nicholas, Siân. "'Brushing Up Your Empire': Dominion and Colonial Propaganda on the BBC's Home Services, 1939–45." *Journal of Imperial and Commonwealth History* 31, no. 2 (2003): 207–30.

Nolte, Insa. *Obafemi Awolowo and the Making of Remo: The Local Politics of a Nigerian Nationalist*. Trenton, NJ: Africa World Press, 2010.

Nwabughuogu, Anthony I. "The Role of Propaganda in the Development of Indirect Rule in Nigeria, 1890–1929." *International Journal of African Historical Studies* 14, no. 1 (1981): 65–92.

Nwafor, Okechukwu. "The Fabric of Friendship: Aso Ebi and the Moral Economy of Amity in Nigeria." *African Studies* 72, no. 1 (2013): 1–18.

Ochonu, Moses E. *Colonialism by Proxy: Hausa Imperial Agents and Middle Belt Consciousness in Nigeria*. Bloomington: Indiana University Press, 2014.

———. *Colonial Meltdown: Northern Nigeria in the Great Depression*. Athens: Ohio University Press, 2009.

Oguamanam, Chidi, and W. Wesley Pue. "Lawyers' Professionalism, Colonialism, State Formation, and National Life in Nigeria, 1900–1960: 'The Fighting Brigade of the People.'" *Social Identities* 13, no. 6 (2007): 769–85.

Oguntomisin, G. O. "Political Change and Adaptation in Yorubaland in the Nineteenth Century." *Canadian Journal of African Studies* 15, no. 2 (1981): 223–37.

Okafor, F. O. E. *The Nigerian Youth Movement, 1934–44: A Re-Appraisal of the Historiography*. Onitsha, Nigeria: Etukokwu Press, 1989.

Okonjo, I. M. *British Administration in Nigeria, 1900–1950: A Nigerian View*. New York: NOK, 1974.

Okonkwo, Rina. "A Jamaican Export to Nigeria! The Life of Amos Stanley Wynter Shackleford." *Caribbean Quarterly* 30, no. 2 (1984): 48–59.

Olorunfemi, A. "Effects of War-Time Trade Controls on Nigerian Cocoa Traders and Producers, 1939–45: A Case-Study of the Hazards of a Dependent Economy." *International Journal of African Historical Studies* 13, no. 4 (1980): 672–87.

Olukoju, Ayodeji. "'Buy British, Sell Foreign': External Trade Control Policies in Nigeria during World War II and Its Aftermath, 1939–1950." *International Journal of African Historical Studies* 35, no. 2/3 (2002): 363–84.

Olusanya, G. O. *The Second World War and Politics in Nigeria, 1939–1953*. London: Evans Bros. for the University of Lagos, 1973.

Omu, Fred I. A. *Press and Politics in Nigeria, 1880–1937*. Atlantic Highlands, NJ: Humanities Press, 1978.

Oriola, Temitope. "'I Acted Like a Man': Exploring Female Ex-Insurgents' Narratives on Nigeria's Oil Insurgency." *Review of African Political Economy* 43, no. 149 (2016): 451–69.

Osuntokun, Akinjide. *Nigeria in the First World War*. Atlantic Highlands, NJ: Humanities Press, 1979.

Oyemakinde, Wale. "The Pullen Marketing Scheme: A Trial in Food Price Control in Nigeria, 1941–1947." *Journal of the Historical Society of Nigeria* 6, no. 4 (1973): 413–23.

Pallinder-Law, Agneta. "Aborted Modernization in West Africa? The Case of Abeokuta." *Journal of African History* 15, no. 1 (1974): 65–82.

——. "Adegboyega Edun: Black Englishman and Yoruba Cultural Patriot." In de Moraes Farias and Barber, *Self-Assertion and Brokerage*, 11–34.

Parsons, Timothy. "The Military Experiences of Ordinary Africans in World War II." In Byfield et al., *Africa and World War II*, 3–23.

Partridge, C. "Native Law and Custom in Egbaland." *Journal of the Royal African Society* 10, no. 40 (1911): 422–33.

Pearce, Robert. "The Colonial Economy: Nigeria and the Second World War." In *Development Studies and Colonial Policy*, edited by Barbara Ingham and Colin Simmons, 263–92. London: Frank Cass, 1987.

Peel, J. D. Y. "Gender in Yoruba Religious Change." *Journal of Religion in Africa* 32, fasc. 2 (May 2002): 136–66.

——. *Religious Encounter and the Making of the Yoruba*. Bloomington: Indiana University Press, 2000.

Peterson, Derek R. *Ethnic Patriotism and the East African Revival: A History of Dissent, c. 1935–1972*. New York: Cambridge University Press, 2012.

Pierson, Ruth Roach, and Nupur Chaudhuri, eds. With the assistance of Beth McAauley. *Nation, Empire, Colony: Historicizing Gender and Race*. Bloomington: Indiana University Press, 1998.

Purvis, June. "Past Papers, Future Thinking: Sylvia Pankhurst (1882–1960), Suffragette, Political Activist, Artist and Writer." *Gender and Education* 20, no. 1 (2008): 81–87.

Putnam, Aric. "Ethiopia Is Now: J. A. Rogers and the Rhetoric of Black Anti-colonialism during the Great Depression." *Rhetoric and Public Affairs* 10, no. 3 (2007): 419–44.

Rassool, Ciraj, and Leslie Witz. "The 1952 Jan Van Riebeeck Tercentenary Festival: Constructing and Contesting Public National History in South Africa." *Journal of African History* 34, no. 3 (1993): 447–68.

Redding, Sean. "Legal Minors and Social Children: Rural African Women and Taxation in the Transkei, South Africa." *African Studies Review* 36, no. 3 (December 1993): 49–74.

Roitman, Janet. *Anti-Crisis*. Durham, NC: Duke University Press, 2014.

———. *Fiscal Disobedience: An Anthropology of Economic Regulation in Central Africa*. Princeton, NJ: Princeton University Press, 2005.

Rooth, Tim. "Economic Tensions and Conflict in the Commonwealth, 1945–c. 1951." *Twentieth Century British History* 13, no. 2 (2002): 121–43.

Roy, Srirupa. *Beyond Belief: India and the Politics of Postcolonial Nationalism*. Durham, NC: Duke University Press, 2007.

Royster, Francesca T. "*Fela!*: Fela Kuti, Bill T. Jones, and the Marketing of Black Masculine Excess on Broadway." *Biography* 34, no. 3 (2011): 492–517.

Russell, E. John. "Sir John Maynard and His Studies of the Russian Peasant." *Slavonic and East European Review* 24, no. 63 (1946): 56–65.

Salhi, Zahia Smail. "The Algerian Feminist Movement between Nationalism, Patriarchy and Islamism." *Women's Studies International Forum* 33, no. 2 (2010): 113–24.

Scarnecchia, Timothy. "Poor Women and Nationalist Politics: Alliances and Fissures in the Formation of a Nationalist Political Movement in Salisbury, Rhodesia, 1950–6." *Journal of African History* 37, no. 2 (1996): 283–310.

———. *The Urban Roots of Democracy and Political Violence in Zimbabwe: Harare and Highfield, 1940–1964*. Rochester, NY: University of Rochester Press, 2008.

Schmidt, Elizabeth. *Mobilizing the Masses: Gender, Ethnicity, and Class in the Nationalist Movement in Guinea, 1939–1958*. Portsmouth, NH: Heinemann, 2005.

Scott, James C. *Seeing Like a State: How Certain Schemes to Improve the Human Condition Have Failed*. New Haven, CT: Yale University Press, 1998.

Scott, William R. *The Sons of Sheba's Race: African-Americans and the Italo-Ethiopian War, 1935–1941*. 2nd ed. Hollywood, CA: Tsehai Publishers, 2006.

Shack, William. *Harlem in Montmartre: A Paris Jazz Story between the Great Wars*. Berkeley: University of California Press, 2001.

Shonekan, Stephanie. "Fela's Foundation: Examining the Revolutionary Songs of Funmilayo Ransome-Kuti and the Abeokuta Market Women's Movement in 1940s Western Nigeria." *Black Music Research Journal* 29, no. 1 (2009): 127–44.

Sklar, Richard L. *Nigerian Political Parties: Power in an Emergent African Nation.* 1963. Reprint, Trenton, NJ: Africa World Press, 2004.

Slogar, Christopher. "Carved Ogboni Figures from Abeokuta, Nigeria." *African Arts* 35, no. 4 (2002): 14–27, 91–92.

Smith, Anthony D. *The Ethnic Origins of Nations.* Oxford: Basil Blackwell, 1988.

Smyke, Raymond J. "A History of the Nigeria Union of Teachers." *West African Journal of Education* 16, no. 3 (1972): 393–404.

Smyke, Raymond J., and Denis C. Storer. *Nigeria Union of Teachers: An Official History.* Ibadan: Oxford University Press, 1974.

Sommer, Doris. *Foundational Fictions: The National Romances of Latin America.* Berkeley: University of California Press, 1991.

———. "Irresistible Romance: The Foundational Fictions of Latin America." In Bhaba, *Nation and Narration,* 71–98.

Soyinka, Wole. *Aké: The Years of Childhood.* New York: Random House, 1981.

Spear, Thomas. "Neo-Traditionalism and the Limits of Invention in British Colonial Africa." *Journal of African History* 44, no. 1 (2003): 3–27.

Spitzer, Leo. *The Creoles of Sierra Leone: Responses to Colonialism, 1870–1945.* Madison: University of Wisconsin Press, 1974.

Summers, Carol. "Ugandan Politics and World War II (1939–1949)." In Byfield et al., *Africa and World War II,* 480–500.

Táíwò, Olúfémi. *How Colonialism Preempted Modernity in Africa.* Bloomington: Indiana University Press, 2010.

Tamuno, Tekena N. "The Role of the Legislative Council in the Administration of Lagos, 1886–1913." *Journal of the Historical Society of Nigeria* 4, no. 4 (1969): 555–70.

Templin, J. Alton. "The Ideology of a Chosen People: Afrikaner Nationalism and the Ossewa Trek, 1938." *Nations and Nationalism* 5, no. 3 (1999): 397–417.

Terretta, Meredith. "'God of Independence, God of Peace': Village Politics and Nationalism in the *Maquis* of Cameroon, 1957–71." *Journal of African History* 46, no. 1 (2005): 75–101.

———. *Petitioning for Our Rights, Fighting for Our Nation: The History of the Democratic Union of Cameroonian Women, 1949–1960.* Bamenda, Cameroon: Langaa Research and Publishing Common Initiative Group, 2013.

Thapar, Suruchi. "Women as Activists; Women as Symbols: A Study of the Indian Nationalist Movement." *Feminist Review,* no. 44 (Summer 1993): 81–96.

Thompson, O. O., S. A. Afolabi, and O. G. F. Nwaorgu. "Sweeter with Age: The Enigmatic Miss Jane McCotter in the Colonial Services of the Egba Native Administration in Abeokuta, Nigeria, 1929–1955." *Journal of International Women's Studies* 20, no. 7 (2019): 334–48.

Tidjani-Serpos, Nouréini. "The Postcolonial Condition: The Archaeology of African Knowledge: From the Feat of Ogun and Sango to the Postcolonial Creativity of Obatala." *Research in African Literatures* 27, no. 1 (1996): 3–16.

Tonukari, Nyerhovwo John. "Cassava and the Future of Starch." *Electronic Journal of Biotechnology* 7, no. 1 (2004). DOI: 10.2225/vol7-issue1-fulltext-i02.

Trouillot, Michel-Rolph. *Silencing the Past: Power and the Production of History*. Boston: Beacon Press, 1995.

Turino, Thomas. *Nationalists, Cosmopolitans, and Popular Music in Zimbabwe*. Chicago: University of Chicago Press, 2000.

Van Allen, Judith. "'Aba Riots' or Igbo 'Women's War'? Ideology, Stratification, and the Invisibility of Women." In *Women in Africa: Studies in Social and Economic Change*, edited by Nancy J. Hafkin and Edna G. Bay, 59–85. Palo Alto, CA: Stanford University Press, 1976.

van Hensbroek, Pieter Boele. *Political Discourses in African Thought: 1860 to the Present*. Westport, CT: Praeger, 1999.

Vaughan, Olufemi. *Nigerian Chiefs: Traditional Power in Modern Politics, 1890s–1990s*. Rochester, NY: University of Rochester Press, 2000.

Vella, J. M. "Acton's Political Trajectory." *Modern Age* 46, no. 3 (2004): 256–58.

Waetjen, Thembisa. "The Limits of Gender Rhetoric for Nationalism: A Case Study from Southern Africa." *Theory and Society* 30, no. 1 (February 2001): 121–52.

Wallace, Adryan. "Influencing the Political Agenda from the Outside: A Comparative Study of Hausa Women's NGOs and CBOs in Kano, Nigeria." *National Political Science Review* (2014): 67–80.

Weisbord, Robert. "British West Indian Reaction to the Italian-Ethiopian War: An Episode in Pan-Africanism." *Caribbean Studies* 10, no. 1 (1970): 34–41.

Wills, Gary. *Inventing America: Jefferson's Declaration of Independence*. Garden City, NY: Doubleday, 1978.

Willis, John Thabiti. *Masquerading Politics: Kinship, Gender, and Ethnicity in a Yoruba Town*. Bloomington: Indiana University Press, 2018.

Woldermariam, Metasebia. "Alternative Representations of War in Africa: New Times and Ethiopia News Coverage of the 1935–41 Italian-Ethiopian War." In *Narrating War and Peace in Africa*, edited by Toyin Falola and Hetty ter Haar, 44–55. Rochester, NY: Rochester University Press, 2010.

Yemitan, Oladipo. *Madame Tinubu: Merchant and King-Maker*. Ibadan: University Press, 1987.

Zachernuk, Philip S. *Colonial Subjects: An African Intelligentsia and Atlantic Ideas*. Charlottesville: University of Virginia Press, 2000.

——. "The Lagos Intelligentsia and the Idea of Progress, ca. 1860–1960." In *Yoruba Historiography*, edited by Toyin Falola, 148–54. Madison: University of Wisconsin Press, 1991.

Index

Page numbers in italics refer to figures and tables.

Abdelwahid, Mustafa, 100

Abeokuta: British control of, 23–24, 28, 64; British in, 25; British treaty with, 39, 237n71; as Christian Egba theocracy, 30; Christianity in, 3, 6; closing courts of, 74–75; defense of, 44, 239n107; depression in, 183–84, 190; economic development of, 31; as Egba nation, 13; elites of, 68–69, 79; establishment of, 6, 27–28; Ethiopia and, 113; ethnic makeup of, 6; Europeans' presence in, 45, 74, 234n11, 234n27; farmland supporting, 237n78; foreign soldiers in, 129; general strike's effect on, 164; generational tensions in, 46; global political engagement of, 20; historians from, 9–10, 66, 80–96; independence of, from Oyo, 9, 80; Lagos compared to, 43; military recruitment in, 127, 130; modernity of, 9; nationalism, 8, 23–24; NCBWA branch in, 102; Nigerian nationalism in, 3–4; political administration of, 6, 39; political fault lines of, 160; precolonial history of, 6; religious diversity of, 70, 78, 198, 205; soldiers from, 130, 146; sovereignty of, denied, 50; as success story for indirect rule, 72; wartime reallocation of funds in, 133; World War II's impact on, 124–48. *See also* Egba United Government (EUG)

Abeokuta, centenary of, 11–12, 24, 64–97, 210, 215; activities of, 87–96; Ademola and, 69, 80, 88, 90–92, 93; anthems of, 89–90, 96, 252nn125–26; British attending, 88, 90, 93–94; British paternalism reinforced by, 66, 68–69; British stake in, 72; cenotaph, 88, 92, 94, 97; cloth manufactured for, 89, 95–96, 97; cost of, 67; criticism of, in media, 94–96; critiques of, 94–96; as display of state-making, 66; the Great Depression and, 67, 68; independence and, 68–69; invitations to, 87, 251n108; local histories written for, 24, 80–87; masculinity and, 66; media reports of, 92–94, 252n118; as money-making scheme, 95–96; numbers attending, 92; schoolchildren at, 89; sovereignty as central concern of, 98; state drums at, 88, 93, 98, 251n108; thanksgiving for tax revolt and, 204, 210, 215; values of, challenged, 122–23; women omitted from, 94, 96, 97; women planning, 87–88; Women's Centenary Celebration Committee for, 70–71. *See also* Centenary Hall

Abeokuta Centenary and Its Celebrations (Ajisafe), 94–95

Abeokuta Educated Elements, 198, 199, 223, 278n72

Abeokuta Grammar School (AGS), 43

Abeokuta Industrial Institute, 43

Abeokuta Ladies Club (ALC): Ademola as patron of, 171, 173; agenda of, 171–72; founding of, 170–71; literacy and, 172–73; rice trade and, 167–68; on taxation of women, 171–72, 173–74

Abeokuta Patriotic Association, 7

Abeokuta Province, 50–56; food production in, 143–44; troops in, 144

Abeokuta Society of Union and Progress, 80, 198

Abeokuta Union of Teachers, 132

Abeokuta Urban District Council (AUDC), 224

Abeokuta Women's Union (AWU): Ademola accused by, 2, 25, 185; Ademola's silence regarding, 1–2; blaming of, 25; celebrating Ademola's abdication, 11, 204–7; council attempting to control, 192; demographics of, 2; Egba Council meeting with, 187–88; erasure of, 18; F. Ransome-Kuti celebrated by, 175; market women as core of, 2, 223; merging with NWU, 2, 216–17; as a political movement, 221; on the salt trade, 142; and sole native authority system, 197–98, 201, 223. *See also* tax revolt

Abosede, M. A., 157

Abubaharu, Alhaji, 215–16

accounting, 22

Action Group (AG), 18, 218, 221

activism: the dead's role in, 178–79; and government roles, conflation of, 222; in Ijemo, 47–48; on a national level, 3

Acton, John (Lord Acton), 207, 280n111

Adams, F. B., 71, 80

Adebanwi, Wale, 11; on the dead's role in activism, 179; on death rituals, 12; on narrative and nationhood, 13–14; on newspapers, 220

Adebayo, Isaiah, 130

Adedamola, Suberu, 71, 77–78, 94, 247n31

Adedoyin, Adeleke, 160, 161

Adekogba, Elizabeth, 216, 220

Ademola, Adegbola, 129, 201, 202

Ademola, Adetokunbo, 203, 275n19

Ademola, Kunle, 275n19

Ademola, Omoba Remi, 117

Ademola I (*alake*), 31

Ademola II (*alake*), 73; abdication of, 1–2, 201, 202, 209, 211; and Abeokuta's independence, 64, 176; Ajisafe's criticism of, 94–95; authoritarianism of, 199; AWU's accusations against, 2, 25, 185; Blaize and, 81, 82; British honors given to, 147, 153; British support of, 194–95; the centenary and, 69, 80, 88, 90–92, 93; challengers to, diversity of, 78–79; challenges to authority of, 77–79, 179; coronation of, 67–68, 73; corruption of, 2, 179, 185, 201, 202; early life of, 81–82; economic affairs of, 81–82, 184–85, 193, 251n88; financial misdeeds attributed to, 82,

185, 278n77; Gbadebo and, 81; grievances against, 185, 187–88, 192–93, 194, 197, 201; Haile Selassie and, 121–22; histories commissioned by, 66, 80–87; improvements introduced by, 86; income of, 184–85; as independent sovereign, 73–74, 77; literacy of, 79; message of, to king of England, 93; as patron of ALC, 171, 173; plot against, 78; Ransome-Kutis and, 142, 164–65, 167–68, 173–75, 179–80, 189, 191–92, 214; removal of, from palace, 201–2, 203; return of, 25, 211–12, 217; and rice collection, 166–67; Shackleford and, 119, 120; and Subuola, 77, 78, 249n52, 249n60; succession of, 24, 64, 72–74, 77; suicidality of, 203; supporters of, 199, 202, 211–12; taxation and, 134, 135, 137, 164–66; tax revolt and, 185–86, 187–88, 189, 191–93; thanksgiving for abdication of, 4, 11, 204–7, 210; trading by, in wartime, 142, 146, 147; UNIA members meeting with, 100; wives of, trading his goods, 185; women meeting with, 164–65; in World War II, 130, 132, 133

Adeniyi-Jones, C. C., 104, 184

Adeoshun, Amusa, 168

Aderinto, Saheed, 16, 110

Adesina (*olowu*), 250n69

Adeyinka, Pa Michael, 130

Adeyinka, S. F., 170

Adubi War, 24, 28, 55–56, 102, 178, 206; commission on, 56–61; forced labor and, 56–58; native courts and, 58–60; *ogboni* chiefs and, 59–60; rural-urban tensions leading to, 60; sanitation fines and, 58–59; women's voices on, absence of, 60–61

adult suffrage, 21, 219–21, 283n41

afin (*alake*'s palace): protests outside, 47–48, 165, 179, 185–86, 191, 201; Ransome-Kuti banned from, 192; school in, 251n106

Africa: and African history, 8; French colonies in, 127–28; imports to, postwar, 152, 156–57, 170; marginalization of, in World War II histories, 124

African diaspora: invasion of Ethiopia and, 113–21; Nigerian, 10, 38–39

Agbe, Omo, 167, 272n78

Agbor, women of, 216

agidi (corn porridge), 53–54

the blitzkrieg, 126
Boer Wars, 246n3
Bornu, the *shehu* of, 87, 251n108
Bourdillon, Bernard, 119, 120, 155, 159, 162, 224, 283n41
Brackenbury, E. A., 77, 78
Britain, postwar debts of, 149, 150–52, 175. *See also* the colonial state
British Cameroon, 231n60
British Ex-Service Men's Union, 121
"brotherhood," 14
Brown, Oliver, 162
Buganda, 28, 62
burglaries, 133
Burma, fighting in, 130
Burton, Antoinette, 8
Bush, Barbara, 22, 23
Buthelezi, Mangosuthu, 17

Cahill, Patrick J., 162
Cameron, Donald, 72, 107, 162, 248n38
Cameron, T. K., 103
Cameroon Campaign, 53
Cameroons, unification of, 231n60
Campbell, Benjamin, 235n33
capital, crisis of, 99
Carr, Henry, 103
cassava starch. *See* starch
"Celebration of Egba Freedom," 204–5
censuses, 177
centenaries, 11–12; collective identities and, 65; gendered nature of, 12, 97
Centenary Hall, 65; cost of, 67; opening of, 88; photographs in, 88, 97. *See also* Abeokuta, centenary of
centralization of political authority, 76–77
Chatterjee, Partha, 5, 14, 66
Chazan, Naomi, 223
chiefs: colonial administration and, 9, 227n2; colonial policy mediated by, 112; colonial support of, 153; council limiting powers of, 71; deposition or suspension of, 71, 107; as district heads, 54; EUG created by, 27; Gbadebo challenged by, 76–77; and indirect rule, 197–98; labor extraction expected of, 57; private courts of, 76; Saros trusted by, 32; taxation powers of, curtailed, 21; trade, 36, 40, 54, 70; waning influence of, 45; women's grievances and, 188; on women's status in their districts, 174. See also *ogboni* (civil authority); *olorogun* (military titlehold-

ers); sole native authority system
children, grown, 45
child street hawking, 109–10
Christianity: in Abeokuta, 3, 6, 30; in Ademola's centenary speech, 91; Ajisafe on, 95; and churches' reactions to the tax revolt, 191, 277n50; and domestic slavery, 36–37; Egba, 30, 83, 85; in Empress Menen's "Appeal," 116; gender roles in, 7–8, 33–38; as "higher" than Islam, 83; independent Yoruba churches and, 259n84; male vs. female converts to, 37; monogamy and, 34; nationalism and, 33–38; separatist African churches, 10; Yoruba nationalism shaped by, 7. *See also* missionaries
Church Missionary Society (CMS), 29, 252n125; antislavery stance of, 33; Johnson superintendent of, 32–33; Saros affiliated with, 31–32
Circle for the Liberation of Ethiopia, 117–18
citizenship, taxation and, 175–76, 223
civil service, Africans in, 102, 105, 274n12
Clauson, J. E., 240n129
Clifford, Hugh, 58, 59–60, 107, 240n129, 241n139, 241n141
cloth: dyers, 40, 67, 112, 122, 139, 172, 257n57; family, 95–96, 97, 253n146; prices, 156–57
coal miners' strike, 18
cocoa, 40, 44, 184; export duties on, 52; falling prices of, 66, 127, 140; migrant labor for, 44–45; women and, 40, 139, 237n79; in World War II, 127, 140
Cohen, A. B., 270n52
Cohen, Robin, 159, 268n29
Coker, J. K., 70, 73, 74, 77, 247n31; Ademola and, 73, 74, 78, 82; libel suit against, 78
Coker, Mary, 37, 38, 236n63
Cole, A. M., 117
Coleman, James S., 18, 19, 163
Colonial Development and Welfare Act, 150, 194–95, 267n3
Colonial Development Corporation, 195
the colonial state, 2–3; in Abeokuta, 6, 24; Abeokuta's chiefs negotiating with, 39, 237n71; Abeokuta's founding and, 27–28; Africanization of, 274n12; the *alake* in, 24, 28–29, 72–73, 76, 196–97, 214–15; as authoritarian, 223–24; "Bolshevik" criticism of, 73; chiefs

Eden, Anthony, 120
education: CMS supporting, 32; about
colonialism, 104; in the EUG, 42–43;
of girls and women, 43, 46, 92, 97, 109,
240n119; Great Depression affecting,
103–4; literacy and, 79; mass, 104–5;
nationalism and, 43, 104–5; scholarships and, 86; and school history textbooks, 9; teachers' organizations and,
103, 154; Western, critique of, 95
Edun, Adegboyega (Jacob Henryson
Samuel), 42, 238n83; Ajisafe's criticism
of, 94; in London, 41, 42, 81; Northern
Nigeria toured by, 51–52; Ponlade and,
47–48; as secretary of the ENA, 50;
taxation under, 55, 243n167
Egba Central Council, 67, 85, 198–200;
Ademola and, 76, 78, 188–89, 195–96,
207–9; in Ademola's centenary speech,
90–91; becoming Abeokuta Urban
District Council, 224; Blair on role
of, 196–97, 199; hearing grievances,
197; inauguration of, in 1949, 210–11;
involvement of, in management,
79–80; literacy of members of, 79, 172,
200, 211, 281n119; as male domain, 71,
86–87, 200; membership on, 69–70,
71, 198–99, 215, 247n20; restructuring
of, 199–201, 207–8; taxation and representation on, 137–38, 208; tax revolt
discussed by, 189–90, 191–92; and
township councils, 279n85; women's
representation on, 182, 192, 193, 196,
210, 211, 223, 224; women's taxation discussed by, 182, 186, 187–89, 191–93, 210
Egba constitutional law, 30, 82–87
Egba Deputation and National Club,
38–39
Egba Division, 50; human geography of,
60; wartime fundraising of, 132. See
also Abeokuta
Egba Interim Council, 210
Egba Native Authority/Administration
(ENA), 50–56, 210, 215; Ademola and,
77; council of, 69–72, 76; council
separated from, 198–99; educated
and indigenous elites on, 77, 249n59;
financial crisis of, 182–83; the Great
Depression's impact on, 67; nomenclature of, 241n144; rice trade policed
by, 145, 146, 147, 166–67, 171; seizure of
goods by, 168–69; strike not supported
by, 164; taxation and, 133–34, 182, 188,

217; during World War II, 125, 130–31,
133–34, 135–36, 264n73; as a Yoruba
state, 71
Egba Oke-Ona, 6
Egba rising of 1918, 202
Egbas, 7, 20; anthem of, 89–90, 96; British mistrusted by, 234n11; Christianity
and, 30, 83, 85; constitution, 30, 85;
constitutional law and, 82–87; dominance of, in Abeokuta, 12, 30; history
of, 80–87, 90, 214; of Lagos, 38–39, 73,
74, 77–78, 190, 198; and Oyos, cultural
identities of, 85
Egba Treaty of Independence, 23
Egba United Board of Management
(EUBM), 30–31, 38–39, 234n11
Egba United Government (EUG),
23–24, 27–63; the *alake* and, 39, 44,
49, 50, 81, 84; breakdown of the family
in, 45–46; British encroachment on,
46–50, 241n141, 241nn138–39; changes
in Abeokuta wrought by, 41–42; class
and gender in, 44–46; demise of, 49–
50, 62; the economy and, 43–44; flag
of, 62, 84; formation of, 27–28, 38–44;
gazette of, 242n144; growth of administration of, 42; independence of,
28–29, 62, 241n141, 241nn138–39; Lagos
government and, 39, 40, 48, 49–50; in
the Lagos press, 41, 43, 49–50; officers
of, 42; railway and, 239n117; symbols
of, at centenary, 89; taxation in, 43–44,
52–53; women's representation in,
23, 39–40, 62–63; women titleholders
excluded from, 39–40, 62–63
Egba Women's Union, 19
*Egba-Yoruba Constitutional Law and Its
Historical Development, The* (Solanke), 9, 82–87
Egbe Atunluse, 211–12
Egberongbe, Alfa, 248n40
Egberongbe, Raheem, 249n60
Egberongbe, Subuola, 77, 78, 96,
248n40, 249n52, 249n60
egusi oil, 126, 261n10
Egypt, women in, 15
Egypt as a Woman (Baron), 15
Eighty-First West Africa Division, 130,
146
Ekpo, Margaret, 218
elections, 198–99, 200, 210–11, 247n20,
255n19; 1951, 221; council, chiefs
controlling, 70; indirect, 224; Richards

Infant Welfare Center, 71–72
infrastructure, 53–54
Inkatha, 17
interwar period, 24–25, 98–123
Islam, 29; in 1920s Lagos, 106; Ali lectur-
ing on, 100; Oyo constitution and, 83
Italo-Abyssinian War: African diaspora
responding to, 116–21; colonialism
critiqued in light of, 121; impact of,
on nationalist thought, 24, 120–22;
Italian atrocities in, 113–14, 118, 119, 121;
Nigeria responding to, 118–21; racial
identity and, 115–16; women's roles in,
113–16, 118–20
Itoku *ogboni* house, closure of, 78
Itori Township, kingling of, 76
iya egbes (leaders of women's associations), 173
iyalode, 32, 39, 235n53, 259n82; definition
of, 40; resuscitation of office of, 182.
See also Tinubu, Madam Efunroye

James, C. L. R., 117, 258n72
Jefferson, Thomas, 206–7
Johnson, G. W., 30–31, 33, 38, 234n12
Johnson, James, 7, 32–33; on female slave-
owners, 36–37, 236n61; polygamists not
tolerated by, 34; women opposing, 37
Johnson, Samuel, 8, 9–10, 84
Johnson-Odim, Cheryl, 165, 167–68,
277n55
Jojolola, Madam, 39, 61, 70, 96, 182
judicial system, 76–77

Kale, Paul M., 160
Kano, Aminu, 221
Karlström, Mikael, 97
Kenny, J. B., 38
Kenya, 127
Keynes, John Maynard, 150
King, John F., 32
kings and kingship: and the *alake*'s
primacy, 39, 66, 84, 85, 196; literacy
and, 79, 95; royal installations and, 11,
39, 67–68, 73–74; Tinubu and, 209;
women's absence from discussions of,
86–87; Zulu, 249n59
Kinoshi, Emanuel (seriki), 160
kirikiri, 47
Kirk, J. H., 76
kola nuts, 40, 44
Kramer, Lloyd, 13
Kuforiji, M., 198

Kuku, S. B., 156–57
Kuti, Fela, 213

labor: marriage as strategy to acquire, 45;
of slaves, unavailability of, 45; wage, 51
labor extraction: as "civic duty," 61,
245n206; colonial expectation of, 56–61;
economic losses resulting from, 58; fines
for avoiding, 57, 59; increase in, during
World War II, 124; for road-building, 44,
45, 56–57; taxation and, 56; tax evasion
punished with, 136; terms of, 56–57
labor unions, 150; arrests of leaders of,
155; cooperation among, 159; NCNC
and, 154–55; strikes and, 154–59
Ladipo, J. A., 167, 272n80
Lafenwa Barracks, 129
Lagos: Abeokuta compared to, 43; annexation of, 234n11; blackmarketing in,
during war, 129, 145; Egbas of, 38–39,
73, 74, 77–78, 190, 198; elite women
in, 16; food prices in, 144–45; "foreigners" in, 110; intellectual developments
in, 99–100; Legislative Council of, 102,
255n19; political agitation in, 106–7,
125; Saros settling in, 233n6; strikes,
149–50, 154–59; taxation in, generally,
184; taxation of women in, 108; tax
protest in, 222; voting rights in, 102,
255n19; West Indians in, 100, 233n6
Lagos Egba Society, 77
Lagos Ethiopia Defence Committee
(LEDC), 118
Lagos Ladies League, 109
Lagos Market and Trading Women As-
sociation, 106
Lagos Times, 42, 82
Lagos Union of Teachers (LUT), 103
Lagos Women's League, 109–10, 111
Lagos Youth Movement, 105. *See also*
Nigerian Youth Movement (NYM)
Lamb, G. F. W., 268n28
land acquisition, 79
Lane-Joynt, Philip, 202
Law, Robin, 8, 9
*Laws and Customs of the Yoruba People,
The* (Ajisafe), 9
League of Nations, 119, 120
Legislative Council: Abeokuta's seat on,
102; NNDP and, 105; NUT and, 104
Lentz, Carola, 65
Likaka, Osumaka, 176
Lindsay, Lisa, 16

Lisabi, 80, 88, 205, 206, 250n80; "children of," 89, 90

Lisabi Mills Orchestra, 279n103

literacy, 79, 172–73, 211, 281n119; of Ademola, 79; and the ALC, 172–73; of Egba Council members, 79, 172, 200, 211, 281n119; and kingship, 79, 95; of market women, 172–73

literary works, 10; gendered binary of, 17–18; genres of, 10–11

Lloyd, Thomas, 270n52

Local Defense Volunteer Force, 132

Local Government Law (1954), 224

locusts, 67

Lonsdale, John, 68

"Lori Oke Ati Petele" (On the hills and in the valleys), 89–90

Losi, John B., 9

Lucas, J. O., 103

Lugard, Frederick, 22, 24, 241n144; durbar staged by, 246n4; enduring legacy of, 79, 233n2; Gbadebo and, 53–54; Ijemo conflict and, 49, 50, 240n129, 241n138; infrastructure threatened by, 53; taxation under, 52, 53–54

Lyttleton Constitution, 220–21

Mabogunje, Akin, 60

Macauley, Herbert, 24, 75, 100, 106, 249n52; colonial government criticized by, 107; market women supported by, 108, 109; and the NCNC, 154

MacCallum, Henry, 81

MacGregor, William, 28–29, 40–41, 50, 62, 81, 197

Macpherson, B. W., 88, 94

Macpherson, John Stuart, 195, 217

Macpherson Constitution, 25–26, 217–18, 219–20

maize, 143, 168

Majekodunmi, E. B., 171

Majekodunmi, J. B., 121, 273n98

Majeobaje Society, 179–80, 191, 194, 204, 210, 211–12, 217, 274n5

"male breadwinner," 16, 181, 190

Maltby, Josephine, 22, 23

Mann, D. O., 78

Mann, Kristin, 36

maps, 177

marketing boards, 152

markets: construction of, 40; and "market masters," 138–39

market women: Abeokuta protests of,

111–12, 122; associations of, 103, 107, 108–9, 111, 122, 172–73; as British citizens, 139; concerns of, vs. elite women's concerns, 110–11; and educated women, united, 172, 273n103; fines on, 59; goods traded by, 40; literacy of, 172–73; and "market masters," 138–39; nationalist, 106; the NNDP supported by, 108; political strategies of, 108–9; rice traded by, 166–67; taxation threatening, 23, 108, 111, 223; tax revolts led by, 222; World War II's effects on, 20, 125, 138–39, 142, 147. See also tax revolt

marriage: divorce and, 46; financial challenges of, 111; as labor acquisition, 45; Yoruba, 36, 236n59. See also wives, Christian

Martin, Susan, 284n44

Martins, August Anthony, 241n135

Martins, P. P., 42

masculinity: Abeokuta's centenary and, 66; and competing masculinities, 17; in Empress Menen's "Appeal," 116; and the labor movement, 16–17; and the male breadwinner, 16, 181, 190; Zulu, 17

Matero, Marc, 117

Matory, J. Lorand, 7

Maynard, John, 268n30

Mba, Nina Emma, 111, 165, 167–68, 274n5, 277n55

McCallum, Henry, 39

McClintock, Anne, 14, 65

McCotter, Jane, 174–75

McIntosh, Marjorie, 273n103

memoirs and diaries, 10

Menelik, 258n64

Menen, Empress, 113–14

methodology: literatures drawn on, 4–5, 177; multidisciplinary approach, 4; structure, 23–26

micronationalism, 9

migrant labor, 16; on cocoa farms, 44–45; labor shortages caused by, 126–27; taxation and, 22, 51

migration: to Abeokuta, 80, 90, 110; water rates causing, 138

military: *balogun* of, 29, 32, 78, 186, 190, 239n107; Christians in ranks of, 31–32; on council, 39, 69–70, 90; presence, during World War II, 144, 145; recruitment, 126–27; weakened position of, 46–47, 196. See also *olorogun* (military titleholders)

Miller, E. A., 134
Ministry of Food and Supply, 125
missionaries, 6, 29; distrust of, 32, 33, 234n11; expulsion of, 30, 31; and military elites, ties between, 33; *ogboni* titles given to, 249n61; Ogundipe and, 31, 32, 33, 37–38; return of, 31; schools of, 42, 43; social revolution pursued by, 33–34, 37–38; wives of, 34–36
Mobilizing the Masses (Schmidt), 15
Mockler, Anthony, 113
moneylending, 82
Moore, C. B., 42
Moore, Modupe, 119
Moore, O., 121
Moore, William, 31
Moorhouse, Harry, 48, 240n129, 241n139
Moorman, Marissa, 5
motherhood, 116, 120
Motor Union strike, 105
Movement for the Emancipation of the Niger Delta, 284n48
Murray, A. E. F., 249n61
Muslims: education of, 43; on the ENA Council, 54. *See also* Islam
Mylius, E. N., 165, 192–93

Naanen, Ben, 222
Nagel, Joane, 16
Nardal, Paulette, 117
narratives: centrality of, to nations, 13, 18; control of, 18–19; family in, 17–18; gendered nature of, 3–4, 13–19, 209–10; importance of, in Abeokuta, 3–4; of male political domination, 220; newspapers helping to create, 11, 220; on the tax revolt, 25, 205–7, 215
the nation: gendered concept of, 8, 14; and performance of nationhood, 65; polyphony of voices on, 5; as text, 13–14
National Congress of British West Africa (NCBWA), 101–2
National Council of British West Africa, 163–64
National Council of Nigeria and the Cameroons (NCNC): Action Group vs., 221; Azikiwe heading up, 163, 218, 270n51; British tour of, 160–62, 163, 270nn51–52; formation of, 18, 150, 153–54; as Igbo party, 218; mandates of, 160, 269n48; militancy of, 154–55, 175; moribund state of, 3, 163, 215; panethnic coalition of, 26; Richards Constitu-

tion and, 159–63; trade unions and, 154–59; women pressured by, 218
National Council of Women's Societies, 273n103
nationalism: Christianity and, 33–38; competing masculinities of, 17, 66; cultural history of, 5–6, 10; education at center of, 104–5; Ethiopian invasion and, 24, 120–22; and fear of communism, 248n44; fluidity of, 86; gender dynamics of, 4, 14–15, 218–19; intelligentsia and, 10, 86; in the interwar period, 99–123; narrative approaches to, 13–19; of the NCNC, 153–54, 218; political intervention and, 6; postwar period crystallizing, 150, 176; ritual and, 11–12, 90, 204–7, 210, 215; the tax revolt and, 179, 208–9; and unity, 105, 153, 176; women's movements and, 106, 209–10, 214, 221, 224. *See also* Yoruba nationalism
nationality, definition of, 5–6
National Union of Teachers of England and Wales, 104
Nation and Its Fragments, The (Chatterjee), 5
Nation and Narration (Bhabha), 13, 18
nation-building: commemorations as, 65, 246n3; erasure of women in, 5, 7–8; unearthing women's role in, 10
Native Authority Ordinance, 198, 224, 227n2, 241n144
native courts: female assessors on, 211; sanitation fines imposed by, 58–59, 244n190
Native Revenue Ordinance, 184
Nazi Germany, 121, 140
Neu, Dean, 22
newspapers, 11; and the creation of narratives, 11, 220; English vs. Yoruba, 11; and the Esugbayi affair, 107; in Lagos, 99, 107; partisan politics and, 13, 220; place of, in nationalist organizing, 13, 220; Ransome-Kuti on, 220; rice trade and, 167, 168; World War II and, 131
New Times and Ethiopia News (NT & EN), 117–18
Nigeria: Abeokuta as constituency of, 176; defense of, 132; modern, women's movements in, 225, 284n48; politics of, postwar, 153–59; wartime food production in, 126, 142–43. *See also* nationalism

Nigeria, scholarship on: gendered narratives in, 3–4; teleological bent of, 3; women's roles ignored by, 18–19
Nigeria Anti-Transfer Committee, 121
Nigerian Commoners' Party, 221
Nigerian Defense Regulations of 1939, 125
Nigerian National Democratic Party (NNDP), 19, 24, 100; Abeokuta branch of, 106, 108, 164; coalitions forming core of, 107–8; diversity of membership in, 102–3; formation of, 102–3, 122; NYM and, 105; women in, 106, 108, 109
Nigerian Reconstruction Group, 153
Nigerians, diasporic, 10, 38–39
Nigerian Sunshine (newspaper), 220, 283n28
Nigerian Supply Board, 126, 260n6
Nigerian Union of Students (NUS), 153, 267n14
Nigerian Union of Teachers (NUT), 103–4, 122, 255n26; NCNC and, 154; rice traders supported by, 167–68; strikers supported by, 104, 156; WASU and, 104, 105, 122
Nigerian Youth Movement (NYM), 18, 24; Abeokuta branch of, 106, 164; leadership of, 105–6; and the NCNC, 154; women's wing of, 105
Nigeria Women's Union (NWU): Abeokuta conference of, 219; AWU merging with, 2, 216–17; erasure of, 18; formation of, 2–3, 4; party formation undermining, 26, 218
Nkrumah, Kwame, 121
Nolte, Insa, 16–17, 217, 221
Northern Elements Progressive Union, 221
Northern People's Congress, 218
Nwabughuogu, Anthony I., 79, 222
Nwafor, Okechukwu, 253n146
Nyobé, Ruben Um, 231n60

obas (kings), 67, 69–70; in the EUG, 39, 84, 237n74; hierarchy of, under ENA, 50–51, 85, 94–95, 242n146; political affiliation with, 60; relocation of, 54; as subordinate to *alake*, 84
Ochonu, Moses, 22
Odowu, 76
Oduntan, Oluwatoyin B., 79, 252n125; on the Adubi War, 242n146; on Egba nationalism, 98; on Folarin, 80–81; on Lisabi, 250n80

Odutola, Timothy Adeola, 145
Odwira festival, 66, 246n4
ogboni (civil authority), 39, 78, 211–12; breaking with the *alake*, 201; British curtailing power of, 51, 59–60; centenary celebrations including, 88, 93, 98; Coker and, 82; EUG usurping, 47; European missionaries joining, 249n61; Ijemo protests and, 47, 48; I. Ransome-Kuti and, 201; native courts usurping revenue of, 59–60; regalia, 249n61; women overthrowing, 186–87
Ogunbisi, M. S., 262n32
Ogundipe, 31, 32; enslaved people mistreated by, 37–38; missionaries and, 31, 32, 33, 37–38; Wood and, 33
Ogunsheye, Felelis, 156, 268n30
Ogunye, Madam, 188, 189
Ojugun, O. N., 163
Oke, G. A., 177–78, 205, 206, 280n106
Okenla, John, 31–32, 239n107
Oke-Ona, 42, 70
Okonjo, I. M., 159
Okonkwo, Rina, 100
Okukenu (*alake*), 91
Olajide, Josie A., 279n103
Olaniji, Lamide, 168
Olaosebiken, Mrs., 142
olopa (native police), 134
Olori Erelu (chief of the women), 39–40
olorogun (military titleholders), 39; on council, 70, 78; weakened position of, 46
Olorunfemi, A., 243n158
Olorun-Nimbe, Abu Bakry Ibiyinka, 160
olowu (king of Owu quarter), 6, 38; crowned, 250n69, 251n99; made lowest-ranking king, 50–51; taxation and, 54, 137
Olubaka, Shefiatu, 218
Olumo Rock, 87, 90, 92, 94
oluwo (head of the *ogboni* or civil chiefs), 48–49, 240n123, 242n146,
Oluwole, Adunni, 221
Oluwole, Isaac, 88
Onatolu, Seriki, 54, 55–56, 58
Onitsha protest, 111
orisas, 37, 187
oro rites, 48, 186–87, 190, 209, 211
oshile/osile, 6, 42, 94, 251n99; as "insubordinate," 71; taxation and, 54
Oshogbo, 1, 202, 203, 227n2
Osindero, J. M., 156

support of the alakeship erased by, 84–85; centenary lectures of, 88, 89; on centrality of the *alake*, 84–85; on constitutional development, 83–84, 89; history of, as call to action, 86; male-centric nationalism of, 86–87; the Ransome-Kutis and, 104, 208–9, 281n114; WASU and, 153, 255n28; and the Westminster model, 224

sole native authority system, 1, 161, 180; AWU and, 197–98, 201, 223; end of, 195–204, 208–9; indirect rule and, 112, 196–97, 199, 200; taxation and, 208–9, 223. *See also* Ademola II (*alake*); tax revolt

Somoye, Oladipo, 132

Sorunke, Emanuel (chief), 129, 191

South Africa, 17; Boer Wars commemorated by, 246n3; taxation in, 51

Southern Rhodesia, 16

Sowole, M. S., 157

Sowunmi, O., 170

Soyinka, Eniola, 171, 187, 188, 189, 190, 276n33

Soyinka, Wole, 2, 129, 130, 171; on AWU's tax revolt, 185–86, 187; memoir of, 185–86, 213

Spitfire *Nigeria*, 132

starch, 140–41, 264n95, 265n97

the state: legibility of, 177; purpose of, 207

Stooke, George Beresford, 166

Storer, Denis, 103

strikes: Abeokuta affected by, 164; commission investigating, 156–58, 158; in Lagos, 154–59

Suny, Ronald, 5

Syer, W. C., 57, 58, 244n190

Tamuno, Tekena, 102

Tanganyika African National Union (TANU), 15

Tanzania, women in, 15

taxation: British ideological foundations of, 20–21; bureaucracy of, 187–88; and categories of taxpayer, 136–37, 137; centrality of, to narrative, 5, 20; and citizenship, 175–76, 223; colonial state's use of, 21–22, 51–56, 133–39, 148; community belonging and, 23; continuity in practices of, 134; control exercised through, 21–22; demands to halve, 75; democracy and, 21, 51,

180, 209, 223; double assessment and, 60; economic conditions affecting, 20, 182, 183–84, 190; ENA and, 51, 54, 133–34, 182, 188, 217; in EUG, 43–44, 52–53; exemption from, 190, 276n45; expectations of the state linked to, 61, 148, 175–76, 180, 223; during the Great Depression, 23, 134; implementation of, 54; inconsistent policies of, 217; increased, 164–65, 188–89, 191; indirect rule and, 222–23; Johnson recommending, 31; labor extraction and, 56; under Lugard, 53, 54–55; of market women, 138–39; modification of, following Adubi War, 60; modification of modes of, 135; native courts and, 58–59; in Northern vs. Southern Nigeria, 66–67; and political participation, 21, 23, 137–39, 184, 225; polygyny discouraged by, 22, 51; scholarship on, 22; and sole native authority system, 208–9, 223; tax collection and, 54, 66, 165–66, 173–74, 182–83, 187–89; and tax revolts generally, 222; and tolls, 52–53; and universal suffrage, 21; urban-rural tensions from, 60, 181; wage labor force created by, 51; World War II and, 126, 133–39, 137, 148; in Yorubaland, precolonial, 52. *See also* Adubi War; income tax; taxation of women; tax revolt

taxation of women, 2, 23, 54–55, 60–61, 148, 165–66, 173–74, 179–212; in Lagos, 108; moral efficacy of, 245n205; suspension of, 191, 201, 210, 217. *See also* tax revolt

tax collectors: commissions received by, 135, 188, 190, 276n33; girls stripped by, 173; salaries paid to, 189

tax evasion: coercive methods of combating, 182–83; olopa combating, 134; prosecution for, 134–35, 136, 182–83, 189, 191; release of prisoners for, 191

taxpayers: as householders, 52; money extracted from, 137; representation of, 101, 175–76, 209, 210–11, 223, 224; and tax evasion, 182–83; women's status as, 55, 61, 139, 148, 223, 224; World War II and, 133–39

Tax Payers Movement, 216

tax resistance, 22–23; and the Adubi War, 24, 28, 55–56; against French colonial powers, 23

NUT, 104, 105, 122; women belonging to, 255n28
Western House of Assembly, 182, 190
West Indian Association, 100
West Indians, 100, 233n6
the Westminster model, 224
White, Anne, 36
White, James, 36
Whiteley, G. C., 155, 199
Wilson, Lieutenant, 48–49
Wingate, Orde, 146, 266n131
wives, Christian, 34; African women adopting values of, 36; domestic role of, 35, 36; of missionaries, 34–36; work of, 35–36
Woldemariam, Metasehia, 118
women: Christian cultural place of, 8, 33–38; colonization worsening lot of, 173–74; combatants, 225, 284n48; on councils, 39–40, 196, 219, 224; in decolonization movements, 15; as dependent, 224–25, 284n44; economic enterprise of, 34, 36–37; elite, feminism of, 109; erasure of, 2–3, 5, 14, 25–26, 213–14; expectations of, from the state, 61; financial independence of, 54–55; fines on, 58–59; in the Macpherson Constitution, 219–20; nationalism and, 150; as nation-makers, 209–10; *ogboni* symbolically overthrown by, 186–87; *orisas* propitiated by, 37; poor, 16, 110, 171–72, 188; postwar organizing of, 170–75; public and private spheres of, intertwined, 111; as symbols, 3, 14–15, 111, 209; taxation's indirect effects on, 51; titles of, 20, 39–40, 62, 70–71, 87, 97, 247n26, 259n82; transgressing gender expectations, 209–10; Victorian mores of, 16, 36, 109–10; wartime economy and, 139–42, 215; wealth created by, 173; wealth of, vs. men, 180–81. *See also* market women; women, political activity of; women's associations
women, political activity of: British reports on, 39–40, 179–80; centenary ignoring, 96, 97; and growth of women's groups, 216–17; household management as preparation for, 219; ideological foundations of, 206–7; Italo-Abyssinian War and, 118–20; marginalization of, 4–5, 15, 19, 26, 62–63, 205, 214–15, 221; men's support or dismissal of, 218–19; motherhood as

metaphor for, 120; narrative of, 209–10, 213–18; partisanism and, 26, 218–22
women's associations: alliances between, 172–73; as democratic, 19; the FNWS bringing together, 219–22; in Great Britain, 160. *See also* market women; *specific organizations*
Women's Centenary Celebration Committee, 70–71
women's movements, nationalism and, 106, 221, 224
Women's Party, 111
Women's Social Day, 173
women's suffrage: constitutional debate on, lacking, 219–20; Northern leaders opposed to, 3, 220–21
Women's War (1929), 25, 103, 111, 122, 198, 222, 223, 245n205, 275n18
women titleholders: the centenary and, 70–71; ENA excluding, 70; EUG excluding, 39–40, 62–63
Wood, J. B., 7, 33, 41, 249n61
Wood, Mrs. J. B., 96
Woolner, Christopher, 130
Working with Gender (Nagel), 16
World War I, 52, 115
World War II, 123–48; Africa marginalized in histories of, 124; command economy and, 124–25, 126; cost of, 133–39; decolonization and, 124; effects of, on market women, 20, 125, 138–39, 142, 147; end of, 149; experiences of, 128–33; farmers and farming in, 124, 125, 126, 127, 131, 140, 142–46; food rationing during, 129, 262n32; food trade during, 141–42, 256n52; fundraising, 132; impact of, on Africa generally, 125–26, 175; labor shortage during, 126–27; market and elite women's cooperation during, 111; material conditions of, 12, 20, 25, 124–48; Nigerians and the buildup to, 121; political mobilization spurred by, 18; political tensions exacerbated by, 147; and the postwar interlude, 149–76; price controls during, 111, 124–25, 133, 141–42, 144–46, 147–48, 256n52; profiteering during, 141–42, 146; propaganda, 131; radio's role in, 131; rice production and, 126, 142–46, 147; taxation during, 126, 133–39, 137, 148; travel during, dangers of, 128; wage freeze during, 256n52; water rates during, 138

the Woro, 89, 97

Yaba Higher College, 105
Yoruba: aesthetics of power, 98; Christianity and, 7–8; cultural identities, 7; diaspora, 233n6; gender ideology, 36, 38; marriage, 36, 236n59; religion, 31, 37; urbanization, 40, 237n78. *See also* Egbas; Saros
Yorubaland: history of, 8; returnees to, 8, 28, 29, 233n6; taxation in, precolonial, 52; taxation in, under Lugard, 53, 54–55

Yoruba language, 7, 10, 11
Yoruba nationalism, 12–13; Christianity in, 7–8; gender in, 8; history of, 7; narratives contributing to, 8
Yoruba Wars, 6, 80
Young, Pelham, 47, 48, 240n129
Young Men's Christian Association of Breadfruit Church, 7

Zachernuk, Philip, 10, 84, 99–100; on NYM, 105–6
Zulu kingship, 249n59